Presented To:

_____

From:

_____

Date:

_____

SIMPLE PRAYERS

A DAYBOOK OF
CONVERSATIONS WITH GOD

by

KENNETH AND KAREN BOA

Unless otherwise indicated, all Scripture passages are paraphrased by the authors.

2nd Printing

Simple Prayers
A Daybook of Conversations With God
ISBN 1-56292-367-6
Copyright © 1997 by Kenneth and Karen Boa
4600 Morton Road
Alpharetta, Georgia 30022

Published by Honor Books, Inc.
P. O. Box 3588
Tulsa, Oklahoma 74155

Printed in the United States of America.

DEDICATION

Karen and I lovingly dedicate this daybook of conversations with God to our children Heather and Matthew.

INTRODUCTION

The Purpose of *Simple Prayers*

The concept of communicating with God — talking directly and openly with Him just as we would talk with an intimate friend — is one of the great experiences of the Christian life. And just as the key to quality relationships is time spent effectively communicating with other people, so the key to a growing personal relationship with God is time invested conversing with Him in prayer and listening to His voice in Scripture.

Most of us want to pray more than we do, but we often find our prayers are unsatisfying and sporadic. *Simple Prayers* was designed to make prayer a more enriching and satisfying experience by providing both form and freedom. The form is Scripture itself, and the freedom is your own thoughts and prayers in response to the truths of Scripture.

One problem with prayer is that it is easy to slip into the extreme of all form and no freedom, or the opposite extreme of all freedom and no form. All form leads to a rote or impersonal approach to prayer, while all freedom produces an unbalanced and undisciplined prayer life that can degenerate into a series of one "gimme" after another.

Simple Prayers is a tool that guides you through the process of praying Scripture back to God. This enables you to think God's thoughts and personalize them in your own words. It also provides a balanced diet of prayer by leading you through different kinds of prayer. Because it is based on Scripture, your prayers will be pleasing to God. That knowledge and experience will encourage you in your daily walk with God.

The Structure of *Simple Prayers*

Each of the 365 days of *Simple Prayers* uses the same four-part structure: Lord, I Draw Near to You; Thank You, Lord, for What You Have Done; Lord, I Listen to Your Words of Truth; and Lord, I Respond to Your Instruction.

You will progress from focusing on God, to focusing on yourself, to finally focusing on others. As you grow in your understanding of God, then of yourself as His child, you can then be free to be a "giver" instead of a "grabber," in prayer as well as in life. You will be able to love and serve God and others as He has called us all to do.

To create this collection of biblical prayers and affirmations, I consulted several translations as well as the original language of every passage. The result is essentially my own translation, though it shares much in common with existing translations. My intention in doing this was to remain as close to the biblical text as possible, while still retaining clarity and readability. I then adapted the passages into a personalized format so they could be used readily in the context of individual and group prayer. A number of these prayers and affirmations were derived from negative statements and evaluations in the Bible and turned into positive statements. In other cases, principles have been derived from the lives of biblical characters.

How To Use Simple Prayers

- As you read the words, it is important that you also take time to pray them into your life. In this way, you personalize them so they can be incorporated in your own thoughts and experience.

- The opening words, "Lord, I Draw Near to You," bring you closer to God and help you personalize the scriptural prayers which follow. You may want to read these prayers more than once. The prompt that follows the prayers invites you to pause and add your own thoughts and prayers before moving on to the next part.

- Having drawn near to God, it is now appropriate for you to say, "Thank You, Lord, for What You Have Done." Read these affirmations and turn them into your own prayer.

- Next you say, "Lord, I Listen to Your Words of Truth." As you listen to what Scripture tells you about your relationship with the Lord, pause briefly and consider what you have heard before moving on.

- Each day concludes with, "Lord, I Respond to Your Instruction," a personal response to God concerning your character or relationships. After reflecting on these passages, use the closing prayer to summarize the last three parts. It is helpful to pray this closing prayer out loud.

You can adapt the prayers in each day to differing time formats. They can be used profitably in a short period of time, or you can move through them more slowly, as you see fit. Although you can tie these daily prayers to the day of the year, there is no need to do so, particularly if you find yourself falling behind. You may decide to mark your place and continue wherever you left off.

Consider making a journal to add your own thoughts and prayers as they come to mind when using *Simple Prayers*. You can also use this journal to record a list of prayers for yourself and for others, as well as specific answers to prayer.

Many of the affirmations are expressed as desires; you will be affirming that these are the things you want to be true of your life. Using this book on a regular basis will be a faith-building exercise that will make these affirmations increasingly real in your life.

SIMPLE PRAYERS

A DAYBOOK OF
CONVERSATIONS WITH GOD

DAY 1

PURIFYING MY HEART

~&

LORD, I DRAW NEAR TO YOU

Lord, I give thanks for Your greatness, Your goodness, and Your love, and I now draw near to enjoy Your presence.

I will exalt You, my God and King;
I will bless Your name for ever and ever.
Every day I will bless You,
And I will praise Your name for ever and ever.
Great is the Lord and most worthy of praise;
His greatness is unsearchable. (Psalm 145:1-3)

Take a moment to consider God's awesome majesty and thank Him that He loves you and wants an intimate relationship with you.

THANK YOU, LORD, FOR WHAT YOU HAVE DONE

In Your unfailing love You have led the people You have redeemed. In Your strength, You have guided them to Your holy dwelling. You brought them in and planted them in the mountain of Your inheritance—the place, O Lord, You made for Your dwelling; the sanctuary, O Lord, Your hands have established. (Exodus 15:13,17)

11
~&

LORD, I LISTEN TO YOUR WORDS OF TRUTH

Many, O Lord my God, are the wonders You have done, and Your thoughts toward us no one can recount to You; were I to speak and tell of them, they would be too many to declare. (Psalm 40:5)

LORD, I RESPOND TO YOUR INSTRUCTION

Direct my footsteps according to Your Word, and let no iniquity have dominion over me. (Psalm 119:133)

Who may ascend the hill of the Lord? Who may stand in His holy place? He who has clean hands and a pure heart, who has not lifted up his soul to an idol or sworn by what is false. (Psalm 24:3-4)

~&

Lord, I thank You for Your beloved Son, for Your unfailing love, and for Your wonderful thoughts. Help me to follow Your word and walk in purity of heart.

DAY 2

REDEEMING MY PAST

❧

LORD, I DRAW NEAR TO YOU

I am grateful to You, O God, for the blessing of Your forgiveness. I thank You that in Christ, You set me free from the guilt of the past and give me hope for the future.

For as high as the heavens are above the earth,
So great is Your love for those who fear You;
As far as the East is from the West,
So far have You removed our transgressions from us.
As a father has compassion on his children,
So the Lord has compassion on those who fear Him. (Psalm 103:11-13)

Take a moment to ask the Spirit to search your heart and reveal any areas of unconfessed sin. Acknowledge these to the Lord and thank Him for His forgiveness.

THANK YOU, LORD, FOR WHAT YOU HAVE DONE

❧

The Lord is near to all who call upon Him, to all who call upon Him in truth. He fulfills the desire of those who fear Him; He hears their cry and saves them. The Lord preserves all who love Him, but all the wicked He will destroy. (Psalm 145:18-20)

LORD, I LISTEN TO YOUR WORDS OF TRUTH

You know how I am formed; You remember that I am dust. As for man, his days are like grass; he flourishes like a flower of the field. The wind passes over it and it is gone, and its place remembers it no more. But the lovingkindness of the Lord is from everlasting to everlasting on those who fear Him, and His righteousness with their children's children, to those who keep His covenant and remember to obey His precepts. (Psalm 103:14-18)

LORD, I RESPOND TO YOUR INSTRUCTION

A friend loves at all times, and a brother is born for adversity. (Proverbs 17:17)

❧

Lord, I thank You for Your righteousness, for Your nearness to all who call upon You, and for Your everlasting lovingkindness. Redeem my past and teach me to hope in You.

DAY 3

FOLLOWING THE PATH OF LOVE

❧

LORD, I DRAW NEAR TO YOU

I praise You, Lord, that You are intimately acquainted with my ways and that You always love me and have my best interests at heart.

May I let the fear of the Lord be upon me, and be careful in what I do, for with the Lord my God there is no injustice or partiality or bribery. (2 Chronicles 19:7)

Take a moment to offer this day to the Lord and ask Him for the grace to grow in your knowledge and love for Him.

THANK YOU, LORD, FOR WHAT YOU HAVE DONE

Who is a God like You, who pardons iniquity and passes over the transgression of the remnant of His inheritance? You do not stay angry forever but delight to show mercy. You will have compassion on Your people; You will tread their iniquities underfoot and hurl all their sins into the depths of the sea. (Micah 7:18-19)

13
❧

LORD, I LISTEN TO YOUR WORDS OF TRUTH

I have been loved by God and called to be a saint; grace and peace have been given to me from God our Father and the Lord Jesus Christ. (Romans 1:7)

LORD, I RESPOND TO YOUR INSTRUCTION

The foremost commandment is this: "Hear, O Israel; the Lord our God, the Lord is one; and you shall love the Lord your God with all your heart and with all your soul and with all your mind and with all your strength." The second is this: "You shall love your neighbor as yourself." There is no commandment greater than these. To love God with all the heart and with the understanding and with all the strength, and to love one's neighbor as himself are more important than all burnt offerings and sacrifices. (Mark 12:29-31,33)

❧

Lord, I thank You for Your power, for Your patience, and for Your compassion. I thank You that I have been loved by You, and I ask You to help me walk in the path of love with You and with others.

DAY 4

SURRENDERING MY WAYS

❧

LORD, I DRAW NEAR TO YOU

As I approach Your throne of grace today, I am grateful that You care about the things that concern me and that You want me to offer them up to You.

May I follow Abraham's example of willingness to offer all that I have to You, holding nothing back and trusting in Your character and in Your promises. (Genesis 22:2-12,16)

Take a moment to share your personal needs with God, including your physical, emotional, relational, and spiritual concerns.

THANK YOU, LORD, FOR WHAT YOU HAVE DONE

God is not a man, that He should lie, nor a son of man, that He should change His mind. Has He spoken and not done it? Has He promised and not fulfilled it? (Numbers 23:19)

14
❧

The foolishness of God is wiser than men, and the weakness of God is stronger than men. But God chose the foolish things of the world to shame the wise, and God chose the weak things of the world to shame the strong; and the lowly things of this world and the despised things God has chosen, and the things that are not, to nullify the things that are, so that no one may boast before Him. (1 Corinthians 1:25,27-29)

LORD, I LISTEN TO YOUR WORDS OF TRUTH

God will keep me strong to the end, so that I will be blameless on the day of our Lord Jesus Christ. God is faithful, through Whom I was called into fellowship with His Son, Jesus Christ our Lord.
(1 Corinthians 1:8-9)

LORD, I RESPOND TO YOUR INSTRUCTION

I should let my gentleness be evident to all men; the Lord is near. (Philippians 4:5)

❧

Lord, I thank You for the certainty of Your promises and for the wisdom of Your ways. I thank You for keeping me strong to the end, so I may be a gentle and loving person.

DAY 5

EXTENDING GOD'S HAND OF MERCY
❧

LORD, I DRAW NEAR TO YOU

Lord, You have invited me to pray for the needs of others, and since You desire what is best for them, I take this opportunity to bring these requests to You.

Since we were called into fellowship with the Lord Jesus Christ, all of us should agree with one another, so that there may be no divisions among us, and that we may be perfectly joined together in the same mind and in the same judgment. (1 Corinthians 1:9-10)

Take a moment to lift up the needs of your family and friends, and to offer up any additional burdens for others that the Lord brings to mind.

THANK YOU, LORD, FOR WHAT YOU HAVE DONE

When I consider Your heavens, the work of Your fingers, the moon and the stars, which You have set in place, what is man that You are mindful of him, and the son of man that You care for him? You made him a little lower than the heavenly beings and crowned him with glory and honor. You made him ruler over the works of Your hands, and You put everything under his feet. (Psalm 8:3-6)

15
❧

LORD, I LISTEN TO YOUR WORDS OF TRUTH

The God of all grace, who called me to His eternal glory in Christ, after I have suffered a little while, will Himself perfect, confirm, strengthen, and establish me. (1 Peter 5:10)

LORD, I RESPOND TO YOUR INSTRUCTION

You have shown me what is good; and what does the Lord require of me but to act justly and to love mercy and to walk humbly with my God? (Micah 6:8)

You have given us a new commandment to love one another even as You have loved us; so we must love one another. By this all men will know that we are Your disciples, if we have love for one another. (John 13:34-35)
❧

Lord, I thank You for Your awesome majesty and creative power. I thank You that You will perfect me in Christ Jesus, so I may demonstrate Your mercy and love to others.

DAY 6

WALKING IN GOD'S TRUTH

~

LORD, I DRAW NEAR TO YOU

Lord, I want Your Word to be deeply implanted in me so that I will know the truth and be able to express it in the way I live.

The Lord is my portion and my inheritance. (Numbers 18:20)

The steps of a man are ordered by the Lord,
And He will delight in his way;
Though he stumbles, he will not be cast down,
For the Lord upholds him with His hand. (Psalm 37:23-24)

Take a moment to affirm the truth of these words from Scripture and ask God to make them a growing reality in your life.

THANK YOU, LORD, FOR WHAT YOU HAVE DONE

God so loved the world that He gave His only begotten Son, that whoever believes in Him should not perish but have eternal life. For God did not send His Son into the world to condemn the world, but to save the world through Him. (John 3:16-17)

LORD, I LISTEN TO YOUR WORDS OF TRUTH

God lifted me out of the slimy pit, out of the mud and mire; He set my feet on a rock and gave me a firm place to stand. He put a new song in my mouth, a hymn of praise to our God. Many will see and fear and put their trust in the Lord. (Psalm 40:2-3)

LORD, I RESPOND TO YOUR INSTRUCTION

The hour has come for me to wake up from sleep, for my salvation is nearer now than when I first believed. The night is nearly over; the day is almost here. Therefore, I will cast off the works of darkness and put on the armor of light. (Romans 13:11-12)
My love must be sincere. I will hate what is evil and cling to what is good. (Romans 12:9)

~

Lord, I thank You for always being with me, for sending Your Son to give me the gift of eternal life, and for putting a new song in my mouth. Help me to cast off the works of darkness and cling to what is good.

DAY 7

RECEIVING GOD'S BLESSINGS

~

LORD, I DRAW NEAR TO YOU

O Lord, I am deeply grateful for Your wonderful acts, for Your abundant promises, and for the gift of my relationship with You through the merits of Christ.

We give thanks to You, Lord God Almighty, the One who is and who was, because You have taken Your great power and have begun to reign. (Revelation 11:17)

Blessed be the name of God for ever and ever,
For wisdom and power belong to You. (Daniel 2:20)

Take a moment to express your gratitude for the many blessings that you have received from the Lord.

THANK YOU, LORD, FOR WHAT YOU HAVE DONE

You are the high and lofty One who inhabits eternity, Whose name is holy. You live in a high and holy place but also with him who is contrite and lowly in spirit, to revive the spirit of the lowly and to revive the heart of the contrite. (Isaiah 57:15)

God promised the gospel beforehand through His prophets in the Holy Scriptures, concerning His Son—Who was a descendant of David according to the flesh, and Who was declared with power to be the Son of God, according to the Spirit of holiness, by His resurrection from the dead—Jesus Christ our Lord. (Romans 1:2-4)

LORD, I LISTEN TO YOUR WORDS OF TRUTH

Blessed be the Lord; day by day He bears our burdens, the God of our salvation. Our God is the God of salvation, and to God the Lord belongs escape from death. (Psalm 68:19-20)

LORD, I RESPOND TO YOUR INSTRUCTION

I will owe nothing to anyone except to love them, for he who loves his neighbor has fulfilled the law. (Romans 13:8)

~

Lord, I thank You for reviving the spirit of the lowly and for raising Your Son from the dead. I thank You for bearing my burdens and pouring out Your blessings on me as I seek to serve You by loving others.

DAY 8

LOVING OTHERS

❧

LORD, I DRAW NEAR TO YOU

Lord, I give thanks for Your greatness, Your goodness, and Your love, and I now draw near to enjoy Your presence.

O Lord, God of Israel, there is no God like You in heaven above or on earth below; You keep Your covenant and mercy with Your servants who walk before You with all their heart. (1 Kings 8:23; 2 Chronicles 6:14)

Take a moment to consider God's awesome majesty and thank Him that He loves you and wants an intimate relationship with you.

THANK YOU, LORD, FOR WHAT YOU HAVE DONE

The Word of God is living and active and sharper than any double-edged sword, piercing even to the dividing of soul and spirit and of joints and marrow, and it judges the thoughts and attitudes of the heart. And there is no creature hidden from His sight, but everything is uncovered and laid bare before the eyes of Him to Whom we must give account. (Hebrews 4:12-13)

The law was added that the transgression might increase. But where sin increased, grace abounded all the more, so that just as sin reigned in death, so also grace might reign through righteousness to bring eternal life through Jesus Christ our Lord. (Romans 5:20-21)

LORD, I LISTEN TO YOUR WORDS OF TRUTH

O Lord, You are our Father. We are the clay; You are the potter; we are all the work of Your hand. (Isaiah 64:8)

LORD, I RESPOND TO YOUR INSTRUCTION

There is only one Lawgiver and Judge, the One who is able to save and to destroy. Who am I to judge my neighbor? (James 4:12)

The one who loves his brother abides in the light, and there is no cause for stumbling in him. (1 John 2:10)

❧

Lord, I thank You for the living power of Your Word and for the abundance of Your grace. I thank You for creating and loving me. I will love others as You have commanded.

18

DAY 9

SEEKING GOD'S GOOD PURPOSE

LORD, I DRAW NEAR TO YOU

I am grateful to You, O God, for the blessing of Your forgiveness. I thank You that in Christ, You set me free from the guilt of the past and give me hope for the future.

A person's wickedness will punish him;
His backsliding will reprove him.
I know therefore and see that it is evil and bitter
To forsake the Lord my God
And have no fear of Him. (Jeremiah 2:19)

Take a moment to ask the Spirit to search your heart and reveal any areas of unconfessed sin. Acknowledge these to the Lord and thank Him for His forgiveness.

THANK YOU, LORD, FOR WHAT YOU HAVE DONE

The Lord, the Lord God, is compassionate and gracious, slow to anger, and abounding in lovingkindness and truth, maintaining love to thousands, and forgiving iniquity, transgression, and sin. (Exodus 34:6-7)

19

LORD, I LISTEN TO YOUR WORDS OF TRUTH

Unless one is born again, he cannot see the kingdom of God; unless one is born of water and the Spirit, he cannot enter into the kingdom of God. That which is born of the flesh is flesh, and that which is born of the Spirit is spirit. The wind blows wherever it pleases, and we hear its sound, but we cannot tell where it comes from, or where it is going. So it is with everyone born of the Spirit. (John 3:3,5-6,8)

LORD, I RESPOND TO YOUR INSTRUCTION

Since I have been approved by God to be entrusted with the gospel, I speak not as pleasing men but God, who tests my heart. I will not seek glory from men. (1 Thessalonians 2:4,6)

I will work out my salvation with fear and trembling, for it is God who works in me to will and to act according to His good purpose. (Philippians 2:12-13)

Lord, I thank You for Your compassion and graciousness and for the authority of the resurrected Christ. I seek to do Your will according to Your good purpose.

DAY 10

DETERMINING TO DO GOOD

❧

LORD, I DRAW NEAR TO YOU

I praise You, Lord, that You are intimately acquainted with my ways and that You always love me and have my best interests at heart.

May I be anxious for nothing, but in everything by prayer and petition with thanksgiving, may I let my requests be known to God. And the peace of God, which transcends all understanding, will guard my heart and my mind in Christ Jesus. (Philippians 4:6-7)

Take a moment to offer this day to the Lord and ask Him for the grace to grow in your knowledge and love for Him.

THANK YOU, LORD, FOR WHAT YOU HAVE DONE

Since God's children have partaken of flesh and blood, He too shared in their humanity so that by His death He might destroy him who holds the power of death, that is, the devil, and free those who all their lives were held in slavery by their fear of death. (Hebrews 2:14-15)

LORD, I LISTEN TO YOUR WORDS OF TRUTH

You are the door; whoever enters through You will be saved and will come in and go out and find pasture. The thief comes only to steal and kill and destroy; You have come that we may have life and have it abundantly. (John 10:9-10)

LORD, I RESPOND TO YOUR INSTRUCTION

As one who has believed in God, I want to be careful to devote myself to doing what is good. These things are good and profitable for everyone. (Titus 3:8)

In this is love, not that we loved God, but that He loved us and sent His Son to be the propitiation for our sins. Since God so loved us, we also ought to love one another. No one has ever seen God; but if we love one another, God abides in us, and His love is perfected in us. (1 John 4:10-12)

❧

Lord, I thank You that You have delivered me from the slavery of death. I thank You that Christ is the door of salvation. I choose this day to devote myself to doing good and loving others as You have loved me.

DAY 11

DISCOVERING GOD'S FAITHFULNESS

&

LORD, I DRAW NEAR TO YOU

As I approach Your throne of grace today, I am grateful that You care about the things that concern me and that You want me to offer them up to You.

When I ask, it will be given to me; when I seek, I will find; when I knock, the door will be opened to me. For everyone who asks, receives; he who seeks, finds; and to him who knocks, the door will be opened. (Matthew 7:7-8; Luke 11:9-10)

Take a moment to share your personal needs with God, including your physical, emotional, relational, and spiritual concerns.

THANK YOU, LORD, FOR WHAT YOU HAVE DONE

The Word of the Lord is upright, and all His work is done in faithfulness. He loves righteousness and justice; the earth is full of the lovingkindness of the Lord. (Psalm 33:4-5)

LORD, I LISTEN TO YOUR WORDS OF TRUTH

In Christ I have redemption through His blood, the forgiveness of sins, in accordance with the riches of God's grace that He lavished on me with all wisdom and understanding. (Ephesians 1:7-8)

LORD, I RESPOND TO YOUR INSTRUCTION

Whoever would love life and see good days must keep his tongue from evil and his lips from speaking guile. He must turn from evil and do good; he must seek peace and pursue it. For the eyes of the Lord are on the righteous, and His ears attend to their prayer, but the face of the Lord is against those who do evil. (1 Peter 3:10-12)

I will not let love and truth leave me; I will bind them around my neck and write them on the tablet of my heart. (Proverbs 3:3)

&

Lord, I thank You for Your faithfulness and for fully bearing my sins. I thank You for Your gift of redemption and forgiveness. Help me to turn away from evil and cling to the path of love and truth.

DAY 12

SOWING GOOD SEED

LORD, I DRAW NEAR TO YOU

Lord, You have invited me to pray for the needs of others, and since You desire what is best for them, I take this opportunity to bring these requests to You.

If it is possible, as far as it depends on me, let me live at peace with all men. (Romans 12:18)

Take a moment to lift up the needs of your family and friends, and to offer up any additional burdens for others that the Lord brings to mind.

THANK YOU, LORD, FOR WHAT YOU HAVE DONE

I will sing of the mercies of the Lord forever; with my mouth I will make Your faithfulness known through all generations. (Psalm 89:1)

From the rising to the setting of the sun, Your name will be great among the nations. In every place incense and pure offerings will be brought to Your name, for Your name will be great among the nations. (Malachi 1:11)

LORD, I LISTEN TO YOUR WORDS OF TRUTH

When the kindness and love of God my Savior appeared, He saved me, not by works of righteousness which I have done, but according to His mercy. He saved me through the washing of regeneration and renewal by the Holy Spirit Whom He poured out on me abundantly through Jesus Christ my Savior, so that having been justified by His grace, I might become an heir according to the hope of eternal life. (Titus 3:4-7)

LORD, I RESPOND TO YOUR INSTRUCTION

I will give generously to others without a grudging heart. (Deuteronomy 15:10)

He who sows sparingly will also reap sparingly, and he who sows bountifully will also reap bountifully. (2 Corinthians 9:6)

Lord, I thank You for Your mercies and faithfulness and for the greatness of Your name. I thank You for the washing of regeneration and renewal by the Holy Spirit. Teach me to sow bountifully by being generous to others.

DAY 13

BELIEVING GOD'S PROMISES

~&~

LORD, I DRAW NEAR TO YOU

Lord, I want Your Word to be deeply implanted in me so that I will know the truth and be able to express it in the way I live.

When I seek the Lord my God, I will find Him if I seek Him with all my heart and with all my soul. (Deuteronomy 4:29)

As for me and my household, we will serve the Lord. (Joshua 24:15)

Take a moment to affirm the truth of these words from Scripture and ask God to make them a growing reality in your life.

THANK YOU, LORD, FOR WHAT YOU HAVE DONE

I will give thanks to the Lord, for He is good; His lovingkindness endures forever. I will give thanks to the Lord for His unfailing love and His wonderful acts to the children of men, for He satisfies the thirsty soul and fills the hungry soul with good things. (Psalm 107:1,8-9)

23
~&~

LORD, I LISTEN TO YOUR WORDS OF TRUTH

God is my strong fortress, and He sets the blameless free in His way. He makes my feet like the feet of a deer; He enables me to stand on the heights. He trains my hands for battle, so that my arms can bend a bow of bronze. You give me Your shield of victory; You stoop down to make me great. You broaden the path beneath me, and my feet have not slipped. (2 Samuel 22:33-37)

LORD, I RESPOND TO YOUR INSTRUCTION

The Lord is my portion; I have promised to keep Your words. I considered my ways and turned my steps to Your testimonies. (Psalm 119:57,59)

I will devote myself to prayer, being watchful in it with thanksgiving. (Colossians 4:2)

~&~

Lord, I thank You for Your goodness and unfailing love and for being my strong fortress. I am devoted to knowing and following You.

DAY 14

EXTOLLING GOD'S GOODNESS

LORD, I DRAW NEAR TO YOU

O Lord, I am deeply grateful for Your wonderful acts, for Your abundant promises, and for the gift of my relationship with You through the merits of Christ.

You are the God who works wonders;
You have revealed Your strength among the peoples.
You redeemed Your people with Your power. (Psalm 77:14-15)

Take a moment to express your gratitude for the many blessings that you have received from the Lord.

THANK YOU, LORD, FOR WHAT YOU HAVE DONE

I will express the memory of Your abundant goodness and joyfully sing of Your righteousness. The Lord is gracious and compassionate, slow to anger, and great in lovingkindness. The Lord is good to all, and His tender mercies are over all His works. (Psalm 145:7-9)

LORD, I LISTEN TO YOUR WORDS OF TRUTH

I lift up my eyes to the hills—where does my help come from? My help comes from the Lord, Who made heaven and earth. He will not allow my foot to slip; He Who watches over me will not slumber. The Lord is my keeper; the Lord is my shade at my right hand. The sun will not harm me by day, nor the moon by night. The Lord will keep me from all evil; He will preserve my soul. The Lord will watch over my coming and going from this time forth and forever. (Psalm 121:1-3,5-8)

LORD, I RESPOND TO YOUR INSTRUCTION

Love is patient, love is kind, it does not envy; love does not boast, it is not arrogant, it does not behave rudely; it does not seek its own, it is not provoked, it keeps no record of wrongs; it does not rejoice in unrighteousness but rejoices with the truth; it bears all things, believes all things, hopes all things, endures all things. Love never fails.
(1 Corinthians 13:4-8)

Lord, I thank You for Your abundant goodness, and for Your protection. Show me how to walk in love each and every day.

DAY 15

PUTTING ON CHRIST

❧

LORD, I DRAW NEAR TO YOU

Lord, I give thanks for Your greatness, Your goodness, and Your love, and I now draw near to enjoy Your presence.

Are You a God nearby,
And not a God far away?
Can anyone hide in secret places
So that You cannot see him?
Do You not fill heaven and earth? (Jeremiah 23:23-24)

Take a moment to consider God's awesome majesty and thank Him that He loves you and wants an intimate relationship with you.

THANK YOU, LORD, FOR WHAT YOU HAVE DONE

We are looking for the blessed hope and the glorious appearing of our great God and Savior, Christ Jesus, who gave Himself for us to redeem us from all iniquity and to purify for Himself a people for His own possession, zealous for good works. (Titus 2:13-14)

25
❧

LORD, I LISTEN TO YOUR WORDS OF TRUTH

The Spirit helps me in my weakness, for I do not know what I ought to pray for, but the Spirit Himself intercedes for me with groans that words cannot express. And He who searches the hearts knows the mind of the Spirit, because the Spirit intercedes for the saints according to the will of God. (Romans 8:26-27)

LORD, I RESPOND TO YOUR INSTRUCTION

As one who has been chosen of God, holy and beloved, I will put on a heart of compassion, kindness, humility, gentleness, and patience, bearing with others and forgiving others even as the Lord forgave me; and above all these things, I will put on love, which is the bond of perfection. (Colossians 3:12-14)

❧

Lord, I thank You for the unbounded dominion of Jesus Christ and for the hope of His glorious coming. I thank You for the ministry of Your Holy Spirit, as I strive to be compassionate and forgiving toward others.

DAY 16

SEARCHING MY HEART

❧

LORD, I DRAW NEAR TO YOU

I am grateful to You, O God, for Your forgiveness. I thank You that in Christ, You have set me free from the past and given me hope for the future.

The fear of the Lord is to hate evil;
Wisdom hates pride and arrogance
And the evil way and the perverse mouth. (Proverbs 8:13)

Take a moment to ask the Spirit to search your heart and reveal any areas of unconfessed sin. Acknowledge these to the Lord and thank Him for His forgiveness.

THANK YOU, LORD, FOR WHAT YOU HAVE DONE

Ah, Lord God! You have made the heavens and the earth by Your great power and outstretched arm. Nothing is too difficult for You. You are the great and mighty God, Whose name is the Lord of hosts. You are great in counsel and mighty in deed, and Your eyes are open to all the ways of the sons of men; You reward everyone according to his ways and according to the fruit of his deeds. (Jeremiah 32:17-19)

You are the Alpha and the Omega, the Beginning and the End. To him who is thirsty, You will give to drink without cost from the spring of the water of life. (Revelation 21:6)

LORD, I LISTEN TO YOUR WORDS OF TRUTH

I want to know God and serve Him with a whole heart and with a willing mind; for the Lord searches all hearts and understands every motive behind the thoughts. (1 Chronicles 28:9)

LORD, I RESPOND TO YOUR INSTRUCTION

This is love: that I walk in obedience to God's commandments. And this is the commandment: that as I have heard from the beginning, I should walk in love. (2 John 6)

❧

Lord, I thank You that You are great in counsel and mighty in deed and that You are the Alpha and the Omega. I thank You for searching my heart, and I ask that I might walk in love and serve others in light of eternity.

DAY 17

SEIZING THE DAY

❧

LORD, I DRAW NEAR TO YOU

I praise You, Lord, that You are intimately acquainted with my ways and that You always love me and have my best interests at heart.

May I not trust in myself or in my own righteousness, nor view others with contempt. (Luke 18:9)

Take a moment to offer this day to the Lord and ask Him for the grace to grow in your knowledge and love for Him.

THANK YOU, LORD, FOR WHAT YOU HAVE DONE

All men are like grass, and all their glory is like the flower of the field. The grass withers and the flower fades, because the breath of the Lord blows on it. Surely the people are grass. The grass withers and the flower fades, but the Word of our God stands forever. (Isaiah 40:6-8)

Where is the wise man? Where is the scholar? Where is the disputer of this age? Has not God made foolish the wisdom of the world? But to those whom God has called, both Jews and Greeks, Christ is the power of God and the wisdom of God. (1 Corinthians 1:20,24)

27
❧

LORD, I LISTEN TO YOUR WORDS OF TRUTH

I have set the Lord always before me; because He is at my right hand, I will not be shaken. Therefore my heart is glad, and my glory rejoices; my body also will rest in hope. You will make known to me the path of life; in Your presence is fullness of joy; in Your right hand are pleasures forever. (Psalm 16:8-9,11)

LORD, I RESPOND TO YOUR INSTRUCTION

I will not take revenge, but leave room for the wrath of God, for it is written: "Vengeance is Mine; I will repay," says the Lord. I will not be overcome by evil, but overcome evil with good. (Romans 12:19,21)

❧

Lord, I thank You for Your eternal Word and for the power and wisdom of Jesus Christ. I thank You for the joy of Your presence, and I ask that I would grasp the brevity of life and desire to overcome evil with good.

DAY 18

REVERENCING THE KING

LORD, I DRAW NEAR TO YOU

As I approach Your throne of grace today, I am grateful that You care about the things that concern me and that You want me to offer them up to You.

May I keep Your statutes and Your commandments and be careful to do as the Lord my God has commanded me; may I not turn aside to the right or to the left. (Deuteronomy 4:40; 5:32)

Take a moment to share your personal needs with God, including your physical, emotional, relational, and spiritual concerns.

THANK YOU, LORD, FOR WHAT YOU HAVE DONE

When we were helpless, at the right time, Christ died for the ungodly. For rarely will anyone die for a righteous man, though perhaps for a good man someone would even dare to die. But God demonstrates His own love for us in that while we were still sinners, Christ died for us. (Romans 5:6-8)

LORD, I LISTEN TO YOUR WORDS OF TRUTH

My flesh and my heart may fail, but God is the strength of my heart and my portion forever. Those who are far from You will perish; You have cut off all who are unfaithful to You. But as for me, the nearness of God is my good. I have made the Lord God my refuge, that I may tell of all Your works. (Psalm 73:26-28)

LORD, I RESPOND TO YOUR INSTRUCTION

The Lord gives wisdom; from His mouth come knowledge and understanding. He stores up sound wisdom for the upright; He is a shield to those who walk in integrity, guarding the paths of justice and protecting the way of His saints. Then I will understand righteousness and justice and honesty—every good path. For wisdom will enter my heart, and knowledge will be pleasant to my soul. Discretion will protect me, and understanding will guard me. (Proverbs 2:6-11)

Lord, I thank You that You are majestic and yet You reached down in love to save us. I thank You that Your nearness is my good, and I ask that I might receive Your wisdom and reverence You, my King, above all else.

DAY 19

ACKNOWLEDGING MY NEED

~&

LORD, I DRAW NEAR TO YOU

Lord, You have invited me to pray for the needs of others, and since You desire what is best for them, I take this opportunity to bring these requests to You.

The Spirit helps me in my weakness, for I do not know what I ought to pray for, but the Spirit Himself intercedes for me with groans that words cannot express. And He who searches the hearts knows the mind of the Spirit, because the Spirit intercedes for the saints according to the will of God. (Romans 8:26-27)

Take a moment to lift up the needs of your family and friends, and to offer up any additional burdens for others that the Lord brings to mind.

THANK YOU, LORD, FOR WHAT YOU HAVE DONE

O Lord, the God of our fathers, are You not the God who is in heaven? Are You not the ruler over all the kingdoms of the nations? Power and might are in Your hand, and no one is able to withstand You. (2 Chronicles 20:6)

I will tell of the lovingkindnesses of the Lord, the praises of the Lord, according to all the Lord has done for us, and the great goodness toward the house of Israel, which He has bestowed on them according to His mercies, and according to the multitude of His lovingkindnesses. (Isaiah 63:7)

LORD, I LISTEN TO YOUR WORDS OF TRUTH

"The Lord is my portion," says my soul; "therefore, I will wait for Him." The Lord is good to those who wait for Him, to the soul who seeks Him. It is good to hope silently for the salvation of the Lord. (Lamentations 3:24-26)

LORD, I RESPOND TO YOUR INSTRUCTION

No one should seek his own good, but the good of others. (1 Corinthians 10:24)

~&

Lord, I thank You for Your power and might and for Your lovingkindness. I thank You for being my portion. Teach me always to be mindful of the needs of others.

DAY 20

PRAISING THE GREAT CREATOR

LORD, I DRAW NEAR TO YOU

Lord, I want Your Word to be deeply implanted in me so that I will know the truth and be able to express it in the way I live.

You will honor those who honor You, but those who despise You will be disdained. (1 Samuel 2:30)

The Lord rewards every man for his righteousness and faithfulness. (1 Samuel 26:23)

Take a moment to affirm the truth of these words from Scripture and ask God to make them a growing reality in your life.

THANK YOU, LORD, FOR WHAT YOU HAVE DONE

Every creature in heaven and on earth and under the earth and on the sea and all that is in them, will sing: "To Him who sits on the throne and to the Lamb be blessing and honor and glory and power for ever and ever!" (Revelation 5:13)

30

LORD, I LISTEN TO YOUR WORDS OF TRUTH

As the Father has loved You, You also have loved me. I must abide in Your love. If I keep Your commandments, I will abide in Your love, just as You kept Your Father's commandments and abide in His love. You have told me this so that Your joy may be in me and that my joy may be full. (John 15:9-11)

LORD, I RESPOND TO YOUR INSTRUCTION

I will guard my heart with all diligence, for out of it flow the issues of life. (Proverbs 4:23)

The fear of the Lord is the beginning of wisdom, and the knowledge of the Holy One is understanding. (Proverbs 9:10)

Lord, I thank You for Your surpassing loftiness and for Your dominion over the heavens. I thank You for loving me in Christ Jesus. I promise to guard my heart and purpose to know You better.

DAY 21

BEING TRANSFORMED BY THE WORD

LORD, I DRAW NEAR TO YOU

O Lord, I am deeply grateful for Your wonderful acts, for Your abundant promises, and for the gift of my relationship with You through the merits of Christ.

I will sing to the Lord, for He is highly exalted.
The Lord is my strength and my song;
He has become my salvation.
He is my God, and I will praise Him,
My father's God, and I will exalt Him. (Exodus 15:1-2)

Take a moment to express your gratitude for the many blessings that you have received from the Lord.

THANK YOU, LORD, FOR WHAT YOU HAVE DONE

The Word became flesh and dwelt among us. We have seen His glory, the glory of the only begotten of the Father, full of grace and truth. (John 1:14)

31

LORD, I LISTEN TO YOUR WORDS OF TRUTH

I do not want to be conformed to the pattern of this world but to be transformed by the renewing of my mind, that I may prove that the will of God is good and acceptable and perfect. (Romans 12:2)

LORD, I RESPOND TO YOUR INSTRUCTION

I will obey those who are in authority over me with fear and trembling and with sincerity of heart, as to Christ; not with external service as a pleaser of men, but as a slave of Christ, doing the will of God from my heart. With good will I will serve as to the Lord and not to men, knowing that I will receive back from the Lord whatever good I do. (Ephesians 6:5-8)

Lord, I thank You for the glory of the incarnate Word, for Your incomparable grandeur, and for the transforming power of Your truth. Help me to order my steps in humility and in gentleness.

DAY 22

EXTOLLING THE AUTHOR OF LIFE

❧

LORD, I DRAW NEAR TO YOU

Lord, I give thanks for Your greatness, Your goodness, and Your love, and I now draw near to enjoy Your presence.

O Lord, You have searched me and You know me.
You know when I sit down and when I rise up;
You understand my thoughts from afar.
You scrutinize my path and my lying down
And are acquainted with all my ways.
Before a word is on my tongue,
O Lord, You know it completely.
You have enclosed me behind and before,
And laid Your hand upon me. (Psalm 139:1-5)

Take a moment to consider God's awesome majesty and thank Him that He loves you and wants an intimate relationship with you.

32
❧

THANK YOU, LORD, FOR WHAT YOU HAVE DONE

The Lord has established His throne in heaven, and His kingdom rules over all. (Psalm 103:19)

LORD, I LISTEN TO YOUR WORDS OF TRUTH

Though I have not seen Jesus, I love Him; and though I do not see Him now but believe in Him, I rejoice with joy inexpressible and full of glory, for I am receiving the end of my faith, the salvation of my soul. (1 Peter 1:8-9)

LORD, I RESPOND TO YOUR INSTRUCTION

I will submit myself for the Lord's sake to every human authority, whether to a king as being supreme, or to governors as sent by him to punish evildoers and to praise those who do right; for it is the will of God that by doing good I may silence the ignorance of foolish men. (1 Peter 2:13-15)

❧

Lord, I thank You for Your unbounded kingdom and for Your sovereignty over nature. I thank You for Jesus, the Savior of my soul, and I ask that I would have the wisdom to acknowledge Your designated spheres of authority.

DAY 23

RESPONDING TO GOD'S WORD

LORD, I DRAW NEAR TO YOU

I am grateful to You, O God, for the blessing of Your forgiveness. I thank You that in Christ, You set me free from the guilt of the past and give me hope for the future.

Good and upright is the Lord;
Therefore He instructs sinners in His ways.
The Lord guides the humble in what is right
And teaches the humble His way. (Psalm 25:8-9)

Take a moment to ask the Spirit to search your heart and reveal any areas of unconfessed sin. Acknowledge these to the Lord and thank Him for His forgiveness.

THANK YOU, LORD, FOR WHAT YOU HAVE DONE

You have chosen me as Your witness and servant so that I may know and believe You and understand that You are the Lord. Before You no God was formed, nor will there be one after You. (Isaiah 43:10)

You answer us with awesome deeds of righteousness, O God of our salvation, You who are the hope of all the ends of the earth and of the farthest seas; You formed the mountains by Your strength, having armed Yourself with power; and You stilled the roaring of the seas, the roaring of their waves, and the tumult of the people. (Psalm 65:5-7)

LORD, I LISTEN TO YOUR WORDS OF TRUTH

I will give thanks to the Lord, call upon His name, and make known to others what He has done. I will sing to Him, sing praises to Him, and tell of all His wonderful acts. (1 Chronicles 16:8-9)

LORD, I RESPOND TO YOUR INSTRUCTION

Like the Bereans, I want the nobility of mind to receive the Word with great eagerness and to examine the Scriptures daily. (Acts 17:11)

Lord, I thank You for choosing me and for Your awesome deeds of righteousness. I thank You for Your wonderful acts, and I ask that You would increase my eagerness to respond to Your Word.

DAY 24

SEEKING THE WALK OF OBEDIENCE
～❧

LORD, I DRAW NEAR TO YOU

I praise You, Lord, that You are intimately acquainted with my ways and that You always love me and have my best interests at heart.

May I be more concerned about the things of God than the things of men. (Mark 8:33)

Take a moment to offer this day to the Lord and ask Him for the grace to grow in your knowledge and love for Him.

THANK YOU, LORD, FOR WHAT YOU HAVE DONE

I will ascribe to the Lord glory and strength. I will ascribe to the Lord the glory due His name and worship the Lord in the beauty of holiness. (Psalm 96:7-9)

The Lord led His people all the way in the wilderness for forty years, to humble them and to test them in order to know what was in their heart, whether or not they would keep His commands. He humbled them, allowing them to hunger and then feeding them with manna, which neither they nor their fathers had known, to teach them that man does not live on bread alone; but man lives by every word that proceeds from the mouth of the Lord. (Deuteronomy 8:2-3)

LORD, I LISTEN TO YOUR WORDS OF TRUTH

I will praise You, O Lord my God, with all my heart, and I will glorify Your name forever. For great is Your love toward me, and You have delivered my soul from the depths of the grave. (Psalm 86:12-13)

LORD, I RESPOND TO YOUR INSTRUCTION

Like Abraham, I should direct my children and my household after me to keep the way of the Lord by doing what is right and just. (Genesis 18:19)

～❧

Lord, I thank You for Your splendor and majesty and for every word that proceeds from Your mouth. I thank You for delivering my soul from the depths of the grave. From this day forth, I will obey Your commandments to serve those in my family.

DAY 25

WALKING IN THE COVENANT

❧

LORD, I DRAW NEAR TO YOU

As I approach Your throne of grace today, I am grateful that You care about the things that concern me and that You want me to offer them up to You.

Turn to me and be gracious to me,
For I am lonely and afflicted.
The troubles of my heart have multiplied;
Free me from my distresses.
Look on my affliction and my pain,
And forgive all my sins. (Psalm 25:16-18)

Take a moment to share your personal needs with God, including your physical, emotional, relational, and spiritual concerns.

THANK YOU, LORD, FOR WHAT YOU HAVE DONE

I will sing to the Lord, for He is highly exalted. The Lord is my strength and my song; He has become my salvation. He is my God, and I will praise Him, my father's God, and I will exalt Him. (Exodus 15:1-2)

LORD, I LISTEN TO YOUR WORDS OF TRUTH

We should not get drunk on wine, for that is dissipation. Instead, we should be filled with the Spirit, speaking to one another with psalms, hymns, and spiritual songs; singing and making music in our hearts to the Lord, always giving thanks to God the Father for everything, in the name of our Lord Jesus Christ. (Ephesians 5:18-20)

LORD, I RESPOND TO YOUR INSTRUCTION

If I lack wisdom, I should ask of God, who gives generously to all without reproach, and it will be given to me. (James 1:5)

I will watch carefully how I walk, not as the unwise but as wise, making the most of every opportunity, because the days are evil. I will not be foolish, but understand what the will of the Lord is. (Ephesians 5:15-17)

❧

Lord, I thank You that You are my strength and my song and for filling me with Your Holy Spirit. I ask that You guide my steps according to Your wisdom.

DAY 26

RESTING IN CHRIST

LORD, I DRAW NEAR TO YOU

Lord, You have invited me to pray for the needs of others, and since You desire what is best for them, I take this opportunity to bring these requests to You.

O Lord, the great and awesome God, who keeps His covenant and lovingkindness with those who love Him and with those who obey His commandments, we have sinned and committed iniquity; we have been wicked and have rebelled, even turning away from Your commandments. (Daniel 9:4)

Take a moment to lift up the needs of your family and friends, and to offer up any additional burdens for others that the Lord brings to mind.

THANK YOU, LORD, FOR WHAT YOU HAVE DONE

O Lord, You have searched me and You know me. You know when I sit down and when I rise up; You understand my thoughts from afar. You scrutinize my path and my lying down and are acquainted with all my ways. Before a word is on my tongue, O Lord, You know it completely. (Psalm 139:1-4)

Lord, You have said, "Come to Me, all you who labor and are heavy laden, and I will give you rest. Take My yoke upon you and learn from Me, for I am gentle and humble in heart, and you will find rest for your souls. For My yoke is easy, and My burden is light." (Matthew 11:28-30)

LORD, I LISTEN TO YOUR WORDS OF TRUTH

You have asked the Father, and He has given me another Comforter to be with me forever, even the Spirit of truth, whom the world cannot receive, because it neither sees Him nor knows Him. But I know Him, for He lives in me. (John 14:16-17)

LORD, I RESPOND TO YOUR INSTRUCTION

I will learn to fear You all the days I live on the earth and teach Your words to my children. (Deuteronomy 4:10)

Lord, I thank You for searching and knowing me and for giving me rest in Christ. I thank You for the indwelling Comforter, who helps me observe Your Word and teach it to others.

DAY 27

IDENTIFYING WITH CHRIST

❧

LORD, I DRAW NEAR TO YOU

Lord, I want Your Word to be deeply implanted in me so that I will know the truth and be able to express it in the way I live.

You are my lamp, O Lord;
The Lord turns my darkness into light.
With Your help I can advance against a troop;
With my God I can leap over a wall. (2 Samuel 22:29-30)

The joy of the Lord is my strength. (Nehemiah 8:10)

Take a moment to affirm the truth of these words from Scripture and ask God to make them a growing reality in your life.

THANK YOU, LORD, FOR WHAT YOU HAVE DONE

No one has ever seen God, but the only begotten Son, who is in the bosom of the Father, has made Him known. (John 1:18)

The Son of Man did not come to be served, but to serve, and to give His life as a ransom for many. (Matthew 20:28)

LORD, I LISTEN TO YOUR WORDS OF TRUTH

If I died with Christ, I believe that I will also live with Him, knowing that Christ, having been raised from the dead, cannot die again; death no longer has dominion over Him. For the death that He died, He died to sin once for all; but the life that He lives, He lives to God. In the same way, I must consider myself to be dead to sin, but alive to God in Christ Jesus. (Romans 6:8-11)

LORD, I RESPOND TO YOUR INSTRUCTION

I will lay up Your words in my heart and in my soul and teach them to my children, talking about them when I sit in my house and when I walk along the way and when I lie down and when I rise up. (Deuteronomy 11:18-19)

❧

Lord, I thank You for Jesus Christ who made You known and gave His life for me. I thank You for my new identity in Christ, as I serve others by making Your Word known to them.

37

DAY 28

WALKING IN THE LIGHT

LORD, I DRAW NEAR TO YOU

O Lord, I am deeply grateful for Your wonderful acts, for Your abundant promises, and for the gift of my relationship with You through the merits of Christ.

The Lord my God is the faithful God, who keeps His covenant and His lovingkindness to a thousand generations of those who love Him and keep His commands. (Deuteronomy 7:9)

Take a moment to express your gratitude for the many blessings that you have received from the Lord.

THANK YOU, LORD, FOR WHAT YOU HAVE DONE

How great are God's signs, and how mighty are His wonders! His kingdom is an eternal kingdom; His dominion endures from generation to generation. (Daniel 4:3)

The Lord said, "I have come as a light into the world, that whoever believes in Me should not stay in darkness. And if anyone hears My words but does not keep them, I do not judge him; for I did not come to judge the world, but to save the world." (John 12:46-47)

LORD, I LISTEN TO YOUR WORDS OF TRUTH

It is because of God that I am in Christ Jesus, who has become for me wisdom from God and righteousness and sanctification and redemption. (1 Corinthians 1:30)

LORD, I RESPOND TO YOUR INSTRUCTION

I will not show partiality in judgment; I will hear both small and great alike. I will not be afraid of any man, for judgment belongs to God. (Deuteronomy 1:17)

Lord, I thank You for Your great signs and wonders and for the light of Christ. I thank You that I am in Christ Jesus, and I pray that I would be impartial in judgment.

DAY 29

HEARING THE VOICE OF THE GOOD SHEPHERD

~&~

LORD, I DRAW NEAR TO YOU

Lord, I give thanks for Your greatness, Your goodness, and Your love, and I now draw near to enjoy Your presence.

Where can I go from Your Spirit?
Or where can I flee from Your presence?
If I ascend to heaven, You are there;
If I make my bed in Sheol, You are there.
If I take the wings of the dawn,
If I dwell in the furthest part of the sea,
Even there Your hand will lead me;
Your right hand will lay hold of me. (Psalm 139:7-10)

Take a moment to consider God's awesome majesty and thank Him that He loves you and wants an intimate relationship with you.

THANK YOU, LORD, FOR WHAT YOU HAVE DONE

39

Who is like You, O Lord? Who is like You—majestic in holiness, awesome in praises, working wonders? (Exodus 15:11)

I am the good Shepherd; I know My sheep and My sheep know Me—just as the Father knows Me and I know the Father—and I lay down My life for the sheep." (John 10:11,14-15)

LORD, I LISTEN TO YOUR WORDS OF TRUTH

If anyone is in Christ, he is a new creation; the old things are passed away; behold, all things have become new. (2 Corinthians 5:17)

LORD, I RESPOND TO YOUR INSTRUCTION

May those who hope in You not be ashamed because of me, O Lord God of hosts; may those who seek You not be dishonored because of me, O God of Israel. (Psalm 69:6)

~&~

Lord, I thank You for Your majestic holiness and for Jesus, the good Shepherd. I thank You that I am a new creation in Christ, and I pray that people would honor You because of the way I live.

DAY 30

PARTAKING IN SPIRITUAL BLESSING

LORD, I DRAW NEAR TO YOU

I am grateful to You, O God, for the blessing of Your forgiveness. I thank You that in Christ, You set me free from the guilt of the past and give me hope for the future.

Those whom You love You rebuke and discipline. Therefore may I be zealous and repent. (Revelation 3:19)

This is the one You esteem:
He who is humble and contrite of spirit,
And who trembles at Your word. (Isaiah 66:2)

Take a moment to ask the Spirit to search your heart and reveal any areas of unconfessed sin. Acknowledge these to the Lord and thank Him for His forgiveness.

THANK YOU, LORD, FOR WHAT YOU HAVE DONE

40

God set forth Christ to be a propitiation through faith in His blood. He did this to demonstrate His righteousness, because in His forbearance He passed over the sins committed beforehand; He did it to demonstrate His righteousness at the present time, that He might be just and the justifier of those who have faith in Jesus. Where, then, is boasting? It is excluded. By what law? Of works? No, but by a law of faith. For we maintain that a man is justified by faith apart from works of the law. (Romans 3:25-28)

LORD, I LISTEN TO YOUR WORDS OF TRUTH

Blessed be the God and Father of our Lord Jesus Christ, who has blessed me with every spiritual blessing in the heavenly realms in Christ. (Ephesians 1:3)

LORD, I RESPOND TO YOUR INSTRUCTION

The integrity of the upright guides them, but the unfaithful are destroyed by their duplicity. (Proverbs 11:3)

Lord, I thank You for the blood of Christ that makes me righteous in Your sight. I thank You that You have blessed me with every spiritual blessing. Help me to live in integrity.

DAY 31

PURSUING GOD'S PEACE

⤳

LORD, I DRAW NEAR TO YOU

I praise You, Lord, that You are intimately acquainted with my ways and that You always love me and have my best interests at heart.

Teach me Your way, O Lord;
I will walk in Your truth;
Unite my heart to fear Your name. (Psalm 86:11)

Take a moment to offer this day to the Lord and ask Him for the grace to grow in your knowledge and love for Him.

THANK YOU, LORD, FOR WHAT YOU HAVE DONE

The Lord reigns forever; He has established His throne for judgment. He will judge the world in righteousness, and He will govern the people with justice. The Lord will also be a refuge for the oppressed, a stronghold in times of trouble. Those who know Your name will trust in You, for You, Lord, have never forsaken those who seek You. (Psalm 9:7-10)

41
⤳

What the law was powerless to do in that it was weakened through the flesh, God did by sending His own Son in the likeness of sinful flesh, on account of sin. (Romans 8:3)

LORD, I LISTEN TO YOUR WORDS OF TRUTH

God raised me up with Christ and seated me with Him in the heavenly realms in Christ Jesus, in order that in the coming ages He might show the surpassing riches of His grace in kindness toward me in Christ Jesus. (Ephesians 2:6-7)

LORD, I RESPOND TO YOUR INSTRUCTION

I will pursue the things that lead to peace and to mutual edification. (Romans 14:19)

⤳

Lord, I thank You that You are a refuge for the oppressed and that You sent Your Son on my behalf. I thank You for raising me up with Christ. Help me to pursue peace with others.

DAY 32

SEEKING HEAVENLY THINGS

❧

LORD, I DRAW NEAR TO YOU

As I approach Your throne of grace today, I am grateful that You care about the things that concern me and that You want me to offer them up to You.

I was once darkness, but now I am light in the Lord. May I walk as a child of light (for the fruit of the light consists in all goodness and righteousness and truth), learning what is pleasing to the Lord. (Ephesians 5:8-10)

Take a moment to share your personal needs with God, including your physical, emotional, relational, and spiritual concerns.

THANK YOU, LORD, FOR WHAT YOU HAVE DONE

You, O Lord, are a compassionate and gracious God, slow to anger, and abounding in lovingkindness and truth. (Psalm 86:15)

42

My attitude should be the same as that of Christ Jesus, who, being in the form of God, did not consider equality with God something to be grasped, but emptied Himself, taking the form of a servant, being made in the likeness of men. And being found in appearance as a man, He humbled Himself and became obedient to death, even death on a cross. (Philippians 2:5-8)

LORD, I LISTEN TO YOUR WORDS OF TRUTH

Since I have been raised with Christ, I should seek the things above, where Christ is seated at the right hand of God. I will set my mind on the things above, not on the things on the earth, for I died, and my life is now hidden with Christ in God. When Christ who is my life appears, then I also will appear with Him in glory. (Colossians 3:1-4)

LORD, I RESPOND TO YOUR INSTRUCTION

I will not set my heart on evil things, or be an idolater, or commit sexual immorality. (1 Corinthians 10:6-8)

❧

Lord, I thank You for Your lovingkindness and truth and for Christ's willingness to humble Himself on behalf of others. I thank You for seating me at Your right hand in Christ, and I am determined to set my heart on heavenly things.

DAY 33

LIVING IN THE LIGHT

LORD, I DRAW NEAR TO YOU

Lord, You have invited me to pray for the needs of others, and since You desire what is best for them, I take this opportunity to bring these requests to You.

If we extend our souls to the hungry
And satisfy the afflicted soul,
Then our light will rise in the darkness,
And our gloom will become like the noonday. (Isaiah 58:10)

Take a moment to lift up the needs of your family and friends, and to offer up any additional burdens for others that the Lord brings to mind.

THANK YOU, LORD, FOR WHAT YOU HAVE DONE

Christ died for sins once for all, the righteous for the unrighteous, to bring me to God. Having been put to death in the body but made alive by the Spirit, He has gone into heaven and is at the right hand of God, after angels and authorities and powers were made subject to Him. (1 Peter 3:18,22)

43

LORD, I LISTEN TO YOUR WORDS OF TRUTH

The Lord is my light and my salvation; whom shall I fear? The Lord is the strength of my life; of whom shall I be afraid? (Psalm 27:1)

LORD, I RESPOND TO YOUR INSTRUCTION

Whatever is true, whatever is noble, whatever is right, whatever is pure, whatever is lovely, whatever is of good report—if anything is excellent or praiseworthy—I will think about such things. The things I have learned and received and heard and seen in those who walk with Christ I will practice, and the God of peace will be with me. (Philippians 4:8-9)

Lord, I thank You that Your righteousness endures forever and that Christ died for sins once for all. I thank You for being my light and salvation. Teach me to set my mind on those things that are pleasing to You.

DAY 34

TRUSTING IN GOD

❧

LORD, I DRAW NEAR TO YOU

Lord, I want Your Word to be deeply implanted in me so that I will know the truth and be able to express it in the way I live.

The Lord is the portion of my inheritance and my cup;
You uphold my destiny.
The boundary lines have fallen for me in pleasant places;
Surely I have a beautiful inheritance. (Psalm 16:5-6)

It is God who arms me with strength
And makes my way perfect. (Psalm 18:32)

Take a moment to affirm the truth of these words from Scripture and ask God to make them a growing reality in your life.

THANK YOU, LORD, FOR WHAT YOU HAVE DONE

44
❧

The Lord is righteous in all His ways and gracious in all His works. (Psalm 145:17)

LORD, I LISTEN TO YOUR WORDS OF TRUTH

I will trust in the Lord and do good; I will dwell in the land and feed on His faithfulness. I will delight myself in the Lord, and He will give me the desires of my heart. I will commit my way to the Lord and trust in Him, and He will bring it to pass. I will rest in the Lord and wait patiently for Him; I will not fret because of him who prospers in his way, with the man who practices evil schemes. (Psalm 37:3-5,7)

LORD, I RESPOND TO YOUR INSTRUCTION

This is the will of God, my sanctification, that I abstain from immorality and learn to possess my own vessel in sanctification and honor. For God did not call me to be impure, but to live a holy life. (1 Thessalonians 4:3-4, 7)

❧

Lord, I thank You that You are righteous and gracious to all Your works. Help me to trust and rest in You, as I purpose to live in sanctification and honor.

DAY 35

RECEIVING GOD'S MERCY

LORD, I DRAW NEAR TO YOU

O Lord, I am deeply grateful for Your wonderful acts, for Your abundant promises, and for the gift of my relationship with You through the merits of Christ.

We know the grace of our Lord Jesus Christ, that though He was rich, yet for our sakes He became poor, that we through His poverty might become rich. (2 Corinthians 8:9)

Thanks be to God for His indescribable gift! (2 Corinthians 9:15)

Take a moment to express your gratitude for the many blessings that you have received from the Lord.

THANK YOU, LORD, FOR WHAT YOU HAVE DONE

Great and marvelous are Your works, Lord God Almighty! Righteous and true are Your ways, King of the nations! Who will not fear You, O Lord, and glorify Your name? For You alone are holy. All nations will come and worship before You, for Your righteous acts have been revealed. (Revelation 15:3-4)

45

LORD, I LISTEN TO YOUR WORDS OF TRUTH

Though I walk in the midst of trouble, You will revive me; You will stretch out Your hand against the anger of my foes, and Your right hand will save me. The Lord will perfect His work in me; Your mercy, O Lord, endures forever; You will not abandon the works of Your hands. (Psalm 138:7-8)

LORD, I RESPOND TO YOUR INSTRUCTION

I have been born again, not of perishable seed, but of imperishable, through the living and abiding Word of God. Therefore, I will put away all malice and all guile and hypocrisy and envy and all slander. (1 Peter 1:23; 2:1)

Lord, I thank You that Your ways are righteous and true. Your mercy has revived me and delivered me from my troubles. Help me to put away malice and walk in love.

DAY 36

SPEAKING TRUTHFULLY

LORD, I DRAW NEAR TO YOU

Lord, I give thanks for Your greatness, Your goodness, and Your love, and I now draw near to enjoy Your presence.

You formed my inward parts;
You wove me together in my mother's womb.
I thank You because I am fearfully and wonderfully made;
Your works are wonderful,
And my soul knows it full well.
My frame was not hidden from You
When I was made in secret
And skillfully wrought in the depths of the earth.
Your eyes saw my embryo,
And all the days ordained for me
Were written in Your book
Before one of them came to be. (Psalm 139:13-16)

Take a moment to consider God's awesome majesty and thank Him that He loves you and wants an intimate relationship with you.

46

THANK YOU, LORD, FOR WHAT YOU HAVE DONE

After His baptism and temptation, Jesus began to preach and say, "Repent, for the kingdom of heaven is at hand." (Matthew 4:17)

LORD, I LISTEN TO YOUR WORDS OF TRUTH

I will trust in the Lord with all my heart and lean not on my own understanding; in all my ways I will acknowledge Him, and He will make my paths straight. I will not be wise in my own eyes, but I will fear the Lord and depart from evil. (Proverbs 3:5-7)

LORD, I RESPOND TO YOUR INSTRUCTION

Each of us must put off falsehood and speak truthfully to his neighbor, for we are members of one another. (Ephesians 4:25)

Lord, I thank You for Your Son Jesus and for His earthly ministry. I thank You for being worthy of my complete trust and that my speech will not be corrupt but truthful.

DAY 37

COMING AS A CHILD

LORD, I DRAW NEAR TO YOU

I am grateful to You, O God, for the blessing of Your forgiveness. I thank You that in Christ, You set me free from the guilt of the past and give me hope for the future.

I return to the Lord my God,
For I have stumbled because of my iniquity.
I take words with me and return to the Lord,
Saying, "Take away all iniquity and receive me graciously,
That I may offer the fruit of my lips." (Hosea 14:1-2)

Take a moment to ask the Spirit to search your heart and reveal any areas of unconfessed sin. Acknowledge these to the Lord and thank Him for His forgiveness.

THANK YOU, LORD, FOR WHAT YOU HAVE DONE

To whom can I liken You or count You equal? To whom can I compare You that You may be alike? (Isaiah 46:5)

47

LORD, I LISTEN TO YOUR WORDS OF TRUTH

Lord Jesus, You have said that unless I am converted and become like a little child, I will never enter the kingdom of heaven. Therefore, whoever humbles himself like a child is the greatest in the kingdom of heaven. (Matthew 18:3-4)

LORD, I RESPOND TO YOUR INSTRUCTION

Reckless words pierce like a sword, but the tongue of the wise brings healing. (Proverbs 12:18)

We should let the word of Christ dwell in us richly as we teach and admonish one another with all wisdom and as we sing psalms, hymns, and spiritual songs with gratitude in our hearts to God. (Colossians 3:16)

Lord, I thank You that You are incomparable. Help me to come to You as a little child. Teach me to speak words that will build others up rather than tear them down.

DAY 38

PARTAKING OF THE BREAD OF LIFE

~&

LORD, I DRAW NEAR TO YOU

I praise You, Lord, that You are intimately acquainted with my ways and that You always love me and have my best interests at heart.

May I be strong in the grace that is in Christ Jesus. (2 Timothy 2:1)

Take a moment to offer this day to the Lord and ask Him for the grace to grow in your knowledge and love for Him.

THANK YOU, LORD, FOR WHAT YOU HAVE DONE

The Lord of hosts has sworn, "Surely, as I have thought, so it will be; and as I have purposed, so it will stand. For the Lord of hosts has purposed, and who can annul it? His hand is stretched out, and who can turn it back? (Isaiah 14:24,27)

48

There will no longer be any curse. The throne of God and of the Lamb will be in the new Jerusalem, and His servants will serve Him. They will see His face, and His name will be on their foreheads. And there will be no night there; they will not need the light of a lamp or the light of the sun, for the Lord God will give them light. And they shall reign for ever and ever. (Revelation 22:3-5)

LORD, I LISTEN TO YOUR WORDS OF TRUTH

The bread of God is He who comes down from heaven and gives life to the world. You are the bread of life. He who comes to You will never hunger, and he who believes in You will never thirst. (John 6:33,35)

LORD, I RESPOND TO YOUR INSTRUCTION

A gentle answer turns away wrath, but a harsh word stirs up anger. The tongue of the wise uses knowledge rightly, but the mouth of the fool pours out folly. (Proverbs 15:1-2)

~&

Lord, I thank You that Your purposes are unchangeable and that You will create new heavens and a new earth. I thank You for Jesus, the Bread of Life, and I pray that my speech would be wise.

DAY 39

WALKING IN PEACE

❧

LORD, I DRAW NEAR TO YOU

As I approach Your throne of grace today, I am grateful that You care about the things that concern me and that You want me to offer them up to You.

We are all sons of the light and sons of the day. We do not belong to the night or to the darkness. So then, let us not be like others who are asleep, but let us be alert and self-controlled. (1 Thessalonians 5:5-6)

Take a moment to share your personal needs with God, including your physical, emotional, relational, and spiritual concerns.

THANK YOU, LORD, FOR WHAT YOU HAVE DONE

All Your works will praise you, O Lord, and Your saints will bless You. They will speak of the glory of Your kingdom and talk of Your power, so that all men may know of Your mighty acts and the glorious majesty of Your kingdom. Your kingdom is an everlasting kingdom, and Your dominion endures through all generations. (Psalm 145:10-13)

49
❧

The first man is of the dust of the earth; the second Man is from heaven. As was the earthly man, so are those who are of the earth; and as is the Man from heaven, so also are those who are of heaven. And just as we have borne the image of the earthly man, so shall we bear the likeness of the heavenly Man. (1 Corinthians 15:47-49)

LORD, I LISTEN TO YOUR WORDS OF TRUTH

Peace You leave with me; Your peace You give to me. Not as the world gives, do You give to me. I will not let my heart be troubled nor let it be fearful. (John 14:27)

LORD, I RESPOND TO YOUR INSTRUCTION

We should always pray for other believers, that our God may count them worthy of His calling and fulfill every desire for goodness and every work of faith with power. (2 Thessalonians 1:11)

❧

Lord, I thank You for Your glorious works and for Christ, the Man from heaven. I thank You for the peace Jesus gives me, as I continually remember other believers in my prayers.

DAY 40

ABIDING IN CHRIST

LORD, I DRAW NEAR TO YOU

Lord, You have invited me to pray for the needs of others, and since You desire what is best for them, I take this opportunity to bring these requests to You.

Defend the weak and the fatherless;
Do justice to the afflicted and destitute.
Rescue the poor and needy;
Deliver them from the hand of the wicked. (Psalm 82:3-4)

Take a moment to lift up the needs of your family and friends, and to offer up any additional burdens for others that the Lord brings to mind.

THANK YOU, LORD, FOR WHAT YOU HAVE DONE

Nothing is too difficult for the Lord. (Genesis 18:14)

According to the Lord's own word, we who are alive and remain until the coming of the Lord will not precede those who have fallen asleep. For the Lord Himself will come down from heaven, with a loud command, with the voice of the archangel, and with the trumpet of God, and the dead in Christ will rise first. Then we who are alive and remain will be caught up together with them in the clouds to meet the Lord in the air. And so we will be with the Lord forever.
(1 Thessalonians 4:15-17)

LORD, I LISTEN TO YOUR WORDS OF TRUTH

If I abide in You, and Your words abide in me, I can ask whatever I wish, and it will be done for me. As I ask in Your name, I will receive, that my joy may be full. (John 15:7; 16:24)

LORD, I RESPOND TO YOUR INSTRUCTION

I will remember those who led me, who spoke the Word of God to me. I will consider the outcome of their way of life and imitate their faith. (Hebrews 13:7)

Lord, I thank You that nothing is too difficult for You and that Christ will return to raise us from the dead. I choose this day to abide in Christ and to order my steps in righteousness and service to others.

DAY 41

CONFESSING AND BELIEVING

~

LORD, I DRAW NEAR TO YOU

Lord, I want Your Word to be deeply implanted in me so that I will know the truth and be able to express it in the way I live.

You preserve my life, and I am devoted to You. You are my God; You will save Your servant who trusts in You. (Psalm 86:2)

Take a moment to affirm the truth of these words from Scripture and ask God to make them a growing reality in your life.

THANK YOU, LORD, FOR WHAT YOU HAVE DONE

God is the blessed and only Sovereign, the King of kings and Lord of lords, Who alone has immortality and dwells in unapproachable light, Whom no one has seen or can see. To Him be honor and eternal dominion. (1 Timothy 6:15-16)

You are worthy to take the scroll and to open its seals, because You were slain, and with Your blood You purchased men for God from every tribe and language and people and nation. You have made them to be a kingdom and priests to serve our God, and they will reign on the earth. (Revelation 5:9-10)

51
~

LORD, I LISTEN TO YOUR WORDS OF TRUTH

If I confess with my mouth the Lord Jesus and believe in my heart that God raised Him from the dead, I will be saved. For it is with my heart that I believe unto righteousness, and it is with my mouth that I confess unto salvation. As the Scripture says, "Whoever trusts in Him will not be put to shame." (Romans 10:9-11)

LORD, I RESPOND TO YOUR INSTRUCTION

We should all be of one mind and be sympathetic, loving as brothers, compassionate, and humble. (1 Peter 3:8)

~

Lord, I thank You for Your majesty and for the saving work of Your Son. I thank You that I have confessed the Lord Jesus with my mouth, and I ask for the power to restrain my tongue and to be compassionate to others.

DAY 42

WALKING IN THE SPIRIT

LORD, I DRAW NEAR TO YOU

O Lord, I am deeply grateful for Your wonderful acts, for Your abundant promises, and for the gift of my relationship with You through the merits of Christ.

Who is like the Lord among the sons of the mighty?
God is greatly feared in the council of the holy ones
And more awesome than all who surround Him.
O Lord God of hosts, who is like You? Your faithfulness also
surrounds You. (Psalm 89:6-8)

Take a moment to express your gratitude for the many blessings that you have received from the Lord.

THANK YOU, LORD, FOR WHAT YOU HAVE DONE

In the beginning was the Word, and the Word was with God, and the Word was God. He was in the beginning with God. (John 1:1-2)

Christ suffered for me, leaving me an example that I should follow in His steps. (1 Peter 2:21)

LORD, I LISTEN TO YOUR WORDS OF TRUTH

As I walk in the Spirit, I will not fulfill the desires of the flesh. For the flesh desires what is contrary to the Spirit, and the Spirit what is contrary to the flesh; for they oppose each other, so that I may not do the things that I wish. But if I am led by the Spirit, I am not under the law. (Galatians 5:16-18)

LORD, I RESPOND TO YOUR INSTRUCTION

When I am blessed with abundance, I will beware lest my heart becomes proud, and I forget the Lord my God Who provided all good things, thinking that it was my power and the strength of my hand that brought this wealth. (Deuteronomy 8:12-14,17)

Lord, I thank You for Christ, the incarnate Word and for His sufferings on my behalf. I thank You that I have the power to walk in the Spirit, and I acknowledge You as the source of every good thing. All I have comes from You so I will be generous to others.

DAY 43

WALKING IN HUMILITY

ক্

Lord, I give thanks for Your greatness, Your goodness, and Your love, and I now draw near to enjoy Your presence.

How precious are Your thoughts to me, O God!
How vast is the sum of them!
If I should count them, they would outnumber the grains of sand.
When I awake, I am still with You. (Psalm 139:17-18)

Take a moment to consider God's awesome majesty and thank Him that He loves you and wants an intimate relationship with you.

THANK   YOU,   LORD,   FOR   WHAT   YOU   HAVE   DONE

I have come to Mount Zion, to the heavenly Jerusalem, the city of the living God, to myriads of angels, and to the assembly and church of the firstborn, who are enrolled in heaven. I have come to God, the Judge of all men, to the spirits of righteous men made perfect, to Jesus the mediator of a new covenant, and to the sprinkled blood that speaks better things than the blood of Abel. (Hebrews 12:22-24)

53
ক্

LORD,   I   LISTEN   TO   YOUR   WORDS   OF   TRUTH

Since I have a great high priest who has passed through the heavens, Jesus the Son of God, I will hold firmly to the faith I confess. For I do not have a high priest Who is unable to sympathize with my weaknesses, but one who has been tempted in every way, just as I am, yet without sin. Therefore, I will approach the throne of grace with confidence, so that I may receive mercy and find grace to help in time of need. (Hebrews 4:14-16)

LORD,   I   RESPOND   TO   YOUR   INSTRUCTION

Before his downfall the heart of a man is haughty, but humility comes before honor. (Proverbs 18:12)

ক্

Lord, I thank You for Your incomparable greatness and for Jesus the mediator of the new covenant. I thank You that He is my great high priest, and this day I choose to walk in humility rather than arrogance.

DAY 44

SPEAKING THE WORD

~

LORD, I DRAW NEAR TO YOU

I am grateful to You, O God, for the blessing of Your forgiveness. I thank You that in Christ, You set me free from the guilt of the past and give me hope for the future.

You, my Redeemer, will come to those who turn from their transgressions. (Isaiah 59:20)

Take a moment to ask the Spirit to search your heart and reveal any areas of unconfessed sin. Acknowledge these to the Lord and thank Him for His forgiveness.

THANK YOU, LORD, FOR WHAT YOU HAVE DONE

To the Lord my God belongs the heavens, even the highest heavens, the earth and everything in it. (Deuteronomy 10:14)

We see Jesus, who was made a little lower than the angels, now crowned with glory and honor because He suffered death, that by the grace of God He might taste death for everyone. For it was fitting for Him, for Whom are all things and through Whom are all things, in bringing many sons to glory, to make the author of their salvation perfect through sufferings. (Hebrews 2:9-10)

LORD, I LISTEN TO YOUR WORDS OF TRUTH

I will not let Your word depart from my mouth, but I will meditate on it day and night, so that I may be careful to do according to all that is written in it; for then I will make my way prosperous, and I will act wisely. (Joshua 1:8)

LORD, I RESPOND TO YOUR INSTRUCTION

I should offer petitions, prayers, intercessions, and thanksgiving on behalf of all men, for kings and all those who are in authority, that we may live peaceful and quiet lives in all godliness and reverence. This is good and acceptable in the sight of God our Savior, who desires all men to be saved and to come to the knowledge of the truth. (1 Timothy 2:1-4)

~

Lord, I thank You for Your rule over all things and for the earthly ministry of Jesus. I thank You for the power of Your Word, as I intercede in prayer for others.

DAY 45

FEARING THE LORD

⁓

LORD, I DRAW NEAR TO YOU

I praise You, Lord, that You are intimately acquainted with my ways and that You always love me and have my best interests at heart.

May I fear the Lord and serve You in truth with all my heart, for I consider what great things You have done for me. (1 Samuel 12:24)

Take a moment to offer this day to the Lord and ask Him for the grace to grow in your knowledge and love for Him.

THANK YOU, LORD, FOR WHAT YOU HAVE DONE

The Lord is great and greatly to be praised; He is to be feared above all gods. For all the gods of the nations are idols, but the Lord made the heavens. Splendor and majesty are before Him; strength and joy are in His place. I will ascribe to the Lord glory and strength. I will ascribe to the Lord the glory due His name and worship the Lord in the beauty of holiness. (1 Chronicles 16:25-29)

By common confession, great is the mystery of godliness: He who was revealed in the flesh, vindicated in the Spirit, seen by angels, preached among the nations, believed on in the world, taken up in glory. (1 Timothy 3:16)

55
⁓

LORD, I LISTEN TO YOUR WORDS OF TRUTH

Naked I came from my mother's womb, and naked I will depart. The Lord gives, and the Lord takes away; blessed be the name of the Lord. (Job 1:21)

LORD, I RESPOND TO YOUR INSTRUCTION

I will be of the same mind with others; I will not be haughty in mind or wise in my own estimation, but I will associate with the humble. (Romans 12:16)

⁓

Lord, I thank You for Your splendor and majesty and for the mystery of godliness in Christ. I thank You that Your name is to be blessed in all things. Teach me to treat others with compassion and dignity.

DAY 46

WAITING FOR THE PROMISE

❧

LORD, I DRAW NEAR TO YOU

As I approach Your throne of grace today, I am grateful that You care about the things that concern me and that You want me to offer them up to You.

By God's grace I want to live to the end in faith, knowing that I will not receive the promises on earth, but seeing them and welcoming them from a distance, I confess that I am a stranger and a pilgrim on the earth. Instead, I long for a better country, a heavenly one. In this way, God will not be ashamed to be called my God, for He has prepared a city for me. Like Moses, may I esteem reproach for the sake of Christ as of greater value than the treasures of this world, because I am looking to the reward. (Hebrews 11:13,16,26)

Take a moment to share your personal needs with God, including your physical, emotional, relational, and spiritual concerns.

THANK YOU, LORD, FOR WHAT YOU HAVE DONE

In the past, God overlooked the times of ignorance, but now He commands all people everywhere to repent. For He has set a day when He will judge the world with justice by the Man He has appointed. He has given assurance of this to all men by raising Him from the dead. (Acts 17:30-31)

LORD, I LISTEN TO YOUR WORDS OF TRUTH

He who does not take his cross and follow after You is not worthy of You. He who finds his life will lose it, and he who loses his life for Your sake will find it. (Matthew 10:38-39)

LORD, I RESPOND TO YOUR INSTRUCTION

For it is not the one who commends himself who is approved, but the one whom the Lord commends. (2 Corinthians 10:18)

❧

Lord, I thank You for Your authority over the nations and for the righteous judgment that You will bring to the world. I thank You that You have called me to find my life in Christ. Help me to love others and boast only in Him.

DAY 47

WALKING WORTHY OF CHRIST

~

LORD, I DRAW NEAR TO YOU

---

*Lord, You have invited me to pray for the needs of others, and since You desire
what is best for them, I take this opportunity to bring these requests to You.*

In God is my salvation and my glory;
My rock of strength, my refuge is in God.
Trust in Him at all times, O people;
Pour out your heart before Him;
God is our refuge. (Psalm 62:7-8)

*Take a moment to lift up the needs of your family and friends, and to offer up any
additional burdens for others that the Lord brings to mind.*

THANK YOU, LORD, FOR WHAT YOU HAVE DONE

The light has come into the world, but men loved darkness rather than
light because their deeds were evil. For everyone who does evil hates
the light and will not come into the light for fear that his deeds will be
exposed. But whoever practices the truth comes into the light, so that
his deeds may be clearly seen as having been done through God. (John
3:19-21)

LORD, I LISTEN TO YOUR WORDS OF TRUTH

May God fill me with the knowledge of His will through all spiritual
wisdom and understanding, so that I may walk worthy of the Lord and
please Him in every way, bearing fruit in every good work, and
growing in the knowledge of God; strengthened with all power
according to His glorious might, so that I may have great endurance
and patience with joy. (Colossians 1:9-11)

LORD, I RESPOND TO YOUR INSTRUCTION

The brother in humble circumstances should glory in his high position,
and the one who is rich should glory in his humiliation, because he will
pass away like a flower of the field. (James 1:9-10)

~

*Lord, I thank You for Your unrivaled splendor. I thank You for the power of
Christ in me. I choose to walk in humility and love.*

DAY 48

HUMBLING MYSELF

LORD, I DRAW NEAR TO YOU

Lord, I want Your Word to be deeply implanted in me so that I will know the truth and be able to express it in the way I live.

You are my hiding place and my shield;
I have put my hope in Your Word. (Psalm 119:114)

My help is in the name of the Lord,
Who made heaven and earth. (Psalm 124:8)

Take a moment to affirm the truth of these words from Scripture and ask God to make them a growing reality in your life.

THANK YOU, LORD, FOR WHAT YOU HAVE DONE

The heart is deceitful above all things and incurably sick. Who can understand it? You, the Lord, search the heart and test the mind to reward a man according to his ways, according to the fruit of his deeds. (Jeremiah 17:9-10)

The Father judges no one, but has given all judgment to the Son, that all may honor the Son just as they honor the Father. He who does not honor the Son does not honor the Father who sent Him. (John 5:22-23)

LORD, I LISTEN TO YOUR WORDS OF TRUTH

From everyone who has been given much, much will be required, and from the one who has been entrusted with much, much more will be asked. (Luke 12:48)

LORD, I RESPOND TO YOUR INSTRUCTION

I will humble myself under the mighty hand of God, that He may exalt me in due time, casting all my anxiety upon Him, because He cares for me. (1 Peter 5:6-7)

I will love my enemies and pray for those who persecute me. (Matthew 5:44)

Lord, I thank You that You search the heart and that all judgment has been given to Your merciful Son. I thank You for giving me so much in Christ. I will humble myself, lean on You, and love my enemies.

DAY 49

BEARING MUCH FRUIT

~&~

LORD, I DRAW NEAR TO YOU

O Lord, I am deeply grateful for Your wonderful acts, for Your abundant promises, and for the gift of my relationship with You through the merits of Christ.

I will exult in the Lord;
I will rejoice in the God of my salvation.
The Lord God is my strength;
He makes my feet like the feet of a deer
And enables me to go on the heights. (Habakkuk 3:18-19)

Take a moment to express your gratitude for the many blessings that you have received from the Lord.

THANK YOU, LORD, FOR WHAT YOU HAVE DONE

God numbers even the very hairs of my head. (Matthew 10:30; Luke 12:7)

LORD, I LISTEN TO YOUR WORDS OF TRUTH

Unless a grain of wheat falls to the ground and dies, it remains alone. But if it dies, it bears much fruit. The one who loves his life will lose it, and the one who hates his life in this world will keep it for eternal life. (John 12:24-25)

LORD, I RESPOND TO YOUR INSTRUCTION

He who heeds instruction is on the path of life, but he who refuses correction goes astray. (Proverbs 10:17)

I will not judge, so that I will not be judged. For in the same way I judge others, I will be judged; and with the measure I use, it will be measured to me. (Matthew 7:1-2)

~&~

Lord, I thank You that You know me intimately and that Jesus serves people with love and compassion. I thank You that You call me to bear much fruit. Give me a humble heart that responds to Your rebuke and keep me from judging others.

DAY 50
HEEDING CORRECTION

LORD, I DRAW NEAR TO YOU

Lord, I give thanks for Your greatness, Your goodness, and Your love, and I now draw near to enjoy Your presence.

The multitudes who went before Jesus and those who followed shouted,
"Hosanna to the Son of David!
Blessed is he who comes in the name of the Lord!
Hosanna in the highest!" (Matthew 21:9)

Take a moment to consider God's awesome majesty and thank Him that He loves you and wants an intimate relationship with you.

THANK YOU, LORD, FOR WHAT YOU HAVE DONE

With the Lord one day is like a thousand years, and a thousand years are like one day. (2 Peter 3:8)

The Son of Man went up to Jerusalem where He was delivered to the chief priests and to the scribes. They condemned Him to death and handed Him over to the Gentiles, who mocked Him and spat upon Him, and scourged Him and killed Him. But on the third day He rose again. (Mark 10:33-34)

LORD, I LISTEN TO YOUR WORDS OF TRUTH

I am committed to God and to the word of His grace, which is able to build me up and give me an inheritance among all those who are sanctified. (Acts 20:32)

LORD, I RESPOND TO YOUR INSTRUCTION

I will not judge my brother or regard him with contempt. Instead of judging him, I will resolve not to put a stumbling block or obstacle in my brother's way. (Romans 14:10,13)

Lord, I thank You that You are not bound by the limits of time and that Jesus suffered for me. I thank You for giving me an inheritance. Help me to respond to correction and keep me from hindering others.

DAY 51

BEARING THE PEACEABLE FRUIT OF RIGHTEOUSNESS

❧

LORD, I DRAW NEAR TO YOU

I am grateful to You, O God, for the blessing of Your forgiveness. I thank You that in Christ, You set me free from the guilt of the past and give me hope for the future.

You, the Lord, search the heart
And test the mind
To reward a man according to his ways,
According to the fruit of his deeds. (Jeremiah 17:10)

Take a moment to ask the Spirit to search your heart and reveal any areas of unconfessed sin. Acknowledge these to the Lord and thank Him for His forgiveness.

THANK YOU, LORD, FOR WHAT YOU HAVE DONE

The Lord my God is the faithful God, who keeps His covenant and His lovingkindness to a thousand generations of those who love Him and keep His commands. (Deuteronomy 7:9)

LORD, I LISTEN TO YOUR WORDS OF TRUTH

I will not let sin reign in my mortal body that I should obey its lusts. Nor will I present the members of my body to sin, as instruments of wickedness, but I will present myself to God as one who is alive from the dead and my members as instruments of righteousness to God. (Romans 6:12-13)

LORD, I RESPOND TO YOUR INSTRUCTION

Our fathers disciplined us for a little while as they thought best, but God disciplines us for our good, that we may share in His holiness. No discipline seems pleasant at the time, but painful; later on, however, it produces the peaceable fruit of righteousness for those who have been trained by it. (Hebrews 12:10-11)

❧

Lord, I thank You for Your faithfulness and for the powerful ministry of Jesus. I thank You for making me alive to You. Help me to respond well to Your discipline and to bear the peaceable fruit of righteousness.

DAY 52

LAYING A FIRM FOUNDATION

LORD, I DRAW NEAR TO YOU

I praise You, Lord, that You are intimately acquainted with my ways and that You always love me and have my best interests at heart.

You are the Lord my God; may I consecrate myself and be holy, because You are holy. (Leviticus 11:44)

Take a moment to offer this day to the Lord and ask Him for the grace to grow in your knowledge and love for Him.

THANK YOU, LORD, FOR WHAT YOU HAVE DONE

During His trials, some began to spit at Jesus and blindfold Him and strike Him with their fists and say to Him, "Prophesy!" And the guards received Him with slaps in the face. The soldiers put a purple robe on Him, then twisted together a crown of thorns and set it on Him. And they began to call out to Him, "Hail, King of the Jews!" Again and again they struck Him on the head with a staff and spit on Him, and bending their knees, they paid mock homage to Him. When they crucified Him, those who passed by hurled insults at Him, wagging their heads and saying, "Ha! You who are going to destroy the temple and build it in three days, save Yourself and come down from the cross!" And at the ninth hour Jesus cried out in a loud voice, "Eloi, Eloi, lama sabachthani?" which means, "My God, My God, why have You forsaken Me?" (Mark 14:65; 15:17-19,29-30,34)

LORD, I LISTEN TO YOUR WORDS OF TRUTH

I desire not only to call You Lord but to do what You say. By Your grace, I will come to You, hear Your words, and put them into practice. Then I will be like a man building a house, who dug down deep and laid the foundation on rock, and when a flood came, the torrent struck that house but could not shake it, because it was well built. (Luke 6:46-48)

LORD, I RESPOND TO YOUR INSTRUCTION

In obedience to the truth I will purify my soul for a sincere love of the brethren, and I will love others fervently from the heart. (1 Peter 1:22)

Lord, I thank You for Jesus' sufferings on my behalf. I thank You that Your Word gives me a firm foundation, and I ask that You would increase my love for others.

DAY 53

APPLYING GOD'S WORD TO MY LIFE

❧

LORD, I DRAW NEAR TO YOU

As I approach Your throne of grace today, I am grateful that You care about the things that concern me and that You want me to offer them up to You.

Your mercy, O Lord, endures forever;
You will not abandon the works of Your hands. (Psalm 138:8)

Take a moment to share your personal needs with God, including your physical, emotional, relational, and spiritual concerns.

THANK YOU, LORD, FOR WHAT YOU HAVE DONE

Jesus took bread, gave thanks, and broke it, and gave it to His disciples, saying, "Take and eat; this is My body." Then He took the cup, gave thanks, and offered it to them, saying, "Drink from it, all of you. This is My blood of the new covenant, which is poured out for many for the forgiveness of sins." (Matthew 26:26-28)

63
❧

LORD, I LISTEN TO YOUR WORDS OF TRUTH

I want to be a doer of the Word and not merely a hearer who deceives himself. For if anyone is a hearer of the Word and not a doer, he is like a man who looks at his natural face in a mirror, and after looking at himself, goes away, and immediately forgets what kind of person he was. But the one who looks intently into the perfect law of freedom and continues in it and is not a forgetful hearer but a doer of the Word, this one will be blessed in what he does. (James 1:22-25)

LORD, I RESPOND TO YOUR INSTRUCTION

I will not wear myself out to get rich; I will have the understanding to cease. I will not set my desire on what flies away, for wealth surely sprouts wings and flies into the heavens like an eagle. (Proverbs 23:4-5)

He who oppresses the poor reproaches his Maker, but whoever is kind to the needy honors Him. (Proverbs 14:31)

❧

Lord, I thank You for Your glory and faithfulness and for Christ's body and blood. I thank You that You want me to apply Your Word in my life, and I ask that You keep me from greed and give me a generous heart.

DAY 54

LAYING UP TREASURES IN HEAVEN

～❧

LORD, I DRAW NEAR TO YOU

Lord, You have invited me to pray for the needs of others, and since You desire what is best for them, I take this opportunity to bring these requests to You.

The God of Israel spoke,
The Rock of Israel said to me:
"He who rules over men in righteousness,
Who rules in the fear of God,
Is like the light of morning when the sun rises,
A morning without clouds,
Like the tender grass springing out of the earth
Through the sunshine after rain." (2 Samuel 23:3-4)

Take a moment to lift up the needs of your family and friends, and to offer up any additional burdens for others that the Lord brings to mind.

THANK YOU, LORD, FOR WHAT YOU HAVE DONE

Rejoice greatly, O daughter of Zion! Shout, O daughter of Jerusalem! Behold, Your King is coming to you; He is just and having salvation, humble and riding on a donkey, on a colt, the foal of a donkey. He will proclaim peace to the nations; His dominion will extend from sea to sea and from the river to the ends of the earth. (Zechariah 9:9-10)

LORD, I LISTEN TO YOUR WORDS OF TRUTH

I know that my Redeemer lives and that in the end He will stand upon the earth. (Job 19:25)

LORD, I RESPOND TO YOUR INSTRUCTION

I will not lay up for myself treasures on earth, where moth and rust destroy and where thieves break in and steal. But I will lay up for myself treasures in heaven, where moth and rust do not destroy and where thieves do not break in and steal. For where my treasure is, there my heart will be also. (Matthew 6:19-21; Luke 12:34)

～❧

Lord, I thank You for Your righteous rule over us, and for Jesus who came in humility as a servant. Help me to lay up spiritual treasures; for where my treasure is, there my heart will be also.

DAY 55

FINDING COMFORT IN HOPE

~❧

LORD, I DRAW NEAR TO YOU

Lord, I want Your Word to be deeply implanted in me so that I will know the truth and be able to express it in the way I live.

Blessed is everyone who fears the Lord,
Who walks in His ways. (Psalm 128:1)

The Lord takes pleasure in those who fear Him,
Who put their hope in His unfailing love. (Psalm 147:11)

Take a moment to affirm the truth of these words from Scripture and ask God to make them a growing reality in your life.

THANK YOU, LORD, FOR WHAT YOU HAVE DONE

Your Word is settled in heaven forever, O Lord. Your faithfulness continues through all generations; You established the earth, and it stands. They continue to this day according to Your ordinances, for all things serve You. (Psalm 119:89-91)

65
~❧

LORD, I LISTEN TO YOUR WORDS OF TRUTH

Why are you downcast, O my soul? Why are you disturbed within me? Hope in God, for I will yet praise Him for the help of His presence. O my God, my soul is downcast within me; therefore I will remember You. Why are you downcast, O my soul? Why are you disturbed within me? Hope in God, for I will yet praise Him, the help of my countenance and my God. (Psalm 42:5-6,11)

LORD, I RESPOND TO YOUR INSTRUCTION

I will not worry about tomorrow, for tomorrow will worry about itself. Each day has enough trouble of its own. (Matthew 6:34)

I do not want to lay up treasure for myself without being rich toward God. (Luke 12:21)

~❧

Lord, I thank You that all things serve You and that You and Your works are wonderful. I thank You that I can find comfort through hope in You. I will not worry about worldly things, but will seek to be rich toward You.

DAY 56

REMEMBERING THE WORKS
OF THE LORD

LORD, I DRAW NEAR TO YOU

O Lord, I am deeply grateful for Your wonderful acts, for Your abundant promises, and for the gift of my relationship with You through the merits of Christ.

Lovingkindness and truth have met together;
Righteousness and peace have kissed each other.
Truth shall spring forth from the earth,
And righteousness looks down from heaven. (Psalm 85:10-11)

Take a moment to express your gratitude for the many blessings that you have received from the Lord.

THANK YOU, LORD, FOR WHAT YOU HAVE DONE

The Lord longs to be gracious and rises to show compassion. For the Lord is a God of justice; blessed are all those who wait for Him! (Isaiah 30:18)

LORD, I LISTEN TO YOUR WORDS OF TRUTH

There is no one who has left house, or brothers, or sisters, or mother, or father, or children, or fields for Your sake and the gospel's, who will not receive a hundred times as much in this present age—houses, brothers, sisters, mothers, children, and fields, along with persecutions—and in the age to come, eternal life. (Mark 10:29-30)

LORD, I RESPOND TO YOUR INSTRUCTION

I will not withhold good from those to whom it is due, when it is in my power to act. (Proverbs 3:27)

He who is kind to the poor lends to the Lord, and He will reward him for what he has done. (Proverbs 19:17)

Lord, I thank You that You rise to show compassion and reward me for my commitment to Christ. Help me to be just and kind to others.

DAY 57

HOPING IN THE RESURRECTION

~&

LORD, I DRAW NEAR TO YOU

Lord, I give thanks for Your greatness, Your goodness, and Your love, and I now draw near to enjoy Your presence.

I will proclaim the name of the Lord and praise the greatness of my God. (Deuteronomy 32:3)

Take a moment to consider God's awesome majesty and thank Him that He loves you and wants an intimate relationship with you.

THANK YOU, LORD, FOR WHAT YOU HAVE DONE

My soul magnifies the Lord and my spirit rejoices in God my Savior, for the Mighty One has done great things for me, and holy is His name. His mercy is on those who fear Him, from generation to generation. (Luke 1:46-47,49-50)

In the past God spoke to the fathers through the prophets at many times and in various ways, but in these last days He has spoken to us by His Son, whom He appointed heir of all things, and through Whom He made the universe. (Hebrews 1:1-2)

67
~&

LORD, I LISTEN TO YOUR WORDS OF TRUTH

Having the firstfruits of the Spirit, I groan inwardly as I wait eagerly for my adoption, the redemption of my body. For in hope I have been saved, but hope that is seen is not hope; for who hopes for what he sees? But if I hope for what I do not yet see, I eagerly wait for it with perseverance. (Romans 8:23-25)

LORD, I RESPOND TO YOUR INSTRUCTION

Godliness with contentment is great gain. For I brought nothing into the world, and I can take nothing out of it. But if I have food and clothing, with these I will be content. (1 Timothy 6:6-8)

~&

Lord, I thank You for Your goodness to me and for the revelation of Your Son. I thank You for the hope of my resurrection. I will be content with what You have given me.

DAY 58

KNOWING CHRIST FULLY

❧

LORD, I DRAW NEAR TO YOU

I am grateful to You, O God, for the blessing of Your forgiveness. I thank You that in Christ, You set me free from the guilt of the past and give me hope for the future.

O Lord, do not rebuke me in Your wrath,
And do not chasten me in Your anger.
For Your arrows have pierced me deeply,
And Your hand has pressed down upon me.
There is no health in my body because of Your wrath,
Nor peace in my bones because of my sin.
For my iniquities have gone over my head;
As a heavy burden, they weigh too much for me. (Psalm 38:1-4)

Take a moment to ask the Spirit to search your heart and reveal any areas of unconfessed sin. Acknowledge these to the Lord and thank Him for His forgiveness.

THANK YOU, LORD, FOR WHAT YOU HAVE DONE

Christ is the image of the invisible God, the firstborn over all creation. For by Him all things were created that are in heaven and on earth, visible and invisible, whether thrones or dominions or rulers or authorities; all things were created by Him and for Him. And He is before all things, and in Him all things hold together. (Colossians 1:15-17)

LORD, I LISTEN TO YOUR WORDS OF TRUTH

Now I see dimly, as in a mirror, but then I shall see face to face. Now I know in part, but then I shall know fully, even as I am fully known. (1 Corinthians 13:12)

LORD, I RESPOND TO YOUR INSTRUCTION

I will keep my life free from the love of money and be content with what I have, for You have said, "I will never leave you, nor will I forsake you." (Hebrews 13:5)

❧

Lord, I thank You for Christ and for His authority over all things. I thank You that I will know Jesus fully. Help me to be content with what I have and to do good deeds toward others.

DAY 59

DELIGHTING IN THE LAW
OF THE LORD

❧

LORD, I DRAW NEAR TO YOU

I praise You, Lord, that You are intimately acquainted with my ways and that You always love me and have my best interests at heart.

As a servant of Christ and a steward of His possessions, it is required that I be found faithful. (1 Corinthians 4:1-2)

Take a moment to offer this day to the Lord and ask Him for the grace to grow in your knowledge and love for Him.

THANK YOU, LORD, FOR WHAT YOU HAVE DONE

God, who made the world and everything in it, since He is Lord of heaven and earth, does not dwell in temples built by hands. And He is not served by human hands, as though He needed anything, since He Himself gives all men life and breath and everything else. (Acts 17:24-25)

69
❧

LORD, I LISTEN TO YOUR WORDS OF TRUTH

I know that if my earthly house, or tent, is destroyed, I have a building from God, a house not made with hands, eternal in the heavens. For in this house I groan, longing to be clothed with my heavenly dwelling, because when I am clothed, I will not be found naked. For while I am in this tent, I groan, being burdened, because I do not want to be unclothed but to be clothed, so that what is mortal may be swallowed up by life. Now it is God who has made me for this very purpose and has given me the Spirit as a guarantee. (2 Corinthians 5:1-5)

LORD, I RESPOND TO YOUR INSTRUCTION

I will contribute to the needs of the saints and practice hospitality. (Romans 12:13)

❧

Lord, I thank You that Your judgments are true and righteous and that You give life to all things. I thank You for the hope of the resurrection. I delight in Your Word and will serve the needs of others as You lead me.

DAY 60

SITTING IN HEAVENLY PLACES

LORD, I DRAW NEAR TO YOU

As I approach Your throne of grace today, I am grateful that You care about the things that concern me and that You want me to offer them up to You.

Oh, that You would bless me and enlarge my territory! Let Your hand be with me and keep me from evil, so it may not grieve me. (1 Chronicles 4:10)

Take a moment to share your personal needs with God, including your physical, emotional, relational, and spiritual concerns.

THANK YOU, LORD, FOR WHAT YOU HAVE DONE

All authority in heaven and on earth has been given to the Son of God. (Matthew 28:18)

While Jesus was eating His last Passover meal with His disciples, He took bread, blessed it, and broke it, and gave it to His disciples, saying, "Take it; this is My body." Then He took the cup, and when He had given thanks He gave it to them, and they all drank from it. And He said to them, "This is My blood of the covenant, which is poured out for many." (Mark 14:22-24)

LORD, I LISTEN TO YOUR WORDS OF TRUTH

My citizenship is in heaven, from which I also eagerly await a Savior, the Lord Jesus Christ, who will transform my lowly body and conform it to His glorious body, according to the exertion of His ability to subject all things to Himself. (Philippians 3:20-21)

LORD, I RESPOND TO YOUR INSTRUCTION

A hot-tempered man stirs up dissension, but he who is slow to anger calms a quarrel. (Proverbs 15:18)

I will not mistreat my neighbor, but I will fear my God; for You are the Lord my God. (Leviticus 25:17)

Lord, I thank You that Christ has been given all authority and that His body and blood purchased my salvation. I thank You for my heavenly citizenship. I stand in awe of You and will always treat You with respect. Help me to be slow to anger.

DAY 61

PRACTICING SELF CONTROL

LORD, I DRAW NEAR TO YOU

Lord, You have invited me to pray for the needs of others, and since You desire what is best for them, I take this opportunity to bring these requests to You.

O Lord, God of our fathers Abraham, Isaac, and Israel, keep this desire in the hearts of Your people forever, and keep their hearts loyal to You. (1 Chronicles 29:18)

Hear from heaven, Your dwelling place, and forgive and deal with each man according to all he does, since You know his heart (for You alone know the hearts of men). (2 Chronicles 6:30)

Take a moment to lift up the needs of your family and friends, and to offer up any additional burdens for others that the Lord brings to mind.

THANK YOU, LORD, FOR WHAT YOU HAVE DONE

God gives strength to the weary and increases the power of the weak. Even youths grow tired and weary, and young men stumble and fall; but those who wait for the Lord will renew their strength; they will mount up with wings like eagles; they will run and not grow weary; they will walk and not be faint. (Isaiah 40:29-31)

LORD, I LISTEN TO YOUR WORDS OF TRUTH

Those who are rich in this present world should not be arrogant or set their hope on the uncertainty of riches but on God, who richly provides us with everything for our enjoyment. They should do good, be rich in good works, and be generous and willing to share. In this way they will lay up treasure for themselves as a firm foundation for the future, so that they may lay hold of true life. (1 Timothy 6:17-19)

LORD, I RESPOND TO YOUR INSTRUCTION

Starting a quarrel is like breaching a dam, so I will stop a quarrel before it breaks out. (Proverbs 17:14)

Lord, I thank You for Your sovereign power and for Your promise of complete renewal. I thank You for the many things You have given me. Help me to be self-controlled and live in peace with others.

DAY 62

RESTING IN GOD'S PROMISES

❧

LORD, I DRAW NEAR TO YOU

Lord, I want Your Word to be deeply implanted in me so that I will know the truth and be able to express it in the way I live.

I will incline my ear and come to You;
I will hear You, that my soul may live. (Isaiah 55:3)

I will seek the Lord while He may be found
And call upon Him while He is near. (Isaiah 55:6)

Take a moment to affirm the truth of these words from Scripture and ask God to make them a growing reality in your life.

THANK YOU, LORD, FOR WHAT YOU HAVE DONE

Though the Lord is on high, yet He looks upon the lowly, but the proud He knows from afar. (Psalm 138:6)

LORD, I LISTEN TO YOUR WORDS OF TRUTH

By God's grace I want to live to the end in faith, knowing that I will not receive the promises on earth, but seeing them and welcoming them from a distance, I confess that I am a stranger and a pilgrim on the earth. Instead, I long for a better country, a heavenly one. In this way, God will not be ashamed to be called my God, for He has prepared a city for me. Like Moses, I esteem reproach for the sake of Christ as of greater value than the treasures of this world, because I am looking to the reward. (Hebrews 11:13,16,26)

LORD, I RESPOND TO YOUR INSTRUCTION

I want to be above reproach, temperate, sensible, respectable, hospitable, able to teach, not given to drunkenness, not violent but gentle, not quarrelsome, not a lover of money, one who manages his own family well, and who keeps his children under control with proper respect. And I want a good reputation with outsiders, so that I will not fall into disgrace and the snare of the devil. (1 Timothy 3:2-4,7)

❧

Lord, I thank You that You look upon the lowly and that Christ serves the lowly in the power of Your Spirit. I thank You for the certainty of Your promises, as I purpose to live in a way that is pleasing to You and beneficial to others.

DAY 63
SEEKING GOD'S APPROVAL

LORD, I DRAW NEAR TO YOU

O Lord, I am deeply grateful for Your wonderful acts, for Your abundant promises, and for the gift of my relationship with You through the merits of Christ.

Blessed be the Lord, the God of Israel,
Because He has visited us and has redeemed His people.
He has raised up a horn of salvation for us
In the house of His servant David. (Luke 1:68-69)

Take a moment to express your gratitude for the many blessings that you have received from the Lord.

THANK YOU, LORD, FOR WHAT YOU HAVE DONE

You are the righteous God, who searches the hearts and secret thoughts. (Psalm 7:9)

You set before Your people life and prosperity, death and destruction; and You commanded them to love You, the Lord their God, to walk in Your ways, and to keep Your commandments, statutes, and judgments, so that they would live and multiply and that You would bless them in the land they were entering to possess. (Deuteronomy 30:15-16)

LORD, I LISTEN TO YOUR WORDS OF TRUTH

Now I am a child of God, and what I shall be has not yet been revealed. I know that when He is revealed, I shall be like Him, for I shall see Him as He is. And everyone who has this hope in Him purifies himself, just as He is pure. (1 John 3:2-3)

LORD, I RESPOND TO YOUR INSTRUCTION

I will be diligent to present myself approved to God, a workman who does not need to be ashamed and who correctly handles the Word of truth. (2 Timothy 2:15)

Lord, I thank You for knowing me perfectly and for desiring my highest good. I thank You that I am Your child, and I seek Your approval in all things that I would handle the Word of truth correctly.

DAY 64

CELEBRATING GOD'S GOODNESS

LORD, I DRAW NEAR TO YOU

Lord, I give thanks for Your greatness, Your goodness, and Your love, and I now draw near to enjoy Your presence.

You alone are the Lord.
You made the heavens,
The heaven of heavens, and all their host,
The earth and all that is on it,
The seas and all that is in them.
You give life to all that is in them,
And the host of heaven worships You. (Nehemiah 9:6)

Take a moment to consider God's awesome majesty and thank Him that He loves you and wants an intimate relationship with you.

THANK YOU, LORD, FOR WHAT YOU HAVE DONE

74

With the kind You show Yourself kind; with the blameless You show Yourself blameless; with the pure You show Yourself pure; but to the crooked You show Yourself shrewd. You save the humble, but Your eyes are on the haughty to bring them low. (2 Samuel 22:26-28)

LORD, I LISTEN TO YOUR WORDS OF TRUTH

How great is Your goodness, which You have stored up for those who fear You, which You have prepared for those who take refuge in You before the sons of men! (Psalm 31:19)

LORD, I RESPOND TO YOUR INSTRUCTION

I will not repay evil for evil to anyone, but I will pursue what is good for others. (1 Thessalonians 5:15)

I will treat subordinates with respect, not threatening them, knowing that both their Master and mine is in heaven, and there is no partiality with Him. (Ephesians 6:9)

Lord, I thank You that You are the ruler of all things and that You save the humble. I thank You for Your goodness. Help me to pursue what is in the best interests of others.

DAY 65

STANDING FIRM IN MY FAITH

~

LORD, I DRAW NEAR TO YOU

I am grateful to You, O God, for the blessing of Your forgiveness. I thank You that in Christ, You set me free from the guilt of the past and give me hope for the future.

Peter came to Jesus and asked, "Lord, how often shall my brother sin against me, and I forgive him? Up to seven times?" Jesus said to him, "I tell you, not seven times, but up to seventy times seven." (Matthew 18:21-22)

Take a moment to ask the Spirit to search your heart and reveal any areas of unconfessed sin. Acknowledge these to the Lord and thank Him for His forgiveness.

THANK YOU, LORD, FOR WHAT YOU HAVE DONE

After His resurrection, Jesus said to the two disciples on the road to Emmaus, "Did not the Christ have to suffer these things and then enter His glory?" And beginning with Moses and all the prophets, He explained to them what was said in all the Scriptures concerning Himself. Later, He appeared to His disciples and said to them, "These are the words I spoke to you while I was still with you, that everything must be fulfilled that is written about Me in the law of Moses, the prophets and the psalms." (Luke 24:26-27,44)

75
~

LORD, I LISTEN TO YOUR WORDS OF TRUTH

Because I love You, You will deliver me; You will protect me, for I acknowledge Your name. I will call upon You, and You will answer me; You will be with me in trouble, You will deliver me and honor me. (Psalm 91:14-15)

LORD, I RESPOND TO YOUR INSTRUCTION

I will prepare my mind for action and be self-controlled, setting my hope fully on the grace to be brought to me at the revelation of Jesus Christ. (1 Peter 1:13)

~

Lord, I thank You that the resurrected Christ perfectly fulfilled the Scriptures. I thank You for Your deliverance, as I stand firm in my faith.

DAY 66

HOPING IN MY GOD

LORD, I DRAW NEAR TO YOU

I praise You, Lord, that You are intimately acquainted with my ways and that You always love me and have my best interests at heart.

I desire not only to call You Lord but to do what You say. By Your grace, I will come to You, hear Your words, and put them into practice. Then I will be like a man building a house, who dug down deep and laid the foundation on rock, and when a flood came, the torrent struck that house but could not shake it, because it was well built. (Luke 6:46-48)

Take a moment to offer this day to the Lord and ask Him for the grace to grow in your knowledge and love for Him.

THANK YOU, LORD, FOR WHAT YOU HAVE DONE

Jesus is Your beloved Son in whom You are well pleased. (Matthew 3:17; Mark 1:11; Luke 3:22)

Apart from the law the righteousness of God has been made known, being witnessed by the law and the prophets, even the righteousness of God through faith in Jesus Christ to all who believe. For there is no difference, for all have sinned and fall short of the glory of God, being justified freely by His grace through the redemption that is in Christ Jesus. (Romans 3:21-24)

LORD, I LISTEN TO YOUR WORDS OF TRUTH

You have loved me with an everlasting love; You have drawn me with lovingkindness. (Jeremiah 31:3)

LORD, I RESPOND TO YOUR INSTRUCTION

What is my hope or joy or crown of rejoicing in the presence of the Lord Jesus at His coming? My glory and joy are the people in whose lives I have been privileged to have a ministry. (1 Thessalonians 2:19-20)

Lord, I thank You for Your beloved Son and for the righteousness which comes through faith in Him. I thank You for loving me with an everlasting love. I will act with courage and hope because You are with me.

DAY 67

HOLDING TO THE TRUTH

~

LORD, I DRAW NEAR TO YOU

*As I approach Your throne of grace today, I am grateful that You care about the
things that concern me and that You want me to offer them up to You.*

Guard my soul and rescue me;
Let me not be ashamed, for I take refuge in You.
May integrity and uprightness protect me,
For I wait for You. (Psalm 25:20-21)

*Take a moment to share your personal needs with God, including your physical,
emotional, relational, and spiritual concerns.*

THANK YOU, LORD, FOR WHAT YOU HAVE DONE

During the days of His flesh, Jesus offered up prayers and petitions
with loud cries and tears to the One who could save Him from death,
and He was heard because of His devoutness. Although He was a Son,
He learned obedience by the things which He suffered; and being
perfected, He became the source of eternal salvation for all who obey
Him, being designated by God as an high priest according to the order
of Melchizedek. (Hebrews 5:7-10)

77
~

LORD, I LISTEN TO YOUR WORDS OF TRUTH

Having been justified by faith, I have peace with God through the Lord
Jesus Christ, through whom I have gained access by faith into this
grace in which I stand; and I rejoice in the hope of the glory of God.
(Romans 5:1-2)

LORD, I RESPOND TO YOUR INSTRUCTION

Thanks be to God, who gives us the victory through our Lord Jesus
Christ. Therefore, I will be steadfast, immovable, abounding in the
work of the Lord, knowing that my labor in the Lord is not in vain.
(1 Corinthians 15:57-58)

~

*Lord, I thank You that You are worthy of all praise and that Jesus became the
source of eternal salvation for all who obey Him. I thank You for the peace and
hope I enjoy in Him, and I ask that I would abound in the work of the Lord and
hold firmly to the truth.*

DAY 68

ESTABLISHING MY HEART
BEFORE GOD

LORD, I DRAW NEAR TO YOU

Lord, You have invited me to pray for the needs of others, and since You desire what is best for them, I take this opportunity to bring these requests to You.

The Lord has said, "If My people who are called by My name will humble themselves and pray and seek My face and turn from their wicked ways, then I will hear from heaven and will forgive their sin and heal their land." (2 Chronicles 7:14)

Take a moment to lift up the needs of your family and friends, and to offer up any additional burdens for others that the Lord brings to mind.

THANK YOU, LORD, FOR WHAT YOU HAVE DONE

The Lord Most High is awesome, the great King over all the earth! God is the King of all the earth, and I will sing His praise. God reigns over the nations; God is seated on His holy throne. (Psalm 47:2,7-8)

As living stones, we are being built into a spiritual house to be a holy priesthood, offering spiritual sacrifices acceptable to God through Jesus Christ. We are a chosen people, a royal priesthood, a holy nation, a people for God's own possession, that we may declare the praises of Him who called us out of darkness into His marvelous light. (1 Peter 2:5,9)

LORD, I LISTEN TO YOUR WORDS OF TRUTH

Thanks be to God, who always leads us in triumph in Christ and through us spreads everywhere the fragrance of the knowledge of Him. (2 Corinthians 2:14)

LORD, I RESPOND TO YOUR INSTRUCTION

I want the Lord to establish my heart as blameless and holy before our God and Father at the coming of our Lord Jesus with all His saints. (1 Thessalonians 3:13)

Lord, I thank You for Your awesome dominion and for creating a people for Your own possession. I thank You for leading me in Christ's triumph. Establish my heart as blameless and holy before You.

DAY 69

FIGHTING THE GOOD FIGHT

❧

LORD, I DRAW NEAR TO YOU

Lord, I want Your Word to be deeply implanted in me so that I will know the truth and be able to express it in the way I live.

I will call upon You and come and pray to You, and You will listen to me. I will seek You and find You when I search for You with all my heart. (Jeremiah 29:12-13)

Take a moment to affirm the truth of these words from Scripture and ask God to make them a growing reality in your life.

THANK YOU, LORD, FOR WHAT YOU HAVE DONE

Christ has been raised from the dead, the firstfruits of those who have fallen asleep. For since death came through a man, the resurrection of the dead comes also through a Man. For as in Adam all die, so in Christ all will be made alive. But each in his own order: Christ, the firstfruits; afterward, those who are Christ's at His coming. Then the end will come, when He delivers the kingdom to God the Father, when He has abolished all rule and all authority and power. For He must reign until He has put all His enemies under His feet. The last enemy that will be destroyed is death. (1 Corinthians 15:20-26)

79

LORD, I LISTEN TO YOUR WORDS OF TRUTH

In Christ I have obtained an inheritance, having been predestined according to the plan of Him who works all things according to the counsel of His will, that we who have trusted in Christ should be to the praise of His glory. (Ephesians 1:11-12)

LORD, I RESPOND TO YOUR INSTRUCTION

I will fight the good fight of faith and lay hold of the eternal life to which I was called when I made the good confession in the presence of many witnesses. (1 Timothy 6:12)

❧

Lord, I thank You that You alone are God and that the resurrected Christ is the firstfruits of those who will be raised from the dead. I thank You for the inheritance You have given to me. Help me to remain faithful in the good fight of faith.

DAY 70

ABOUNDING IN GRACE

❧

LORD, I DRAW NEAR TO YOU

O Lord, I am deeply grateful for Your wonderful acts, for Your abundant promises, and for the gift of my relationship with You through the merits of Christ.

You are the God Who answered me in the day of my distress and have been with me wherever I have gone. (Genesis 35:3)

Take a moment to express your gratitude for the many blessings that you have received from the Lord.

THANK YOU, LORD, FOR WHAT YOU HAVE DONE

The holy city, new Jerusalem, will come down out of heaven from God, prepared as a bride adorned for her husband. A loud voice from the throne will say, "Behold, the tabernacle of God is with men, and He will dwell with them, and they will be His people, and God Himself will be with them and be their God, and He will wipe every tear from their eyes. There will be no more death or mourning or crying or pain, for the first things have passed away." He who is seated on the throne will say, "Behold, I make all things new." (Revelation 21:2-5)

LORD, I LISTEN TO YOUR WORDS OF TRUTH

The grace of my Lord was poured out on me abundantly, along with the faith and love that are in Christ Jesus. (1 Timothy 1:14)

LORD, I RESPOND TO YOUR INSTRUCTION

He who loves his own wife loves himself; for no one ever hated his own flesh, but nourishes and cherishes it, just as Christ also does the church, for we are members of His body. (Ephesians 5:28-30)

As the church is subject to Christ, so also wives should be to their husbands in everything. (Ephesians 5:24)

❧

Lord, I thank You for Your greatness and for the indescribable joy of Your new creation. I thank You for the abundance of grace I have received in Christ Jesus, as I purpose to be faithful and loving in my family relationships and in service to others.

DAY 71

CELEBRATING THE GIFT OF LIFE

❧

LORD, I DRAW NEAR TO YOU

Lord, I give thanks for Your greatness, Your goodness, and Your love, and I now draw near to enjoy Your presence.

The Lord shall reign for ever and ever. (Exodus 15:18)

Take a moment to consider God's awesome majesty and thank Him that He loves you and wants an intimate relationship with you.

THANK YOU, LORD, FOR WHAT YOU HAVE DONE

My Redeemer, the Lord of hosts is Your name; You are the Holy One of Israel. (Isaiah 47:4)

The Lord God formed man from the dust of the ground and breathed into his nostrils the breath of life; and man became a living being. And out of the ground the Lord God made every tree grow that is pleasing to the eye and good for food. In the middle of the garden were the tree of life and the tree of the knowledge of good and evil. Then the Lord God took the man and put him in the Garden of Eden to cultivate it and take care of it. (Genesis 2:7,9,15)

81
❧

LORD, I LISTEN TO YOUR WORDS OF TRUTH

Because I am a son, God has sent the Spirit of His Son into my heart, crying, "Abba, Father." So I am no longer a slave, but a son; and if a son, then an heir through Christ. (Galatians 4:6-7)

LORD, I RESPOND TO YOUR INSTRUCTION

Blessed is the man who perseveres under trial, because when he has been approved, he will receive the crown of life that God has promised to those who love Him. (James 1:12)

❧

Lord, I thank You that You are my Redeemer and that You gave me the gift of life. I thank You for making me Your child and heir. By Your grace I will persevere under trials and receive the crown of life.

DAY 72

DECLARING GOD'S
WONDROUS DEEDS

❧

LORD, I DRAW NEAR TO YOU

I am grateful to You, O God, for the blessing of Your forgiveness. I thank You that in Christ, You set me free from the guilt of the past and give me hope for the future.

Heal me, O Lord, and I will be healed;
Save me, and I will be saved,
For You are my praise. (Jeremiah 17:14)

Take a moment to ask the Spirit to search your heart and reveal any areas of unconfessed sin. Acknowledge these to the Lord and thank Him for His forgiveness.

THANK YOU, LORD, FOR WHAT YOU HAVE DONE

No one has ever seen God, but the only begotten Son, who is in the bosom of the Father, and has made Him known. (John 1:18)

O Lord, how manifold are Your works! In wisdom You made them all; the earth is full of Your possessions. (Psalm 104:24)

LORD, I LISTEN TO YOUR WORDS OF TRUTH

My mouth will tell of Your righteousness and of Your salvation all day long, though I know not its measure. I will come in the strength of the Lord God; I will proclaim Your righteousness, Yours alone. Since my youth, O God, You have taught me, and to this day I declare Your wondrous deeds. (Psalm 71:15-17)

LORD, I RESPOND TO YOUR INSTRUCTION

The father of the righteous will greatly rejoice, and he who begets a wise son will be glad in him. May my father and mother be glad; may she who gave me birth rejoice. (Proverbs 23:24-25)

❧

Lord, I thank You for Your manifold wisdom and works and for the way Your Son has made You known. I thank You for Your righteousness and wonderful deeds. Teach me to live a life that would honor my parents.

DAY 73

GROWING IN GODLINESS

❦

LORD, I DRAW NEAR TO YOU

I praise You, Lord, that You are intimately acquainted with my ways and that You always love me and have my best interests at heart.

Since I call on the Father who judges each man's work impartially, may I conduct myself in fear of the Lord during the time of my sojourn on earth. (1 Peter 1:17)

Take a moment to offer this day to the Lord and ask Him for the grace to grow in your knowledge and love for Him.

THANK YOU, LORD, FOR WHAT YOU HAVE DONE

The Son is the radiance of God's glory and the exact representation of His being, upholding all things by His powerful Word. After He cleansed our sins, He sat down at the right hand of the Majesty on high, having become as much superior to angels as the name He has inherited is more excellent than theirs. (Hebrews 1:3-4)

Since the creation of the world God's invisible attributes—His eternal power and divine nature—have been clearly seen, being understood from what has been made, so that men are without excuse. (Romans 1:20)

83

❦

LORD, I LISTEN TO YOUR WORDS OF TRUTH

"Come now, let us reason together," says the Lord. "Though your sins are like scarlet, they shall be as white as snow; though they are red as crimson, they shall be like wool." (Isaiah 1:18)

LORD, I RESPOND TO YOUR INSTRUCTION

I desire to be righteous before You in my generation. (Genesis 7:1)

Since the day of the Lord will come like a thief, what kind of person should I be in holy conduct and godliness as I look for and hasten the coming of the day of God? (2 Peter 3:10-12)

❦

Lord, I thank You for Your glorious attributes that have been revealed in creation and most clearly in Your perfect Son. I thank You for the forgiveness of my sins, and I will be diligent to conduct myself before You in godliness.

DAY 74

WALKING IN RIGHTEOUSNESS

❧

LORD, I DRAW NEAR TO YOU

As I approach Your throne of grace today, I am grateful that You care about the things that concern me and that You want me to offer them up to You.

I lift up my eyes to You,
To You who dwell in heaven.
As the eyes of servants look to the hand of their master,
As the eyes of a maid look to the hand of her mistress,
So my eyes look to the Lord my God,
Until He shows me His mercy. (Psalm 123:1-2)

Take a moment to share your personal needs with God, including your physical, emotional, relational, and spiritual concerns.

THANK YOU, LORD, FOR WHAT YOU HAVE DONE

84

The Lord will be gracious to whom He will be gracious, and He will have compassion on whom He will have compassion. (Exodus 33:19)

The Lord upholds all who fall and lifts up all who are bowed down. The eyes of all look to You, and You give them their food at the proper time. You open Your hand and satisfy the desire of every living thing. (Psalm 145:14-16)

LORD, I LISTEN TO YOUR WORDS OF TRUTH

I will greatly rejoice in the Lord; my soul will be joyful in my God. For He has clothed me with garments of salvation and arrayed me in a robe of righteousness, as a bridegroom decks himself with ornaments, and as a bride adorns herself with her jewels. (Isaiah 61:10)

LORD, I RESPOND TO YOUR INSTRUCTION

Foolishness is bound up in the heart of a child, but the rod of discipline will drive it far from him. (Proverbs 22:15)

❧

Lord, I thank You for Your graciousness and for Your loving provision. I thank You for the gift of Your righteousness, and I ask for the strength to discipline and nurture my children in the way of Christ.

DAY 75

BECOMING GOD'S CHILD

LORD, I DRAW NEAR TO YOU

Lord, You have invited me to pray for the needs of others, and since You desire what is best for them, I take this opportunity to bring these requests to You.

Lord, there is no one besides You to help the powerless against the mighty. Help us, O Lord our God, for we rest in You. O Lord, You are our God; do not let man prevail against You. (2 Chronicles 14:11)

Take a moment to lift up the needs of your family and friends, and to offer up any additional burdens for others that the Lord brings to mind.

THANK YOU, LORD, FOR WHAT YOU HAVE DONE

Jesus rejoiced in the Holy Spirit, and said, "I praise You, Father, Lord of heaven and earth, because You have hidden these things from the wise and learned, and revealed them to little children. Yes, Father, for this was well pleasing in Your sight. All things have been delivered to Me by My Father. No one knows the Son except the Father, and no one knows the Father except the Son and those to whom the Son chooses to reveal Him." (Matthew 11:25-27; Luke 10:21-22)

LORD, I LISTEN TO YOUR WORDS OF TRUTH

As many as received Christ, to them He gave the right to become children of God, to those who believe in His name, who were born not of blood, nor of the will of the flesh, nor of the will of man, but of God. (John 1:12-13)

LORD, I RESPOND TO YOUR INSTRUCTION

A fool shows his annoyance at once, but a prudent man overlooks an insult. (Proverbs 12:16)

I will not be quickly provoked in my spirit, for anger rests in the bosom of fools. (Ecclesiastes 7:9)

Lord, I thank You for Your power and greatness and for revealing Yourself through Your Son. I thank You for giving me the right to become Your child. Teach me to practice self-control so that I will not be quickly provoked.

DAY 76

TAKING HOLD OF ETERNAL LIFE

◆

LORD, I DRAW NEAR TO YOU

Lord, I want Your Word to be deeply implanted in me so that I will know the truth and be able to express it in the way I live.

I will not lay up for myself treasures on earth, where moth and rust destroy and where thieves break in and steal. But I will lay up for myself treasures in heaven, where moth and rust do not destroy and where thieves do not break in and steal. For where my treasure is, there my heart will be also. (Matthew 6:19-21; Luke 12:34)

Take a moment to affirm the truth of these words from Scripture and ask God to make them a growing reality in your life.

THANK YOU, LORD, FOR WHAT YOU HAVE DONE

Your throne is established from of old; You are from everlasting. Your testimonies stand firm; holiness adorns Your house, O Lord, forever. (Psalm 93:2,5)

Jesus fulfilled the words of the prophet Isaiah: "The Spirit of the Lord is upon Me, because He has anointed Me to preach good news to the poor. He has sent Me to proclaim freedom for the captives and recovery of sight to the blind, to set free those who are downtrodden, to proclaim the acceptable year of the Lord." (Luke 4:18-19)

LORD, I LISTEN TO YOUR WORDS OF TRUTH

Whoever hears the Word of Jesus and believes Him who sent Him has eternal life and will not come into judgment, but has passed over from death to life. (John 5:24)

LORD, I RESPOND TO YOUR INSTRUCTION

I will train up each child according to His way; even when he is old he will not depart from it. (Proverbs 22:6)

◆

Lord, I thank You that You are clothed with majesty and that Jesus came to set us free. I thank You for Your gift of eternal life through faith in Christ. Guide me as I instruct others in the way of righteousness and truth.

DAY 77

SEEKING REFUGE IN MY GOD

❧

LORD, I DRAW NEAR TO YOU

O Lord, I am deeply grateful for Your wonderful acts, for Your abundant promises, and for the gift of my relationship with You through the merits of Christ.

My heart rejoices in the Lord;
My horn is exalted in the Lord.
My mouth boasts over my enemies,
For I delight in Your salvation. (1 Samuel 2:1)

Take a moment to express your gratitude for the many blessings that you have received from the Lord.

THANK YOU, LORD, FOR WHAT YOU HAVE DONE

The eyes of the Lord are everywhere, keeping watch on the evil and the good. (Proverbs 15:3)

❧

LORD, I LISTEN TO YOUR WORDS OF TRUTH

Since I have been justified by Christ's blood, much more shall I be saved from God's wrath through Him. For if, when I was God's enemy, I was reconciled to Him through the death of His Son, much more, having been reconciled, shall I be saved through His life. And not only this, but I also rejoice in God through my Lord Jesus Christ, through whom I have now received the reconciliation. (Romans 5:9-11)

LORD, I RESPOND TO YOUR INSTRUCTION

It is better to take refuge in the Lord than to trust in man. (Psalm 118:8)

❧

Lord, I thank You for the unlimited love and forgiveness that Jesus offers through His work on the cross. I thank You for making me acceptable in Your sight because of Christ's sacrifice on my behalf. I seek refuge in You and hope in Your salvation.

DAY 78

RECEIVING GOD'S GIFT OF RIGHTEOUSNESS

LORD, I DRAW NEAR TO YOU

Lord, I give thanks for Your greatness, Your goodness, and Your love, and I now draw near to enjoy Your presence.

The Lord God is the Alpha and the Omega, Who is, and Who was, and Who is to come, the Almighty. (Revelation 1:8)

Take a moment to consider God's awesome majesty and thank Him that He loves you and wants an intimate relationship with you.

THANK YOU, LORD, FOR WHAT YOU HAVE DONE

You have sworn by Yourself; the Word has gone out of Your mouth in righteousness and will not return. Every knee will bow before You, and every tongue will acknowledge You. (Isaiah 45:23)

Jesus said to Martha, "I am the resurrection and the life. He who believes in Me will live, even though he dies, and whoever lives and believes in Me will never die." (John 11:25-26)

LORD, I LISTEN TO YOUR WORDS OF TRUTH

God made Him who knew no sin to be sin for me, so that in Him I might become the righteousness of God. (2 Corinthians 5:21)

LORD, I RESPOND TO YOUR INSTRUCTION

The righteousness of the blameless makes a straight way for them, but the wicked will fall by their own wickedness. (Proverbs 11:5)

The path of the righteous is like the first gleam of dawn, shining ever brighter until the full light of day. But the way of the wicked is like darkness; they do not know what makes them stumble. (Proverbs 4:18-19)

Lord, I thank You that Jesus is the resurrection and the life and that every knee will bow before Him. I thank You for the gift of His righteousness. Show me how to walk in His power and light.

DAY 79

RECEIVING FORGIVENESS

~

LORD, I DRAW NEAR TO YOU

I am grateful to You, O God, for the blessing of Your forgiveness. I thank You that in Christ, You set me free from the guilt of the past and give me hope for the future.

I, even I, am He who blots out your transgressions for My own sake, And I will not remember your sins. (Isaiah 43:25)

Take a moment to ask the Spirit to search your heart and reveal any areas of unconfessed sin. Acknowledge these to the Lord and thank Him for His forgiveness.

THANK YOU, LORD, FOR WHAT YOU HAVE DONE

You are the Lord, the God of all mankind. Nothing is too difficult for You. (Jeremiah 32:27)

God sent His Word to the children of Israel, telling the good news of peace through Jesus Christ, who is Lord of all. He commanded the apostles to preach to the people and to testify that He is the One whom God appointed as judge of the living and the dead. To Him all the prophets witness that through His name, everyone who believes in Him receives forgiveness of sins. (Acts 10:36, 42-43)

89
~

LORD, I LISTEN TO YOUR WORDS OF TRUTH

God, who is rich in mercy, because of His great love with which He loved me, made me alive with Christ, even when I was dead in transgressions; it is by grace I have been saved. (Ephesians 2:4-5)

LORD, I RESPOND TO YOUR INSTRUCTION

We must take heed to ourselves and to all the flock of which the Holy Spirit has made us overseers to shepherd the church of God, which He purchased with His own blood. (Acts 20:28)

~

Lord, I thank You that You are the God of all mankind and that everyone who believes in Christ will receive forgiveness of sins. I thank You for the richness of Your mercy, as I take heed to myself and guide others into the truth of Your Word.

DAY 80

EDIFYING OTHERS

❧

LORD, I DRAW NEAR TO YOU

I praise You, Lord, that You are intimately acquainted with my ways and that You always love me and have my best interests at heart.

May I not love with words or tongue, but in deed and in truth. By this I will know that I am of the truth and will assure my heart before Him; for if my heart condemns me, God is greater than my heart, and knows all things. If my heart does not condemn me, I have confidence before God and receive from Him whatever I ask, because I keep His commandments and do the things that are pleasing in His sight. (1 John 3:18-22)

Take a moment to offer this day to the Lord and ask Him for the grace to grow in your knowledge and love for Him.

THANK YOU, LORD, FOR WHAT YOU HAVE DONE

90

If the many died by the trespass of the one man, how much more did the grace of God and the gift that came by the grace of the one Man, Jesus Christ, abound to many. And the gift of God is not like the result of the one man's sin, for the judgment followed one sin and brought condemnation, but the gift followed many trespasses and brought justification. (Romans 5:15-16)

LORD, I LISTEN TO YOUR WORDS OF TRUTH

It is a trustworthy saying, that deserves full acceptance, that Christ Jesus came into the world to save sinners. I obtained mercy as the worst of sinners, so that Christ Jesus might display His unlimited patience as an example for those who would believe on Him for eternal life. (1 Timothy 1:15-16)

LORD, I RESPOND TO YOUR INSTRUCTION

In Christ Jesus, God's whole building is joined together and growing into a holy temple in the Lord, in whom we also are being built together into a dwelling of God in the Spirit. (Ephesians 2:21-22)

❧

Lord, I thank You that You are the eternal King and that the gift of Your grace in Christ Jesus abounded to the many. Help me to edify others for Your glory.

DAY 81

COMMITTING MY WORKS TO GOD

LORD, I DRAW NEAR TO YOU

As I approach Your throne of grace today, I am grateful that You care about the things that concern me and that You want me to offer them up to You.

I called on Your name, O Lord,
From the depths of the pit.
You have heard my voice:
"Do not hide Your ear from my cry for relief,
From my cry for help."
You drew near when I called on You,
And You said, "Do not fear!"
O Lord, You pleaded the cause of my soul;
You redeemed my life. (Lamentations 3:55-58)

Take a moment to share your personal needs with God, including your physical, emotional, relational, and spiritual concerns.

THANK YOU, LORD, FOR WHAT YOU HAVE DONE

The Lord my God is God of gods and Lord of lords, the great God, mighty and awesome, who shows no partiality and accepts no bribes. He executes justice for the fatherless and the widow and loves the alien, giving him food and clothing. (Deuteronomy 10:17-18)

LORD, I LISTEN TO YOUR WORDS OF TRUTH

If I claim to be without sin, I deceive myself, and the truth is not in me. If I confess my sins, He is faithful and just and will forgive me my sins and purify me from all unrighteousness. If I claim I have not sinned, I make Him a liar and His Word is not in me. (1 John 1:8-10)

LORD, I RESPOND TO YOUR INSTRUCTION

I will commit my works to the Lord, and my plans will be established. (Proverbs 16:3)

Lord, I thank You for Your justice and love. I thank You for forgiving my sins, and I commit my plans and my works to You.

DAY 82

EXERCISING MY GOD-GIVEN GIFTS

LORD, I DRAW NEAR TO YOU

Lord, You have invited me to pray for the needs of others, and since You desire what is best for them, I take this opportunity to bring these requests to You.

Salvation belongs to the Lord.
May Your blessing be on Your people. (Psalm 3:8)

Take a moment to lift up the needs of your family and friends, and to offer up any additional burdens for others that the Lord brings to mind.

THANK YOU, LORD, FOR WHAT YOU HAVE DONE

To God belong wisdom and power; counsel and understanding are His. (Job 12:13)

God was pleased to have all His fullness dwell in Christ and through Him to reconcile all things to Himself, whether things on earth or things in heaven, having made peace through the blood of His cross. (Colossians 1:19-20)

LORD, I LISTEN TO YOUR WORDS OF TRUTH

The Lord is my rock and my fortress and my deliverer; my God is my rock; I will take refuge in Him, my shield and the horn of my salvation, my stronghold and my refuge—my Savior, You save me from violence. I call on the Lord, who is worthy of praise, and I am saved from my enemies. (2 Samuel 22:2-4)

LORD, I RESPOND TO YOUR INSTRUCTION

There are different kinds of gifts, but the same Spirit. And there are different kinds of service, but the same Lord. And there are different kinds of working, but the same God works all of them in all people. But to each one the manifestation of the Spirit is given for the common good. (1 Corinthians 12:4-7)

Lord, I thank You for Your wisdom and power and for all the fullness that dwells in Christ. I thank You for being my stronghold and my refuge. Help me to exercise my God-given gifts in the service of others.

DAY 83

LEARNING GOD'S WAYS

꼭

LORD, I DRAW NEAR TO YOU

Lord, I want Your Word to be deeply implanted in me so that I will know the truth and be able to express it in the way I live.

Who is like You, O Lord?
Who is like You—majestic in holiness,
Awesome in praises, working wonders? (Exodus 15:11)

Take a moment to affirm the truth of these words from Scripture and ask God to make them a growing reality in your life.

THANK YOU, LORD, FOR WHAT YOU HAVE DONE

Once God has spoken; twice I have heard this: that power belongs to God, and that You, O Lord, are loving. For You reward each person according to what he has done. (Psalm 62:11-12)

How shall we escape if we ignore God's great salvation? This salvation, which was first announced by the Lord, was confirmed by those who heard Him. God also bore witness to it by signs and wonders and various miracles and gifts of the Holy Spirit distributed according to His will. (Hebrews 2:3-4)

93
꼭

LORD, I LISTEN TO YOUR WORDS OF TRUTH

You will instruct me and teach me in the way I should go; You will counsel me and watch over me. (Psalm 32:8)

LORD, I RESPOND TO YOUR INSTRUCTION

There should be no division in the body, but its members should have the same concern for each other. If one member suffers, all the members suffer with it; if one member is honored, all the members rejoice with it. Now we are the body of Christ, and each one of us is a member of it. (1 Corinthians 12:25-27)

꼭

Lord, I thank You for Your wondrous power and for the greatness of Your salvation in Jesus. I thank You for instructing and teaching me in the way I should go, and I ask that You would put within me a deeper concern for the welfare and unity of the body of Christ.

DAY 84

RESTING IN GOD'S CONTINUAL PRESENCE

LORD, I DRAW NEAR TO YOU

O Lord, I am deeply grateful for Your wonderful acts, for Your abundant promises, and for the gift of my relationship with You through the merits of Christ.

This poor man cried out, and the Lord heard him,
And saved him out of all his troubles.
The angel of the Lord encamps around those who fear Him,
And delivers them. (Psalm 34:6-7)

Take a moment to express your gratitude for the many blessings that you have received from the Lord.

THANK YOU, LORD, FOR WHAT YOU HAVE DONE

94

I will give thanks to the Lord, for He is good; His lovingkindness endures forever. (Psalm 118:1)

Every good and perfect gift is from above, coming down from the Father of lights, with Whom there is no variation, or shifting shadow. Of His own will He brought us forth by the Word of truth, that we might be a kind of firstfruits of His creatures. (James 1:17-18)

LORD, I LISTEN TO YOUR WORDS OF TRUTH

I am continually with You; You hold me by my right hand. You guide me with Your counsel, and afterward You will take me to glory. (Psalm 73:23-24)

LORD, I RESPOND TO YOUR INSTRUCTION

Cursed is the one who trusts in man, who depends on flesh for his strength and whose heart turns away from the Lord. But blessed is the man who trusts in the Lord, whose confidence is in Him. (Jeremiah 17:5,7)

Lord, I thank You that Your lovingkindness endures forever and that Your perfect gifts flow out of Your unchanging character. I thank You for Your continual presence. Help me to keep my trust in You rather than in the promises of people.

DAY 85

RELYING ON MY GOD

❧

LORD, I DRAW NEAR TO YOU

Lord, I give thanks for Your greatness, Your goodness, and Your love, and I now draw near to enjoy Your presence.

A great multitude, which no one could number, from all nations and tribes and peoples and languages will stand before the throne and before the Lamb, clothed with white robes with palm branches in their hands, and will cry out with a loud voice, "Salvation belongs to our God, who sits on the throne, and to the Lamb!" (Revelation 7:9-10)

Take a moment to consider God's awesome majesty and thank Him that He loves you and wants an intimate relationship with you.

THANK YOU, LORD, FOR WHAT YOU HAVE DONE

How precious are Your thoughts to me, O God! How vast is the sum of them! If I should count them, they would outnumber the grains of sand. When I awake, I am still with You. (Psalm 139:17-18)

95

❧

Jesus Christ is the faithful witness, the firstborn from the dead, and the ruler of the kings of the earth. To Him who loves us and has freed us from our sins by His blood and has made us to be a kingdom and priests to serve His God and Father; to Him be glory and power for ever and ever. (Revelation 1:5-6)

LORD, I LISTEN TO YOUR WORDS OF TRUTH

Even to my old age, You are the same, and even to my gray hairs You will carry me. You have made me, and You will bear me; You will sustain me and You will deliver me. (Isaiah 46:4)

LORD, I RESPOND TO YOUR INSTRUCTION

Who among us fears the Lord and obeys the Word of His Servant? Let him who walks in darkness and has no light trust in the name of the Lord and rely upon his God. (Isaiah 50:10)

❧

Lord, I thank You for the vastness of Your thoughts and for the freedom I have received in Christ. I thank You for Your faithful sustenance. I will always rely upon You.

DAY 86

ENCOURAGING OTHERS

LORD, I DRAW NEAR TO YOU

I am grateful to You, O God, for the blessing of Your forgiveness. I thank You that in Christ, You set me free from the guilt of the past and give me hope for the future.

All a man's ways are right in his own eyes,
But the Lord weighs the hearts. (Proverbs 21:2)

Take a moment to ask the Spirit to search your heart and reveal any areas of unconfessed sin. Acknowledge these to the Lord and thank Him for His forgiveness.

THANK YOU, LORD, FOR WHAT YOU HAVE DONE

"My thoughts are not your thoughts, neither are your ways My ways," declares the Lord. "As the heavens are higher than the earth, so are My ways higher than your ways, and My thoughts than your thoughts." (Isaiah 55:8-9)

Behold, the Lord God will come with power, and His arm will rule for Him. Behold, His reward is with Him, and His recompense accompanies Him. He will feed His flock like a shepherd; He will gather the lambs in His arms and carry them close to His heart; He will gently lead those that have young. (Isaiah 40:10-11)

LORD, I LISTEN TO YOUR WORDS OF TRUTH

I know that all things work together for good to those who love God, to those who have been called according to His purpose. (Romans 8:28)

LORD, I RESPOND TO YOUR INSTRUCTION

We must encourage one another daily, as long as it is still called "Today," lest any of us be hardened by the deceitfulness of sin. (Hebrews 3:13)

Lord, I thank You that Your ways are limitless and that You feed Your flock like a shepherd. I thank You for working all things together for my highest good. Help me to be a source of encouragement to others.

DAY 87

GLORIFYING MY GOD

❧

LORD, I DRAW NEAR TO YOU

I praise You, Lord, that You are intimately acquainted with my ways and that You always love me and have my best interests at heart.

May I listen carefully to the voice of the Lord my God and do what is right in Your sight; may I pay attention to Your commandments and keep all Your statutes. (Exodus 15:26)

Take a moment to offer this day to the Lord and ask Him for the grace to grow in your knowledge and love for Him.

THANK YOU, LORD, FOR WHAT YOU HAVE DONE

Jesus is in the Father, and the Father is in Him. He spoke the words of His Father and did the works of His Father who dwells in Him. He told us to believe in Him because He is in the Father and the Father is in Him, and because He proved it through His works. (John 14:10-11)

97
❧

Men will see the Son of Man coming in clouds with great power and glory. And He will send His angels and gather His elect from the four winds, from the ends of the earth to the ends of the heavens. We must take heed and be watchful, for we do not know when that time will come. (Mark 13:26-27,33)

LORD, I LISTEN TO YOUR WORDS OF TRUTH

No temptation has overtaken me except what is common to man. And God is faithful, who will not let me be tempted beyond what I am able, but with the temptation will also provide a way out, so that I may be able to endure it. (1 Corinthians 10:13)

LORD, I RESPOND TO YOUR INSTRUCTION

I do not want to love praise from men more than praise from God. (John 12:43)

❧

Lord, I thank You that Jesus so clearly manifested Your perfection and that He will come again in power and glory. I thank You for Your provision in times of temptation, and I ask for the grace to seek Your praise rather than that of people.

DAY 88

SEEKING HIDDEN TREASURE

LORD, I DRAW NEAR TO YOU

As I approach Your throne of grace today, I am grateful that You care about the things that concern me and that You want me to offer them up to You.

May I watch carefully how I walk, not as the unwise but as wise, making the most of every opportunity, because the days are evil. May I not be foolish, but understand what the will of the Lord is. (Ephesians 5:15-17)

Take a moment to share your personal needs with God, including your physical, emotional, relational, and spiritual concerns.

THANK YOU, LORD, FOR WHAT YOU HAVE DONE

In Christ are hidden all the treasures of wisdom and knowledge. (Colossians 2:3)

98

As the lightning comes from the east and flashes to the west, so will be the coming of the Son of Man. The sign of the Son of Man will appear in the sky, and all the nations of the earth will mourn, and they will see the Son of Man coming on the clouds of the sky with power and great glory. (Matthew 24:27,30)

LORD, I LISTEN TO YOUR WORDS OF TRUTH

God's divine power has given me all things that pertain to life and godliness, through the knowledge of Him who called me by His own glory and virtue. Through these He has given me His very great and precious promises, so that through them I may be a partaker of the divine nature, having escaped the corruption that is in the world by lust. (2 Peter 1:3-4)

LORD, I RESPOND TO YOUR INSTRUCTION

I will not seek my own interests, but those of Christ Jesus. (Philippians 2:21)

Lord, I thank You that all the treasures of wisdom and knowledge are hidden in Christ and He will return with power and great glory. I thank You for Your power and Your precious promises, as I seek the interests of Christ.

DAY 89

PROCLAIMING GOD'S SALVATION

༄

LORD, I DRAW NEAR TO YOU

Lord, You have invited me to pray for the needs of others, and since You desire what is best for them, I take this opportunity to bring these requests to You.

Many are saying, "Who will show us any good?"
O Lord, lift up the light of Your countenance upon us. (Psalm 4:6)

The eyes of the Lord are on the righteous,
And His ears are attentive to their cry. (Psalm 34:15)

Take a moment to lift up the needs of your family and friends, and to offer up any additional burdens for others that the Lord brings to mind.

THANK YOU, LORD, FOR WHAT YOU HAVE DONE

God is light; in Him there is no darkness at all. (1 John 1:5)

Everything exposed by the light becomes visible, for it is light that makes everything visible. For this reason it says, "Awake, you who sleep; arise from the dead, and Christ will shine on you." (Ephesians 5:13-14)

LORD, I LISTEN TO YOUR WORDS OF TRUTH

I want to love the Lord my God, obey His voice, and hold fast to Him. For the Lord is my life and the length of my days. (Deuteronomy 30:20)

LORD, I RESPOND TO YOUR INSTRUCTION

I want to be an example for other believers in speech, in behavior, in love, in faith, and in purity. (1 Timothy 4:12)

How beautiful on the mountains are the feet of those who bring good news, who proclaim peace, who bring good tidings, who proclaim salvation. (Isaiah 52:7; Nahum 1:15)

༄

Lord, I thank You for the light of Christ and that all things will become visible in Him. Help me to be an example for others and proclaim Your salvation.

DAY 90

ENTERING INTO THE HARVEST

LORD, I DRAW NEAR TO YOU

Lord, I want Your Word to be deeply implanted in me so that I will know the truth and be able to express it in the way I live.

There is no one holy like the Lord;
There is no one besides You;
Nor is there any Rock like our God. (1 Samuel 2:2)

Take a moment to affirm the truth of these words from Scripture and ask God to make them a growing reality in your life.

THANK YOU, LORD, FOR WHAT YOU HAVE DONE

All things are possible with God. (Matthew 19:26; Mark 10:27)

Like the roar of rushing waters and like loud peals of thunder, a great multitude will shout, "Hallelujah! For the Lord God Almighty reigns. Let us rejoice and be glad and give Him glory! For the marriage of the Lamb has come, and His bride has made herself ready." Blessed are those who are invited to the marriage supper of the Lamb. (Revelation 19:6-7,9)

LORD, I LISTEN TO YOUR WORDS OF TRUTH

Better is one day in Your courts than a thousand elsewhere; I would rather be a doorkeeper in the house of my God than dwell in the tents of the wicked. For the Lord God is a sun and shield; the Lord will give grace and glory; no good thing does He withhold from those who walk in integrity. O Lord of hosts, blessed is the man who trusts in You! (Psalm 84:10-12)

LORD, I RESPOND TO YOUR INSTRUCTION

The harvest is plentiful, but the workers are few. Therefore, I will pray that the Lord of the harvest will send out workers into His harvest. (Matthew 9:37-38; Luke 10:2)

Lord, I thank You that You reign over all things and that Christ is preparing us for union with Him. I thank You that You give grace and glory, and I ask that I would be privileged to participate in Your harvest.

DAY 91

WALKING IN THE LIGHT

~&~

LORD, I DRAW NEAR TO YOU

O Lord, I am deeply grateful for Your wonderful acts, for Your abundant promises, and for the gift of my relationship with You through the merits of Christ.

Bless the Lord, O my soul;
And all that is within me, bless His holy name.
Bless the Lord, O my soul, And forget not all His benefits;
Who forgives all your iniquities And heals all your diseases;
Who redeems your life from the pit
And crowns you with love and compassion;
Who satisfies your desires with good things,
So that your youth is renewed like the eagle's. (Psalm 103:1-5)

Take a moment to express your gratitude for the many blessings that you have received from the Lord.

THANK YOU, LORD, FOR WHAT YOU HAVE DONE

Jesus Christ is coming with the clouds, and every eye will see Him, even those who pierced Him; and all the people of the earth will mourn because of Him. Even so, Amen. (Revelation 1:7)

LORD, I LISTEN TO YOUR WORDS OF TRUTH

He who loves his father or mother more than You is not worthy of You; he who loves his son or daughter more than You is not worthy of You. (Matthew 10:37)

LORD, I RESPOND TO YOUR INSTRUCTION

If I say that I have fellowship with Christ and yet walk in the darkness, I lie and do not practice the truth. But if I walk in the light, as He is in the light, we have fellowship with one another, and the blood of Jesus His Son purifies me from all sin. (1 John 1:6-7)

~&~

Lord, I thank You for the promise of Christ's return in power. I desire to love You more than anyone else and to walk in the light.

DAY 92

BEARING FRUIT THAT REMAINS

LORD, I DRAW NEAR TO YOU

Lord, I give thanks for Your greatness, Your goodness, and Your love, and I now draw near to enjoy Your presence.

Blessed is the man who fears the Lord,
Who finds great delight in His commands. (Psalm 112:1)

Take a moment to consider God's awesome majesty and thank Him that He loves you and wants an intimate relationship with you.

THANK YOU, LORD, FOR WHAT YOU HAVE DONE

Heaven and earth will pass away, but the words of the Lord Jesus will never pass away. (Matthew 24:35; Luke 21:33)

The day of the Lord will come like a thief, in which the heavens will pass away with a roar, and the elements will be destroyed by intense heat, and the earth and its works will be laid bare. The day of God will bring about the destruction of the heavens by fire, and the elements will melt with intense heat. (2 Peter 3:10,12)

LORD, I LISTEN TO YOUR WORDS OF TRUTH

We are Your friends if we do what You command. No longer do You call us servants, because a servant does not know what his master is doing. Instead, You have called us friends, for everything that You learned from Your Father, You have made known to us. We did not choose You, but You chose us and appointed us to go and bear fruit, and that our fruit should remain, that whatever we ask the Father in Your name, He may give to us. (John 15:14-16)

LORD, I RESPOND TO YOUR INSTRUCTION

I will not be ashamed to testify about our Lord, but I will join with others in suffering for the gospel according to the power of God. (2 Timothy 1:8)

Lord, I thank You that Your promises are sure and that You will create new heavens and a new earth. I thank You for choosing me to bear fruit that remains. I will acknowledge Jesus Christ before others at every opportunity.

DAY 93

GATHERING TOGETHER IN CHRIST

◆❧

LORD, I DRAW NEAR TO YOU

I am grateful to You, O God, for the blessing of Your forgiveness. I thank You that in Christ, You set me free from the guilt of the past and give me hope for the future.

I confess my iniquity;
I am troubled by my sin.
O Lord, do not forsake me;
O my God, be not far from me!
Make haste to help me,
O Lord my salvation. (Psalm 38:18,21-22)

Take a moment to ask the Spirit to search your heart and reveal any areas of unconfessed sin. Acknowledge these to the Lord and thank Him for His forgiveness.

THANK YOU, LORD, FOR WHAT YOU HAVE DONE

There will be no temple in the new Jerusalem, because the Lord God Almighty and the Lamb are its temple. The city will not need the sun or the moon to shine on it, for the glory of God gives it light, and the Lamb is its lamp. The nations will walk by its light, and the kings of the earth will bring their splendor into it. And its gates will never be shut by day, for there will be no night there. (Revelation 21:22-25)

LORD, I LISTEN TO YOUR WORDS OF TRUTH

God made known to us the mystery of His will according to His good pleasure, which He purposed in Himself, that in the stewardship of the fullness of the times, He might gather together all things in Christ, things in the heavens and things upon the earth. (Ephesians 1:9-10)

LORD, I RESPOND TO YOUR INSTRUCTION

I will not let love and truth leave me; I will bind them around my neck and write them on the tablet of my heart. (Proverbs 3:3)

◆❧

Lord, I thank You for Your promise of future glory. I thank You for gathering all things together in Christ. Help me to be loving and truthful.

DAY 94

SHARING CHRIST'S MESSAGE

❧

LORD, I DRAW NEAR TO YOU

I praise You, Lord, that You are intimately acquainted with my ways and that You always love me and have my best interests at heart.

May I be a faithful person who fears God. (Nehemiah 7:2)

I have hope in God, that there will be a resurrection of both the righteous and the wicked. In view of this, may I strive always to keep my conscience blameless before God and men. (Acts 24:15-16)

Take a moment to offer this day to the Lord and ask Him for the grace to grow in your knowledge and love for Him.

THANK YOU, LORD, FOR WHAT YOU HAVE DONE

Who has measured the waters in the hollow of His hand, or marked off the heavens with the breadth of his hand? Who has calculated the dust of the earth in a measure, or weighed the mountains in the balance and the hills in scales? (Isaiah 40:12)

LORD, I LISTEN TO YOUR WORDS OF TRUTH

May our hearts be encouraged, being joined together in love, so that we may have the riches of the full assurance of understanding. (Colossians 2:2)

LORD, I RESPOND TO YOUR INSTRUCTION

You have called us to go and make disciples of all nations, baptizing them in the name of the Father, and of the Son, and of the Holy Spirit, teaching them to observe everything You have commanded us. And surely You are with us always, even to the end of the age. (Matthew 28:19-20)

As the Father sent the Son into the world, He also has sent us into the world. And He has prayed for those who will believe in Him through our message. (John 17:18,20)

❧

Lord, I thank You for the glory of Your majesty and for Your incomparable power and dominion. I will be encouraged in Your love as I participate in Your Great Commission by sharing the message of Christ with others.

DAY 95

WALKING IN FAITH AND LOVE

❧

LORD, I DRAW NEAR TO YOU

As I approach Your throne of grace today, I am grateful that You care about the things that concern me and that You want me to offer them up to You.

As one who has been chosen of God, holy and beloved, may I put on a heart of compassion, kindness, humility, gentleness, and patience, bearing with others and forgiving others even as the Lord forgave me; and above all these things, may I put on love, which is the bond of perfection. (Colossians 3:12-14)

Take a moment to share your personal needs with God, including your physical, emotional, relational, and spiritual concerns.

THANK YOU, LORD, FOR WHAT YOU HAVE DONE

The Word that goes forth from Your mouth will not return to You empty but will accomplish what You desire and achieve the purpose for which You sent it. (Isaiah 55:11)

105
❧

God has made everything beautiful in its time. He has also set eternity in the hearts of men; yet they cannot fathom what God has done from beginning to end. (Ecclesiastes 3:11)

LORD, I LISTEN TO YOUR WORDS OF TRUTH

Those who obey Christ's commandments abide in Him, and He in them. And this is how I know that He abides in me: by the Spirit Whom He has given me. (1 John 3:24)

LORD, I RESPOND TO YOUR INSTRUCTION

I will keep the pattern of sound teaching that I have heard, in faith and love which are in Christ Jesus. (2 Timothy 1:13)

I want everything I do to be done in love. (1 Corinthians 16:14)

❧

Lord, I thank You that Your Word never returns empty and that You have set eternity in our hearts. I thank You that You have given me Your Holy Spirit, and I choose to walk in faith and in love every day.

DAY 96

PROCLAIMING GOD'S KINGDOM

༒

LORD, I DRAW NEAR TO YOU

*Lord, You have invited me to pray for the needs of others, and since You desire
what is best for them, I take this opportunity to bring these requests to You.*

God be gracious to us and bless us,
And make His face shine upon us;
That Your way may be known on earth,
Your salvation among all nations. (Psalm 67:1-2)

Help me, O God of my salvation, for the glory of Your name;
Deliver me and forgive my sins for Your name's sake. (Psalm 79:9)

*Take a moment to lift up the needs of your family and friends, and to offer up any
additional burdens for others that the Lord brings to mind.*

THANK YOU, LORD, FOR WHAT YOU HAVE DONE

Many are the plans in a man's heart, but it is the counsel of the Lord
that will stand. (Proverbs 19:21)

The Lord is the great God, the great King above all gods. In His hand
are the depths of the earth, and the summits of the mountains are His
also. The sea is His, for He made it, and His hands formed the dry
land. He is our God and we are the people of His pasture and the
sheep under His care. (Psalm 95:3-5, 7)

LORD, I LISTEN TO YOUR WORDS OF TRUTH

Glory in the holy name of the Lord; let the hearts of those who seek the
Lord rejoice. Seek the Lord and His strength; seek His face always.
Remember the wonderful works He has done, His miracles, and the
judgments He pronounced. (1 Chronicles 16:10-12)

LORD, I RESPOND TO YOUR INSTRUCTION

You have called me to go and proclaim the kingdom of God. (Luke 9:60)

༒

*Lord, I thank You that Your counsel will stand and that Your dominion extends
to the ends of the earth. I thank You for Your wonderful works and for the power
You have given me to proclaim Your kingdom.*

DAY 97

NUMBERING MY DAYS

LORD, I DRAW NEAR TO YOU

Lord, I want Your Word to be deeply implanted in me so that I will know the truth and be able to express it in the way I live.

Because the Lord God helps me,
I will not be disgraced.
Therefore I have set my face like flint,
And I know I will not be put to shame.
He who vindicates me is near;
Who will contend with me?
Surely the Lord God will help me;
Who is he that will condemn me? (Isaiah 50:7-9)

Take a moment to affirm the truth of these words from Scripture and ask God to make them a growing reality in your life.

THANK YOU, LORD, FOR WHAT YOU HAVE DONE

Whatever the Lord pleases He does, in the heavens and on the earth, in the seas and all their depths. (Psalm 135:6)

LORD, I LISTEN TO YOUR WORDS OF TRUTH

I will sing of Your strength, yes, I will sing of Your mercy in the morning, for You have been my stronghold, my refuge in times of trouble. To You, O my Strength, I will sing praises, for God is my fortress, my loving God. (Psalm 59:16-17)

LORD, I RESPOND TO YOUR INSTRUCTION

Teach me to number my days, that I may gain a heart of wisdom. (Psalm 90:12)

The fear of the Lord, that is wisdom, and to depart from evil is understanding. (Job 28:28)

Lord, I thank You that You are the Lord of the heavens and the earth. I thank You for Your mercy and faithfulness. Help me to recognize the brevity of my earthly sojourn and live in wisdom.

DAY 98

LOVING MY NEIGHBOR

❧

O Lord, I am deeply grateful for Your wonderful acts, for Your abundant promises, and for the gift of my relationship with You through the merits of Christ.

Shout for joy, O heavens! Rejoice, O earth!
Break out into singing, O mountains!
For the Lord has comforted His people
And will have compassion on His afflicted. (Isaiah 49:13)

I will greatly rejoice in the Lord;
My soul will be joyful in my God.
For He has clothed me with garments of salvation
And arrayed me in a robe of righteousness,
As a bridegroom decks himself with ornaments,
And as a bride adorns herself with her jewels. (Isaiah 61:10)

Take a moment to express your gratitude for the many blessings that you have received from the Lord.

THANK YOU, LORD, FOR WHAT YOU HAVE DONE

You alone are the Lord. You made the heavens, even the heaven of heavens, and all their starry host, the earth and all that is on it, the seas and all that is in them. You give life to all that is in them, and the host of heaven worships You. (Nehemiah 9:6)

LORD, I LISTEN TO YOUR WORDS OF TRUTH

I will sing to the Lord as long as I live; I will sing praise to my God while I have my being. May my meditation be pleasing to Him; I will be glad in the Lord. (Psalm 104:33-34)

LORD, I RESPOND TO YOUR INSTRUCTION

Whatever I want others to do to me, I will also do to them, for this is the law and the prophets. (Matthew 7:12)

❧

Lord, I thank You for making all things. I ask that I would be glad in You and that I would serve others in the way I wish them to treat me.

DAY 99

APPLYING MY HEART TO UNDERSTANDING

LORD, I DRAW NEAR TO YOU

Lord, I give thanks for Your greatness, Your goodness, and Your love, and I now draw near to enjoy Your presence.

The Son of Man will come with the clouds of heaven. In the presence of the Ancient of Days, He will be given dominion and glory and a kingdom, so that all peoples, nations, and men of every language will worship Him. His dominion is an everlasting dominion that will not pass away, and His kingdom is one that will never be destroyed. (Daniel 7:13-14)

Take a moment to consider God's awesome majesty and thank Him that He loves you and wants an intimate relationship with you.

THANK YOU, LORD, FOR WHAT YOU HAVE DONE

The heavens declare the glory of God, and the skies proclaim the work of His hands. Day after day they pour forth speech; night after night they reveal knowledge. (Psalm 19:1-2)

LORD, I LISTEN TO YOUR WORDS OF TRUTH

I will rejoice always, pray without ceasing, and give thanks in all circumstances, for this is God's will for us in Christ Jesus. (1 Thessalonians 5:16-18)

LORD, I RESPOND TO YOUR INSTRUCTION

I will receive the words of wisdom and treasure her commands within me, turning my ear to wisdom and applying my heart to understanding. If I cry for discernment and lift up my voice for understanding, if I seek her as silver and search for her as for hidden treasures, then I will understand the fear of the Lord and find the knowledge of God. (Proverbs 2:1-5)

Lord, I thank You for Your sovereign majesty and for the heavens that proclaim the work of Your hands. I will rejoice and be thankful in all things, listen to wisdom, and apply my heart to understanding.

DAY 100

STUDYING GOD'S WORD

LORD, I DRAW NEAR TO YOU

I am grateful to You, O God, for the blessing of Your forgiveness. I thank You that in Christ, You set me free from the guilt of the past and give me hope for the future.

Who may ascend the hill of the Lord?
Who may stand in His holy place?
He who has clean hands and a pure heart,
Who has not lifted up his soul to an idol
Or sworn by what is false. (Psalm 24:3-4)

Take a moment to ask the Spirit to search your heart and reveal any areas of unconfessed sin. Acknowledge these to the Lord and thank Him for His forgiveness.

THANK YOU, LORD, FOR WHAT YOU HAVE DONE

God is wise in heart and mighty in strength. Who has resisted Him without harm? (Job 9:4)

O Lord of hosts, God of Israel, enthroned between the cherubim, You alone are God over all the kingdoms of the earth. You have made heaven and earth. (Isaiah 37:16)

LORD, I LISTEN TO YOUR WORDS OF TRUTH

God both raised the Lord and will also raise me up through His power. (1 Corinthians 6:14)

LORD, I RESPOND TO YOUR INSTRUCTION

Like Ezra, I want to set my heart to study the Word of the Lord, and to do it, and to teach it to others. (Ezra 7:10)

I want to be a person of faith, who does not doubt the promises of God, and not a double-minded man, who is unstable in all his ways. (James 1:6,8)

Lord, I thank You for Your wisdom and strength and for Your authority over all things. I thank You for the assurance of the resurrection. Teach me Your Word that I may find hope in Your promises.

DAY 101

WALKING IN NEWNESS OF LIFE

～

LORD, I DRAW NEAR TO YOU

I praise You, Lord, that You are intimately acquainted with my ways and that You always love me and have my best interests at heart.

As one who knows righteousness, who has Your law in my heart, may I not fear the reproach of men or be terrified by their revilings. (Isaiah 51:7)

Take a moment to offer this day to the Lord and ask Him for the grace to grow in your knowledge and love for Him.

THANK YOU, LORD, FOR WHAT YOU HAVE DONE

Lord, You have been our dwelling place throughout all generations. Before the mountains were born or You brought forth the earth and the world, from everlasting to everlasting, You are God. You turn men back into dust, and say, "Return, O children of men." For a thousand years in Your sight are like yesterday when it passes by or like a watch in the night. (Psalm 90:1-4)

111
～

Multitudes who sleep in the dust of the earth will awake, some to everlasting life, others to shame and everlasting contempt. Those who are wise will shine like the brightness of the heavens, and those who lead many to righteousness like the stars for ever and ever. (Daniel 12:2-3)

LORD, I LISTEN TO YOUR WORDS OF TRUTH

All of us who were baptized into Christ Jesus were baptized into His death. I was therefore buried with Him through baptism into death, in order that just as Christ was raised from the dead through the glory of the Father, so I too may walk in newness of life. (Romans 6:3-4)

LORD, I RESPOND TO YOUR INSTRUCTION

Whoever is wise understands these things; whoever is discerning knows them. The ways of the Lord are right; the righteous will walk in them, but transgressors will stumble in them. (Hosea 14:9)

～

Lord, I thank You that You are everlasting and that You promise to raise me from the dead so that I can dwell with You forever. I thank You for newness of life in Christ, as I strive to walk in wisdom.

DAY 102

LOVING AND FORGIVING

LORD, I DRAW NEAR TO YOU

As I approach Your throne of grace today, I am grateful that You care about the things that concern me and that You want me to offer them up to You.

May I be above reproach, temperate, sensible, respectable, hospitable, able to teach, not given to drunkenness, not violent but gentle, not quarrelsome, not a lover of money, one who manages my own family well, and who keeps my children under control with proper respect. Grant me a good reputation with outsiders, so that I will not fall into disgrace and the snare of the devil. (1 Timothy 3:2-4, 7)

Take a moment to share your personal needs with God, including your physical, emotional, relational, and spiritual concerns.

THANK YOU, LORD, FOR WHAT YOU HAVE DONE

112

Long ago You ordained Your plan, and now You are bringing it to pass. (2 Kings 19:25; Isaiah 37:26)

The Lord who created the heavens, He is God. He fashioned and made the earth and established it; He did not create it to be empty but formed it to be inhabited. He is the Lord, and there is no other. (Isaiah 45:18)

LORD, I LISTEN TO YOUR WORDS OF TRUTH

If Christ is in me, my body is dead because of sin, yet my spirit is alive because of righteousness. And if the Spirit of Him who raised Jesus from the dead is living in me, He who raised Christ from the dead will also give life to my mortal body through His Spirit, who lives in me. (Romans 8:10-11)

LORD, I RESPOND TO YOUR INSTRUCTION

If I forgive men for their transgressions, my heavenly Father will also forgive me. (Matthew 6:14)

Lord, I thank You for Your eternal plan and for creating the heavens and the earth. I thank You that the Holy Spirit lives in me. I will strive to love and forgive others just as I have been loved and forgiven by You.

DAY 103

PRACTICING WISDOM FROM ABOVE

～◆

LORD, I DRAW NEAR TO YOU

Lord, You have invited me to pray for the needs of others, and since You desire what is best for them, I take this opportunity to bring these requests to You.

Blessed are those whose strength is in You,
Who have set their hearts on pilgrimage. (Psalm 84:5)

O Lord, be gracious to us; we have hoped in You.
Be our strength every morning,
Our salvation in time of distress. (Isaiah 33:2)

Take a moment to lift up the needs of your family and friends, and to offer up any additional burdens for others that the Lord brings to mind.

THANK YOU, LORD, FOR WHAT YOU HAVE DONE

Your hand laid the foundations of the earth, and Your right hand spread out the heavens; when You summon them, they all stand up together. (Isaiah 48:13)

LORD, I LISTEN TO YOUR WORDS OF TRUTH

God Who said, "Let light shine out of darkness" made His light shine in my heart to give me the light of the knowledge of the glory of God in the face of Christ. But I have this treasure in an earthen vessel to show that this all-surpassing power is from God and not from me. (2 Corinthians 4:6-7)

LORD, I RESPOND TO YOUR INSTRUCTION

The wisdom that comes from above is first pure, then peaceable, gentle, submissive, full of mercy and good fruits, without partiality and hypocrisy. And the fruit of righteousness is sown in peace by those who make peace. (James 3:17-18)

I will examine all things, hold fast to the good, and abstain from every form of evil. (1 Thessalonians 5:21-22)

～◆

Lord, I thank You for Your magnificent work in creation and for making the light of the knowledge of Christ shine in my heart. Teach me to practice the wisdom that comes from above clinging to the good and avoiding every form of evil.

DAY 104

FORBEARING AND FORGIVING

❧

LORD, I DRAW NEAR TO YOU

Lord, I want Your Word to be deeply implanted in me so that I will know the truth and be able to express it in the way I live.

I will both lie down in peace and sleep,
For You alone, O Lord, make me dwell in safety. (Psalm 4:8)

I have set the Lord always before me;
Because He is at my right hand, I will not be shaken.
Therefore my heart is glad, and my glory rejoices;
My body also will rest in hope.
You will make known to me the path of life;
In Your presence is fullness of joy;
In Your right hand are pleasures forever. (Psalm 16:8-9,11)

Take a moment to affirm the truth of these words from Scripture and ask God to make them a growing reality in your life.

THANK YOU, LORD, FOR WHAT YOU HAVE DONE

Heaven is Your throne, and the earth is Your footstool. Your hand made all these things, and so they came into being. (Isaiah 66:1-2)

LORD, I LISTEN TO YOUR WORDS OF TRUTH

I am God's workmanship, created in Christ Jesus for good works, which God prepared beforehand for me to do. (Ephesians 2:10)

LORD, I RESPOND TO YOUR INSTRUCTION

I will love my enemies, do good to them, and lend to them, expecting nothing in return. Then my reward will be great, and I will be a child of the Most High; for He is kind to the ungrateful and evil. I will be merciful just as my Father is merciful. (Luke 6:35-36)

I will bear with others and forgive whatever complaints I have against them; I will forgive just as the Lord forgave me. (Colossians 3:13)

❧

Lord, I thank You for Your righteous and glorious throne and for creating me in Christ Jesus for good works. Help me to be merciful and love those who do not love me and demonstrate forbearance and forgiveness.

DAY 105

KNOWING CHRIST

꘎

LORD, I DRAW NEAR TO YOU

O Lord, I am deeply grateful for Your wonderful acts, for Your abundant promises, and for the gift of my relationship with You through the merits of Christ.

I will sing to the Lord and give praise to the Lord,
For He has rescued the life of the needy
From the hands of evildoers. (Jeremiah 20:13)

The Lord is good,
A refuge in times of trouble;
He knows those who trust in Him. (Nahum 1:7)

Take a moment to express your gratitude for the many blessings that you have received from the Lord.

THANK YOU, LORD, FOR WHAT YOU HAVE DONE

Great is our Lord and mighty in power; His understanding is infinite. (Psalm 147:5)

Through Christ all things were made, and without Him nothing was made that has been made. In Him was life, and the life was the light of men. (John 1:3-4)

LORD, I LISTEN TO YOUR WORDS OF TRUTH

I want to know Christ and the power of His resurrection and the fellowship of His sufferings, being conformed to His death, that I may attain to the resurrection from the dead. (Philippians 3:10-11)

LORD, I RESPOND TO YOUR INSTRUCTION

I will not be dishonest in judgment, in measurement of weight or quantity. I will be honest and just in my business affairs. (Leviticus 19:35-36)

꘎

Lord, I thank You that You are mighty in power and that You created all things through Your Son. I ask that I might know Christ more intimately and be a person of character and integrity.

DAY 106

PUTTING AWAY BITTERNESS
AND WRATH

❧

LORD, I DRAW NEAR TO YOU

Lord, I give thanks for Your greatness, Your goodness, and Your love, and I now draw near to enjoy Your presence.

Where were you when I laid the foundations of the earth?
Tell Me, if you have understanding.
Who determined its measurements?
Surely you know!
Or who stretched the line across it?
On what were its bases sunk,
Or who laid its cornerstone,
When the morning stars sang together
And all the sons of God shouted for joy? (Job 38:4-7)

Take a moment to consider God's awesome majesty and thank Him that He loves you and wants an intimate relationship with you.

THANK YOU, LORD, FOR WHAT YOU HAVE DONE

You declare the end from the beginning, and from ancient times things that have not yet been done, saying, "My purpose will stand, and I will do all My pleasure." (Isaiah 46:10)

LORD, I LISTEN TO YOUR WORDS OF TRUTH

God has given me eternal life, and this life is in His Son. He who has the Son has life; he who does not have the Son of God does not have life. Since I believe in the name of the Son of God, I know that I have eternal life. (1 John 5:11-13)

LORD, I RESPOND TO YOUR INSTRUCTION

I will put away all bitterness and anger and wrath and shouting and slander, along with all malice. And I will be kind and compassionate to others, forgiving them just as God in Christ also forgave me. (Ephesians 4:31-32)

❧

Lord, I thank You that Your eternal purpose will stand. I ask You to help me put away bitterness and wrath and show kindness and compassion to others.

DAY 107

RESTING IN GOD'S STRENGTH

❧

LORD, I DRAW NEAR TO YOU

I am grateful to You, O God, for the blessing of Your forgiveness. I thank You that in Christ, You set me free from the guilt of the past and give me hope for the future.

You have been just in all that has happened to me; You have acted faithfully, while I did wrong. (Nehemiah 9:33)

Take a moment to ask the Spirit to search your heart and reveal any areas of unconfessed sin. Acknowledge these to the Lord and thank Him for His forgiveness.

THANK YOU, LORD, FOR WHAT YOU HAVE DONE

To the only God our Savior, through Jesus Christ our Lord, be glory, majesty, dominion, and authority before all ages and now and forever. Amen. (Jude 25)

The Scriptures predicted that the Christ should suffer and rise from the dead on the third day, and that repentance and forgiveness of sins should be preached in His name to all nations, beginning at Jerusalem. (Luke 24:46-47)

117
❧

LORD, I LISTEN TO YOUR WORDS OF TRUTH

The Lord is my strength and my shield; my heart trusts in Him, and I am helped. My heart greatly rejoices, and I will give thanks to Him in song. (Psalm 28:7)

LORD, I RESPOND TO YOUR INSTRUCTION

There are six things the Lord hates, seven that are detestable to Him: haughty eyes, a lying tongue, hands that shed innocent blood, a heart that devises wicked plans, feet that run swiftly to evil, a false witness who breathes lies, and one who causes strife among brothers. (Proverbs 6:16-19)

❧

Lord, I thank You for the glory and majesty of Jesus Christ and for the gift of forgiveness through His death and resurrection. I thank You that You are my strength and my shield. I choose not to do those things that are displeasing to You.

DAY 108

CHOOSING TO DO GOOD
❧

LORD, I DRAW NEAR TO YOU

I praise You, Lord, that You are intimately acquainted with my ways and that You always love me and have my best interests at heart.

As I walk in the Spirit, I will not fulfill the desires of the flesh. For the flesh desires what is contrary to the Spirit, and the Spirit what is contrary to the flesh; for they oppose each other, so that I may not do the things that I wish. But if I am led by the Spirit, I am not under the law. (Galatians 5:16-18)

Take a moment to offer this day to the Lord and ask Him for the grace to grow in your knowledge and love for Him.

THANK YOU, LORD, FOR WHAT YOU HAVE DONE

O Lord, God of heaven, You are the great and awesome God, keeping Your covenant of loyal love with those who love You and obey Your commands. (Nehemiah 1:5)

118

The Lord said, "In My Father's house are many dwellings; if it were not so, I would have told you. I am going there to prepare a place for you. And if I go and prepare a place for you, I will come again and receive you to Myself, that you also may be where I am." (John 14:2-3)

LORD, I LISTEN TO YOUR WORDS OF TRUTH

When I am afraid, I will trust in You. In God, Whose Word I praise, in God I have put my trust. I will not fear; what can mortal man do to me? (Psalm 56:3-4)

LORD, I RESPOND TO YOUR INSTRUCTION

I will not forget to do good and to share with others, for with such sacrifices God is well pleased. (Hebrews 13:16)
❧

Lord, I thank You that You are the great and awesome God and that Jesus is preparing a heavenly dwelling for me. I thank You that I can trust in You, and I will not forget to do good and share with others.

DAY 109

FIXING MY THOUGHTS ON JESUS

❧

LORD, I DRAW NEAR TO YOU

As I approach Your throne of grace today, I am grateful that You care about the things that concern me and that You want me to offer them up to You.

Since I have a great cloud of witnesses surrounding me, may I lay aside every impediment and the sin that so easily entangles, and run with endurance the race that is set before me, fixing my eyes on Jesus, the author and perfecter of my faith, Who for the joy set before Him endured the cross, despising the shame, and sat down at the right hand of the throne of God. May I consider Him who endured such hostility from sinners so that I will not grow weary and lose heart. (Hebrews 12:1-3)

Take a moment to share your personal needs with God, including your physical, emotional, relational, and spiritual concerns.

THANK YOU, LORD, FOR WHAT YOU HAVE DONE

Jesus told His disciples, "The Spirit will glorify Me by taking from what is Mine and making it known to you. All that belongs to the Father is Mine. Therefore, I said that He will take from what is Mine and make it known to you." (John 16:14-15)

LORD, I LISTEN TO YOUR WORDS OF TRUTH

You are my lovingkindness and my fortress, my high tower and my deliverer, my shield, in whom I take refuge. (Psalm 144:2)

LORD, I RESPOND TO YOUR INSTRUCTION

The thoughts of the righteous are just, but the advice of the wicked is deceitful. (Proverbs 12:5)

I will walk properly as in the daytime, not in revellings and drunkenness, not in promiscuity and debauchery, not in strife and jealousy. Rather, I will put on the Lord Jesus Christ and make no provision to gratify the lusts of the flesh. (Romans 13:13-14)

❧

Lord, I thank You for the gift of Your indwelling Holy Spirit. I thank You that You are my high tower and my deliverer, and I ask You to help me keep my thoughts and actions honorable to the Lord Jesus Christ.

DAY 110

SHOWING KINDNESS

❧

LORD, I DRAW NEAR TO YOU

Lord, You have invited me to pray for the needs of others, and since You desire what is best for them, I take this opportunity to bring these requests to You.

Restore us again, O God of our salvation,
And put away Your anger toward us.
Will You be angry with us forever?
Will You prolong Your anger to all generations?
Will You not revive us again,
That Your people may rejoice in You?
Show us Your lovingkindness, O Lord,
And grant us Your salvation. (Psalm 85:4-7)

Take a moment to lift up the needs of your family and friends, and to offer up any additional burdens for others that the Lord brings to mind.

THANK YOU, LORD, FOR WHAT YOU HAVE DONE

It is good to give thanks to the Lord and to sing praises to Your name, O Most High, to declare Your lovingkindness in the morning and Your faithfulness at night. (Psalm 92:1-2)

Through Jesus the forgiveness of sins is proclaimed, that through Him everyone who believes is justified from all things from which they could not be justified by the law of Moses. (Acts 13:38-39)

LORD, I LISTEN TO YOUR WORDS OF TRUTH

Because the Lord God helps me, I will not be disgraced. Therefore I have set my face like flint, and I know I will not be put to shame. He who vindicates me is near; who will contend with me? Surely the Lord God will help me; who is he that will condemn me? (Isaiah 50:7-9)

LORD, I RESPOND TO YOUR INSTRUCTION

I will remember those in prison as though bound with them, and those who are mistreated, since I myself am also in the body. (Hebrews 13:3)

❧

Lord, I thank You for Your lovingkindness and faithfulness and for Your provision of forgiveness through Jesus Christ. I thank You that You help and vindicate me. I will show hospitality kindness to others as a testimony to You.

DAY 111

FLEEING TEMPTATION

~❧~

LORD, I DRAW NEAR TO YOU

Lord, I want Your Word to be deeply implanted in me so that I will know the truth and be able to express it in the way I live.

Save Your people and bless Your inheritance;
Be their shepherd and carry them forever. (Psalm 28:9)

Take a moment to affirm the truth of these words from Scripture and ask God to make them a growing reality in your life.

THANK YOU, LORD, FOR WHAT YOU HAVE DONE

Your merciful love is higher than the heavens, and Your truth reaches to the skies. (Psalm 108:4)

If by the trespass of the one man, death reigned through that one man, much more will those who receive the abundance of grace and of the gift of righteousness reign in life through the one Man, Jesus Christ. Consequently, just as the result of one trespass was condemnation for all men, so also the result of one act of righteousness was justification that brings life for all men. For just as through the disobedience of the one man the many were made sinners, so also through the obedience of the one Man the many will be made righteous. (Romans 5:17-19)

121
~❧~

LORD, I LISTEN TO YOUR WORDS OF TRUTH

You have said, "Whatever you ask for in prayer, believe that you have received it, and it will be yours." (Mark 11:24)

LORD, I RESPOND TO YOUR INSTRUCTION

I will not say when I am tempted, "I am being tempted by God;" for God cannot be tempted by evil, nor does He tempt anyone. But each one is tempted when he is drawn away and enticed by his own lust. Then, after lust has conceived, it gives birth to sin; and sin, when it is full-grown, gives birth to death. (James 1:13-15)

~❧~

Lord, I thank You for Your merciful love and truth and for the perfect obedience of Your Son Jesus Christ. I thank You that You invite me to offer my requests to You. I will flee from sin and turn to You in times of temptation.

DAY 112

WORSHIPPING GOD IN SPIRIT AND TRUTH

❧

LORD, I DRAW NEAR TO YOU

O Lord, I am deeply grateful for Your wonderful acts, for Your abundant promises, and for the gift of my relationship with You through the merits of Christ.

Surely the Lord's hand is not too short to save,
Nor His ear too dull to hear.
But our iniquities have separated us from our God;
Our sins have hidden His face from us, so that He will not hear.
Yet the Lord saw that there was no one to intervene;
So His own arm worked salvation for Him,
And His righteousness sustained Him. (Isaiah 59:1-2,16)

Take a moment to express your gratitude for the many blessings that you have received from the Lord.

122

THANK YOU, LORD, FOR WHAT YOU HAVE DONE

God is able to do immeasurably more than all that we ask or think, according to His power that is at work within us. To Him be glory in the Church and in Christ Jesus throughout all generations, for ever and ever. (Ephesians 3:20-21)

LORD, I LISTEN TO YOUR WORDS OF TRUTH

The hour is coming and now is, when true worshipers will worship the Father in spirit and truth, for the Father is seeking such to worship Him. God is spirit, and those who worship Him must worship in spirit and truth. (John 4:23-24)

LORD, I RESPOND TO YOUR INSTRUCTION

A virtuous wife is the crown of her husband, but she who causes shame is like decay in his bones. (Proverbs 12:4)

❧

Lord, I thank You for Your power to do immeasurably more than all that I ask or think. I thank You for calling me to worship You in spirit and truth. Help me to be virtuous in my relationships with others.

DAY 113

CONSIDERING MY STEPS

❧

LORD, I DRAW NEAR TO YOU

Lord, I give thanks for Your greatness, Your goodness, and Your love, and I now draw near to enjoy Your presence.

You are the living God,
And there is no god besides You.
You put to death and You bring to life,
You have wounded and You will heal,
And no one can deliver from Your hand. (Deuteronomy 32:39)

Take a moment to consider God's awesome majesty and thank Him that He loves you and wants an intimate relationship with you.

THANK YOU, LORD, FOR WHAT YOU HAVE DONE

The Lord is our judge, the Lord is our lawgiver, the Lord is our king; it is He who will save us. (Isaiah 33:22)

Christ is the head of the body, the church; He is the beginning and the firstborn from among the dead, so that in everything He might have the supremacy. (Colossians 1:18)

LORD, I LISTEN TO YOUR WORDS OF TRUTH

Unless I eat the flesh of the Son of Man and drink His blood, I have no life in me. Whoever eats Your flesh and drinks Your blood has eternal life, and You will raise him up at the last day. For Your flesh is true food, and Your blood is true drink. Whoever eats Your flesh and drinks Your blood abides in You, and You in him. As the living Father sent You, and You live because of the Father, so the one who feeds on You will live because of You. (John 6:53-57)

LORD, I RESPOND TO YOUR INSTRUCTION

A simple man believes everything, but a prudent man considers his steps. (Proverbs 14:15)

❧

Lord, I thank You that You are my King and that Christ is supreme in all things. I thank You for the body and blood of the Lord Jesus. I will carefully consider my steps.

123
❧

DAY 114
ABIDING IN CHRIST
❧

LORD, I DRAW NEAR TO YOU

I am grateful to You, O God, for the blessing of Your forgiveness. I thank You that in Christ, You set me free from the guilt of the past and give me hope for the future.

When I sin against the Lord, I may be sure that my sin will find me out. (Numbers 32:23)

Take a moment to ask the Spirit to search your heart and reveal any areas of unconfessed sin. Acknowledge these to the Lord and thank Him for His forgiveness.

THANK YOU, LORD, FOR WHAT YOU HAVE DONE

The Lord is good, a refuge in times of trouble; He knows those who trust in Him. (Nahum 1:7)

124
❧

The faith of those chosen of God and the knowledge of the truth, which is according to godliness, is a faith and knowledge resting in the hope of eternal life, which God, who does not lie, promised before the beginning of time. At the appointed time, He manifested His Word through the preaching entrusted to the apostles by the command of God our Savior. (Titus 1:1-3)

LORD, I LISTEN TO YOUR WORDS OF TRUTH

You are the true vine, and Your Father is the vinedresser. He cuts off every branch in You that bears no fruit, while every branch that does bear fruit He prunes, that it may bear more fruit. I will abide in You, and You will abide in me. As the branch cannot bear fruit of itself, unless it abides in the vine, neither can I, unless I abide in You. (John 15:1-2,4)

LORD, I RESPOND TO YOUR INSTRUCTION

Houses and wealth are inherited from fathers, but a prudent wife is from the Lord. (Proverbs 19:14)

❧

Lord, I thank You that You are a refuge in times of trouble and that I have been chosen by You to receive the gift of eternal life in Your Son. I will abide in Jesus Christ and walk in prudence and the fear of the Lord.

DAY 115
LIVING ACCORDING TO THE SPIRIT

❧

LORD, I DRAW NEAR TO YOU

I praise You, Lord, that You are intimately acquainted with my ways and that You always love me and have my best interests at heart.

May I not be conformed to the pattern of this world but be transformed by the renewing of my mind, that I may prove that the will of God is good and acceptable and perfect. (Romans 12:2)

Take a moment to offer this day to the Lord and ask Him for the grace to grow in your knowledge and love for Him.

THANK YOU, LORD, FOR WHAT YOU HAVE DONE

Blessed be the God and Father of our Lord Jesus Christ, the Father of mercies and the God of all comfort. (2 Corinthians 1:3)

Christ had to be made like His brothers in every way, in order that He might become a merciful and faithful high priest in things pertaining to God, to make propitiation for the sins of the people. Because He Himself suffered when He was tempted, He is able to help those who are being tempted. (Hebrews 2:17-18)

125

LORD, I LISTEN TO YOUR WORDS OF TRUTH

Those who live according to the flesh set their minds on the things of the flesh; but those who live according to the Spirit set their minds on the things of the Spirit. The mind of the flesh is death, but the mind of the Spirit is life and peace. (Romans 8:5-6)

LORD, I RESPOND TO YOUR INSTRUCTION

A prudent man sees evil and hides himself, but the simple keep going and suffer for it. (Proverbs 22:3; 27:12)

A fool has no delight in understanding, but only in airing his own opinions. (Proverbs 18:2)

❧

Lord, I thank You that You are the Father of mercies and that Christ is my merciful and faithful high priest. I choose to live according to the Spirit. I will avoid evil and seek understanding.

DAY 116

BEING OF GOOD COURAGE

LORD, I DRAW NEAR TO YOU

As I approach Your throne of grace today, I am grateful that You care about the things that concern me and that You want me to offer them up to You.

Do not let my heart envy sinners,
But let me live only in the fear of the Lord.
For surely there is a future,
And my hope will not be cut off. (Proverbs 23:17-18)

Take a moment to share your personal needs with God, including your physical, emotional, relational, and spiritual concerns.

THANK YOU, LORD, FOR WHAT YOU HAVE DONE

The Lord of hosts is wonderful in counsel and great in wisdom. (Isaiah 28:29)

Jesus as our high priest meets our needs: He is holy, blameless, undefiled, set apart from sinners, and exalted above the heavens. Unlike the other high priests, He does not need to offer sacrifices day after day, first for His own sins, and then for the sins of the people, for He did this once for all when He offered up Himself. (Hebrews 7:26-27)

LORD, I LISTEN TO YOUR WORDS OF TRUTH

I am always of good courage and know that as long as I am at home in the body, I am away from the Lord. For I live by faith, not by sight. I am of good courage and would prefer to be absent from the body and to be at home with the Lord. (2 Corinthians 5:6-8)

LORD, I RESPOND TO YOUR INSTRUCTION

Since she is a companion and a wife by covenant, a husband should not deal treacherously against the wife of his youth. The Lord God of hosts seeks a godly offspring and hates divorce; therefore we must take heed to our spirit and not deal treacherously. (Malachi 2:14-16)

Lord, I thank You that Jesus my high priest is holy, blameless, and exalted above the heavens. Help me always to be of good courage in Christ and to be faithful in my relationships with others.

DAY 117

APPROACHING THE FATHER BOLDLY

❧

LORD, I DRAW NEAR TO YOU

Lord, You have invited me to pray for the needs of others, and since You desire what is best for them, I take this opportunity to bring these requests to You.

All of us have become like one who is unclean,
And all our righteous acts are like filthy rags;
We all shrivel up like a leaf,
And our iniquities, like the wind, sweep us away.
But now, O Lord, You are our Father.
We are the clay; You are the potter;
We are all the work of Your hand. (Isaiah 64:6,8)

Take a moment to lift up the needs of your family and friends, and to offer up any additional burdens for others that the Lord brings to mind.

THANK YOU, LORD, FOR WHAT YOU HAVE DONE

127
❧

By the will of God, I have been sanctified through the offering of the body of Jesus Christ once for all. And every priest stands daily ministering and offering again and again the same sacrifices, which can never take away sins. But when this Priest had offered for all time one sacrifice for sins, He sat down at the right hand of God, waiting from that time for His enemies to be made a footstool for His feet. For by one offering, He has made perfect forever those who are being sanctified. (Hebrews 10:10-14)

LORD, I LISTEN TO YOUR WORDS OF TRUTH

In Christ Jesus my Lord, I have boldness and confident access through faith in Him. (Ephesians 3:12)

LORD, I RESPOND TO YOUR INSTRUCTION

I will not let any corrupt word come out of my mouth, but only what is helpful for building others up according to their needs, that it may impart grace to those who hear. (Ephesians 4:29)

❧

Lord, I thank You that through my faith in Christ Jesus I may approach the Father with boldness and confidence. Help me always to speak words to others that portray humility and grace.

DAY 118

IMPARTING GOD'S WORD

LORD, I DRAW NEAR TO YOU

Lord, I want Your Word to be deeply implanted in me so that I will know the truth and be able to express it in the way I live.

My soul waits in hope for the Lord;
He is my help and my shield.
My heart rejoices in Him,
Because I trust in His holy name.
Let Your unfailing love be upon us, O Lord,
Even as we put our hope in You. (Psalm 33:20-22)

Take a moment to affirm the truth of these words from Scripture and ask God to make them a growing reality in your life.

THANK YOU, LORD, FOR WHAT YOU HAVE DONE

Your testimonies, which You have commanded, are righteous and trustworthy. Your righteousness is everlasting, and Your law is truth. (Psalm 119:138,142)

LORD, I LISTEN TO YOUR WORDS OF TRUTH

Faith is the reality of things hoped for and the conviction of things not seen. (Hebrews 11:1)

Without faith it is impossible to please God, for he who comes to Him must believe that He exists, and that He is a rewarder of those who earnestly seek Him. (Hebrews 11:6)

LORD, I RESPOND TO YOUR INSTRUCTION

Your commandments will be upon my heart, and I will teach them diligently to my children and talk about them when I sit in my house and when I walk along the way and when I lie down and when I rise up. (Deuteronomy 6:6-7)

Lord, I thank You for Your truth and for Your mighty works on behalf of Your people. My heart's desire is to please You by walking in faith and imparting Your Word to others.

DAY 119

BOASTING ONLY IN GOD

LORD, I DRAW NEAR TO YOU

O Lord, I am deeply grateful for Your wonderful acts, for Your abundant promises, and for the gift of my relationship with You through the merits of Christ.

I will give thanks to the Lord, call upon His name,
And make known to others what He has done.
I will sing to Him, sing praises to Him,
And tell of all His wonderful acts. (1 Chronicles 16:8-9)

Take a moment to express your gratitude for the many blessings that you have received from the Lord.

THANK YOU, LORD, FOR WHAT YOU HAVE DONE

Righteousness and justice are the foundation of Your throne; lovingkindness and truth go before You. (Psalm 89:14)

129

LORD, I LISTEN TO YOUR WORDS OF TRUTH

Everyone who believes that Jesus is the Christ, is born of God; and everyone who loves the Father, loves Him Who is begotten of Him. Whatever is born of God overcomes the world, and this is the victory that has overcome the world—our faith. Who is he who overcomes the world, but he who believes that Jesus is the Son of God. (1 John 5:1, 4-5)

LORD, I RESPOND TO YOUR INSTRUCTION

Thus says the Lord: "Let not the wise man boast of his wisdom, and let not the strong man boast of his strength, and let not the rich man boast of his riches; but let him who boasts, boast about this: that he understands and knows Me, that I am the Lord, who exercises lovingkindness, justice, and righteousness on earth; for in these I delight," declares the Lord. (Jeremiah 9:23-24)

Lord, I thank You for Your loyalty, love, and truth. I thank You that I have been born of God through faith in Christ Jesus. I will boast only in Your lovingkindness, justice, and righteousness..

DAY 120
EMBRACING A SERVANT'S HEART

LORD, I DRAW NEAR TO YOU

Lord, I give thanks for Your greatness, Your goodness, and Your love, and I now draw near to enjoy Your presence.

Who is like the Lord our God,
The One who is enthroned on high,
Who humbles Himself to behold
The things that are in the heavens and in the earth? (Psalm 113:5-6)

Take a moment to consider God's awesome majesty and thank Him that He loves you and wants an intimate relationship with you.

THANK YOU, LORD, FOR WHAT YOU HAVE DONE

The Lord is upright; He is my Rock, and there is no unrighteousness in Him. (Psalm 92:15)

You are the Lord our God, who brought Your people out of Egypt so that they would no longer be their slaves; You broke the bars of their yoke and enabled them to walk with heads held high. (Leviticus 26:13)

LORD, I LISTEN TO YOUR WORDS OF TRUTH

Whoever wishes to become great among others must become their servant, and whoever wishes to be first among them must be their slave. (Matthew 20:26-27; Mark 10:43-44)

LORD, I RESPOND TO YOUR INSTRUCTION

I will not withhold discipline from a child; if I strike him with the rod, he will not die. (Proverbs 23:13)

A fool despises his father's discipline, but whoever heeds correction is prudent. (Proverbs 15:5)

Lord, I thank You that there is no unrighteousness in You and that You enable Your people to walk with heads held high. Teach me to be a servant to others and nurture them in Your truth.

DAY 121

SERVING FAITHFULLY

❦

LORD, I DRAW NEAR TO YOU

I am grateful to You, O God, for the blessing of Your forgiveness. I thank You that in Christ, You set me free from the guilt of the past and give me hope for the future.

"For a brief moment I forsook you,
But with great compassion I will gather you.
In a flood of anger I hid My face from you for a moment,
But I will have compassion on you with everlasting kindness,"
Says the Lord your Redeemer. (Isaiah 54:7-8)

Take a moment to ask the Spirit to search your heart and reveal any areas of unconfessed sin. Acknowledge these to the Lord and thank Him for His forgiveness.

THANK YOU, LORD, FOR WHAT YOU HAVE DONE

The eyes of the Lord move to and fro throughout the whole earth to strengthen those whose hearts are fully committed to Him. (2 Chronicles 16:9)

131
❦

LORD, I LISTEN TO YOUR WORDS OF TRUTH

By Your grace, I want to hear the words, "Well done, good and faithful servant; you have been faithful with a few things; I will put you in charge of many things. Enter into the joy of your Lord." (Matthew 25:21)

LORD, I RESPOND TO YOUR INSTRUCTION

Who makes me different from anyone else? And what do I have that I did not receive? And if I did receive it, why I should I boast as though I had not received it? (1 Corinthians 4:7)

Whoever exalts himself will be humbled, and whoever humbles himself will be exalted. (Matthew 23:12; Luke 14:11; 18:14)

❦

Lord, I thank You for strengthening those whose hearts are committed to You. Help me to be a good and faithful servant, as I humble myself before You. I acknowledge that all things come from You.

DAY 122

SERVING OTHERS BY IMPARTING GOD'S TRUTH

LORD, I DRAW NEAR TO YOU

I praise You, Lord, that You are intimately acquainted with my ways and that You always love me and have my best interests at heart.

I will be careful to lead a blameless life.
May I walk in the integrity of my heart in the midst of my house.
I will set no wicked thing before my eyes.
I hate the work of those who fall away;
Do not let it cling to me. (Psalm 101:2-3)

Take a moment to offer this day to the Lord and ask Him for the grace to grow in your knowledge and love for Him.

THANK YOU, LORD, FOR WHAT YOU HAVE DONE

As for God, His way is perfect; the Word of the Lord is proven. He is a shield to all who take refuge in Him. For who is God besides the Lord? And who is the Rock except our God? (Psalm 18:30-31)

You save the humble but bring low those whose eyes are haughty. (Psalm 18:27)

LORD, I LISTEN TO YOUR WORDS OF TRUTH

The greatest among us should be like the youngest, and the one who rules like the one who serves. For who is greater, the one who is at the table or the one who serves? Is it not the one who is at the table? But Jesus came among us as the One who serves. (Luke 22:26-27)

LORD, I RESPOND TO YOUR INSTRUCTION

I will discipline my child while there is hope and not be a willing party to his death. (Proverbs 19:18)

The rod and reproof impart wisdom, but a child left to himself brings shame to his mother. (Proverbs 29:15)

Lord, I thank You that You are a shield and a refuge and that You save the humble. Just as Jesus came as the One who served, I will serve others by imparting Your truth to them.

DAY 123

WALKING WORTHY OF MY CALLING

*

LORD, I DRAW NEAR TO YOU

As I approach Your throne of grace today, I am grateful that You care about the things that concern me and that You want me to offer them up to You.

Out of the depths I have called to You, O Lord.
O Lord, hear my voice,
And let Your ears be attentive
To the voice of my supplications. (Psalm 130:1-2)

Take a moment to share your personal needs with God, including your physical, emotional, relational, and spiritual concerns.

THANK YOU, LORD, FOR WHAT YOU HAVE DONE

I will give thanks to the Lord according to His righteousness and will sing praise to the name of the Lord Most High. (Psalm 7:17)

As the earth brings forth its sprouts and as a garden causes that which is sown to spring up, so the Lord God will make righteousness and praise spring up before all nations. (Isaiah 61:11)

133

LORD, I LISTEN TO YOUR WORDS OF TRUTH

My body is a temple of the Holy Spirit, who is in me, whom I have from God, and I am not my own. For I was bought at a price; therefore, I will glorify God in my body. (1 Corinthians 6:19-20)

LORD, I RESPOND TO YOUR INSTRUCTION

If anyone thinks he is something when he is nothing, he deceives himself. (Galatians 6:3)

I want to walk in a way that is worthy of the calling with which I was called, with all humility and meekness and patience. (Ephesians 4:1-2)

*

Lord, I thank You for Your righteousness and for Your promise to make righteousness spring up before all nations. I thank You that I was bought at a price. Help me to walk in a way that is worthy of the calling with which I was called.

DAY 124

WEARING GOD'S FULL ARMOR

LORD, I DRAW NEAR TO YOU

Lord, You have invited me to pray for the needs of others, and since You desire what is best for them, I take this opportunity to bring these requests to You.

If two of you agree on earth about anything you may ask, it will be done for you by My Father in heaven. Where two or three come together in My name, I am there in their midst. (Matthew 18:19-20)

May we be devoted to one another in brotherly love, honoring one another above ourselves. (Romans 12:10)

Take a moment to lift up the needs of your family and friends, and to offer up any other burdens for others that the Lord brings to mind.

THANK YOU, LORD, FOR WHAT YOU HAVE DONE

Let me fall into the hands of the Lord, for His mercies are very great; but do not let me fall into the hands of men. (1 Chronicles 21:13)

I will sing to the Lord and give praise to the Lord, for He has rescued the life of the needy from the hands of evildoers. (Jeremiah 20:13)

LORD, I LISTEN TO YOUR WORDS OF TRUTH

My struggle is not against flesh and blood, but against the rulers, against the authorities, against the world rulers of this darkness, against the spiritual forces of evil in the heavenly realms. Therefore, I will put on the full armor of God, so that I may be able to resist in the day of evil, having done all to stand. (Ephesians 6:12-13)

LORD, I RESPOND TO YOUR INSTRUCTION

I want to speak words of encouragement to other believers. (Acts 20:2)

We should encourage one another and build each other up in Christ Jesus. (1 Thessalonians 5:11)

Lord, I thank You for the greatness of Your mercies and for rescuing the lives of the needy. I will put on the full armor of God daily, and I will be a source of encouragement to others.

DAY 125

WALKING IN HOLINESS

LORD, I DRAW NEAR TO YOU

Lord, I want Your Word to be deeply implanted in me so that I will know the truth and be able to express it in the way I live.

Blessed be the Lord, the God of Israel,
From everlasting to everlasting.
Amen and Amen. (Psalm 41:13)

Take a moment to affirm the truth of these words from Scripture and ask God to make them a growing reality in your life.

THANK YOU, LORD, FOR WHAT YOU HAVE DONE

O Lord, God of Israel, there is no God like You in heaven above or on earth below; You keep Your covenant and mercy with Your servants who walk before You with all their heart. (1 Kings 8:23; 2 Chronicles 6:14)

You promised to restore the children of Israel and Judah, saying, "They shall be My people, and I will be their God. And I will give them one heart and one way, so that they will always fear Me for their own good and the good of their children after them." (Jeremiah 32:38-39)

135

LORD, I LISTEN TO YOUR WORDS OF TRUTH

As an obedient child, I will not conform myself to the former lusts I had when I lived in ignorance, but as He Who called me is holy, so I will be holy in all my conduct, because it is written: "You shall be holy, for I am holy." (1 Peter 1:14-16)

LORD, I RESPOND TO YOUR INSTRUCTION

I will submit myself to God and resist the devil, and he will flee from me. I will humble myself before the Lord, and He will exalt me. (James 4:7,10)

Lord, I thank You for Your uniqueness and for the faithfulness of Your promises. Help me to walk in holiness, submit myself to You, and resist the devil.

DAY 126

SUBMITTING ONE TO ANOTHER

❧

LORD, I DRAW NEAR TO YOU

O Lord, I am deeply grateful for Your wonderful acts, for Your abundant promises, and for the gift of my relationship with You through the merits of Christ.

The Lord is the strength of my life;
Of whom shall I be afraid? (Psalm 27:1)

Take a moment to express your gratitude for the many blessings that you have received from the Lord.

THANK YOU, LORD, FOR WHAT YOU HAVE DONE

You must be treated as holy by those who come near You, and before all people, You will be honored. (Leviticus 10:3)

For those who revere Your name, the Son of righteousness will rise with healing in His wings. And they will go out and leap like calves released from the stall. (Malachi 4:2)

LORD, I LISTEN TO YOUR WORDS OF TRUTH

He who has Your commandments and obeys them, he is the one who loves You; and he who loves You will be loved by Your Father, and You will love him and manifest Yourself to him. (John 14:21)

LORD, I RESPOND TO YOUR INSTRUCTION

We ought always to thank God for other believers and pray that their faith would grow more and more, and that the love each of them has toward one another would increase. (2 Thessalonians 1:3)
We should submit to one another out of reverence for Christ. (Ephesians 5:21)

❧

Lord, I am thankful You are worthy of all honor and that the Son of righteousness will rise with healing in His wings. I thank You for manifesting Yourself to those who love You and for the people You place in my life. I commit to pray for them on a regular basis.

136

DAY 127

PRESENTING MY MEMBERS TO GOD

❧

LORD, I DRAW NEAR TO YOU

Lord, I give thanks for Your greatness, Your goodness, and Your love, and I now draw near to enjoy Your presence.

Who has measured the waters in the hollow of His hand,
Or marked off the heavens with the breadth of his hand?
Who has calculated the dust of the earth in a measure,
Or weighed the mountains in the balance
And the hills in scales? (Isaiah 40:12)

Take a moment to consider God's awesome majesty and thank Him that He loves you and wants an intimate relationship with you.

THANK YOU, LORD, FOR WHAT YOU HAVE DONE

The Lord Jesus, who is holy and true, holds the key of David. What He opens no one can shut, and what He shuts no one can open. (Revelation 3:7)

137

Where Jesus went, the blind received sight, the lame walked, the lepers were cured, the deaf heard, the dead were raised up, and the good news was preached to the poor. (Matthew 11:5)

LORD, I LISTEN TO YOUR WORDS OF TRUTH

Just as I presented the members of my body as slaves to impurity and to ever-increasing lawlessness, so I now present my members as slaves to righteousness, leading to holiness. (Romans 6:19)

LORD, I RESPOND TO YOUR INSTRUCTION

The wise in heart accept commands, but a chattering fool will be thrown down. (Proverbs 10:8)

The way of a fool is right in his own eyes, but a wise man listens to counsel. (Proverbs 12:15)

❧

Lord, I thank You that the Lord Jesus holds the key of David that opens doors no one can open and shuts doors no one can shut. I thank You that He is a servant to those in need. I now present my members as slaves to righteousness, and I will be wise in heart and listen to counsel.

DAY 128

WALKING IN UNITY

❧

LORD, I DRAW NEAR TO YOU

I am grateful to You, O God, for the blessing of Your forgiveness. I thank You that in Christ, You set me free from the guilt of the past and give me hope for the future.

I will sacrifice to You
With the voice of thanksgiving.
I will fulfill what I have vowed.
Salvation is from the Lord. (Jonah 2:9)

Take a moment to ask the Spirit to search your heart and reveal any areas of unconfessed sin. Acknowledge these to the Lord and thank Him for His forgiveness.

THANK YOU, LORD, FOR WHAT YOU HAVE DONE

Jesus preached the gospel of the kingdom of God, and said, "The time is fulfilled, and the kingdom of God is at hand. Repent and believe the good news." (Mark 1:14-15)

LORD, I LISTEN TO YOUR WORDS OF TRUTH

No one who waits for You will be ashamed, but those who are treacherous without cause will be ashamed. Show me Your ways, O Lord, teach me Your paths; lead me in Your truth and teach me, for You are the God of my salvation, and my hope is in You all day long. (Psalm 25:3-5)

LORD, I RESPOND TO YOUR INSTRUCTION

If we have any encouragement from being united with Christ, if any comfort from His love, if any fellowship of the Spirit, if any affection and compassion, we should also be like-minded, having the same love, being one in spirit and one in purpose. (Philippians 2:1-2)

❧

Lord, I thank You that Jesus offered the good news of the kingdom. Teach me Your ways and lead me in Your paths, so I may be of one mind and spirit with other believers.

DAY 129

HEEDING GOD'S WORDS

❧

LORD, I DRAW NEAR TO YOU

I praise You, Lord, that You are intimately acquainted with my ways and that You always love me and have my best interests at heart.

I am the salt of the earth, but if the salt loses its flavor, how can it be made salty again? It is no longer good for anything, except to be thrown out and trampled underfoot by men. I am the light of the world. A city set on a hill cannot be hidden. Neither do people light a lamp and put it under a basket, but on a lampstand, and it gives light to all who are in the house. In the same way, I must let my light shine before men, that they may see my good deeds and praise my Father in heaven. (Matthew 5:13-16)

Take a moment to offer this day to the Lord and ask Him for the grace to grow in your knowledge and love for Him.

THANK YOU, LORD, FOR WHAT YOU HAVE DONE

139

❧

You know me, O Lord; You see me and test my thoughts about You. (Jeremiah 12:3)

If anyone is ashamed of You and Your words in this adulterous and sinful generation, the Son of Man will be ashamed of him when He comes in the glory of His Father with the holy angels. (Mark 8:38)

LORD, I LISTEN TO YOUR WORDS OF TRUTH

My soul waits in hope for the Lord; He is my help and my shield. My heart rejoices in Him, because I trust in His holy name. (Psalm 33:20-21)

LORD, I RESPOND TO YOUR INSTRUCTION

The heart of the prudent acquires knowledge, and the ear of the wise seeks knowledge. (Proverbs 18:15)

He who heeds the Word prospers, and blessed is he who trusts in the Lord. (Proverbs 16:20)

❧

Lord, I thank You that You know me and I pray that I would never be ashamed of my relationship with Jesus Christ. I thank You for being my help and my shield. Help me to acquire knowledge and to heed Your Word in everything I do.

DAY 130

EMBRACING GOD'S DISCIPLINE

LORD, I DRAW NEAR TO YOU

As I approach Your throne of grace today, I am grateful that You care about the things that concern me and that You want me to offer them up to You.

O Lord, hear my prayer;
Listen to the voice of my supplications.
In the day of my trouble I will call upon You,
For You will answer me.
You are great and do wondrous deeds;
You alone are God. (Psalm 86:6-7,10)

Take a moment to share your personal needs with God, including your physical, emotional, relational, and spiritual concerns.

THANK YOU, LORD, FOR WHAT YOU HAVE DONE

In his heart a man plans his way, but the Lord determines his steps. (Proverbs 16:9)

The Son of Man knew that He must suffer many things and be rejected by the elders, chief priests, and scribes, and be killed and be raised on the third day. (Luke 9:22)

LORD, I LISTEN TO YOUR WORDS OF TRUTH

You are my hope, O Lord God; You are my trust from my youth. As for me, I will always have hope; I will praise You more and more. (Psalm 71:5,14)

LORD, I RESPOND TO YOUR INSTRUCTION

I will endure discipline, for God is treating me as a son. For what son is not disciplined by his father? If I am without discipline, of which all have become partakers, then I am an illegitimate child and not a true son. Moreover, we have all had human fathers who disciplined us, and we respected them; how much more should I be subjected to the Father of spirits and live? (Hebrews 12:7-9)

Lord, I thank You that the Son of Man was willing to suffer for us. I thank You that You are my hope and my trust. Give me the grace to accept Your discipline in my life.

DAY 131

PROSPERING IN GOD'S PLANS

LORD, I DRAW NEAR TO YOU

Lord, You have invited me to pray for the needs of others, and since You desire what is best for them, I take this opportunity to bring these requests to You.

The harvest is plentiful, but the workers are few. Therefore, I will pray that the Lord of the harvest will send out workers into His harvest. (Matthew 9:37-38; Luke 10:2)

You have called us to go and make disciples of all nations, baptizing them in the name of the Father, and of the Son, and of the Holy Spirit, teaching them to observe everything You have commanded us. And surely You are with us always, even to the end of the age. (Matthew 28:19-20)

Take a moment to lift up the needs of your family and friends, and to offer up any additional burdens for others that the Lord brings to mind.

THANK YOU, LORD, FOR WHAT YOU HAVE DONE

Blessed is the King who comes in the name of the Lord! Peace in heaven and glory in the highest! (Luke 19:38)

LORD, I LISTEN TO YOUR WORDS OF TRUTH

"I know the plans I have for you," declares the Lord, "plans to prosper you and not to harm you, plans to give you a future and a hope." (Jeremiah 29:11)

LORD, I RESPOND TO YOUR INSTRUCTION

I shall not covet my neighbor's house, my neighbor's wife, his manservant or maidservant, his ox or donkey, or anything that belongs to my neighbor. (Exodus 20:17; Deuteronomy 5:21)

I was called to freedom, but I will not use my freedom to indulge the flesh, but through love I will serve others. For the whole law is summed up in this word: "You shall love your neighbor as yourself." (Galatians 5:13-14)

Lord, I thank You that You endure forever and Your plans give me a future and a hope. Help me not to be covetous or to indulge my flesh, but to serve others in love.

DAY 132

ENDURING PERSECUTION FOR CHRIST'S SAKE

LORD, I DRAW NEAR TO YOU

Lord, I want Your Word to be deeply implanted in me so that I will know the truth and be able to express it in the way I live.

When I remember You on my bed,
I meditate on You through the watches of the night.
Because You have been my help,
I will rejoice in the shadow of Your wings.
My soul clings to You;
Your right hand upholds me. (Psalm 63:6-8)

Take a moment to affirm the truth of these words from Scripture and ask God to make them a growing reality in your life.

THANK YOU, LORD, FOR WHAT YOU HAVE DONE

142

Christ was in the world, and the world was made through Him, and the world did not know Him. He came to His own, but His own did not receive Him. (John 1:10-11)

LORD, I LISTEN TO YOUR WORDS OF TRUTH

Blessed are those who are persecuted for the sake of righteousness, for theirs is the kingdom of heaven. Blessed are you when people insult you, persecute you, and falsely say all kinds of evil against you because of Me. Rejoice and be glad, because great is your reward in heaven, for in the same way they persecuted the prophets who were before you. (Matthew 5:10-12)

LORD, I RESPOND TO YOUR INSTRUCTION

I will accept others, just as Christ accepted me to the glory of God. (Romans 15:7)

Lord, I thank You for Christ's service of those who did not realize Who He was. I thank You that You reward those who are persecuted for Your sake. Teach me to show compassion and acceptance to others.

DAY 133

CHOOSING THE GOOD PART

❧

LORD, I DRAW NEAR TO YOU

O Lord, I am deeply grateful for Your wonderful acts, for Your abundant promises, and for the gift of my relationship with You through the merits of Christ.

Many, O Lord my God, are the wonders You have done,
And Your thoughts toward us no one can recount to You;
Were I to speak and tell of them,
They would be too many to declare. (Psalm 40:5)

Take a moment to express your gratitude for the many blessings that you have received from the Lord.

THANK YOU, LORD, FOR WHAT YOU HAVE DONE

The Lord said, "Destroy this temple, and I will raise it again in three days." But He was speaking of the temple of His body. After He was raised from the dead, His disciples remembered that He had said this to them, and they believed the Scripture and the words that Jesus had spoken. (John 2:19, 21-22)

143
❧

LORD, I LISTEN TO YOUR WORDS OF TRUTH

I rejoice in my tribulations, knowing that tribulation produces perseverance; and perseverance, character; and character, hope. And hope does not disappoint, because the love of God has been poured out into my heart through the Holy Spirit who was given to me. (Romans 5:3-5)

LORD, I RESPOND TO YOUR INSTRUCTION

I do not want to be worried and troubled about many things; only one thing is needed. Like Mary, I want to choose the good part, which will not be taken away from me. (Luke 10:41-42)

❧

Lord, I thank You that You raised Your Son Jesus from the dead, and that Your love has been poured out into my heart through the Holy Spirit. I will not be anxious like Martha, but will choose the good part as Mary did and focus my attention on You.

DAY 134

SEEKING GOD'S JOY AND PEACE

❧

LORD, I DRAW NEAR TO YOU

Lord, I give thanks for Your greatness, Your goodness, and Your love, and I now draw near to enjoy Your presence.

John looked and heard the voice of many angels encircling the throne and the living creatures and the elders; and their number was myriads of myriads, and thousands of thousands, saying with a loud voice, "Worthy is the Lamb, who was slain,
To receive power and riches and wisdom
And strength and honor and glory and blessing!" (Revelation 5:11-12)

Take a moment to consider God's awesome majesty and thank Him that He loves you and wants an intimate relationship with you.

THANK YOU, LORD, FOR WHAT YOU HAVE DONE

The Lord will guard the feet of His saints, but the wicked will be silenced in darkness. It is not by strength that one prevails; those who contend with the Lord will be shattered. He will thunder against them from heaven; the Lord will judge the ends of the earth. He will give strength to His king and exalt the horn of His anointed. (1 Samuel 2:9-10)

Just as the Father raises the dead and gives them life, even so the Son gives life to whom He wishes. (John 5:21)

LORD, I LISTEN TO YOUR WORDS OF TRUTH

The God of hope will fill me with all joy and peace as I trust in Him, so that I may overflow with hope by the power of the Holy Spirit. (Romans 15:13)

LORD, I RESPOND TO YOUR INSTRUCTION

I will love my enemies, do good to those who hate me, bless those who curse me, and pray for those who mistreat me. Just as I want others to do to me, I will do to them in the same way. (Luke 6:27-28,31)

❧

Lord, I thank You for guarding the feet of Your saints and for the gift of life in Your Son. I thank You for Your joy and peace. Give me the grace to do good to those who mistreat me.

DAY 135

RENEWING MY SOUL

❧

LORD, I DRAW NEAR TO YOU

I am grateful to You, O God, for the blessing of Your forgiveness. I thank You that in Christ, You set me free from the guilt of the past and give me hope for the future.

I will not forget the exhortation that addresses me as a son:
"My son, do not despise the Lord's discipline,
Nor lose heart when you are rebuked by Him,
For whom the Lord loves He disciplines,
And He chastises every son whom He receives." (Hebrews 12:5-6)

Take a moment to ask the Spirit to search your heart and reveal any areas of unconfessed sin. Acknowledge these to the Lord and thank Him for His forgiveness.

THANK YOU, LORD, FOR WHAT YOU HAVE DONE

When Judas went out to betray Him, Jesus said, "Now is the Son of Man glorified, and God is glorified in Him. If God is glorified in Him, God will glorify the Son in Himself and will glorify Him immediately." (John 13:31-32)

145
❧

LORD, I LISTEN TO YOUR WORDS OF TRUTH

I do not lose heart; even though my outward man is perishing, yet my inner man is being renewed day by day. For this light affliction which is momentary is working for me a far more exceeding and eternal weight of glory, while I do not look at the things which are seen but at the things which are unseen. For the things which are seen are temporary, but the things which are unseen are eternal. (2 Corinthians 4:16-18)

LORD, I RESPOND TO YOUR INSTRUCTION

For the love of money is a root of all kinds of evil, and some by longing for it have wandered from the faith and pierced themselves with many sorrows. But I will flee from these things, and pursue righteousness, godliness, faith, love, patience, and gentleness. (1 Timothy 6:10-11)

❧

Lord, I thank You for Your Son's willingness to glorify You through His death and resurrection. Thank You for daily renewing me within, and I pray I will not succumb to greed but be drawn by love.

DAY 136

TURNING AWAY FROM THE WORLD

LORD, I DRAW NEAR TO YOU

I praise You, Lord, that You are intimately acquainted with my ways and that You always love me and have my best interests at heart.

May I fear God and keep His commandments, for this applies to every person. (Ecclesiastes 12:13)

Incline my heart to Your testimonies
And not to selfish gain.
Turn my eyes away from worthless things,
And revive me in Your way. (Psalm 119:36-37)

Take a moment to offer this day to the Lord and ask Him for the grace to grow in your knowledge and love for Him.

THANK YOU, LORD, FOR WHAT YOU HAVE DONE

146

The Lord Jesus is the first and the last, and the Living One; He was dead, and behold He is alive forevermore and holds the keys of death and of Hades. (Revelation 1:17-18)

Jesus told His opponents, "You are from below; I am from above. You are of this world; I am not of this world. I told you, therefore, that you would die in your sins, for if you do not believe that I AM, you will die in your sins." (John 8:23-24)

LORD, I LISTEN TO YOUR WORDS OF TRUTH

I desire that the God of peace Himself will sanctify me completely, and that my whole spirit, soul, and body will be preserved blameless at the coming of my Lord Jesus Christ. He Who calls me is faithful, Who also will do it. (1 Thessalonians 5:23-24)

LORD, I RESPOND TO YOUR INSTRUCTION

I know that friendship with the world is enmity toward God. Anyone who wants to be a friend of the world makes himself an enemy of God. (James 4:4)

Lord, I thank You that Jesus is the first and the last and that He is the great I AM. I choose not to be a friend of the world, but a friend of those whom You love.

DAY 137

DELIGHTING IN GOD'S DELIVERANCE

❧

LORD, I DRAW NEAR TO YOU

As I approach Your throne of grace today, I am grateful that You care about the things that concern me and that You want me to offer them up to You.

May it be unto me as you said to Jacob, "Behold, I am with you and will watch over you wherever you go; I will not leave you until I have done what I have promised you." (Genesis 28:15)

Take a moment to share your personal needs with God, including your physical, emotional, relational, and spiritual concerns.

THANK YOU, LORD, FOR WHAT YOU HAVE DONE

The Lord God is the Alpha and the Omega, Who is, and Who was, and Who is to come, the Almighty. (Revelation 1:8)

Jesus said, "My Father loves Me because I lay down My life that I may take it up again. No one takes it from Me, but I lay it down of My own accord. I have authority to lay it down and authority to take it up again. This command I received from My Father." (John 10:17-18)

147
❧

LORD, I LISTEN TO YOUR WORDS OF TRUTH

The Lord will deliver me from every evil work and will bring me safely to His heavenly kingdom. To Him be glory forever and ever. (2 Timothy 4:18)

LORD, I RESPOND TO YOUR INSTRUCTION

Whoever gives another a cup of water to drink because of His name as a follower of Christ will by no means lose his reward. (Mark 9:41)

When I give, it will be given to me; good measure, pressed down, shaken together, running over, will be poured into my lap. For with the measure I use, it will be measured back to me. (Luke 6:38)

❧

Lord, I thank You that You are the Alpha and the Omega and that Jesus had the authority to lay down His life and to take it up again. Deliver me from every evil work. I will be generous in my service to others.

DAY 138

HIDING GOD'S WORD IN MY HEART

❦

LORD, I DRAW NEAR TO YOU

Lord, You have invited me to pray for the needs of others, and since You desire what is best for them, I take this opportunity to bring these requests to You.

You have given us a new commandment to love one another even as You have loved us; so we must love one another. By this all men will know that we are Your disciples, if we have love for one another. (John 13:34-35)

This is Your commandment, that we love one another, as You have loved us. (John 15:12)

Take a moment to lift up the needs of your family and friends, and to offer up any additional burdens for others that the Lord brings to mind.

THANK YOU, LORD, FOR WHAT YOU HAVE DONE

Jesus proved through His works that the Father is in Him, and that He is in the Father. (John 10:38)

All these testified that Jesus is the Son of God: John the Baptist, the works that Jesus did, the Father, and the Scriptures. (John 5:31-39)

LORD, I LISTEN TO YOUR WORDS OF TRUTH

You have blessed me and kept me; You have made Your face shine upon me and have been gracious to me; You have turned Your face toward me and given me peace. (Numbers 6:24-26)

LORD, I RESPOND TO YOUR INSTRUCTION

I have kept my feet from every evil path that I might keep Your Word. I gain understanding from Your precepts; therefore, I hate every false way. (Psalm 119:101,104)

I have hidden Your Word in my heart that I might not sin against You. (Psalm 119:11)

❦

Lord, I thank You for blessing and keeping me. Hide Your Word in my heart and keep my feet from every evil path.

DAY 139

ENTERTAINING ANGELS

~&

LORD, I DRAW NEAR TO YOU

Lord, I want Your Word to be deeply implanted in me so that I will know the truth and be able to express it in the way I live.

I will not fear, for You are with me;
I will not be dismayed, for You are my God.
You will strengthen me and help me;
You will uphold me with Your righteous right hand.
For You are the Lord my God, Who takes hold of my right hand
And says to me, "Do not fear; I will help you." (Isaiah 41:10,13)

Take a moment to affirm the truth of these words from Scripture and ask God to make them a growing reality in your life.

THANK YOU, LORD, FOR WHAT YOU HAVE DONE

Jesus knew that the Father had given all things into His hands and that He had come from God and was returning to God. (John 13:3)

He who comes from above is above all; he who is from the earth belongs to the earth, and speaks as one from the earth. He who comes from heaven is above all. He Whom God has sent speaks the words of God, for He gives the Spirit without limit. (John 3:31,34)

149
~&

LORD, I LISTEN TO YOUR WORDS OF TRUTH

I believe that it is through the grace of our Lord Jesus that I am saved. (Acts 15:11)

LORD, I RESPOND TO YOUR INSTRUCTION

I must help the weak and remember the words of the Lord Jesus, "It is more blessed to give than to receive." (Acts 20:35)

I will not forget to show hospitality to strangers, for by so doing some have entertained angels without knowing it. (Hebrews 13:2)

~&

Lord, I thank You that Jesus came from heaven and that You gave all things into His hands. I thank You that I am saved through the grace of the Lord Jesus. I will help the weak and show hospitality to strangers at every opportunity.

DAY 140

WATCHING AND PRAYING

LORD, I DRAW NEAR TO YOU

O Lord, I am deeply grateful for Your wonderful acts, for Your abundant promises, and for the gift of my relationship with You through the merits of Christ.

I will praise You, O Lord my God, with all my heart,
And I will glorify Your name forever.
For great is Your love toward me,
And You have delivered my soul from the depths of the grave. (Psalm 86:12-13)

Take a moment to express your gratitude for the many blessings that you have received from the Lord.

THANK YOU, LORD, FOR WHAT YOU HAVE DONE

Before Abraham was born, Jesus Christ always exists. (John 8:58)

From Christ's fullness we have all received, and grace upon grace. For the law was given through Moses; grace and truth came through Jesus Christ. (John 1:16-17)

LORD, I LISTEN TO YOUR WORDS OF TRUTH

Who shall separate me from the love of Christ? Shall tribulation, or distress, or persecution, or famine, or nakedness, or danger, or sword? As it is written: "For Your sake we face death all day long; we are considered as sheep to be slaughtered." Yet in all these things I am more than a conqueror through Him Who loved me. (Romans 8:35-37)

LORD, I RESPOND TO YOUR INSTRUCTION

I will watch and pray so that I will not fall into temptation; the spirit is willing, but the flesh is weak. (Matthew 26:41)

Lord, I thank You that Jesus Christ has always existed and for the grace I have received from His fullness. I thank You that nothing can separate me from the love of Christ. Help me to watch and pray that I may control my flesh and not fall into temptation.

DAY 141

SUPPLYING THE NEEDS OF THE SAINTS

❦

LORD, I DRAW NEAR TO YOU

Lord, I give thanks for Your greatness, Your goodness, and Your love, and I now draw near to enjoy Your presence.

May I fear You, the Lord my God; may I serve You, hold fast to You, and take my oaths in Your name. For You are my praise, and You are my God, who performed for me these great and awesome wonders which I have seen with my own eyes. (Deuteronomy 10:20-21)

You are the great, the mighty, and the awesome God, who keeps His covenant of lovingkindness. (Nehemiah 9:32)

Take a moment to consider God's awesome majesty and thank Him that He loves you and wants an intimate relationship with you.

THANK YOU, LORD, FOR WHAT YOU HAVE DONE

God raised Jesus from the dead, freeing Him from the agony of death, because it was impossible for Him to be held by it. (Acts 2:24)

LORD, I LISTEN TO YOUR WORDS OF TRUTH

God chose me in Christ before the foundation of the world to be holy and blameless in His sight. In love He predestined me to be adopted as His son through Jesus Christ, according to the good pleasure of His will, to the praise of the glory of His grace, which He bestowed upon me in the One He loves. (Ephesians 1:4-6)

LORD, I RESPOND TO YOUR INSTRUCTION

Because of our ministry of supplying the needs of the saints, they will glorify God for the obedience that accompanies our confession of the gospel of Christ, and for the liberality of sharing with them and with everyone else. (2 Corinthians 9:13)

❦

Lord, I thank You for Your awesome power and for raising Jesus from the dead. I thank You for choosing me in Christ before the foundation of the world. Give me the ability to assist those around me who are in need.

DAY 142

BEING A FAITHFUL STEWARD

LORD, I DRAW NEAR TO YOU

I am grateful to You, O God, for the blessing of Your forgiveness. I thank You that in Christ, You set me free from the guilt of the past and give me hope for the future.

Good and upright is the Lord;
Therefore He instructs sinners in His ways.
The Lord guides the humble in what is right
And teaches the humble His way. (Psalm 25:8-9)

Take a moment to ask the Spirit to search your heart and reveal any areas of unconfessed sin. Acknowledge these to the Lord and thank Him for His forgiveness.

THANK YOU, LORD, FOR WHAT YOU HAVE DONE

I will regard the Lord of hosts as holy; He shall be my fear, and He shall be my dread. (Isaiah 8:13)

Jesus is the stone which was rejected by the builders, but which has become the chief cornerstone. Salvation is found in no one else, for there is no other name under heaven given to men by which we must be saved. (Acts 4:11-12)

LORD, I LISTEN TO YOUR WORDS OF TRUTH

By grace I have been saved through faith, and this not of myself; it is the gift of God, not of works, so that no one can boast. (Ephesians 2:8-9)

LORD, I RESPOND TO YOUR INSTRUCTION

As each of us has received a gift, we should use it to serve others, as good stewards of the manifold grace of God. (1 Peter 4:10)

I want to be worthy of respect, not double-tongued, not addicted to wine, not fond of dishonest gain, but holding the mystery of the faith with a clear conscience. (1 Timothy 3:8-9)

Lord, I thank You that You are holy and that Jesus is the source of eternal salvation. I thank You that You have saved me by grace through faith. Help me to be a faithful steward of the gifts You have given me.

DAY 143

ANSWERING MY HOLY CALLING

❧

LORD, I DRAW NEAR TO YOU

I praise You, Lord, that You are intimately acquainted with my ways and that You always love me and have my best interests at heart.

I will not let sin reign in my mortal body that I should obey its lusts. Nor will I present the members of my body to sin, as instruments of wickedness, but I will present myself to God as one who is alive from the dead and my members as instruments of righteousness to God. (Romans 6:12-13)

May I put away all filthiness and the overflow of wickedness, and in meekness accept the Word planted in me, which is able to save my soul. (James 1:21)

Take a moment to offer this day to the Lord and ask Him for the grace to grow in your knowledge and love for Him.

THANK YOU, LORD, FOR WHAT YOU HAVE DONE

---

153 ❧

Holy, Holy, Holy is the Lord of hosts; the whole earth is full of His glory. (Isaiah 6:3)

Our Lord Jesus Christ gave Himself for our sins to rescue us from the present evil age, according to the will of our God and Father, to Whom be glory for ever and ever. (Galatians 1:3-5)

LORD, I LISTEN TO YOUR WORDS OF TRUTH

God has saved me and called me with a holy calling, not according to my works but according to His own purpose and grace. (2 Timothy 1:9)

LORD, I RESPOND TO YOUR INSTRUCTION

A righteous man guides his friends, but the way of the wicked leads them astray. (Proverbs 12:26)

I will not plan evil against my neighbor, since he lives trustfully by me. (Proverbs 3:29)

❧

Lord, I thank You for the richness of Your glory and for rescuing me from the present evil age. I thank You for saving me and calling me with a holy calling. I will be gracious and live in peace with my friends and neighbors.

DAY 144

ABIDING IN GOD'S LOVE

❧

LORD, I DRAW NEAR TO YOU

As I approach Your throne of grace today, I am grateful that You care about the things that concern me and that You want me to offer them up to You.

Show me Your ways, O Lord,
Teach me Your paths;
Lead me in Your truth and teach me,
For You are the God of my salvation,
And my hope is in You all day long. (Psalm 25:4-5)

Take a moment to share your personal needs with God, including your physical, emotional, relational, and spiritual concerns.

THANK YOU, LORD, FOR WHAT YOU HAVE DONE

I know that You alone, Whose name is the Lord, are the Most High over all the earth. (Psalm 83:18)

154

God placed all things under Christ's feet and gave Him to be head over all things to the Church, which is His body, the fullness of Him Who fills all in all. (Ephesians 1:22-23)

LORD, I LISTEN TO YOUR WORDS OF TRUTH

We have known and have believed the love God has for us. God is love, and he who abides in love abides in God, and God in him. In this way, love has been perfected among us so that we may have confidence in the day of judgment; because as He is, so are we in this world. There is no fear in love, but perfect love casts out fear, because fear involves punishment, and the one who fears has not been perfected in love. (1 John 4:16-18)

LORD, I RESPOND TO YOUR INSTRUCTION

I will be strong and courageous, being careful to obey Your Word; I will not turn from it to the right or to the left, that I may act wisely wherever I go. (Joshua 1:7)

❧

Lord, I thank You that You are the Most High over all the earth and that You placed all things under Christ's feet. I ask for the grace to abide in Your love and obey Your Word.

DAY 145

SPEAKING THE TRUTH IN LOVE

◈

LORD, I DRAW NEAR TO YOU

Lord, You have invited me to pray for the needs of others, and since You desire what is best for them, I take this opportunity to bring these requests to You.

The Lord Jesus prayed these words for the unity of all who would believe in Him: "I ask that all of them may be one, Father, just as You are in Me and I am in You, that they also may be in Us, that the world may believe that You sent Me. And the glory which You gave Me I have given to them, that they may be one, just as We are one: I in them, and You in Me, that they may be perfected in one, that the world may know that You have sent Me and have loved them, even as You have loved Me." (John 17:21-23)

Take a moment to lift up the needs of your family and friends, and to offer up any additional burdens for others that the Lord brings to mind.

THANK YOU, LORD, FOR WHAT YOU HAVE DONE

O Lord, our Lord, how majestic is Your name in all the earth! You have set Your glory above the heavens! (Psalm 8:1)

The wrath of God is revealed from heaven against all the godlessness and unrighteousness of men who suppress the truth by their unrighteousness, since what may be known about God is manifest in them, because God has manifested it to them. (Romans 1:18-19)

LORD, I LISTEN TO YOUR WORDS OF TRUTH

The salvation of the righteous comes from the Lord; He is their stronghold in time of trouble. The Lord helps them and delivers them; He delivers them from the wicked and saves them, because they take refuge in Him. (Psalm 37:39-40)

LORD, I RESPOND TO YOUR INSTRUCTION

I will not hate my brother in my heart, but I will reprove my neighbor frankly and not incur sin because of him. (Leviticus 19:17)

◈

Lord, I thank You that You have revealed Your majesty and glory to all people. I thank You for Your salvation and deliverance. I will speak the truth to others in love.

DAY 146

STANDING FIRM IN MY FAITH

LORD, I DRAW NEAR TO YOU

Lord, I want Your Word to be deeply implanted in me so that I will know the truth and be able to express it in the way I live.

Father in heaven,
Hallowed be Your name.
Your kingdom come;
Your will be done
On earth as it is in heaven. (Matthew 6:9-10)

Take a moment to affirm the truth of these words from Scripture and ask God to make them a growing reality in your life.

THANK YOU, LORD, FOR WHAT YOU HAVE DONE

Your righteousness, O God, reaches to the heavens, You Who have done great things. O God, who is like You? (Psalm 71:19)

We know that whatever the law says, it says to those who are under the law, that every mouth may be silenced, and the whole world held accountable to God; because no one will be justified in His sight by the works of the law, for through the law comes the knowledge of sin. (Romans 3:19-20)

LORD, I LISTEN TO YOUR WORDS OF TRUTH

For as high as the heavens are above the earth, so great is His love for those who fear Him; as far as the East is from the West, so far has He removed our transgressions from us. As a father has compassion on His children, so the Lord has compassion on those who fear Him. (Psalm 103:11-13)

LORD, I RESPOND TO YOUR INSTRUCTION

I will be on my guard, stand firm in the faith, act with courage, and be strong. (1 Corinthians 16:13)

Lord, I thank You for the great things You have done and for the power of Your revealed Word. I thank You for Your limitless compassion. I will act with courage and stand firm in my faith.

DAY 147

EXAMINING MY WAYS

❧

LORD, I DRAW NEAR TO YOU

O Lord, I am deeply grateful for Your wonderful acts, for Your abundant promises, and for the gift of my relationship with You through the merits of Christ.

All the kings of the earth will give thanks to You, O Lord,
When they hear the words of Your mouth.
Yes, they sing of the ways of the Lord,
For the glory of the Lord is great.
Though the Lord is on high,
Yet He looks upon the lowly,
But the proud He knows from afar. (Psalm 138:4-6)

Take a moment to express your gratitude for the many blessings that you have received from the Lord.

THANK YOU, LORD, FOR WHAT YOU HAVE DONE

O Sovereign Lord, You are God! Your words are true, and You have promised good things to Your servant. (2 Samuel 7:28)

God will impute righteousness to us who believe in Him Who raised Jesus our Lord from the dead, Who was delivered over to death because of our sins and was raised because of our justification. (Romans 4:24-25)

LORD, I LISTEN TO YOUR WORDS OF TRUTH

Why should any living man complain when punished for his sins? Let us search out and examine our ways, and let us return to the Lord. (Lamentations 3:39-40)

LORD, I RESPOND TO YOUR INSTRUCTION

I will trust in You enough to honor You as holy in the sight of others. (Numbers 20:12)

❧

Lord, I thank You that Your words are true and that You credit righteousness to those who trust in Christ. Guide me back to You when I fall into disobedience, and teach me how to examine my ways.

DAY 148

DRINKING LIVING WATER

❧

LORD, I DRAW NEAR TO YOU

Lord, I give thanks for Your greatness, Your goodness, and Your love, and I now draw near to enjoy Your presence.

The word of the Lord is upright,
And all His work is done in faithfulness.
He loves righteousness and justice;
The earth is full of the lovingkindness of the Lord. (Psalm 33:4-5)

Once God has spoken;
Twice I have heard this:
That power belongs to God,
And that You, O Lord, are loving.
For You reward each person according to what he has done. (Psalm 62:11-12)

Take a moment to consider God's awesome majesty and thank Him that He loves you and wants an intimate relationship with you.

158

THANK YOU, LORD, FOR WHAT YOU HAVE DONE

I will arise and bless the Lord, my God, Who is from everlasting to everlasting. Blessed be Your glorious name, which is exalted above all blessing and praise! (Nehemiah 9:5)

LORD, I LISTEN TO YOUR WORDS OF TRUTH

Everyone who drinks ordinary water will be thirsty again, but whoever drinks the water You give will never thirst. Indeed, the water You give becomes in us a spring of water welling up to eternal life. (John 4:13-14)

LORD, I RESPOND TO YOUR INSTRUCTION

I will be self-controlled in all things, endure hardship, do the work of an evangelist, and fulfill my ministry. (2 Timothy 4:5)

❧

Lord, I thank You that Your glorious name is exalted and for the living water that Jesus offers. Help me to persevere and fulfill my calling no matter what the cost may be.

DAY 149

LIVING IN PEACE WITH ALL MEN

ᴄ᷅ᴗ

LORD, I DRAW NEAR TO YOU

I am grateful to You, O God, for the blessing of Your forgiveness. I thank You that in Christ, You set me free from the guilt of the past and give me hope for the future.

When I have sinned against You, hear from heaven and forgive my sin and restore me. Teach me the good way in which I should walk. When I sin against You—for there is no one who does not sin—may I return to You with all my heart and with all my soul. (1 Kings 8:33-34,36,46,48)

Take a moment to ask the Spirit to search your heart and reveal any areas of unconfessed sin. Acknowledge these to the Lord and thank Him for His forgiveness.

THANK YOU, LORD, FOR WHAT YOU HAVE DONE

God will have mercy on whom He has mercy, and He will have compassion on whom He has compassion. It does not depend on human desire or effort, but on God's mercy. (Romans 9:15,16)

159

LORD, I LISTEN TO YOUR WORDS OF TRUTH

Lord Jesus, all that the Father gives You will come to You, and whoever comes to You, You will never cast out. For You have come down from heaven not to do Your own will, but the will of Him who sent You. And this is the will of Him Who sent You, that You will lose none of all that He has given You, but raise them up at the last day. For Your Father's will is that everyone who looks to the Son and believes in Him may have eternal life, and You will raise him up at the last day. (John 6:37-40)

LORD, I RESPOND TO YOUR INSTRUCTION

If it is possible, as far as it depends on me, I will live at peace with all men. (Romans 12:18)

ᴄ᷅ᴗ

Lord, I thank You that You show mercy and compassion according to Your perfect will. I thank You that You will never cast out anyone who looks to Your Son and believes in Him. Help me to live at peace with others continually.

DAY 150

RUNNING WITH ENDURANCE

LORD, I DRAW NEAR TO YOU

I praise You, Lord, that You are intimately acquainted with my ways and that You always love me and have my best interests at heart.

Like Noah, may I be a righteous person, blameless among the people of my time, and one who walks with God. (Genesis 6:9)

May I do according to all that the Lord commands me. (Exodus 39:42; 40:16)

Take a moment to offer this day to the Lord and ask Him for the grace to grow in your knowledge and love for Him.

THANK YOU, LORD, FOR WHAT YOU HAVE DONE

You revealed Yourself to Moses as "I AM WHO I AM." (Exodus 3:14)

LORD, I LISTEN TO YOUR WORDS OF TRUTH

Your sheep hear Your voice, and You know them, and they follow You. You give them eternal life, and they shall never perish; no one can snatch them out of Your hand. The Father, Who has given them to You, is greater than all; no one can snatch them out of the Father's hand. (John 10:27-29)

LORD, I RESPOND TO YOUR INSTRUCTION

Since I have a great cloud of witnesses surrounding me, I want to lay aside every impediment and the sin that so easily entangles, and run with endurance the race that is set before me, fixing my eyes on Jesus, the author and perfecter of my faith, Who for the joy set before Him endured the cross, despising the shame, and sat down at the right hand of the throne of God. I will consider Him Who endured such hostility from sinners, so that I will not grow weary and lose heart. (Hebrews 12:1-3)

Lord, I thank You that You know and protect Your sheep. I will run with endurance the race that is set before me and commit myself to doing good.

DAY 151

BEING CONFORMED TO CHRIST'S LIKENESS

֎

LORD, I DRAW NEAR TO YOU

As I approach Your throne of grace today, I am grateful that You care about the things that concern me and that You want me to offer them up to You.

O continue Your lovingkindness to those who know You,
And Your righteousness to the upright in heart.
Do not let the foot of pride come against me,
And let not the hand of the wicked drive me away. (Psalm 36:10-11)

Take a moment to share your personal needs with God, including your physical, emotional, relational, and spiritual concerns.

THANK YOU, LORD, FOR WHAT YOU HAVE DONE

But when He, the Spirit of truth, comes, He will guide you into all the truth; for He will not speak on His own initiative, but whatever He hears, He will speak; and He will disclose to you what is to come. He shall glorify Me; for He shall take of Mine, and shall disclose it to you. (John 16:13-14)

161

LORD, I LISTEN TO YOUR WORDS OF TRUTH

Those God foreknew, He also predestined to be conformed to the likeness of His Son, that He might be the firstborn among many brothers. And those He predestined, He also called; those He called, He also justified; those He justified, He also glorified. (Romans 8:29-30)

LORD, I RESPOND TO YOUR INSTRUCTION

To the law and to the testimony! If men do not speak according to Your Word, they have no light of dawn. (Isaiah 8:20)

You are the stability of our times, a wealth of salvation, wisdom, and knowledge; the fear of the Lord is the key to this treasure. (Isaiah 33:6)

֎

Lord, I thank You for sending Your Holy Spirit to guide us into all truth and for Your purpose in conforming me to the likeness of Your Son. Teach me to speak according to the wisdom of Your Word.

DAY 152

KEEPING MYSELF IN GOD'S LOVE

LORD, I DRAW NEAR TO YOU

Lord, You have invited me to pray for the needs of others, and since You desire what is best for them, I take this opportunity to bring these requests to You.

Jesus said, "As the Father has sent Me, I also send you." (John 20:21)

Grant that I may be used to open the eyes of others and to turn them from darkness to light, and from the power of satan to God, so that they may receive forgiveness of sins and an inheritance among those who have been sanctified by faith in Jesus. (Acts 26:18)

Take a moment to lift up the needs of your family and friends, and to offer up any additional burdens for others that the Lord brings to mind.

THANK YOU, LORD, FOR WHAT YOU HAVE DONE

Jesus is the way, and the truth, and the life. No one comes to the Father except through Him. (John 14:6)

The angel said to the shepherds, "Do not be afraid. I bring you good news of great joy that will be for all the people. For today in the city of David a Savior has been born to you, Who is Christ the Lord." (Luke 2:10-11)

LORD, I LISTEN TO YOUR WORDS OF TRUTH

I must not receive God's grace in vain. For He says, "In the acceptable time I heard you, and in the day of salvation I helped you." Now is the time of God's favor; now is the day of salvation. (2 Corinthians 6:1-2)

LORD, I RESPOND TO YOUR INSTRUCTION

Like Noah, I want to be a righteous person, blameless among the people of my time, and one who walks with God. (Genesis 6:9)

Being built up in the most holy faith and praying in the Holy Spirit, I want to keep myself in the love of God as I wait for the mercy of our Lord Jesus Christ to eternal life. (Jude 20-21)

Lord, I thank You for the good news that Jesus is the way, the truth, and the life. I thank You for the grace of Your salvation. Help me to keep myself in Your love.

DAY 153

FULFILLING GOD'S LAW

LORD, I DRAW NEAR TO YOU

Lord, I want Your Word to be deeply implanted in me so that I will know the truth and be able to express it in the way I live.

May our Lord Jesus Christ Himself and God our Father, who has loved us and has given us eternal consolation and good hope by grace, comfort our hearts and strengthen us in every good work and word. (2 Thessalonians 2:16-17)

Take a moment to affirm the truth of these words from Scripture and ask God to make them a growing reality in your life.

THANK YOU, LORD, FOR WHAT YOU HAVE DONE

The Lord is the Spirit, and where the Spirit of the Lord is, there is freedom. (2 Corinthians 3:17)

When He was asked by the Pharisees when the kingdom of God would come, Jesus replied, "The kingdom of God does not come with obser-vation, nor will people say, 'Here it is,' or 'There it is,' for behold, the kingdom of God is within you." (Luke 17:20-21)

163

LORD, I LISTEN TO YOUR WORDS OF TRUTH

We were dead in our trespasses and sins, in which we used to live when we followed the course of this world and of the ruler of the kingdom of the air, the spirit who is now at work in the sons of disobedience. All of us also lived among them at one time, gratifying the cravings of our flesh and of the mind, and were by nature children of wrath. (Ephesians 2:1-3)

LORD, I RESPOND TO YOUR INSTRUCTION

I will owe nothing to anyone except to love them; by loving my neighbor, I fulfill Your law. (Romans 13:8)

Lord, I thank You for the freedom of Your Spirit and for the reality of Your kingdom. I thank You for delivering me from bondage to the world, the flesh, and the devil. I will strive to love my neighbors.

DAY 154

SPEAKING WISELY

LORD, I DRAW NEAR TO YOU

O Lord, I am deeply grateful for Your wonderful acts, for Your abundant promises, and for the gift of my relationship with You through the merits of Christ.

The Lord upholds all who fall
And lifts up all who are bowed down.
The eyes of all look to You,
And You give them their food at the proper time.
You open Your hand
And satisfy the desire of every living thing. (Psalm 145:14-16)

Take a moment to express your gratitude for the many blessings that you have received from the Lord.

THANK YOU, LORD, FOR WHAT YOU HAVE DONE

164

The Lord does not see as man sees. Man looks at the outward appearance, but the Lord looks at the heart. (1 Samuel 16:7)

Jesus knew all men, and had no need for anyone's testimony about man, for He knew what was in man. (John 2:24-25)

LORD, I LISTEN TO YOUR WORDS OF TRUTH

Once I was alienated from God and was an enemy in my mind because of my evil works. But now He has reconciled me by His fleshly body through death to present me holy and blameless in His sight and free from reproach. (Colossians 1:21-22)

LORD, I RESPOND TO YOUR INSTRUCTION

The mouth of the righteous speaks wisdom, and his tongue speaks what is just. The law of his God is in his heart; his steps do not slide. (Psalm 37:30-31)

Lord, I thank You that You look at the heart and not at outward appearances. I thank You for reconciling me to You through the death of Your Son. Help me to keep my steps on the right path and to speak wisdom.

DAY 155

SPURNING SELFISH AMBITION

⤚❧

LORD, I DRAW NEAR TO YOU

Lord, I give thanks for Your greatness, Your goodness, and Your love, and I now draw near to enjoy Your presence.

How great are Your works, O Lord!
Your thoughts are very deep.
The senseless man does not know;
Fools do not understand
That when the wicked spring up like grass
And all the evildoers flourish,
They will be destroyed forever.
But You, O Lord, are exalted forever. (Psalm 92:5-8)

You are the Lord, that is Your name.
You will not give Your glory to another,
Or Your praise to idols. (Isaiah 42:8)

Take a moment to consider God's awesome majesty and thank Him that He loves you and wants an intimate relationship with you.

165
❧

THANK YOU, LORD, FOR WHAT YOU HAVE DONE

I know that You can do all things and that no purpose of Yours can be thwarted. (Job 42:2)

LORD, I LISTEN TO YOUR WORDS OF TRUTH

I was not redeemed with perishable things such as silver or gold from the aimless way of life handed down to me from my forefathers, but with the precious blood of Christ, as of a lamb without blemish or defect. (1 Peter 1:18-19)

LORD, I RESPOND TO YOUR INSTRUCTION

I will do nothing out of selfish ambition or vain conceit, but in humility I will esteem others as more important than myself. I will look not only to my own interests, but also to the interests of others. (Philippians 2:3-4)

⤚❧

Lord, I thank You that Your purposes will be established and for redeeming me with the precious blood of Christ. I am determined not to be selfishly ambitious, but to consider the interests of others above my own.

DAY 156

DWELLING IN YOUR PRESENCE

❧

LORD, I DRAW NEAR TO YOU

I am grateful to You, O God, for the blessing of Your forgiveness. I thank You that in Christ, You set me free from the guilt of the past and give me hope for the future.

I will endure discipline, for God is treating me as a son. For what son is not disciplined by his father? If I am without discipline, of which all have become partakers, then I am an illegitimate child and not a true son. Moreover, we have all had human fathers who disciplined us, and we respected them; how much more should I be subjected to the Father of spirits and live? (Hebrews 12:7-9)

Take a moment to ask the Spirit to search your heart and reveal any areas of unconfessed sin. Acknowledge these to the Lord and thank Him for His forgiveness.

THANK YOU, LORD, FOR WHAT YOU HAVE DONE

❧

He Who is the Glory of Israel does not lie or change His mind, for He is not a man, that He should change His mind. (1 Samuel 15:29)

The Lord by wisdom founded the earth; by understanding He established the heavens; by His knowledge the deeps were divided, and the clouds drop down the dew. (Proverbs 3:19-20)

LORD, I LISTEN TO YOUR WORDS OF TRUTH

The Lord Himself goes before me and will be with me; He will never leave me nor forsake me. I will not be afraid or be dismayed. (Deuteronomy 31:8)

LORD, I RESPOND TO YOUR INSTRUCTION

Surely the righteous will give thanks to Your name; the upright will dwell in Your presence. (Psalm 140:13)

❧

Lord, I thank You that Your purposes never change and that You established the heavens and the earth in wisdom. I thank You that You will never leave me nor forsake me, as I dwell in Your presence.

DAY 157

TURNING FROM DARKNESS TO THE LIGHT

LORD, I DRAW NEAR TO YOU

I praise You, Lord, that You are intimately acquainted with my ways and that You always love me and have my best interests at heart.

You are the true vine, and Your Father is the vinedresser. He cuts off every branch in You that bears no fruit, while every branch that does bear fruit He prunes, that it may bear more fruit. May I abide in You, and You in me. As the branch cannot bear fruit of itself, unless it abides in the vine, neither can I, unless I abide in You. (John 15:1-2,4)

Take a moment to offer this day to the Lord and ask Him for the grace to grow in your knowledge and love for Him.

THANK YOU, LORD, FOR WHAT YOU HAVE DONE

The eyes of the Lord are in every place, watching the good and the evil. (Proverbs 15:3)

The Son of Man is going to come in the glory of His Father with His angels, and then He will reward each person according to his works. (Matthew 16:27)

LORD, I LISTEN TO YOUR WORDS OF TRUTH

You are my lamp, O Lord; the Lord turns my darkness into light. With Your help I can advance against a troop; with my God I can leap over a wall. (2 Samuel 22:29-30)

LORD, I RESPOND TO YOUR INSTRUCTION

An anxious heart weighs a man down, but a good word makes him glad. (Proverbs 12:25)

God comforts us in all our afflictions, so that we can comfort those in any affliction with the comfort we ourselves have received from God. (2 Corinthians 1:4)

Lord, I thank You that the Son of Man will reward each person according to his works. Thank You for turning my darkness into light, and for comforting me in my afflictions so that I may comfort and encourage others.

DAY 158

WEIGHING MY HEART

LORD, I DRAW NEAR TO YOU

As I approach Your throne of grace today, I am grateful that You care about the things that concern me and that You want me to offer them up to You.

Let me hear Your unfailing love in the morning,
For I have put my trust in You.
Show me the way I should walk,
For to You I lift up my soul. (Psalm 143:8)

Take a moment to share your personal needs with God, including your physical, emotional, relational, and spiritual concerns.

THANK YOU, LORD, FOR WHAT YOU HAVE DONE

All a man's ways are right in his own eyes, but the Lord weighs the hearts. (Proverbs 21:2)

Nothing is hidden that will not be revealed, and nothing is secret that will not be known and come out into the open. (Luke 8:17)

LORD, I LISTEN TO YOUR WORDS OF TRUTH

Lord, there is no one besides You to help the powerless against the mighty. Help us, O Lord our God, for we rest in You. O Lord, You are our God; do not let man prevail against You. (2 Chronicles 14:11)

LORD, I RESPOND TO YOUR INSTRUCTION

In the way of righteousness there is life, and in that pathway there is no death. (Proverbs 12:28)

I will let my eyes look straight ahead, and fix my gaze straight before me. I will ponder the path of my feet so that all my ways will be established. I will not turn to the right or to the left but keep my foot from evil. (Proverbs 4:25-27)

Lord, I thank You that You weigh the hearts and that all things will be revealed by the light of Christ. I thank You for helping the powerless against the mighty. Help me to walk in righteousness that my ways may be established in You.

DAY 159

FOLLOWING THE GOOD SHEPHERD

~&~

LORD, I DRAW NEAR TO YOU

---

*Lord, You have invited me to pray for the needs of others, and since You desire
what is best for them, I take this opportunity to bring these requests to You.*

May I help the weak and remember the words of the Lord Jesus, that
He said, "It is more blessed to give than to receive." (Acts 20:35)

*Take a moment to lift up the needs of your family and friends, and to offer up any
additional burdens for others that the Lord brings to mind.*

THANK YOU, LORD, FOR WHAT YOU HAVE DONE

Before You formed me in the womb, You knew me; before I was born,
You set me apart. (Jeremiah 1:5)

Because Jesus lives forever, He has a permanent priesthood. Therefore,
He is also able to save completely those who come to God through
Him, since He always lives to intercede for them. (Hebrews 7:24-25)

169
~&~

LORD, I LISTEN TO YOUR WORDS OF TRUTH

The Lord is my shepherd; I shall not be in want. He makes me lie
down in green pastures; He leads me beside quiet waters; He restores
my soul. He guides me in the paths of righteousness for His name's
sake. Even though I walk through the valley of the shadow of death, I
will fear no evil, for You are with me; Your rod and Your staff, they
comfort me. You prepare a table before me in the presence of my
enemies. You anoint my head with oil; my cup overflows. Surely
goodness and mercy will follow me all the days of my life, and I will
dwell in the house of the Lord forever. (Psalm 23:1-6)

LORD, I RESPOND TO YOUR INSTRUCTION

Whatever I do, I will work at it with all my heart, as to the Lord and
not to men, knowing that I will receive the reward of the inheritance
from the Lord. It is the Lord Christ I am serving. (Colossians 3:23-24)

~&~

*Lord, I thank You that Jesus saves and intercedes for me. I thank You that You
guide and protect me as my shepherd. Help me to be more concerned about
pleasing You than impressing people.*

DAY 160

FINDING REFUGE IN MY GOD

LORD, I DRAW NEAR TO YOU

Lord, I want Your Word to be deeply implanted in me so that I will know the truth and be able to express it in the way I live.

To the King eternal, immortal, invisible, the only God, be honor and glory forever and ever. (1 Timothy 1:17)

The God of all grace, who called me to His eternal glory in Christ, after I have suffered a little while, will Himself perfect, confirm, strengthen, and establish me. To Him be the glory and dominion for ever and ever. Amen. (1 Peter 5:10-11)

Take a moment to affirm the truth of these words from Scripture and ask God to make them a growing reality in your life.

THANK YOU, LORD, FOR WHAT YOU HAVE DONE

I know, O Lord, that a man's way is not his own; it is not in a man who walks to direct his steps. (Jeremiah 10:23)

The god of this age has blinded the minds of unbelievers, so that they cannot see the light of the gospel of the glory of Christ, Who is the image of God. (2 Corinthians 4:4)

LORD, I LISTEN TO YOUR WORDS OF TRUTH

God is my refuge and strength, an ever-present help in trouble. Therefore, I will not fear, though the earth changes and the mountains slip into the heart of the sea. (Psalm 46:1-2)

LORD, I RESPOND TO YOUR INSTRUCTION

Blessed is the man who always fears God, but he who hardens his heart falls into trouble. (Proverbs 28:14)

A person's wickedness will punish him; his backsliding will reprove him. I know, therefore, and see that it is evil and bitter to forsake the Lord my God and have no fear of Him. (Jeremiah 2:19)

Lord, I thank You that You direct my steps and illuminate me with the gospel of the glory of Christ. I thank You for being my refuge and strength. I will fear You and never forsake You.

DAY 161
DELIGHTING IN GOD'S DISCIPLINE
❦

LORD, I DRAW NEAR TO YOU

*O Lord, I am deeply grateful for Your wonderful acts, for Your abundant
promises, and for the gift of my relationship with You through the merits of
Christ.*

The Lord is close to the brokenhearted
And saves those who are crushed in spirit.
Many are the afflictions of the righteous,
But the Lord delivers him out of them all. (Psalm 34:18-19)

*Take a moment to express your gratitude for the many blessings that you have
received from the Lord.*

THANK YOU, LORD, FOR WHAT YOU HAVE DONE

I will give thanks to the Lord, for He is good; His love endures forever.
(1 Chronicles 16:34)

Jesus did not ask that the Father should take us out of the world, but
that He protect us from the evil one. He prayed, "Father, I desire those
You have given Me to be with Me where I am, that they may behold
My glory, the glory You have given Me because You loved Me before
the foundation of the world." (John 17:15,24)

LORD, I LISTEN TO YOUR WORDS OF TRUTH

I will not despise the discipline of the Lord nor resent His correction;
for the Lord disciplines those He loves, as a father the son he delights
in. (Proverbs 3:11-12)

LORD, I RESPOND TO YOUR INSTRUCTION

I will do all things without complaining or arguing, so that I may
become blameless and pure, a child of God without fault in the midst of
a crooked and perverse generation, among whom I shine as a light in
the world, holding fast the Word of life. (Philippians 2:14-16)
❦

*Lord, I thank You for Your goodness and everlasting love and for Jesus' desire for
us to be with Him and behold His glory. I thank You for the discipline You send
for my good. I will pursue purity in my character continuously.*

171
❦

DAY 162

SEEKING GOD'S KINGDOM

LORD, I DRAW NEAR TO YOU

Lord, I give thanks for Your greatness, Your goodness, and Your love, and I now draw near to enjoy Your presence.

The Lord Most High is awesome,
The great King over all the earth!
God is the King of all the earth,
And I will sing His praise.
God reigns over the nations;
God is seated on His holy throne. (Psalm 47:2,7-8)

Take a moment to consider God's awesome majesty and thank Him that He loves you and wants an intimate relationship with you.

THANK YOU, LORD, FOR WHAT YOU HAVE DONE

Lovingkindness and truth have met together; righteousness and peace have kissed each other. Truth shall spring forth from the earth, and righteousness looks down from heaven. (Psalm 85:10-11)

The Lord prayed, "I glorified You on the earth by completing the work You gave Me to do. And now, Father, glorify Me in Your presence with the glory I had with You before the world began." (John 17:4-5)

LORD, I LISTEN TO YOUR WORDS OF TRUTH

I will not fear, for You are with me; I will not be dismayed, for You are my God. You will strengthen me and help me; You will uphold me with Your righteous right hand. For You are the Lord my God, Who takes hold of my right hand and says to me, "Do not fear; I will help you." (Isaiah 41:10,13)

LORD, I RESPOND TO YOUR INSTRUCTION

I will seek first Your kingdom and Your righteousness; and all these things shall be added to me. Therefore, I will not be anxious for tomorrow; for tomorrow will care for itself. (Matthew 6:33-34)

Lord, I thank You for Your lovingkindness and truth and for the perfection of Christ's completed work. I thank You for strengthening and upholding me. I will seek Your righteousness and Your kingdom.

DAY 163

HONORING ALL PEOPLE

～

LORD, I DRAW NEAR TO YOU

I am grateful to You, O God, for the blessing of Your forgiveness. I thank You that in Christ, You set me free from the guilt of the past and give me hope for the future.

Lord, I have heard of Your fame, and I stand in awe of Your deeds.
O Lord, revive Your work in the midst of the years,
In our time make them known;
In wrath remember mercy. (Habakkuk 3:2)

Take a moment to ask the Spirit to search your heart and reveal any areas of unconfessed sin. Acknowledge these to the Lord and thank Him for His forgiveness.

THANK YOU, LORD, FOR WHAT YOU HAVE DONE

You, Lord, are good and ready to forgive and abundant in mercy to all who call upon You. (Psalm 86:5)

Peter told the council, "The God of our fathers raised up Jesus Whom you had killed by hanging Him on a tree. God exalted Him to His own right hand as Prince and Savior, that He might give repentance and forgiveness of sins to Israel." (Acts 5:30-31)

173

～

LORD, I LISTEN TO YOUR WORDS OF TRUTH

If God is for me, who can be against me? He Who did not spare His own Son, but delivered Him up for us all, how will He not, also with Him, freely give us all things? (Romans 8:31-32)

LORD, I RESPOND TO YOUR INSTRUCTION

Those younger should be submissive to those who are older, and all of us should clothe ourselves with humility toward one another, for "God opposes the proud but gives grace to the humble." (1 Peter 5:5)

I will honor all people, love the brotherhood of believers, fear God, and honor the king. (1 Peter 2:17)

～

Lord, I thank You for Your mercy and forgiveness and for exalting Jesus to Your right hand as Prince and Savior. I thank You for freely giving me all things in Christ. I will clothe myself with humility and love toward others.

DAY 164

BEING FULL OF THE SPIRIT

❧

LORD, I DRAW NEAR TO YOU

I praise You, Lord, that You are intimately acquainted with my ways and that You always love me and have my best interests at heart.

May I not turn aside from following the Lord, but serve the Lord with all my heart. May I not turn aside to go after worthless things which do not profit or deliver, because they are useless. (1 Samuel 12:20-21)

Take a moment to offer this day to the Lord and ask Him for the grace to grow in your knowledge and love for Him.

THANK YOU, LORD, FOR WHAT YOU HAVE DONE

I will sing of Your lovingkindness and justice; to You, O Lord, I will sing praises. (Psalm 101:1)

As the gospel spread to the Gentiles, many rejoiced and glorified the Word of the Lord, and all who were appointed for eternal life believed. (Acts 13:48)

LORD, I LISTEN TO YOUR WORDS OF TRUTH

Who will bring a charge against those whom God has chosen? It is God Who justifies. Who is he who condemns? It is Christ Jesus Who died, Who was furthermore raised to life, Who is at the right hand of God and is also interceding for me. (Romans 8:33-34)

LORD, I RESPOND TO YOUR INSTRUCTION

I must not test the Lord or grumble as some of the Israelites did. (1 Corinthians 10:9-10)

Like Barnabas, I want to be a good person, full of the Holy Spirit and of faith. (Acts 11:24)

❧

Lord, I thank You for Your lovingkindness and justice and for the priceless gift of eternal life in Christ. I thank You that in Christ Jesus I cannot be condemned. Help me not to grumble about my circumstances but be full of the Holy Spirit and faith.

DAY 165

BEING FAITHFUL IN SERVICE TO OTHERS

~&~

LORD, I DRAW NEAR TO YOU

As I approach Your throne of grace today, I am grateful that You care about the things that concern me and that You want me to offer them up to You.

May my conscience testify that I have conducted myself in the world in the holiness and sincerity that are from God, not in fleshly wisdom but in the grace of God, especially in my relations with others. (2 Corinthians 1:12)

Take a moment to share your personal needs with God, including your physical, emotional, relational, and spiritual concerns.

THANK YOU, LORD, FOR WHAT YOU HAVE DONE

The Lord executes righteousness and justice for all who are oppressed. The Lord is compassionate and gracious, slow to anger, and abounding in lovingkindness. (Psalm 103:6,8)

Both Jews and Greeks must turn to God in repentance and have faith in our Lord Jesus Christ. (Acts 20:21)

175
~&~

LORD, I LISTEN TO YOUR WORDS OF TRUTH

The Lord is faithful, Who will strengthen me and protect me from the evil one. (2 Thessalonians 3:3)

LORD, I RESPOND TO YOUR INSTRUCTION

The husband should fulfill his marital duty to his wife, and likewise the wife to her husband. The wife's body does not belong to her alone, but also to her husband. In the same way, the husband's body does not belong to him alone, but also to his wife. (1 Corinthians 7:3-4)

Each husband must love his own wife as he loves himself, and each wife must respect her husband. (Ephesians 5:33)

~&~

Lord, I thank You for being compassionate and gracious and for Your gift of repentance and faith in Jesus Christ. I thank You for protecting me from the evil one. Help me to be faithful in my service to others.

DAY 166

SOWING AND REAPING

LORD, I DRAW NEAR TO YOU

Lord, You have invited me to pray for the needs of others, and since You desire what is best for them, I take this opportunity to bring these requests to You.

Let love be without hypocrisy. Abhor what is evil; cling to what is good.
Be devoted to one another in brotherly love; give preference to one another in honor. (Romans 12:9-10)

Take a moment to lift up the needs of your family and friends, and to offer up any additional burdens for others that the Lord brings to mind.

THANK YOU, LORD, FOR WHAT YOU HAVE DONE

The Lord's lovingkindness is great toward us, and the truth of the Lord endures forever. Praise the Lord! (Psalm 117:2)

Those who show contempt for the riches of God's kindness, forbearance, and patience do not realize that the kindness of God leads toward repentance. (Romans 2:4)

LORD, I LISTEN TO YOUR WORDS OF TRUTH

The Lord my God wants me to fear Him, to walk in all His ways, to love Him, and to serve the Lord my God with all my heart and with all my soul. (Deuteronomy 10:12)

LORD, I RESPOND TO YOUR INSTRUCTION

God is not mocked, for whatever I sow, this I will also reap. If I sow to please my flesh, I will reap corruption; If I sow to please the Spirit, I will of the Spirit reap eternal life. (Galatians 6:7-8)

Whatever I do, whether in word or in deed, I will do all in the name of the Lord Jesus, giving thanks to God the Father through Him. (Colossians 3:17)

Lord, I thank You for the riches of Your kindness, forbearance, and patience. I will walk in Your ways by loving and serving You, sowing to please the Spirit, and doing all things in the name of the Lord Jesus.

DAY 167

SEEKING TO KNOW GOD

❧

LORD, I DRAW NEAR TO YOU

Lord, I want Your Word to be deeply implanted in me so that I will know the truth and be able to express it in the way I live.

May the God of peace, Who through the blood of the eternal covenant brought back from the dead our Lord Jesus, that great Shepherd of the sheep, equip us in every good thing to do His will, working in us what is pleasing in His sight, through Jesus Christ, to Whom be glory forever and ever. (Hebrews 13:20-21)

Take a moment to affirm the truth of these words from Scripture and ask God to make them a growing reality in your life.

THANK YOU, LORD, FOR WHAT YOU HAVE DONE

The sum of Your words is truth, and all of Your righteous judgments are eternal. (Psalm 119:160)

177
❧

You will punish the world for its evil, the wicked for their iniquity. You will put an end to the arrogance of the haughty and will humble the pride of the ruthless. (Isaiah 13:11)

LORD, I LISTEN TO YOUR WORDS OF TRUTH

My soul yearns for You in the night; my spirit within me diligently seeks You. When Your judgments come upon the earth, the inhabitants of the world learn righteousness. (Isaiah 26:9)

LORD, I RESPOND TO YOUR INSTRUCTION

Wives should be submissive to their own husbands, so that even if any of them disobey the Word, they may be won without a word by the behavior of their wives, when they see their purity and reverence. (1 Peter 3:1-2)

Husbands should be considerate as they live with their wives and treat them with respect as the weaker vessel and as co-heirs of the grace of life. (1 Peter 3:7)

❧

Lord, I thank You that Your righteous judgments are eternal and that You will put an end to iniquity. I thank You for the desire to seek and to know You. Help me to be faithful in my commitment to serve others.

DAY 168

PURSUING RIGHTEOUSNESS

~

LORD, I DRAW NEAR TO YOU

O Lord, I am deeply grateful for Your wonderful acts, for Your abundant promises, and for the gift of my relationship with You through the merits of Christ.

Rejoice greatly, O daughter of Zion!
Shout, O daughter of Jerusalem!
Behold, Your King is coming to you;
He is just and having salvation,
Humble and riding on a donkey,
On a colt, the foal of a donkey.
He will proclaim peace to the nations;
His dominion will extend from sea to sea
And from the river to the ends of the earth. (Zechariah 9:9-10)

Take a moment to express your gratitude for the many blessings that you have received from the Lord.

THANK YOU, LORD, FOR WHAT YOU HAVE DONE

O Lord of hosts, You judge righteously and test the heart and mind; to You I have committed my cause. (Jeremiah 11:20)

The Lord of hosts has planned it, to bring low the pride of all glory and to humble all who are renowned on the earth. (Isaiah 23:9)

LORD, I LISTEN TO YOUR WORDS OF TRUTH

I do not want to be like those who draw near to You with their mouths and honor You with their lips, but whose hearts are far from You, and whose reverence for You is made up only of rules taught by men. (Isaiah 29:13)

LORD, I RESPOND TO YOUR INSTRUCTION

I will flee youthful lusts and pursue righteousness, faith, love, and peace, with those who call on the Lord out of a pure heart. (2 Timothy 2:22)

~

Lord, I thank You for Your righteous judgments and for Your plan to humble the proud. I will draw near to You in my heart, not merely my actions, as I pursue righteousness, faith, love, and peace.

DAY 169

ACKNOWLEDGING MY GOD BEFORE MEN

~♥

LORD, I DRAW NEAR TO YOU

Lord, I give thanks for Your greatness, Your goodness, and Your love, and I now draw near to enjoy Your presence.

I will ascribe to the Lord glory and strength.
I will ascribe to the Lord the glory due His name
And worship the Lord in the beauty of holiness.
Tremble before Him, all the earth.
The world is firmly established, it will not be moved. (1 Chronicles 16:28-30)

Take a moment to consider God's awesome majesty and thank Him that He loves you and wants an intimate relationship with you.

THANK YOU, LORD, FOR WHAT YOU HAVE DONE

I call this to mind, and therefore I have hope: The Lord's mercies never cease, for His compassions never fail. They are new every morning; great is Your faithfulness. (Lamentations 3:21-23)

The earth will be filled with the knowledge of the glory of the Lord, as the waters cover the sea. (Habakkuk 2:14)

LORD, I LISTEN TO YOUR WORDS OF TRUTH

Whoever acknowledges You before men, the Son of Man will also acknowledge him before the angels of God. But he who disowns You before men will be denied before the angels of God. (Luke 12:8-9)

LORD, I RESPOND TO YOUR INSTRUCTION

Fathers should not provoke their children to wrath but bring them up in the discipline and instruction of the Lord. (Ephesians 6:4)

~♥

Lord, I thank You for Your compassions and for Your great faithfulness. I will acknowledge You before others. Help me to fulfill my responsibilities to instruct others in Your truth.

DAY 170

ADDING TO MY FAITH

❧

LORD, I DRAW NEAR TO YOU

I am grateful to You, O God, for the blessing of Your forgiveness. I thank You that in Christ, You set me free from the guilt of the past and give me hope for the future.

And my tongue will sing aloud of Your righteousness.
O Lord, open my lips,
And my mouth will declare Your praise.
For You do not desire sacrifice, or I would bring it;
You do not delight in burnt offering.
The sacrifices of God are a broken spirit;
A broken and contrite heart,
O God, You will not despise. (Psalm 51:14-17)

Take a moment to ask the Spirit to search your heart and reveal any areas of unconfessed sin. Acknowledge these to the Lord and thank Him for His forgiveness.

180

THANK YOU, LORD, FOR WHAT YOU HAVE DONE

Your eyes are too pure to look at evil; You cannot look on wickedness. (Habakkuk 1:13)

LORD, I LISTEN TO YOUR WORDS OF TRUTH

This is eternal life: that I may know You, the only true God, and Jesus Christ, Whom You have sent. (John 17:3)

LORD, I RESPOND TO YOUR INSTRUCTION

I will be diligent to add to my faith, virtue; and to virtue, knowledge; and to knowledge, self-control; and to self-control, perseverance; and to perseverance, godliness; and to godliness, brotherly kindness; and to brotherly kindness, love. For if these qualities are mine in increasing measure, they will keep me from being barren and unfruitful in the full knowledge of our Lord Jesus Christ. (2 Peter 1:5-8)

❧

Lord, I thank You for the gift of eternal life in the knowledge of Jesus Christ. Help me to add to my faith those character traits that will bring fruitfulness in the full knowledge of Christ.

DAY 171

APPROVING THE EXCELLENT

LORD, I DRAW NEAR TO YOU

I praise You, Lord, that You are intimately acquainted with my ways and that You always love me and have my best interests at heart.

I will trust in You, Lord, and do good; I will dwell in the land and feed on Your faithfulness. When I delight myself in You, You will give me the desires of my heart. I will commit my way to You and trust in You, and You will bring it to pass. You will bring forth my righteousness like the light, and my justice like the noonday. I will rest in You and wait patiently for You; I will not fret because of him who prospers in his way, with the man who practices evil schemes. (Psalm 37:3-7)

Take a moment to offer this day to the Lord and ask Him for the grace to grow in your knowledge and love for Him.

THANK YOU, LORD, FOR WHAT YOU HAVE DONE

Oh, the depth of the riches both of the wisdom and knowledge of God! How unsearchable are His judgments, and His ways past finding out! For who has known the mind of the Lord? Or who has been His counselor? Or who has first given to Him, that He should repay him? For from Him and through Him and to Him are all things. To Him be the glory forever! Amen. (Romans 11:33-36)

181

LORD, I LISTEN TO YOUR WORDS OF TRUTH

My love abounds more and more in full knowledge and depth of insight, so that I am able to approve the things that are excellent, in order to be sincere and blameless until the day of Christ—having been filled with the fruit of righteousness that comes through Jesus Christ, to the glory and praise of God. (Philippians 1:9-11)

LORD, I RESPOND TO YOUR INSTRUCTION

As we have opportunity, we should do good to all people, especially to those who belong to the family of faith. (Galatians 6:10)

Lord, I thank You for the depth of Your wisdom and knowledge so that I may approve the excellent and be sincere and blameless before You. I pray that my love and knowledge of You would abound, as I minister to the saints.

DAY 172

REJOICING IN MY SALVATION

LORD, I DRAW NEAR TO YOU

As I approach Your throne of grace today, I am grateful that You care about the things that concern me and that You want me to offer them up to You.

I will learn to be content in whatever circumstances I am. Whether I am abased or in abundance, whether I am filled or hungry, let me learn the secret of being content in any and every situation. I can do all things through Him who strengthens me. (Philippians 4:11-13)

Take a moment to share your personal needs with God, including your physical, emotional, relational, and spiritual concerns.

THANK YOU, LORD, FOR WHAT YOU HAVE DONE

The Lord is not slow concerning His promise, as some count slowness, but is patient with us, not wanting anyone to perish, but for all to come to repentance. (2 Peter 3:9)

The Father has sent the Son to be the Savior of the world. Whoever confesses that Jesus is the Son of God, God abides in him and he in God. (1 John 4:14-15)

LORD, I LISTEN TO YOUR WORDS OF TRUTH

I trust in Your loyal love; my heart rejoices in Your salvation. I will sing to the Lord, for He has dealt bountifully with me. (Psalm 13:5-6)

LORD, I RESPOND TO YOUR INSTRUCTION

He who pursues righteousness and love finds life, righteousness, and honor. (Proverbs 21:21)

I will not imitate what is evil but what is good. The one who does good is of God; the one who does evil has not seen God. (3 John 11)

Lord, I thank You for Your desire that all would come to repentance and confess that Jesus is Your Son. I will trust in Your loyal love, rejoice in my salvation, pursue righteousness, and imitate that which is good.

DAY 173

CELEBRATING GOD'S LOVINGKINDNESS

❧

LORD, I DRAW NEAR TO YOU

Lord, You have invited me to pray for the needs of others, and since You desire what is best for them, I take this opportunity to bring these requests to You.

I owe nothing to anyone except to love them, for he who loves his neighbor has fulfilled the law. For the commandments, "You shall not commit adultery," "You shall not murder," "You shall not steal," "You shall not covet," and if there is any other commandment, it is summed up in this saying: "You shall love your neighbor as yourself." Love does no harm to a neighbor; therefore, love is the fulfillment of the law. (Romans 13:8-10)

Take a moment to lift up the needs of your family and friends, and to offer up any additional burdens for others that the Lord brings to mind.

THANK YOU, LORD, FOR WHAT YOU HAVE DONE

I will proclaim the name of the Lord and praise the greatness of my God. (Deuteronomy 32:3)

By this the love of God was manifested to us, that God has sent His only begotten Son into the world that we might live through Him. In this is love, not that we loved God, but that He loved us and sent His Son to be the propitiation for our sins. (1 John 4:9-10)

LORD, I LISTEN TO YOUR WORDS OF TRUTH

Because Your lovingkindness is better than life, my lips will praise You. So I will bless You as long as I live; I will lift up my hands in Your name. (Psalm 63:3-4)

LORD, I RESPOND TO YOUR INSTRUCTION

We should bear with one another in love and make every effort to keep the unity of the Spirit in the bond of peace. (Ephesians 4:2-3)

❧

Lord, I thank You for the love that You manifested in sending Your only begotten Son into the world. I thank You that Your lovingkindness is better than life. I seek to show forbearance to others and live in peaceful unity with them.

DAY 174

PRAISING THE ROCK
OF MY SALVATION

❧

LORD, I DRAW NEAR TO YOU

---

*Lord, I want Your Word to be deeply implanted in me so that I will know the
truth and be able to express it in the way I live.*

You are worthy, our Lord and God,
To receive glory and honor and power,
For You created all things,
And by Your will they were created and have their being.
(Revelation 4:11)

*Take a moment to affirm the truth of these words from Scripture and ask God to
make them a growing reality in your life.*

THANK YOU, LORD, FOR WHAT YOU HAVE DONE

184

"The Lord lives! Blessed be my Rock! Exalted be God, the Rock of my
salvation! (2 Samuel 22:47)

How much more will the blood of Christ, who through the eternal
Spirit offered Himself unblemished to God, cleanse our consciences
from acts that lead to death, so that we may serve the living God?
(Hebrews 9:13-14)

LORD, I LISTEN TO YOUR WORDS OF TRUTH

Blessed are those who have learned to acclaim You, who walk in the
light of Your presence, O Lord. They rejoice in Your name all day long,
and they are exalted in Your righteousness. (Psalm 89:15-16)

LORD, I RESPOND TO YOUR INSTRUCTION

I want to abound in faith, in speech, in knowledge, in all diligence, in
love, and in the grace of giving. (2 Corinthians 8:7)

I want to abound in love and faith toward the Lord Jesus and to all the
saints. (Philemon 5)

❧

*Lord, I thank You that You are the Rock of my salvation and that the blood of
Christ has cleansed my sins. I will learn to acclaim You and to abound in love
and faith.*

DAY 175

ATTAINING THE UNITY
OF THE FAITH

LORD, I DRAW NEAR TO YOU

O Lord, I am deeply grateful for Your wonderful acts, for Your abundant promises, and for the gift of my relationship with You through the merits of Christ.

I will give thanks to the Lord, for He is good;
His lovingkindness endures forever.
I will give thanks to the Lord for His unfailing love
And His wonderful acts to the children of men,
For He satisfies the thirsty soul
And fills the hungry soul with good things. (Psalm 107:1,8-9)

Take a moment to express your gratitude for the many blessings that you have received from the Lord.

THANK YOU, LORD, FOR WHAT YOU HAVE DONE

185

God is exalted beyond our understanding; the number of His years is unsearchable. (Job 36:26)

LORD, I LISTEN TO YOUR WORDS OF TRUTH

I will exult in the Lord; I will rejoice in the God of my salvation. The Lord God is my strength; He makes my feet like the feet of a deer and enables me to go on the heights. (Habakkuk 3:18-19)

LORD, I RESPOND TO YOUR INSTRUCTION

We must all attain to unity of the faith and of the knowledge of the Son of God to a mature man, to the measure of the stature of the fullness of Christ, so that we will no longer be infants, being blown and carried around by every wind of doctrine, by the cunning and craftiness of men in their deceitful scheming; but speaking the truth in love, we must grow up in all things into Him Who is the Head, that is, Christ. (Ephesians 4:13-15)

Lord, I thank You that You are exalted beyond my understanding. Teach me to speak the truth in love as we seek unity in the faith.

DAY 176

PRACTICING GOD'S COMMANDMENTS

❧

LORD, I DRAW NEAR TO YOU

Lord, I give thanks for Your greatness, Your goodness, and Your love, and I now draw near to enjoy Your presence.

My soul magnifies the Lord
And my spirit rejoices in God my Savior,
For the Mighty One has done great things for me,
And holy is His name.
His mercy is on those who fear Him,
From generation to generation. (Luke 1:46-47,49-50)

Take a moment to consider God's awesome majesty and thank Him that He loves you and wants an intimate relationship with you.

THANK YOU, LORD, FOR WHAT YOU HAVE DONE

I will be still and know that You are God; You will be exalted among the nations, You will be exalted in the earth. (Psalm 46:10)

LORD, I LISTEN TO YOUR WORDS OF TRUTH

Since I am receiving a kingdom that cannot be shaken, I will be thankful and so worship God acceptably with reverence and awe, for my God is a consuming fire. (Hebrews 12:28-29)

LORD, I RESPOND TO YOUR INSTRUCTION

The fear of the Lord is the beginning of wisdom; all who practice His commandments have a good understanding. His praise endures forever. (Psalm 111:10)

I ask for a wise and understanding heart to discern between good and evil. (1 Kings 3:9,12)

❧

Lord, I thank You that You will be exalted and reverenced among the nations. I thank You that I am receiving a kingdom that cannot be shaken. I will fear You and practice Your commandments. Give me a wise and understanding heart.

DAY 177

SUBMITTING TO SPIRITUAL AUTHORITY

ॐ

LORD, I DRAW NEAR TO YOU

I am grateful to You, O God, for the blessing of Your forgiveness. I thank You that in Christ, You set me free from the guilt of the past and give me hope for the future.

God's eyes are on the ways of a man,
And He sees all his steps.
There is no darkness or deep shadow
Where the workers of iniquity can hide.
He does not need to examine a man further,
That he should go before God in judgment. (Job 34:21-23)

Take a moment to ask the Spirit to search your heart and reveal any areas of unconfessed sin. Acknowledge these to the Lord and thank Him for His forgiveness.

THANK YOU, LORD, FOR WHAT YOU HAVE DONE

187
ॐ

Great is the Lord, and most worthy of praise in the city of our God, His holy mountain. As is Your name, O God, so is Your praise to the ends of the earth; Your right hand is filled with righteousness. (Psalm 48:1,10)

LORD, I LISTEN TO YOUR WORDS OF TRUTH

If I have been united with Christ in the likeness of His death, I will certainly also be united with Him in the likeness of His resurrection. (Romans 6:5)

LORD, I RESPOND TO YOUR INSTRUCTION

I will obey those who lead me and submit to them, for they keep watch over my soul as those who must give an account. I will obey them, so that they may do this with joy and not with grief, for this would be unprofitable for me. (Hebrews 13:17)

ॐ

Lord, I thank You that You are most worthy of praise and for my identification with Christ in His death and resurrection. I will submit to my spiritual leaders and pray with joy for other believers that love many abound in them.

DAY 178

FINDING WISDOM AND GAINING UNDERSTANDING

❧

LORD, I DRAW NEAR TO YOU

I praise You, Lord, that You are intimately acquainted with my ways and that You always love me and have my best interests at heart.

I will praise the LORD, who counsels me; even at night my heart instructs me. I have set the LORD always before me. Because he is at my right hand, I will not be shaken. (Psalm 16:2, 7-8)

Take a moment to offer this day to the Lord and ask Him for the grace to grow in your knowledge and love for Him.

THANK YOU, LORD, FOR WHAT YOU HAVE DONE

I will trust in the Lord forever, for in Yahweh, the Lord, I have an everlasting Rock. (Isaiah 26:4)

188

Christ is the mediator of a new covenant, by means of death, for the redemption of the transgressions committed under the first covenant, that those who are called may receive the promise of the eternal inheritance. (Hebrews 9:15)

LORD, I LISTEN TO YOUR WORDS OF TRUTH

I know that my old self was crucified with Christ, so that the body of sin might be done away with, that I should no longer be a slave to sin; for the one who has died has been freed from sin. (Romans 6:6-7)

LORD, I RESPOND TO YOUR INSTRUCTION

Blessed is the man who finds wisdom, and the man who gains understanding, for its profit is greater than that of silver, and its gain than fine gold. She is more precious than jewels, and nothing I desire can compare with her. Long life is in her right hand; in her left hand are riches and honor. Her ways are pleasant ways, and all her paths are peace. She is a tree of life to those who embrace her, and happy are those who hold her fast. (Proverbs 3:13-18)

❧

Lord, I thank You that I can trust in You forever and that Christ has promised the gift of an eternal inheritance. I thank You for my deliverance in Christ from the bondage of sin. Help me to find wisdom and gain understanding.

DAY 179

LOVING THE LOST

❧

LORD, I DRAW NEAR TO YOU

As I approach Your throne of grace today, I am grateful that You care about the things that concern me and that You want me to offer them up to You.

We are all sons of the light and sons of the day. We do not belong to the night or to the darkness. So then, let us not be like others who are asleep, but let us be alert and self-controlled. (1 Thessalonians 5:5-6)

Take a moment to share your personal needs with God, including your physical, emotional, relational, and spiritual concerns.

THANK YOU, LORD, FOR WHAT YOU HAVE DONE

You are He; You are the first, and You are also the last. (Isaiah 48:12)

LORD, I LISTEN TO YOUR WORDS OF TRUTH

I have become dead to the law through the body of Christ, that I might belong to another, to Him who was raised from the dead, in order that I might bear fruit to God. But now, by dying to what once bound me, I have been released from the law so that I serve in newness of the Spirit and not in oldness of the letter. (Romans 7:4,6)

LORD, I RESPOND TO YOUR INSTRUCTION

Concerning the lost, Jesus said, "What man among you, if he has a hundred sheep and loses one of them, does not leave the ninety-nine in the open country and go after the one that is lost until he finds it? And when he finds it, he lays it on his shoulders, rejoicing. And when he comes into his house, he calls his friends and neighbors together and says to them, 'Rejoice with me, for I have found my sheep which was lost!' I tell you that in the same way there will be more joy in heaven over one sinner who repents than over ninety-nine righteous persons who need no repentance. There is joy in the presence of the angels of God over one sinner who repents." (Luke 15:4-7,10)

❧

Lord, I thank You that Jesus is the first and the last. I thank You that I now belong to Him Who was raised from the dead. Give me Your heart and concern for the lost.

DAY 180

SPURNING CONDEMNATION

Lord, You have invited me to pray for the needs of others, and since You desire what is best for them, I take this opportunity to bring these requests to You.

May I pursue the things that lead to peace and to mutual edification. (Romans 14:19)

May I accept others, just as Christ accepted me to the glory of God. (Romans 15:7)

Take a moment to lift up the needs of your family and friends, and to offer up any other burdens for others that the Lord brings to mind.

THANK YOU, LORD, FOR WHAT YOU HAVE DONE

Glory to God in the highest, and on earth peace to those on whom His favor rests. (Luke 2:14)

The kingdom of the world has become the kingdom of our Lord and of His Christ, and He will reign for ever and ever. (Revelation 11:15)

LORD, I LISTEN TO YOUR WORDS OF TRUTH

There is now no condemnation for those who are in Christ Jesus, because the law of the Spirit of life in Christ Jesus has set me free from the law of sin and death. (Romans 8:1-2)

LORD, I RESPOND TO YOUR INSTRUCTION

There is a way that seems right to a man, but its end is the way of death. (Proverbs 14:12)

Wisdom is better than jewels, and all desirable things cannot be compared with her. Wisdom dwells together with prudence and finds knowledge and discretion. (Proverbs 8:11-12)

Lord, I thank You that Christ will come again and reign forever. I thank You that there is no condemnation for those who are in Him. Grant me more of Your wisdom that I may find prudence, knowledge, and discretion.

DAY 181

SHARING MY FAITH

❧

LORD, I DRAW NEAR TO YOU

Lord, I want Your Word to be deeply implanted in me so that I will know the truth and be able to express it in the way I live.

Worthy is the Lamb, who was slain,
To receive power and riches and wisdom
And strength and honor and glory and blessing! (Revelation 5:12)

Take a moment to affirm the truth of these words from Scripture and ask God to make them a growing reality in your life.

THANK YOU, LORD, FOR WHAT YOU HAVE DONE

Jesus is the Christ, the Son of the living God. (Matthew 16:16)

God highly exalted Christ Jesus and gave Him the name that is above every name, that at the name of Jesus every knee should bow, in heaven and on earth and under the earth, and every tongue should confess that Jesus Christ is Lord, to the glory of God the Father. (Philippians 2:9-11)

191
❧

LORD, I LISTEN TO YOUR WORDS OF TRUTH

None of us lives to himself alone and none of us dies to himself alone. If we live, we live to the Lord; and if we die, we die to the Lord. So, whether we live or die, we belong to the Lord. (Romans 14:7-8)

LORD, I RESPOND TO YOUR INSTRUCTION

I pray that the sharing of my faith may become effective through the knowledge of every good thing which is in me for Christ's sake. (Philemon 6)

We are the fragrance of Christ to God among those who are being saved and among those who are perishing; to the one an aroma from death to death; to the other, an aroma from life to life. And who is sufficient for these things? (2 Corinthians 2:15-16)

❧

Lord, I thank You that Jesus is the Christ and that You exalted Him above every name. I have chosen to live for Him and to share the fragrance of Christ with those who do not know Him.

DAY 182

KEEPING MY MIND ON THE GOOD

LORD, I DRAW NEAR TO YOU

O Lord, I am deeply grateful for Your wonderful acts, for Your abundant promises, and for the gift of my relationship with You through the merits of Christ.

Blessed is the one You choose and bring near
To live in Your courts.
We will be satisfied with the goodness of Your house,
Of Your holy temple. (Psalm 65:4)

Take a moment to express your gratitude for the many blessings that you have received from the Lord.

THANK YOU, LORD, FOR WHAT YOU HAVE DONE

Anyone who has seen Jesus has seen the Father. (John 14:9)

Jesus will be great and will be called the Son of the Most High. The Lord God will give Him the throne of His father David, and He will reign over the house of Jacob forever, and His kingdom will never end. (Luke 1:32-33)

LORD, I LISTEN TO YOUR WORDS OF TRUTH

We were all baptized by one Spirit into one body—whether Jews or Greeks, slave or free—and we were all given the one Spirit to drink. (1 Corinthians 12:13)

LORD, I RESPOND TO YOUR INSTRUCTION

Whatever is true, whatever is noble, whatever is right, whatever is pure, whatever is lovely, whatever is of good report—if anything is excellent or praiseworthy—I will think about such things. The things I have learned and received and heard and seen in those who walk with Christ I will practice, and the God of peace will be with me. (Philippians 4:8-9)

Lord, I thank You that Jesus has shown us Who You are and for the gift of Your indwelling Holy Spirit. Help me to set my mind on the things that are true, noble, right, pure, lovely, and praiseworthy.

DAY 183

BEING TRANSFORMED BY THE SPIRIT

❧

LORD, I DRAW NEAR TO YOU

Lord, I give thanks for Your greatness, Your goodness, and Your love, and I now draw near to enjoy Your presence.

Oh, the depth of the riches both of the wisdom and knowledge of God! How unsearchable are Your judgments, and Your ways past finding out! For from You and through You and to You are all things. To You be the glory forever! Amen. (Romans 11:33,36)

Hallelujah! Salvation and glory and power belong to our God, because His judgments are true and righteous. (Revelation 19:1-2)

Take a moment to consider God's awesome majesty and thank Him that He loves you and wants an intimate relationship with you.

THANK YOU, LORD, FOR WHAT YOU HAVE DONE

I know that You are a gracious and compassionate God, slow to anger and abounding in lovingkindness, a God who relents from sending calamity. (Jonah 4:2)

193
❧

LORD, I LISTEN TO YOUR WORDS OF TRUTH

We all, with unveiled face beholding as in a mirror the glory of the Lord, are being transformed into the same image from glory to glory, which comes from the Lord, who is the Spirit. (2 Corinthians 3:18)

LORD, I RESPOND TO YOUR INSTRUCTION

All things are from God, who reconciled us to Himself through Christ and gave us the ministry of reconciliation: namely, that God was reconciling the world to Himself in Christ, not counting their trespasses against them. And He has committed to us the message of reconciliation. Therefore, we are ambassadors for Christ, as though God were appealing through us, as we implore others on Christ's behalf to be reconciled to God. (2 Corinthians 5:18-20)

❧

Lord, I thank You that You are gracious and compassionate and for the transforming power of Your Spirit. As an ambassador of Christ, I will lovingly seek to persuade others to be reconciled to You through Him.

DAY 184

FEASTING ON SOLID FOOD

LORD, I DRAW NEAR TO YOU

I am grateful to You, O God, for the blessing of Your forgiveness. I thank You that in Christ, You set me free from the guilt of the past and give me hope for the future.

The Lord your God is gracious and compassionate, and He will not turn His face from you if you return to Him. (2 Chronicles 30:9)

Take a moment to ask the Spirit to search your heart and reveal any areas of unconfessed sin. Acknowledge these to the Lord and thank Him for His forgiveness.

THANK YOU, LORD, FOR WHAT YOU HAVE DONE

Jesus is my Lord and my God. (John 20:28)

Whoever is ashamed of Jesus and His words, the Son of Man will be ashamed of him when He comes in His glory and in the glory of the Father and of the holy angels. (Luke 9:26)

194

LORD, I LISTEN TO YOUR WORDS OF TRUTH

Through the law I died to the law so that I might live for God. I have been crucified with Christ; and it is no longer I who live, but Christ lives in me; and the life which I now live in the flesh, I live by faith in the Son of God, Who loved me and gave Himself for me. (Galatians 2:19-20)

LORD, I RESPOND TO YOUR INSTRUCTION

I will not enter the path of the wicked or walk in the way of evil men. (Proverbs 4:14)

Anyone who partakes only of milk is not accustomed to the Word of righteousness, for he is an infant. But solid food is for the mature, who because of use have their senses trained to distinguish good from evil. Therefore, I will leave the elementary teachings about Christ and go on to maturity. (Hebrews 5:13-6:1)

Lord, I thank You that Jesus is my Lord and my God. I am determined to eat the solid food of the Word so I may go on to maturity in Him.

DAY 185

BOASTING IN THE CROSS

LORD, I DRAW NEAR TO YOU

I praise You, Lord, that You are intimately acquainted with my ways and that You always love me and have my best interests at heart.

Like Josiah, I will do what is right in the sight of the Lord, walking in the ways of David and not turning aside to the right or to the left. Give me a tender and responsive heart, so that I will humble myself before You when I hear Your Word. (2 Chronicles 34:1-2,27)

Take a moment to offer this day to the Lord and ask Him for the grace to grow in your knowledge and love for Him.

THANK YOU, LORD, FOR WHAT YOU HAVE DONE

The God and Father of the Lord Jesus is blessed forever. (2 Corinthians 11:31)
When the fullness of time had come, God sent forth His Son, born of a woman, born under law, to redeem those under law, that we might receive the adoption as sons. (Galatians 4:4-5)

195

LORD, I LISTEN TO YOUR WORDS OF TRUTH

I will never boast except in the cross of our Lord Jesus Christ, through which the world has been crucified to me, and I to the world. (Galatians 6:14)

LORD, I RESPOND TO YOUR INSTRUCTION

I know, my God, that You test the heart and are pleased with integrity. (1 Chronicles 29:17)

I will not pervert justice or show partiality. I will not accept a bribe, for a bribe blinds the eyes of the wise and perverts the words of the righteous. (Deuteronomy 16:19)

Lord, I thank You that You are blessed forever and that You sent Your Son so we could be adopted into Your family. I thank You for the power of the cross of Christ. Help me to walk in integrity and justice.

DAY 186

BEING JUSTIFIED BY FAITH

LORD, I DRAW NEAR TO YOU

As I approach Your throne of grace today, I am grateful that You care about the things that concern me and that You want me to offer them up to You.

I will discipline myself to godliness. For physical exercise profits a little, but godliness is profitable for all things, since it holds promise for both the present life and the life to come. (1 Timothy 4:7-8)

Take a moment to share your personal needs with God, including your physical, emotional, relational, and spiritual concerns.

THANK YOU, LORD, FOR WHAT YOU HAVE DONE

In Christ all the fullness of the Godhead lives in bodily form. (Colossians 2:9)

LORD, I LISTEN TO YOUR WORDS OF TRUTH

Whatever was gain to me I now consider loss for the sake of Christ. What is more, I consider all things loss compared to the surpassing greatness of knowing Christ Jesus my Lord, for Whose sake I have suffered the loss of all things and consider them rubbish, that I may gain Christ and be found in Him, not having a righteousness of my own that comes from the law, but that which is through faith in Christ—the righteousness that comes from God on the basis of faith. (Philippians 3:7-9)

LORD, I RESPOND TO YOUR INSTRUCTION

I should walk in wisdom toward outsiders, making the most of every opportunity. My speech should always be with grace, seasoned with salt, so that I may know how to answer each person. (Colossians 4:5-6)

I will sanctify Christ as Lord in my heart, always being ready to make a defense to everyone who asks me to give the reason for the hope that is in me, but with gentleness and respect. (1 Peter 3:15)

Lord, I thank You that all Your fullness dwells in Christ and that He made it possible for us to be justified by faith. Help me to comprehend the surpassing greatness of knowing Him, and how to use wisdom, tactfulness, and clarity when I tell others about Him.

DAY 187

PUTTING ON THE NEW SELF

❧

LORD, I DRAW NEAR TO YOU

Lord, You have invited me to pray for the needs of others, and since You desire what is best for them, I take this opportunity to bring these requests to You.

We were all baptized by one Spirit into one body—whether Jews or Greeks, slave or free—and we were all given the one Spirit to drink. (1 Corinthians 12:13)

There should be no division in the body, but its members should have the same concern for each other. If one member suffers, all the members suffer with it; if one member is honored, all the members rejoice with it. Now we are the body of Christ, and each one of us is a member of it. (1 Corinthians 12:25-27)

Take a moment to lift up the needs of your family and friends, and to offer up any additional burdens for others that the Lord brings to mind.

THANK YOU, LORD, FOR WHAT YOU HAVE DONE

197 ❧

Jesus Christ is the same yesterday, today, and forever. (Hebrews 13:8)

No one can lay a foundation other than the one already laid, which is Jesus Christ. (1 Corinthians 3:11)

LORD, I LISTEN TO YOUR WORDS OF TRUTH

I have put off the old self with its practices and have put on the new self, who is being renewed in full knowledge according to the image of its Creator. (Colossians 3:9-10)

LORD, I RESPOND TO YOUR INSTRUCTION

If I do not judge, I will not be judged; if I do not condemn, I will not be condemned; if I forgive, I will be forgiven. (Luke 6:37)

We must be devoted to one another in brotherly love, honoring one another above ourselves. (Romans 12:10)

❧

Lord, I thank You that Christ is the sure and unchanging foundation of my faith. I thank You that in Him I have put on the new self. Teach me not to judge others, but to love them with brotherly love and honor them above myself.

DAY 188

BEING EMPOWERED BY THE SPIRIT

LORD, I DRAW NEAR TO YOU

Lord, I want Your Word to be deeply implanted in me so that I will know the truth and be able to express it in the way I live.

Every creature in heaven and on earth and under the earth and on the sea and all that is in them, will sing:
"To Him who sits on the throne and to the Lamb
Be blessing and honor and glory and power
For ever and ever!" (Revelation 5:13)

Take a moment to affirm the truth of these words from Scripture and ask God to make them a growing reality in your life.

THANK YOU, LORD, FOR WHAT YOU HAVE DONE

Your Word is truth. (John 17:17)

198

The things that happened to the Israelites in the wilderness were examples and were written for our admonition, upon whom the fulfillment of the ages has come. (1 Corinthians 10:11)

LORD, I LISTEN TO YOUR WORDS OF TRUTH

"Not by might nor by power, but by My Spirit," says the Lord of hosts. (Zechariah 4:6)

LORD, I RESPOND TO YOUR INSTRUCTION

Wealth gained by dishonesty will dwindle, but he who gathers by labor will increase. (Proverbs 13:11)

A good name is more desirable than great riches; favor is better than silver or gold. (Proverbs 22:1)

Lord, I thank You for the truth of Your Word and for its timeless application to every life. I thank You for the power of Your Spirit. Help me not to sacrifice my integrity to gain wealth.

DAY 189

INCREASING IN LOVE

~&~

LORD, I DRAW NEAR TO YOU

O Lord, I am deeply grateful for Your wonderful acts, for Your abundant promises, and for the gift of my relationship with You through the merits of Christ.

Surely the righteous will give thanks to Your name;
The upright will dwell in Your presence. (Psalm 140:13)

The Lord is near to all who call upon Him,
To all who call upon Him in truth.
He fulfills the desire of those who fear Him;
He hears their cry and saves them.
The Lord preserves all who love Him,
But all the wicked He will destroy. (Psalm 145:18-20)

Take a moment to express your gratitude for the many blessings that you have received from the Lord.

THANK YOU, LORD, FOR WHAT YOU HAVE DONE

Foreigners will rebuild your walls, and their kings will serve you.
Though in anger I struck you, in favor I will show you compassion.
Your gates will always stand open, they will never be shut, day or
night, so that men may bring you the wealth of the nations — their
kings led in triumphal procession. (Isaiah 60:10-11)

LORD, I LISTEN TO YOUR WORDS OF TRUTH

When I ask, it will be given to me; when I seek, I will find; when I
knock, the door will be opened to me. For everyone who asks, receives;
he who seeks, finds; and to him who knocks, the door will be opened.
(Matthew 7:7-8; Luke 11:9-10)

LORD, I RESPOND TO YOUR INSTRUCTION

Concerning brotherly love, we have been taught by God to love each
other, and the Lord urges us to increase more and more.
(1 Thessalonians 4:9-10)

~&~

*Lord, I thank You that You show compassion to Your saints. I am blessed that
You delight in answering my prayers. Help me to increase more and more in my
love for others.*

DAY 190

FLEEING IMPURITY

LORD, I DRAW NEAR TO YOU

Lord, I give thanks for Your greatness, Your goodness, and Your love, and I now draw near to enjoy Your presence.

He who made the Pleiades and Orion
And turns deep darkness into morning
And darkens day into night,
Who calls for the waters of the sea
And pours them out over the face of the earth—
The Lord is His name. (Amos 5:8)

Take a moment to consider God's awesome majesty and thank Him that He loves you and wants an intimate relationship with you.

THANK YOU, LORD, FOR WHAT YOU HAVE DONE

200

Only in the Lord are righteousness and strength. (Isaiah 45:24)

If righteousness could be gained through the law, Christ died for nothing. (Galatians 2:21)

LORD, I LISTEN TO YOUR WORDS OF TRUTH

Whoever does not receive the kingdom of God like a little child will never enter it. (Mark 10:15; Luke 18:17)

LORD, I RESPOND TO YOUR INSTRUCTION

I will keep the feast of Christ, my Passover, not with old leaven, or with the leaven of malice and wickedness, but with the unleavened bread of sincerity and truth. (1 Corinthians 5:7-8)

I do not want even a hint of immorality, or any impurity, or greed in my life, as is proper for a saint. Nor will I give myself to obscenity, foolish talk, or coarse joking, which are not fitting, but rather to giving of thanks. (Ephesians 5:3-4)

Lord, I thank You for Your righteousness and strength and for the sufficiency of Christ's redemptive work. Help me to have childlike faith to be able to receive Your kingdom and give me the strength I need to flee immorality and impurity and pursue sincerity and truth.

DAY 191

MANIFESTING GOD'S LOVE

◦❧

LORD, I DRAW NEAR TO YOU

I am grateful to You, O God, for the blessing of Your forgiveness. I thank You that in Christ, You set me free from the guilt of the past and give me hope for the future.

Let the power of my Lord be great, just as You have spoken, saying, "The Lord is slow to anger and abounding in mercy, forgiving iniquity and transgression." (Numbers 14:17-18)

Take a moment to ask the Spirit to search your heart and reveal any areas of unconfessed sin. Acknowledge these to the Lord and thank Him for His forgiveness.

THANK YOU, LORD, FOR WHAT YOU HAVE DONE

It pleased the Lord for the sake of His righteousness to make His law great and glorious. (Isaiah 42:21)

Is the law opposed to the promises of God? Certainly not! For if a law had been given that could impart life, then righteousness would indeed have been by the law. But the Scripture has confined all under sin, so that the promise by faith in Jesus Christ might be given to those who believe. (Galatians 3:21-22)

LORD, I LISTEN TO YOUR WORDS OF TRUTH

He who believes in God's Son is not condemned, but he who does not believe is condemned already, because he has not believed in the name of the only begotten Son of God. (John 3:18)

LORD, I RESPOND TO YOUR INSTRUCTION

We love, because God first loved us. If anyone says, "I love God," and hates his brother, he is a liar; for the one who does not love his brother whom he has seen, cannot love God Whom he has not seen. And we have this commandment from Him: that the one who loves God must also love his brother. (1 John 4:19-21)

◦❧

Lord, I thank You for the greatness of Your law and that since I believe in Christ, I will not face condemnation. Help me to manifest my love for You by loving others.

DAY 192

LIVING HONORABLY

LORD, I DRAW NEAR TO YOU

I praise You, Lord, that You are intimately acquainted with my ways and that You always love me and have my best interests at heart.

Let the name of the Lord Jesus be magnified in my life. (Acts 19:17)

In view of God's mercy, I present my body as a living sacrifice, holy and pleasing to God, which is my reasonable service. (Romans 12:1)

Take a moment to offer this day to the Lord and ask Him for the grace to grow in your knowledge and love for Him.

THANK YOU, LORD, FOR WHAT YOU HAVE DONE

I know that the Lord will maintain the cause of the afflicted, and justice for the poor. (Psalm 140:12)

Those who had anyone sick with various kinds of diseases brought them to Jesus, and laying His hands on each one, He healed them. (Luke 4:40)

LORD, I LISTEN TO YOUR WORDS OF TRUTH

You are the living bread that came down from heaven. If anyone eats of this bread, he will live forever. This bread is Your flesh, which You have given for the life of the world. (John 6:51)

LORD, I RESPOND TO YOUR INSTRUCTION

I desire to have a clear conscience and to live honorably in all things. (Hebrews 13:18)

As an alien and a stranger in the world, I will abstain from fleshly lusts, which war against my soul. (1 Peter 2:11)

Lord, I thank You for Your compassion for the afflicted and the poor and the way in which Your Son demonstrated that compassion. I thank You that He is the living bread that came down from heaven. Help me to live honorably by abstaining from those things that are displeasing to You.

DAY 193

LOVING AS GOD LOVES

LORD, I DRAW NEAR TO YOU

As I approach Your throne of grace today, I am grateful that You care about the things that concern me and that You want me to offer them up to You.

Since I have a great high priest who has passed through the heavens, Jesus the Son of God, I will hold firmly to the faith I confess. For I do not have a high priest Who is unable to sympathize with my weaknesses, but one Who has been tempted in every way, just as I am, yet without sin. Therefore, I will approach the throne of grace with confidence, so that I may receive mercy and find grace to help in time of need. (Hebrews 4:14-16)

Take a moment to share your personal needs with God, including your physical, emotional, relational, and spiritual concerns.

THANK YOU, LORD, FOR WHAT YOU HAVE DONE

I will exalt the Lord my God and worship Him, for the Lord God is holy. (Psalm 99:9)

The Lord has performed mighty deeds with His arm; He has scattered those who are proud in the thoughts of their heart. He has brought down rulers from their thrones and has lifted up the humble. (Luke 1:51-52)

LORD, I LISTEN TO YOUR WORDS OF TRUTH

It is in You, Lord Jesus, that I have peace. In this world I will have tribulation, but I will be of good cheer, because You have overcome the world. (John 16:33)

LORD, I RESPOND TO YOUR INSTRUCTION

This is the message we heard from the beginning, that we should love one another. We know that we have passed out of death into life, because we love the brethren. The one who does not love abides in death. By this we know love, that Christ laid down His life for us, and we ought to lay down our lives for the brethren. (1 John 3:11,14,16)

Lord, I thank You for Your holiness and for the mighty deeds You have done. Teach me to love others in the same way You have loved me.

DAY 194

PROCLAIMING THE GOSPEL

❧

LORD, I DRAW NEAR TO YOU

Lord, You have invited me to pray for the needs of others, and since You desire what is best for them, I take this opportunity to bring these requests to You.

If I speak in the tongues of men and of angels, but have not love, I am only a resounding gong or a clanging cymbal. And if I have the gift of prophecy and understand all mysteries and all knowledge, and if I have all faith so as to remove mountains, but have not love, I am nothing. And if I give all my possessions to the poor, and if I deliver my body to be burned, but have not love, it profits me nothing. (1 Corinthians 13:1-3)

Take a moment to lift up the needs of your family and friends, and to offer up any additional burdens for others that the Lord brings to mind.

THANK YOU, LORD, FOR WHAT YOU HAVE DONE

204
❧

Good and upright is the Lord; therefore He instructs sinners in His ways. (Psalm 25:8)

Jesus said to the scribes and Pharisees, "It is not the healthy who need a physician, but the sick. I have not come to call the righteous, but sinners." (Mark 2:17)

LORD, I LISTEN TO YOUR WORDS OF TRUTH

I am not ashamed of the gospel, for it is the power of God for salvation to everyone who believes, to the Jew first, and also to the Gentile. For in it the righteousness of God is revealed from faith to faith, just as it is written: "The righteous will live by faith." (Romans 1:16-17)

LORD, I RESPOND TO YOUR INSTRUCTION

I will not go about spreading slander among people, nor will I do anything that endangers the life of my neighbor. (Leviticus 19:16)

He who speaks truth reveals what is right; but a false witness, deceit. (Proverbs 12:17)

❧

Lord, I thank You for instructing sinners in Your ways and for Christ's loving ministry to sinners. I thank You for the power of the gospel of faith in Your Son. I will be truthful in all my words.

DAY 195

BEING LED BY THE SPIRIT

❧

LORD, I DRAW NEAR TO YOU

Lord, I want Your Word to be deeply implanted in me so that I will know the truth and be able to express it in the way I live.

Great and marvelous are Your works,
Lord God Almighty!
Righteous and true are Your ways,
King of the nations!
Who will not fear You, O Lord,
And glorify Your name?
For You alone are holy.
All nations will come and worship before You,
For Your righteous acts have been revealed. (Revelation 15:3-4)

Take a moment to affirm the truth of these words from Scripture and ask God to make them a growing reality in your life.

THANK YOU, LORD, FOR WHAT YOU HAVE DONE

205
❧

You are not a God Who takes pleasure in wickedness; evil cannot dwell with You. (Psalm 5:4)

The Lord of hosts warned the priests of Israel, "If you do not listen, and if you do not set your heart to honor My name, I will send a curse upon you, and I will curse your blessings; indeed, I have already cursed them, because you have not set your heart to honor Me." (Malachi 2:2)

LORD, I LISTEN TO YOUR WORDS OF TRUTH

If I live according to the flesh, I will die; but if by the Spirit I put to death the deeds of the body, I will live. For those who are led by the Spirit of God are sons of God. (Romans 8:13-14)

LORD, I RESPOND TO YOUR INSTRUCTION

The tongue that brings healing is a tree of life, but perverseness in it crushes the spirit. (Proverbs 15:4)

❧

Lord, I thank You that You take no pleasure in wickedness and that You call Your people to honor Your name. I thank You for leading me by Your Spirit. Teach me to edify others in the things I say.

DAY 196

FLEEING ANGER

❧

O Lord, I am deeply grateful for Your wonderful acts, for Your abundant promises, and for the gift of my relationship with You through the merits of Christ.

Because I love You, You will deliver me;
You will protect me, for I acknowledge Your name.
I will call upon You, and You will answer me;
You will be with me in trouble,
You will deliver me and honor me.
With long life You will satisfy me
And show me Your salvation. (Psalm 91:14-16)

Take a moment to express your gratitude for the many blessings that you have received from the Lord.

You, Lord God, take no pleasure in the death of the wicked but rather that the wicked turn from their ways and live. (Ezekiel 18:23; 33:11)

Your grace is sufficient for me, for Your power is made perfect in weakness. Therefore, I will boast all the more gladly in my weaknesses, that the power of Christ may rest upon me. Therefore, I can be content in weaknesses, in insults, in hardships, in persecutions, in difficulties, for Christ's sake. For when I am weak, then I am strong. (2 Corinthians 12:9-10)

Do you see a man who is hasty in his words? There is more hope for a fool than for him. (Proverbs 29:20)

I will put away all of these things: anger, wrath, malice, slander, and abusive language from my mouth. (Colossians 3:8)

❧

Lord, I thank You for Your desire that the wicked would turn from their ways and live. I thank You for Your power that is made perfect in my weakness. Keep me from anger, and teach me to choose my words wisely.

DAY 197

BEARING THE FRUIT OF THE SPIRIT

~&~

LORD, I DRAW NEAR TO YOU

Lord, I give thanks for Your greatness, Your goodness, and Your love, and I now draw near to enjoy Your presence.

You are my hope, O Lord God;
You are my trust from my youth.
As for me, I will always have hope;
I will praise You more and more. (Psalm 71:5,14)

Take a moment to consider God's awesome majesty and thank Him that He loves you and wants an intimate relationship with you.

THANK YOU, LORD, FOR WHAT YOU HAVE DONE

The Lord God promised to gather the children of Israel from the nations and bring them back from the countries where they were scattered. "And I will give them the land of Israel. They will return to it and remove all its detestable images and abominations. I will give them one heart and put a new spirit within them, and I will remove the stony heart out of their flesh and give them a heart of flesh, that they may walk in My statutes and keep My ordinances. They shall be My people, and I will be their God." (Ezekiel 11:17-20)

207
~&~

LORD, I LISTEN TO YOUR WORDS OF TRUTH

The works of the flesh are evident, which are: immorality, impurity, sensuality, idolatry, sorcery, hatred, discord, jealousy, fits of rage, selfish ambition, dissensions, factions, envyings, drunkenness, revelries, and the like. Those who practice such things will not inherit the kingdom of God. But the fruit of the Spirit is love, joy, peace, patience, kindness, goodness, faithfulness, gentleness, self-control; against such things there is no law. (Galatians 5:19-23)

LORD, I RESPOND TO YOUR INSTRUCTION

Better is open rebuke than love that is concealed. (Proverbs 27:5)

~&~

Lord, I thank You for Your promise to gather Your people and put a new spirit within them. I thank You for the fruit of the Spirit. Increase my concern for others.

DAY 198

WALKING IN OBEDIENCE TO GOD'S WORD

❧

LORD, I DRAW NEAR TO YOU

I am grateful to You, O God, for the blessing of Your forgiveness. I thank You that in Christ, You set me free from the guilt of the past and give me hope for the future.

Has the Lord as much delight in burnt offerings and sacrifices
As in obeying the voice of the Lord?
To obey is better than sacrifice,
And to heed is better than the fat of rams.
For rebellion is like the sin of divination,
And stubbornness is as iniquity and idolatry. (1 Samuel 15:22-23)

Take a moment to ask the Spirit to search your heart and reveal any areas of unconfessed sin. Acknowledge these to the Lord and thank Him for His forgiveness.

208

THANK YOU, LORD, FOR WHAT YOU HAVE DONE

The Lord my God is a consuming fire, a jealous God. (Deuteronomy 4:24)

LORD, I LISTEN TO YOUR WORDS OF TRUTH

God will supply all my needs according to His glorious riches in Christ Jesus. To my God and Father be glory for ever and ever. (Philippians 4:19-20)

LORD, I RESPOND TO YOUR INSTRUCTION

Direct my footsteps according to Your Word, and let no iniquity have dominion over me. (Psalm 119:133)

Who may ascend the hill of the Lord? Who may stand in His holy place? He who has clean hands and a pure heart, who has not lifted up his soul to an idol or sworn by what is false. (Psalm 24:3-4)

❧

Lord, I thank You for supplying all my needs. Help me to walk in purity of heart and obedience to Your Word.

DAY 199

LOVING AT ALL TIMES

~❧~

LORD, I DRAW NEAR TO YOU

I praise You, Lord, that You are intimately acquainted with my ways and that You always love me and have my best interests at heart.

Like Enoch, let me walk with God. (Genesis 5:24)

Like Noah, let me find favor in the eyes of the Lord, and do everything just as God commands me. (Genesis 6:8,22; 7:5)

Take a moment to offer this day to the Lord and ask Him for the grace to grow in your knowledge and love for Him.

THANK YOU, LORD, FOR WHAT YOU HAVE DONE

The Lord is a jealous God, punishing the children for the sin of the fathers to the third and fourth generation of those who hate Him, but showing lovingkindness to a thousand generations of those who love Him and keep His commandments. (Exodus 20:5-6; Deuteronomy 5:9-10)

209
~❧~

Lord, I have heard of Your fame, and I stand in awe of Your deeds. O Lord, revive Your work in the midst of the years, in our time make them known; in wrath remember mercy. (Habakkuk 3:2)

LORD, I LISTEN TO YOUR WORDS OF TRUTH

Christ was chosen before the creation of the world but was revealed in these last times for our sake. Through Him I believe in God, who raised Him from the dead and glorified Him, so that my faith and hope are in God. (1 Peter 1:20-21)

LORD, I RESPOND TO YOUR INSTRUCTION

Hatred stirs up strife, but love covers all transgressions. (Proverbs 10:12)

A friend loves at all times, and a brother is born for adversity. (Proverbs 17:17)

~❧~

Lord, I thank You for Your lovingkindness and for Your awesome deeds. I thank You that You revealed Your Son for our sake. I will purpose to love others at all times.

DAY 200

DETERMINING TO BE HOLY

❧

LORD, I DRAW NEAR TO YOU

As I approach Your throne of grace today, I am grateful that You care about the things that concern me and that You want me to offer them up to You.

May I humble myself under the mighty hand of God, that He may exalt me in due time, casting all my anxiety upon Him, because He cares for me. (1 Peter 5:6-7)

Take a moment to share your personal needs with God, including your physical, emotional, relational, and spiritual concerns.

THANK YOU, LORD, FOR WHAT YOU HAVE DONE

Far be it from You to kill the righteous with the wicked, treating the righteous and the wicked alike. Far be it from You! Will not the Judge of all the earth do right? (Genesis 18:25)

210

The Lord relieves the humble, but He casts the wicked to the ground. (Psalm 147:6)

LORD, I LISTEN TO YOUR WORDS OF TRUTH

You are the Lord my God; I will consecrate myself and be holy, because You are holy. You are the Lord who brought Your people up out of Egypt to be their God; therefore I will be holy, because You are holy. (Leviticus 11:44-45; 19:2)

LORD, I RESPOND TO YOUR INSTRUCTION

The foremost commandment is this: "Hear, O Israel; the Lord our God, the Lord is one; and you shall love the Lord your God with all your heart and with all your soul and with all your mind and with all your strength." The second is this: "You shall love your neighbor as yourself." There is no commandment greater than these. To love God with all the heart and with the understanding and with all the strength, and to love one's neighbor as himself are more important than all burnt offerings and sacrifices. (Mark 12:29-31,33)

❧

Lord, I thank You that Your judgments are always right and just. I pray that as I consecrate myself and determine to be holy, I will love You with all my heart, soul, mind, and strength and love my neighbor as myself.

DAY 201

TURNING MY HEART FROM PRIDE

‿

LORD, I DRAW NEAR TO YOU

Lord, You have invited me to pray for the needs of others, and since You desire what is best for them, I take this opportunity to bring these requests to You.

All things are from God, Who reconciled us to Himself through Christ and gave us the ministry of reconciliation: namely, that God was reconciling the world to Himself in Christ, not counting their trespasses against them. And He has committed to us the message of reconciliation. Therefore, we are ambassadors for Christ, as though God were appealing through us, as we implore others on Christ's behalf to be reconciled to God. (2 Corinthians 5:18-20)

Take a moment to lift up the needs of your family and friends, and to offer up any additional burdens for others that the Lord brings to mind.

THANK YOU, LORD, FOR WHAT YOU HAVE DONE

The Father loves the Son and has given all things into His hand. (John 3:35)

211
‿

LORD, I LISTEN TO YOUR WORDS OF TRUTH

Whoever receives a little child in Your name receives You, and whoever receives You receives Him who sent You. For he who is least among us all is the one who is great. (Luke 9:48)

LORD, I RESPOND TO YOUR INSTRUCTION

When pride comes, then comes dishonor, but with humility comes wisdom. (Proverbs 11:2)

The tongue is a small part of the body, but it makes great boasts. Consider what a great forest is set on fire by a small spark. The tongue also is a fire, a world of evil that is set among the parts of the body, that corrupts the whole body, and sets the whole course of our life on fire and is set on fire by hell. (James 3:5-6)

‿

Lord, I thank You that You have given all things into Your Son's hand. Help me to reach out to and receive others in Your name. I will guard myself from pride and boasting that I might gain wisdom.

DAY 202

TRUSTING GOD'S UNFAILING WORD

LORD, I DRAW NEAR TO YOU

Lord, I want Your Word to be deeply implanted in me so that I will know the truth and be able to express it in the way I live.

You are the Alpha and the Omega, the Beginning and the End. To him who is thirsty, You will give to drink without cost from the spring of the water of life. He who overcomes will inherit all this, and You will be his God and he will be Your son. (Revelation 21:6-7)

Take a moment to affirm the truth of these words from Scripture and ask God to make them a growing reality in your life.

THANK YOU, LORD, FOR WHAT YOU HAVE DONE

It is easier for heaven and earth to disappear than for a stroke of a letter of God's law to fail. (Luke 16:17)

Jesus fell with His face to the ground and prayed, "My Father, if it is possible, let this cup pass from Me. Yet not as I will, but as You will." (Matthew 26:39)

LORD, I LISTEN TO YOUR WORDS OF TRUTH

If anyone serves You, he must follow You; and where You are, Your servant also will be. If anyone serves You, the Father will honor him. (John 12:26)

LORD, I RESPOND TO YOUR INSTRUCTION

I do not want to justify myself in the eyes of men; God knows our hearts, and what is highly esteemed among men is detestable in the sight of God. (Luke 16:15)

Peter came to Jesus and asked, "Lord, how often shall my brother sin against me, and I forgive him? Up to seven times?" Jesus said to him, "I tell you, not seven times, but up to seventy times seven." (Matthew 18:21-22)

Lord, I thank You that Your Word will never fail and that Jesus perfectly fulfilled Your will. I will not seek to justify myself before others. Help me to forgive those who have injured me.

DAY 203

USING MY SPIRITUAL WEAPONS

❧

LORD, I DRAW NEAR TO YOU

O Lord, I am deeply grateful for Your wonderful acts, for Your abundant promises, and for the gift of my relationship with You through the merits of Christ.

Surely God is my salvation;
I will trust and not be afraid.
For the Lord God is my strength and my song,
And He has become my salvation. (Isaiah 12:2)

Take a moment to express your gratitude for the many blessings that you have received from the Lord.

THANK YOU, LORD, FOR WHAT YOU HAVE DONE

Nothing is impossible with God. (Luke 1:37)

LORD, I LISTEN TO YOUR WORDS OF TRUTH

I will stand firm, having girded my waist with truth, having put on the breastplate of righteousness, and having shod my feet with the readiness of the gospel of peace; above all, taking up the shield of faith with which I will be able to quench all the fiery darts of the evil one. I will take the helmet of salvation and the sword of the Spirit, which is the Word of God. With all prayer and petition, I will pray always in the Spirit, and to this end I will be watchful with all perseverance and petition for all the saints. (Ephesians 6:14-18)

LORD, I RESPOND TO YOUR INSTRUCTION

Humility and the fear of the Lord bring wealth and honor and life. (Proverbs 22:4)

Woe to those who are wise in their own eyes and clever in their own sight! (Isaiah 5:21)

❧

Lord, I thank You that nothing is impossible with You. Teach me to use the spiritual weapons of warfare that You have provided. Beginning today, I choose not to be wise in my own eyes, but to live in humility and the fear of the Lord.

DAY 204

WALKING HUMBLY WITH MY GOD

LORD, I DRAW NEAR TO YOU

Lord, I give thanks for Your greatness, Your goodness, and Your love, and I now draw near to enjoy Your presence.

Lord, You have been our dwelling place throughout all generations.
Before the mountains were born
Or You brought forth the earth and the world,
From everlasting to everlasting, You are God.
You turn men back into dust,
And say, "Return, O children of men."
For a thousand years in Your sight
Are like yesterday when it passes by
Or like a watch in the night. (Psalm 90:1-4)

Take a moment to consider God's awesome majesty and thank Him that He loves you and wants an intimate relationship with you.

214

THANK YOU, LORD, FOR WHAT YOU HAVE DONE

Where two or three come together in the name of Jesus, He is there in their midst. (Matthew 18:20)

As Moses lifted up the serpent in the desert, so the Son of Man had to be lifted up, that everyone who believes in Him may have eternal life. (John 3:14-15)

LORD, I LISTEN TO YOUR WORDS OF TRUTH

I would have lost heart unless I had believed that I would see the goodness of the Lord in the land of the living. I will hope in the Lord and be of good courage, and He will strengthen my heart; yes, I will hope in the Lord. (Psalm 27:13-14)

LORD, I RESPOND TO YOUR INSTRUCTION

You have shown me what is good; and what does the Lord require of me but to act justly and to love mercy and to walk humbly with my God? (Micah 6:8)

Lord, I thank You for Your promised presence and that I can confidently hope in You. Help me to act justly, love mercy, and walk humbly with You.

DAY 205

WAITING FOR THE LORD

~&~

LORD, I DRAW NEAR TO YOU

I am grateful to You, O God, for the blessing of Your forgiveness. I thank You that in Christ, You set me free from the guilt of the past and give me hope for the future.

God fashions the hearts of all
And understands all their works. (Psalm 33:15)

The Lord does not see as man sees. Man looks at the outward appearance, but the Lord looks at the heart. (1 Samuel 16:7)

Take a moment to ask the Spirit to search your heart and reveal any areas of unconfessed sin. Acknowledge these to the Lord and thank Him for His forgiveness.

THANK YOU, LORD, FOR WHAT YOU HAVE DONE

I will be silent before the Lord, for He is aroused from His holy dwelling place. (Zechariah 2:13)

215
~&~

You are worthy, our Lord and God, to receive glory and honor and power, for You created all things, and by Your will they were created and have their being. (Revelation 4:11)

LORD, I LISTEN TO YOUR WORDS OF TRUTH

I wait for the Lord; my soul waits, and in His Word I put my hope. I hope in the Lord, for with Him is unfailing love and abundant redemption. (Psalm 130:5,7)

LORD, I RESPOND TO YOUR INSTRUCTION

Let him who thinks he stands take heed lest he fall. (1 Corinthians 10:12)

Blessed are the poor in spirit, for theirs is the kingdom of heaven. Blessed are those who mourn, for they will be comforted. Blessed are the meek, for they will inherit the earth. (Matthew 5:3-5)

~&~

Lord, I thank You for Your matchless holiness and for the glory of Your creation. Keep me ever mindful of Your blessings and my complete spiritual bankruptcy apart from the merits of Jesus Christ.

DAY 206

HOPING IN THE RESURRECTION

❧

LORD, I DRAW NEAR TO YOU

I praise You, Lord, that You are intimately acquainted with my ways and that You always love me and have my best interests at heart.

I want to walk in a way that is worthy of the calling with which I was called, with all humility and meekness and patience. (Ephesians 4:1-2)

As one who shares in the heavenly calling, I fix my thoughts on Jesus, the Apostle and High Priest of my confession. (Hebrews 3:1)

Take a moment to offer this day to the Lord and ask Him for the grace to grow in your knowledge and love for Him.

THANK YOU, LORD, FOR WHAT YOU HAVE DONE

Are You a God nearby, and not a God far away? Can anyone hide in secret places so that You cannot see him? Do You not fill heaven and earth? (Jeremiah 23:23-24)

By faith I understand that the universe was formed by the Word of God, so that what is seen was not made out of things which are visible. (Hebrews 11:3)

LORD, I LISTEN TO YOUR WORDS OF TRUTH

I have hope in God, that there will be a resurrection of both the righteous and the wicked. In view of this, I strive always to keep my conscience blameless before God and men. (Acts 24:15-16)

LORD, I RESPOND TO YOUR INSTRUCTION

I should let my gentleness be evident to all men; the Lord is near. (Philippians 4:5)

My love must be sincere. I will hate what is evil and cling to what is good. (Romans 12:9)

❧

Lord, I thank You that You fill heaven and earth and that You formed the universe by the power of Your Word. I thank You for the hope of the resurrection. Help me to be gentle and sincere in my love for people.

DAY 207

CASTING OFF THE WORKS OF DARKNESS

❧

LORD, I DRAW NEAR TO YOU

As I approach Your throne of grace today, I am grateful that You care about the things that concern me and that You want me to offer them up to You.

I wait for the Lord; my soul waits,
And in His Word I put my hope.
I hope in the Lord,
For with Him are unfailing love
And abundant redemption. (Psalm 130:5,7)

Take a moment to share your personal needs with God, including your physical, emotional, relational, and spiritual concerns.

THANK YOU, LORD, FOR WHAT YOU HAVE DONE

God will bring every work into judgment, including every hidden thing, whether it is good or evil. (Ecclesiastes 12:14)

LORD, I LISTEN TO YOUR WORDS OF TRUTH

Since I am a child of God, I am an heir of God and a joint heir with Christ, if indeed I share in His sufferings in order that I may also share in His glory. For I consider that the sufferings of this present time are not worth comparing with the glory that will be revealed to me. (Romans 8:17-18)

LORD, I RESPOND TO YOUR INSTRUCTION

The hour has come for me to wake up from sleep, for my salvation is nearer now than when I first believed. The night is nearly over; the day is almost here. Therefore I will cast off the works of darkness and put on the armor of light. (Romans 13:11-12)

❧

Lord, I thank You that nothing will escape Your perfect judgment and that the sufferings of this present time are not worth comparing with the glory that will be revealed to me. Help me to walk in the light of Your truth and cast off the works of darkness.

DAY 208

LOVING GOD AND MY NEIGHBOR

~

LORD, I DRAW NEAR TO YOU

Lord, You have invited me to pray for the needs of others, and since You desire what is best for them, I take this opportunity to bring these requests to You.

How good and pleasant it is
When brothers live together in unity! (Psalm 133:1)

There is neither Jew nor Greek; there is neither slave nor free; there is neither male nor female; for we are all one in Christ Jesus. (Galatians 3:28)

Take a moment to lift up the needs of your family and friends, and to offer up any additional burdens for others that the Lord brings to mind.

THANK YOU, LORD, FOR WHAT YOU HAVE DONE

I know that whatever God does will remain forever; nothing can be added to it and nothing taken from it. God does it so that men will revere Him. (Ecclesiastes 3:14)

LORD, I LISTEN TO YOUR WORDS OF TRUTH

Whatever things were written in the past were written for our learning, so that through endurance and the encouragement of the Scriptures we might have hope. (Romans 15:4)

LORD, I RESPOND TO YOUR INSTRUCTION

I will owe nothing to anyone except to love them, for he who loves his neighbor has fulfilled the law. For the commandments, "You shall not commit adultery," "You shall not murder," "You shall not steal," "You shall not covet," and if there is any other commandment, it is summed up in this saying: "You shall love your neighbor as yourself." Love does no harm to a neighbor; therefore, love is the fulfillment of the law. (Romans 13:8-10)

~

Lord, I thank You that Your works endure forever and that You do everything well. I thank You for the encouragement of the Scriptures. I seek to please You by loving and serving others as You have commanded.

DAY 209

LOVING INSTRUCTION

<hr>

LORD, I DRAW NEAR TO YOU

Lord, I want Your Word to be deeply implanted in me so that I will know the truth and be able to express it in the way I live.

I call this to mind,
And therefore I have hope:
The Lord's mercies never cease,
For His compassions never fail.
They are new every morning;
Great is Your faithfulness. (Lamentations 3:21-23)

Take a moment to affirm the truth of these words from Scripture and ask God to make them a growing reality in your life.

<hr>

THANK YOU, LORD, FOR WHAT YOU HAVE DONE

The spirit of a man is the lamp of the Lord, searching the inward depths of his being. (Proverbs 20:27)

219

O Lord, what is man that You know him, or the son of man that You think of him? Man is like a breath; his days are like a passing shadow. (Psalm 144:3-4)

<hr>

LORD, I LISTEN TO YOUR WORDS OF TRUTH

Eye has not seen, ear has not heard, nor have entered the heart of man the things that God has prepared for those who love Him. (1 Corinthians 2:9)

<hr>

LORD, I RESPOND TO YOUR INSTRUCTION

A rebuke goes deeper into a wise man than a hundred lashes into a fool. (Proverbs 17:10)

Whoever loves instruction loves knowledge, but he who hates correction is stupid. (Proverbs 12:1)

Lord, I thank You that You know me intimately and still care for me. I thank you, Lord, for what You are preparing for those who love You. Help me to learn wisdom from rebuke and correction.

DAY 210

ABIDING IN THE LIGHT

LORD, I DRAW NEAR TO YOU

O Lord, I am deeply grateful for Your wonderful acts, for Your abundant promises, and for the gift of my relationship with You through the merits of Christ.

The Lord has bared His holy arm
In the sight of all the nations,
And all the ends of the earth will see
The salvation of our God. (Isaiah 52:10)

The Lord has performed mighty deeds with His arm;
He has scattered those who are proud in the thoughts of their heart.
He has brought down rulers from their thrones
And has lifted up the humble. (Luke 1:51-52)

Take a moment to express your gratitude for the many blessings that you have received from the Lord.

THANK YOU, LORD, FOR WHAT YOU HAVE DONE

How great are Your works, O Lord! Your thoughts are very deep. The senseless man does not know; fools do not understand that when the wicked spring up like grass and all the evildoers flourish, they will be destroyed forever. But You, O Lord, are exalted forever. (Psalm 92:5-7)

LORD, I LISTEN TO YOUR WORDS OF TRUTH

I know that He who raised the Lord Jesus will also raise me with Jesus and present me in His presence. (2 Corinthians 4:14)

LORD, I RESPOND TO YOUR INSTRUCTION

The one who loves his brother abides in the light, and there is no cause for stumbling in him. But the one who hates his brother is in the darkness and walks in the darkness and does not know where he is going, because the darkness has blinded his eyes. (1 John 2:10-11)

Lord, I thank You for Your marvelous works and that You will raise me with Jesus. Teach me to abide in the light by loving others.

DAY 211

PLEASING THE LORD

~❧~

LORD, I DRAW NEAR TO YOU

Lord, I give thanks for Your greatness, Your goodness, and Your love, and I now draw near to enjoy Your presence.

O Lord, how manifold are Your works!
In wisdom You made them all;
The earth is full of Your possessions. (Psalm 104:24)

Take a moment to consider God's awesome majesty and thank Him that He loves you and wants an intimate relationship with you.

THANK YOU, LORD, FOR WHAT YOU HAVE DONE

The Lord is the true God; He is the living God and the everlasting King. At His wrath, the earth trembles, and the nations cannot endure His indignation. (Jeremiah 10:10)

You formed my inward parts; You wove me together in my mother's womb. I thank You because I am fearfully and wonderfully made; Your works are wonderful, and my soul knows it full well. (Psalm 139:13-14)

221
~❧~

LORD, I LISTEN TO YOUR WORDS OF TRUTH

I make it my ambition to please the Lord, whether I am at home in the body or away from it. For we must all appear before the judgment seat of Christ, that each one may receive what is due for the things done while in the body, whether good or bad. (2 Corinthians 5:9-10)

LORD, I RESPOND TO YOUR INSTRUCTION

Since I have been approved by God to be entrusted with the gospel, I speak not as pleasing men but God, who tests my heart. I will not seek glory from men. (1 Thessalonians 2:4,6)

I will work out my salvation with fear and trembling, for it is God Who works in me to will and to act according to His good purpose. (Philippians 2:12-13)

~❧~

Lord, I thank You that You are the true and living God and that I am fearfully and wonderfully made. I will make it my ambition to be pleasing to You and will not seek glory from men.

DAY 212

PRESSING TOWARD THE GOAL

LORD, I DRAW NEAR TO YOU

I am grateful to You, O God, for the blessing of Your forgiveness. I thank You that in Christ, You set me free from the guilt of the past and give me hope for the future.

God is wise in heart and mighty in strength.
Who has resisted Him without harm? (Job 9:4)

I know in my heart that as a man disciplines his son, so the Lord my God disciplines me. (Deuteronomy 8:5)

Take a moment to ask the Spirit to search your heart and reveal any areas of unconfessed sin. Acknowledge these to the Lord and thank Him for His forgiveness.

THANK YOU, LORD, FOR WHAT YOU HAVE DONE

Jesus is the Christ, the Son of God, who came into the world. (John 11:27)

LORD, I LISTEN TO YOUR WORDS OF TRUTH

I have not been made perfect, but I press on to lay hold of that for which Christ Jesus also laid hold of me. I do not consider myself yet to have attained it, but one thing I do: forgetting what is behind and stretching forward to what is ahead, I press on toward the goal to win the prize of the upward call of God in Christ Jesus. (Philippians 3:12-14)

LORD, I RESPOND TO YOUR INSTRUCTION

All Scripture is God-breathed and is useful for teaching, for reproof, for correction, for training in righteousness, that the man of God may be thoroughly equipped for every good work. (2 Timothy 3:16-17)

Blessed are the pure in heart, for they shall see God. Blessed are the peacemakers, for they shall be called sons of God. (Matthew 5:8-9)

Lord, I thank You that Your Son came into the world and purchased our salvation. I thank You for the prize of Your upward call in Christ Jesus. I will be responsive to Scripture and pursue purity of heart and peace with others.

DAY 213

SEEKING GOD'S KINGDOM

❧

LORD, I DRAW NEAR TO YOU

I praise You, Lord, that You are intimately acquainted with my ways and that You always love me and have my best interests at heart.

Examine me, O Lord, and try me;
Purify my mind and my heart;
For Your lovingkindness is ever before me,
And I have walked in Your truth. (Psalm 26:2-3)

May I sow righteousness,
Reap the fruit of unfailing love,
And break up my fallow ground;
For it is time to seek the Lord,
Until He comes and rains righteousness on me. (Hosea 10:12)

Take a moment to offer this day to the Lord and ask Him for the grace to grow in your knowledge and love for Him.

223
❧

THANK YOU, LORD, FOR WHAT YOU HAVE DONE

The counsel of the Lord stands firm forever, the plans of His heart through all generations. (Psalm 33:11)

Every animal of the forest is Yours, and the cattle on a thousand hills. (Psalm 50:10)

LORD, I LISTEN TO YOUR WORDS OF TRUTH

My faith in Christ Jesus and love for all the saints spring from the hope that is stored up for me in heaven, of which I have heard in the Word of truth, the gospel. (Colossians 1:4-5)

LORD, I RESPOND TO YOUR INSTRUCTION

I will seek first His kingdom and His righteousness, and all these things will be added to me. (Matthew 6:33; Luke 12:31)

❧

Lord, I thank You that Your counsel stands firm forever and that all things are Yours. I thank You for the Word of truth and my faith in Christ Jesus. I will seek first Your kingdom and Your righteousness.

DAY 214

DEVOTING MYSELF TO DOING GOOD

~~~

LORD, I DRAW NEAR TO YOU

As I approach Your throne of grace today, I am grateful that You care about the things that concern me and that You want me to offer them up to You.

In Your righteousness deliver me and rescue me;
Turn Your ear to me and save me.
Be my rock of refuge, to which I can always go;
You have given the commandment to save me,
For You are my rock and my fortress. (Psalm 71:2-3)

Take a moment to share your personal needs with God, including your physical, emotional, relational, and spiritual concerns.

THANK YOU, LORD, FOR WHAT YOU HAVE DONE

God's voice thunders in marvelous ways; He does great things which we cannot comprehend. (Job 37:5)

The Mighty One, God, the Lord, has spoken and summoned the earth from the rising of the sun to the place where it sets. (Psalm 50:1)

LORD, I LISTEN TO YOUR WORDS OF TRUTH

My hope in God is an anchor of my soul, both sure and steadfast, and it enters the inner sanctuary behind the veil, where Jesus the forerunner has entered on my behalf, having become a high priest forever, according to the order of Melchizedek. (Hebrews 6:19-20)

LORD, I RESPOND TO YOUR INSTRUCTION

As one who has believed in God, I want to be careful to devote myself to doing what is good. These things are good and profitable for everyone. (Titus 3:8)

~~~

Lord, I thank You that You do great things which we cannot comprehend and that You have spoken with crowning authority. I thank You that my hope in Christ is the sure and steadfast anchor of my soul. I will devote myself to doing what is good.

DAY 215

ABIDING IN CONTENTMENT

❧

LORD, I DRAW NEAR TO YOU

Lord, You have invited me to pray for the needs of others, and since You desire what is best for them, I take this opportunity to bring these requests to You.

We should bear one another's burdens and so fulfill the law of Christ. (Galatians 6:2)

As we have opportunity, we should do good to all people, especially to those who belong to the family of faith. (Galatians 6:10)

Take a moment to lift up the needs of your family and friends, and to offer up any other burdens for others that the Lord brings to mind.

THANK YOU, LORD, FOR WHAT YOU HAVE DONE

The heavens and the highest heavens cannot contain the Lord. (2 Chronicles 2:6; 6:18)

It is God the Lord who created the heavens and stretched them out, who spread out the earth and all that comes out of it, who gives breath to its people, and spirit to those who walk on it. (Isaiah 42:5)

225
❧

LORD, I LISTEN TO YOUR WORDS OF TRUTH

Blessed be the God and Father of my Lord Jesus Christ, Who according to His great mercy has given me new birth into a living hope through the resurrection of Jesus Christ from the dead, and into an inheritance that is incorruptible and undefiled and unfading, reserved in heaven for me. (1 Peter 1:3-4)

LORD, I RESPOND TO YOUR INSTRUCTION

I want to learn to be content in whatever circumstances I am. Whether I am abased or in abundance, whether I am filled or hungry, I want to learn the secret of being content in any and every situation. I can do all things through Him who strengthens me. (Philippians 4:11-13)

❧

Lord, I thank You that the highest heavens cannot contain You and that You are the source of all biological and spiritual life. I thank You for the inheritance of those who hope in Christ. I will be content with what You have given me.

DAY 216

CLINGING TO LOVE AND TRUTH

❧

LORD, I DRAW NEAR TO YOU

Lord, I want Your Word to be deeply implanted in me so that I will know the truth and be able to express it in the way I live.

Praise the Lord!
Praise the Lord from the heavens;
Praise Him in the heights.
Praise Him, all His angels;
Praise Him, all His hosts.
Praise Him, sun and moon;
Praise Him, all you shining stars.
Praise Him, you highest heavens
And you waters above the heavens. (Psalm 148:1-4)

Take a moment to affirm the truth of these words from Scripture and ask God to make them a growing reality in your life.

THANK YOU, LORD, FOR WHAT YOU HAVE DONE

The Lord is the God of knowledge, and by Him actions are weighed. (1 Samuel 2:3)

The Lord, He is God. It is He who made us, and not we ourselves; we are His people and the sheep of His pasture. (Psalm 100:3)

LORD, I LISTEN TO YOUR WORDS OF TRUTH

I am convinced that neither death nor life, nor angels nor principalities, nor things present nor things to come, nor powers, nor height nor depth, nor anything else in all creation, will be able to separate me from the love of God that is in Christ Jesus my Lord. (Romans 8:38-39)

LORD, I RESPOND TO YOUR INSTRUCTION

I will not let love and truth leave me; I will bind them around my neck and write them on the tablet of my heart. (Proverbs 3:3)

❧

Lord, I thank You that You are the God of knowledge and that I am part of Your flock. I thank You that nothing can separate me from Your love that is in Christ Jesus. I will cling to Your love and truth.

DAY 217

LOVING MY NEIGHBOR AS MYSELF

LORD, I DRAW NEAR TO YOU

O Lord, I am deeply grateful for Your wonderful acts, for Your abundant promises, and for the gift of my relationship with You through the merits of Christ.

God sent His Word to the children of Israel, telling the good news of peace through Jesus Christ, Who is Lord of all. He commanded the apostles to preach to the people and to testify that He is the One Whom God appointed as judge of the living and the dead. To Him all the prophets witness that through His name, everyone who believes in Him receives forgiveness of sins. (Acts 10:36,42-43)

Take a moment to express your gratitude for the many blessings that you have received from the Lord.

THANK YOU, LORD, FOR WHAT YOU HAVE DONE

God made the earth by His power; He established the world by His wisdom and stretched out the heavens by His understanding. (Jeremiah 10:12)

227

LORD, I LISTEN TO YOUR WORDS OF TRUTH

I thank God because of His grace in Christ Jesus. In Him we have been enriched in every way, in all speech and in all knowledge. We do not lack any spiritual gift, as we eagerly wait for the revelation of our Lord Jesus Christ. (1 Corinthians 1:4-5,7)

LORD, I RESPOND TO YOUR INSTRUCTION

"You shall love the Lord your God with all your heart and with all your soul and with all your mind." This is the first and great commandment. And the second is like it: "You shall love your neighbor as yourself." All the law and the prophets hang on these two commandments. (Matthew 22:37-40)

Lord, I thank You for establishing the heavens by Your wisdom and understanding. I thank You for the riches of Your grace in Christ Jesus. I will love You with all my heart, soul, and mind and love my neighbor as myself.

DAY 218

GIVING GENEROUSLY TO OTHERS

LORD, I DRAW NEAR TO YOU

Lord, I give thanks for Your greatness, Your goodness, and Your love, and I now draw near to enjoy Your presence.

As the deer pants for the water brooks,
So my soul pants for You, O God.
My soul thirsts for God, for the living God.
When shall I come and appear before God? (Psalm 42:1-2)

My soul yearns for You in the night;
My spirit within me diligently seeks You.
When Your judgments come upon the earth,
The inhabitants of the world learn righteousness. (Isaiah 26:9)

Take a moment to consider God's awesome majesty and thank Him that He loves you and wants an intimate relationship with you.

THANK YOU, LORD, FOR WHAT YOU HAVE DONE

We will not all sleep, but we will all be changed, in a moment, in the twinkling of an eye, at the last trumpet. For the trumpet will sound, and the dead will be raised imperishable, and we shall be changed. For this perishable must clothe itself with the imperishable, and this mortal with immortality. (1 Corinthians 15:51-53)

LORD, I LISTEN TO YOUR WORDS OF TRUTH

The grace of the Lord Jesus Christ and the love of God and the fellowship of the Holy Spirit are with me. (2 Corinthians 13:14)

LORD, I RESPOND TO YOUR INSTRUCTION

I will give generously to others without a grudging heart. (Deuteronomy 15:10)

Now He who supplies seed to the sower and bread for food will also supply and increase our seed and will increase the fruits of our righteousness. (2 Corinthians 9:10)

Lord, I thank You for Your promise that You will raise me to immortality and that I will be imperishable in Your presence. I thank You for Your love, grace, and fellowship. I will be generous with the resources You have entrusted to me.

DAY 219

PUTTING ON A HEART OF COMPASSION

LORD, I DRAW NEAR TO YOU

I am grateful to You, O God, for the blessing of Your forgiveness. I thank You that in Christ, You set me free from the guilt of the past and give me hope for the future.

You are the righteous God, who searches the hearts and secret thoughts. (Psalm 7:9)

The spirit of a man is the lamp of the Lord,
Searching the inward depths of his being. (Proverbs 20:27)

Take a moment to ask the Spirit to search your heart and reveal any areas of unconfessed sin. Acknowledge these to the Lord and thank Him for His forgiveness.

THANK YOU, LORD, FOR WHAT YOU HAVE DONE

An hour is coming, and now is, when the dead will hear the voice of the Son of God; and those who hear will live. For as the Father has life in Himself, so He has granted the Son to have life in Himself, and He has given Him authority to execute judgment, because He is the Son of Man. (John 5:25-27)

LORD, I LISTEN TO YOUR WORDS OF TRUTH

I am confident of this, that He Who began a good work in me will carry it on to completion until the day of Christ Jesus. (Philippians 1:6)

LORD, I RESPOND TO YOUR INSTRUCTION

As one who has been chosen of God, holy and beloved, I will put on a heart of compassion, kindness, humility, gentleness, and patience, bearing with others and forgiving others even as the Lord forgave me; and above all these things, I will put on love, which is the bond of perfection. (Colossians 3:12-14)

Lord, I thank You that You have given Your Son the authority to raise all people from the dead. I thank You that You will complete the good work You have begun in me. I will put on a heart of compassion, kindness, humility, gentleness, patience, and most importantly, love.

DAY 220
PRACTICING MERCY AND FAIRNESS

～

LORD, I DRAW NEAR TO YOU

I praise You, Lord, that You are intimately acquainted with my ways and that You always love me and have my best interests at heart.

With regard to my former way of life, may I put off my old self, which is being corrupted by its deceitful desires, and be renewed in the spirit of my mind; and may I put on the new self, which was created according to God in righteousness and true holiness. (Ephesians 4:22-24)

May I be diligent to add to my faith, virtue; and to virtue, knowledge; and to knowledge, self-control; and to self-control, perseverance; and to perseverance, godliness; and to godliness, brotherly kindness; and to brotherly kindness, love. For if these qualities are mine in increasing measure, they will keep me from being barren and unfruitful in the full knowledge of our Lord Jesus Christ. (2 Peter 1:5-8)

Take a moment to offer this day to the Lord and ask Him for the grace to grow in your knowledge and love for Him.

230
～

THANK YOU, LORD, FOR WHAT YOU HAVE DONE

God will judge the secrets of men through Jesus Christ, according to the Gospel. (Romans 2:16)

LORD, I LISTEN TO YOUR WORDS OF TRUTH

My soul silently waits for God alone; my salvation comes from Him. He alone is my rock and my salvation; He is my stronghold; I will never be shaken. (Psalm 62:1-2)

LORD, I RESPOND TO YOUR INSTRUCTION

I will do no injustice in judgment, nor show partiality to the poor or favoritism to the great, but I will judge my neighbor fairly. (Leviticus 19:15)

You desire mercy, not sacrifice, and the knowledge of God more than burnt offerings. (Hosea 6:6)

～

Lord, I thank You for Your eternal Son and that You will judge the secrets of men through Him. I thank You that You alone are my rock and my salvation. Help me to practice fairness and mercy in my dealings with others.

DAY 221

WALKING IN FAITH AND LOVE

❧

LORD, I DRAW NEAR TO YOU

---

*As I approach Your throne of grace today, I am grateful that You care about the
things that concern me and that You want me to offer them up to You.*

Hear my cry, O God,
And listen to my prayer.
From the ends of the earth I call to You
When my heart grows faint;
Lead me to the rock that is higher than I.
You have been a shelter for me
And a strong tower against the enemy.
I will dwell in Your tent forever
And take refuge in the shelter of Your wings. (Psalm 61:1-4)

*Take a moment to share your personal needs with God, including your physical,
emotional, relational, and spiritual concerns.*

THANK YOU, LORD, FOR WHAT YOU HAVE DONE

231
❧

No one has seen the Father, except the One Who is from God; only He
has seen the Father. (John 6:46)

I must be ready, for the Son of Man will come at an hour when I do
not expect Him. (Matthew 24:44; Luke 12:40)

LORD, I LISTEN TO YOUR WORDS OF TRUTH

This is what the Lord God, the Holy One of Israel, says: "In repentance
and rest is your salvation; in quietness and trust is your strength."
(Isaiah 30:15)

LORD, I RESPOND TO YOUR INSTRUCTION

Since I belong to the day, I will be self-controlled, putting on the
breastplate of faith and love, and the hope of salvation as a helmet.
(1 Thessalonians 5:8)

❧

*Lord, I thank You for Your Son who has revealed You and for the truth that He
could come at any time. I thank You that my salvation is in repentance and rest.
I will walk in faith and love.*

DAY 222

WALKING IN POWER

LORD, I DRAW NEAR TO YOU

Lord, You have invited me to pray for the needs of others, and since You desire what is best for them, I take this opportunity to bring these requests to You.

Each of us must put off falsehood and speak truthfully to his neighbor, for we are members of one another. (Ephesians 4:25)

We should submit to one another out of reverence for Christ. (Ephesians 5:21)

Take a moment to lift up the needs of your family and friends, and to offer up any other burdens for others that the Lord brings to mind.

THANK YOU, LORD, FOR WHAT YOU HAVE DONE

Jesus is the Son of God; He is the King of Israel. (John 1:49)

An hour is coming when all who are in the graves will hear the voice of the Son of Man, and will come out—those who have done good to a resurrection of life, and those who have done evil to a resurrection of judgment. (John 5:28-29)

LORD, I LISTEN TO YOUR WORDS OF TRUTH

"Even now," declares the Lord, "return to Me with all your heart, with fasting and weeping and mourning." So rend your heart and not your garments. Return to the Lord your God, for He is gracious and compassionate, slow to anger and abounding in lovingkindness, and He relents from sending calamity. (Joel 2:12-13)

LORD, I RESPOND TO YOUR INSTRUCTION

Laziness casts one into a deep sleep, and an idle person will be hungry. (Proverbs 19:15)

God has not given me a spirit of timidity, but a spirit of power, of love, and of self-control. (2 Timothy 1:7)

Lord, I thank You that Jesus is Your Son and that all who are in the graves will hear His voice. I thank You for Your grace and compassion. I will not succumb to laziness but will walk in power, love, and self-control.

DAY 223

WORKING FOR SPIRITUAL FOOD

❧

LORD, I DRAW NEAR TO YOU

Lord, I want Your Word to be deeply implanted in me so that I will know the truth and be able to express it in the way I live.

Lord Jesus, You are coming quickly. Your reward is with You, and You will give to everyone according to what he has done. You are the Alpha and the Omega, the First and the Last, the Beginning and the End. Yes, You are coming quickly. Amen. Come, Lord Jesus! (Revelation 22:12-13,20)

Take a moment to affirm the truth of these words from Scripture and ask God to make them a growing reality in your life.

THANK YOU, LORD, FOR WHAT YOU HAVE DONE

Jesus of Nazareth, the son of Joseph, is the Messiah (that is, the Christ). He is the One Moses wrote about in the Law, and about whom the prophets also wrote. (John 1:41,45)

233
❧

Behold, a virgin shall be with child and will give birth to a son, and they will call His name Immanuel, which means, "God with us." (Matthew 1:23)

LORD, I LISTEN TO YOUR WORDS OF TRUTH

I should not work for the food that perishes, but for the food that endures to eternal life, which the Son of Man gives me, for God the Father has set His seal on Him. (John 6:27)

LORD, I RESPOND TO YOUR INSTRUCTION

The end of all things is near; therefore, I will be clear minded and self-controlled for prayer. (1 Peter 4:7)

The sons of this world are more shrewd in dealing with their own kind than are the sons of light. I would be wise to use worldly wealth to make friends for myself, so that when it is gone, they may welcome me into the eternal dwellings. (Luke 16:8-9)

❧

Lord, I thank You for Your incarnate Son and for His perfect fulfillment of the law and the prophets. I thank You for the food that endures to eternal life. Help me to be prayerful and prudent in the use of my worldly resources.

DAY 224

OVERCOMING EVIL WITH GOOD

O Lord, I am deeply grateful for Your wonderful acts, for Your abundant promises, and for the gift of my relationship with You through the merits of Christ.

The salvation of the righteous comes from the Lord;
He is their stronghold in time of trouble.
The Lord helps them and delivers them;
He delivers them from the wicked and saves them,
Because they take refuge in Him. (Psalm 37:39-40)

Take a moment to express your gratitude for the many blessings that you have received from the Lord.

THANK YOU, LORD, FOR WHAT YOU HAVE DONE

234

In the resurrection of the dead, the body that is sown is perishable, but it is raised imperishable; it is sown in dishonor, but it is raised in glory; it is sown in weakness, but it is raised in power; it is sown a natural body, but it is raised a spiritual body. If there is a natural body, there is also a spiritual body. (1 Corinthians 15:42-44)

LORD, I LISTEN TO YOUR WORDS OF TRUTH

I shall know the truth, and the truth shall set me free. Everyone who commits sin is a slave of sin. And a slave has no permanent place in the family, but a son belongs to it forever. So if the Son sets me free, I shall be free indeed. (John 8:32,34-36)

LORD, I RESPOND TO YOUR INSTRUCTION

I will not be afraid of my adversaries, but I will remember the Lord, who is great and awesome. (Nehemiah 4:14)

I will not take revenge, but leave room for the wrath of God, for it is written: "Vengeance is Mine; I will repay," says the Lord. I will not be overcome by evil, but overcome evil with good. (Romans 12:19,21)

Lord, I thank You for the resurrected life that You are preparing for Your children. I thank You for the truth that sets me free. I will keep my confidence in You and overcome evil with good.

DAY 225

CONTINUING STEADFASTLY IN PRAYER

❧

LORD, I DRAW NEAR TO YOU

Lord, I give thanks for Your greatness, Your goodness, and Your love, and I now draw near to enjoy Your presence.

Not to us, O Lord, not to us
But to Your name give glory,
Because of Your lovingkindness and truth. (Psalm 115:1)

Praise the Lord!
For it is good to sing praises to our God,
Because praise is pleasant and beautiful. (Psalm 147:1)

Take a moment to consider God's awesome majesty and thank Him that He loves you and wants an intimate relationship with you.

THANK YOU, LORD, FOR WHAT YOU HAVE DONE

You are the Lord; You do not change. (Malachi 3:6)

Blessed be the Lord God, the God of Israel, Who alone does wonderful things. (Psalm 72:18)

LORD, I LISTEN TO YOUR WORDS OF TRUTH

Sin shall not be my master, because I am not under law, but under grace. I have been set free from sin and have become a slave of righteousness. (Romans 6:14,18)

LORD, I RESPOND TO YOUR INSTRUCTION

Lord, make me to know my end and what is the measure of my days; let me know how fleeting is my life. (Psalm 39:4)

I will rejoice in hope, persevere in affliction, and continue steadfastly in prayer. (Romans 12:12)

❧

Lord, I thank You that You do not change and that You alone do wonderful things. I thank You that I am not under law, but under grace. I will live and persevere in light of eternity and continue steadfastly in prayer.

235
❧

DAY 226

SEEKING THE BEST INTERESTS OF OTHERS

❧

LORD, I DRAW NEAR TO YOU

I am grateful to You, O God, for the blessing of Your forgiveness. I thank You that in Christ, You set me free from the guilt of the past and give me hope for the future.

The refining pot is for silver and the furnace for gold,
But the Lord tests the hearts. (Proverbs 17:3)

You have set our iniquities before You,
Our secret sins in the light of Your presence. (Psalm 90:8)

Take a moment to ask the Spirit to search your heart and reveal any areas of unconfessed sin. Acknowledge these to the Lord and thank Him for His forgiveness.

THANK YOU, LORD, FOR WHAT YOU HAVE DONE

236
❧

I will recall to mind the former things, those of long ago; You are God, and there is no other; You are God, and there is none like You. (Isaiah 46:9)

The whole family in heaven and on earth derives its name from the God and Father of our Lord Jesus Christ. (Ephesians 3:14-15)

LORD, I LISTEN TO YOUR WORDS OF TRUTH

I was washed, I was sanctified, I was justified in the name of the Lord Jesus Christ and by the Spirit of our God. (1 Corinthians 6:11)

LORD, I RESPOND TO YOUR INSTRUCTION

We who are strong ought to bear the weaknesses of those who are not strong, and not to please ourselves. Each of us should please his neighbor for his good, to build him up. (Romans 15:1-2)

❧

Lord, I thank You that there is none like You and that the whole family in heaven and earth derives its name from You. I thank You that I have been washed, sanctified, and justified in Christ. I will consider the needs and best interests of others above my own.

DAY 227

ENDURING ALL THINGS FOR CHRIST'S SAKE

❧

LORD, I DRAW NEAR TO YOU

I praise You, Lord, that You are intimately acquainted with my ways and that You always love me and have my best interests at heart.

May I fight the good fight of faith and lay hold of the eternal life to which I was called when I made the good confession in the presence of many witnesses. In the sight of God, Who gives life to all things, and of Christ Jesus, Who testified the good confession before Pontius Pilate, may I keep this command without blemish or reproach until the appearing of our Lord Jesus Christ, which God will bring about in His own time. (1 Timothy 6:12-15)

Take a moment to offer this day to the Lord and ask Him for the grace to grow in your knowledge and love for Him.

THANK YOU, LORD, FOR WHAT YOU HAVE DONE

You are the Lord, that is Your name. You will not give Your glory to another, or Your praise to idols. (Isaiah 42:8)

LORD, I LISTEN TO YOUR WORDS OF TRUTH

The love of Christ compels me, because I am convinced that One died for all, and therefore all died. And He died for all, that those who live should no longer live for themselves but for Him Who died for them and was raised again. (2 Corinthians 5:14-15)

LORD, I RESPOND TO YOUR INSTRUCTION

I am hard pressed on every side, but not crushed; perplexed, but not in despair; persecuted, but not forsaken; struck down, but not destroyed; always carrying about in my body the death of Jesus, so that the life of Jesus may also be revealed in my body. For we who live are always being delivered over to death for Jesus' sake, so that His life may be revealed in our mortal body. (2 Corinthians 4:8-11)

❧

Lord, I thank You that You are worthy of all glory and that You have complete dominion over all things. I thank You for the love of Christ who died for me. Help me not to despair in my adversities but to endure all things for Your sake.

DAY 228

BEING STRENGTHENED IN EVERY GOOD WORK

❧

LORD, I DRAW NEAR TO YOU

As I approach Your throne of grace today, I am grateful that You care about the things that concern me and that You want me to offer them up to You.

Whatever I do, may I do all to the glory of God. (1 Corinthians 10:31)

May everything I do be done in love. (1 Corinthians 16:14)

Take a moment to share your personal needs with God, including your physical, emotional, relational, and spiritual concerns.

THANK YOU, LORD, FOR WHAT YOU HAVE DONE

Your name, O Lord, endures forever, Your renown, O Lord, through all generations. (Psalm 135:13)

238

The Lord made the earth by His power; He established the world by His wisdom and stretched out the heavens by His understanding. (Jeremiah 51:15)

LORD, I LISTEN TO YOUR WORDS OF TRUTH

Godly sorrow brings repentance that leads to salvation and leaves no regret, but worldly sorrow brings death. (2 Corinthians 7:10)

LORD, I RESPOND TO YOUR INSTRUCTION

I will guard my heart with all diligence, for out of it flow the issues of life. (Proverbs 4:23)

May our Lord Jesus Christ Himself and God our Father, Who has loved us and has given us eternal consolation and good hope by grace, comfort our hearts and strengthen us in every good work and word. (2 Thessalonians 2:16-17)

❧

Lord, I thank You for the glory of Your name and for creating the heavens and earth through Your power and wisdom. I thank You that godly sorrow leads to repentance. I will guard my heart and be strengthened in every good work and deed.

DAY 229

DOING THE WILL OF GOD

~

LORD, I DRAW NEAR TO YOU

Lord, You have invited me to pray for the needs of others, and since You desire what is best for them, I take this opportunity to bring these requests to You.

With all prayer and petition, we should pray always in the Spirit, and to this end we should be watchful with all perseverance and petition for all the saints. (Ephesians 6:18)

I pray that words may be given to me, that I may open my mouth boldly to make known the mystery of the gospel. (Ephesians 6:19)

Take a moment to lift up the needs of your family and friends, and to offer up any additional burdens for others that the Lord brings to mind.

THANK YOU, LORD, FOR WHAT YOU HAVE DONE

My flesh trembles for fear of You; I stand in awe of Your judgments. (Psalm 119:120)

239
~

You form the light and create darkness; You bring prosperity and create disaster; You, the Lord, do all these things. (Isaiah 45:7)

LORD, I LISTEN TO YOUR WORDS OF TRUTH

I am no longer a stranger and alien, but a fellow citizen with God's people and a member of God's household, built on the foundation of the apostles and prophets, with Christ Jesus Himself as the chief cornerstone. (Ephesians 2:19-20)

LORD, I RESPOND TO YOUR INSTRUCTION

I will obey those who are in authority over me with fear and trembling and with sincerity of heart, as to Christ; not with external service as a pleaser of men, but as a slave of Christ, doing the will of God from my heart. With good will I will serve as to the Lord and not to men, knowing that I will receive back from the Lord whatever good I do. (Ephesians 6:5-8)

~

Lord, I thank You for Your awesome judgments and for Your sovereign authority over all things. I thank You that You have made me a member of Your household. I will render service to others in Your name and do Your will from my heart.

DAY 230

LEARNING THROUGH MY TRIALS

～❧～

LORD, I DRAW NEAR TO YOU

Lord, I want Your Word to be deeply implanted in me so that I will know the truth and be able to express it in the way I live.

Remember the wonderful works He has done,
His miracles, and the judgments He pronounced. (1 Chronicles 16:12)

Take a moment to affirm the truth of these words from Scripture and ask God to make them a growing reality in your life.

THANK YOU, LORD, FOR WHAT YOU HAVE DONE

Blessed be the Lord, the God of Israel, from everlasting to everlasting.
Praise the Lord. (Psalm 106:48)

LORD, I LISTEN TO YOUR WORDS OF TRUTH

The Father has qualified me to share in the inheritance of the saints in the light. For He has rescued me from the dominion of darkness and brought me into the kingdom of His beloved Son, in Whom I have redemption, the forgiveness of sins. (Colossians 1:12-14)

LORD, I RESPOND TO YOUR INSTRUCTION

I will consider it all joy whenever I fall into various trials, knowing that the testing of my faith produces endurance. And I will let endurance finish its work, so that I may be mature and complete, lacking in nothing. (James 1:2-4)

I will fight the good fight, finish the race, and keep the faith, so that there will be laid up for me the crown of righteousness, which the Lord, the righteous Judge, will award to me on that day; and not only to me, but also to all who have longed for His appearing. (2 Timothy 4:7-8)

～❧～

Lord, I thank You for Your blessed and everlasting name and for qualifying me to share an inheritance in the kingdom of Your beloved Son. Help me to learn endurance through my trials and finish my race well.

DAY 231

ASKING FOR WISDOM

LORD, I DRAW NEAR TO YOU

O Lord, I am deeply grateful for Your wonderful acts, for Your abundant promises, and for the gift of my relationship with You through the merits of Christ.

Blessed be the Lord; day by day He bears our burdens,
The God of our salvation.
Our God is the God of salvation,
And to God the Lord belongs escape from death. (Psalm 68:19-20)

Take a moment to express your gratitude for the many blessings that you have received from the Lord.

THANK YOU, LORD, FOR WHAT YOU HAVE DONE

Who can express the mighty acts of the Lord or fully declare His praise? (Psalm 106:2)

LORD, I LISTEN TO YOUR WORDS OF TRUTH

When I was dead in my trespasses and in the uncircumcision of my flesh, God made me alive with Christ. He forgave me all my trespasses, having canceled the written code, with its regulations, that was against me and was contrary to me; He took it away, nailing it to the cross. And having disarmed the powers and authorities, He made a public spectacle of them, triumphing over them by the cross. (Colossians 2:13-15)

LORD, I RESPOND TO YOUR INSTRUCTION

If I lack wisdom, I should ask of God, who gives generously to all without reproach, and it will be given to me. (James 1:5)

I will watch carefully how I walk, not as the unwise but as wise, making the most of every opportunity, because the days are evil. I will not be foolish, but understand what the will of the Lord is. (Ephesians 5:15-17)

Lord, I thank You for Your mighty acts and for forgiving my trespasses and making me alive in Christ. As I ask for Your wisdom, help me to understand Your will.

DAY 232

DWELLING IN SAFETY

LORD, I DRAW NEAR TO YOU

Lord, I give thanks for Your greatness, Your goodness, and Your love, and I now draw near to enjoy Your presence.

Who has directed the Spirit of the Lord,
Or instructed Him as His counselor?
Whom did the Lord consult to enlighten Him,
And who taught Him the path of justice?
Who taught Him knowledge
Or showed Him the way of understanding?
Surely the nations are like a drop in a bucket
And are regarded as dust on the scales;
He weighs the islands as though they were fine dust.
Before Him all the nations are as nothing;
They are regarded by Him as less than nothing and worthless.
To whom, then, will I compare God?
Or what likeness will I compare with Him? (Isaiah 40:13-15,17-18)

242

Take a moment to consider God's awesome majesty and thank Him that He loves you and wants an intimate relationship with you.

THANK YOU, LORD, FOR WHAT YOU HAVE DONE

God took Abram outside and said, "Look up at the heavens and count the stars if you are able to count them." Then He said to him, "So shall your descendants be." And Abram believed in the Lord, and He credited it to him as righteousness. (Genesis 15:5-6)

LORD, I LISTEN TO YOUR WORDS OF TRUTH

I will both lie down in peace and sleep, for You alone, O Lord, make me dwell in safety. (Psalm 4:8)

LORD, I RESPOND TO YOUR INSTRUCTION

I will be careful not to forget the Lord my God by failing to observe His commandments, His ordinances, and His statutes. (Deuteronomy 8:11)

Lord, I thank You that You are the God of Abraham and that You are faithful to the promises that he received and believed. I thank You for making me dwell in safety. I will be faithful to You.

DAY 233

LEARNING TO FEAR GOD

❧

LORD, I DRAW NEAR TO YOU

I am grateful to You, O God, for the blessing of Your forgiveness. I thank You that in Christ, You set me free from the guilt of the past and give me hope for the future.

There is not a righteous man on earth who continually does good
And never sins. (Ecclesiastes 7:20)

Take a moment to ask the Spirit to search your heart and reveal any areas of unconfessed sin. Acknowledge these to the Lord and thank Him for His forgiveness.

THANK YOU, LORD, FOR WHAT YOU HAVE DONE

The Lord appeared to Abram and said to him, "I am El Shaddai; walk before Me and be blameless. And I will confirm My covenant between Me and you and will greatly increase your numbers." Then Abram fell on his face, and God talked with him, saying, "As for Me, My covenant is with you, and you will be the father of many nations. No longer will you be called Abram; your name will be Abraham, for I have made you a father of many nations. I will make you exceedingly fruitful; I will make nations of you, and kings will come from you. And I will establish My covenant as an everlasting covenant between Me and you and your descendants after you for the generations to come, to be your God and the God of your descendants after you." (Genesis 17:1-7)

243
❧

LORD, I LISTEN TO YOUR WORDS OF TRUTH

Who is the man that fears the Lord? He will instruct him in the way he should choose. (Psalm 25:12)

LORD, I RESPOND TO YOUR INSTRUCTION

I will learn to fear You all the days I live on the earth and teach Your words to my children. (Deuteronomy 4:10)

❧

Lord, I thank You for calling Abraham and his descendants to walk before You and for the covenant promises You made. Instruct me in the way I should go, that I may learn to fear You and teach Your words to others.

DAY 234

LAYING UP GOD'S WORDS IN MY HEART

❧

LORD, I DRAW NEAR TO YOU

I praise You, Lord, that You are intimately acquainted with my ways and that You always love me and have my best interests at heart.

By Your grace, I want to observe Your judgments and keep Your statutes, to walk in them; You are the Lord my God. May I keep Your statutes and Your judgments, by which a man may live if he does them; You are the Lord. (Leviticus 18:4-5)

Take a moment to offer this day to the Lord and ask Him for the grace to grow in your knowledge and love for Him.

THANK YOU, LORD, FOR WHAT YOU HAVE DONE

244 ❧

The Lord said to Abraham, "By Myself I have sworn, that because you have not withheld your son, your only son, I will surely bless you and make your descendants as numerous as the stars in the sky and as the sand on the seashore. Your descendants will take possession of the cities of their enemies, and through your offspring all nations on earth will be blessed, because you have obeyed My voice." (Genesis 22:16-18)

LORD, I LISTEN TO YOUR WORDS OF TRUTH

In You, O Lord, I have taken refuge; let me never be ashamed; deliver me in Your righteousness. Since You are my rock and my fortress, for Your name's sake lead me and guide me. Into Your hands I commit my spirit; redeem me, O Lord, God of truth. (Psalm 31:1,3,5)

LORD, I RESPOND TO YOUR INSTRUCTION

I will lay up Your words in my heart and in my soul and teach them to my children, talking about them when I sit in my house and when I walk along the way and when I lie down and when I rise up. (Deuteronomy 11:18-19)

❧

Lord, I thank You for the covenant You made with Abraham and for the widespread blessings it has produced. I thank You for leading and guiding me. Help me to lay up Your words in my heart and teach them to others.

DAY 235

WALKING UPRIGHTLY

❧

LORD, I DRAW NEAR TO YOU

As I approach Your throne of grace today, I am grateful that You care about the things that concern me and that You want me to offer them up to You.

In Christ Jesus my Lord, I have boldness and confident access through faith in Him. (Ephesians 3:12)

Just as I received Christ Jesus the Lord, so let me walk in Him, rooted and built up in Him, and established in the faith, as I was taught, and abounding in thanksgiving. (Colossians 2:6-7)

Take a moment to share your personal needs with God, including your physical, emotional, relational, and spiritual concerns.

THANK YOU, LORD, FOR WHAT YOU HAVE DONE

The Lord is righteous; He loves righteousness; the upright will see His face. (Psalm 11:7)

245
❧

LORD, I LISTEN TO YOUR WORDS OF TRUTH

I love You, O Lord, my strength. The Lord is my rock and my fortress and my deliverer; my God is my rock, in Whom I take refuge. He is my shield and the horn of my salvation, my stronghold. I call upon the Lord, Who is worthy of praise, and I am saved from my enemies. (Psalm 18:1-3)

LORD, I RESPOND TO YOUR INSTRUCTION

Lord, who may dwell in Your tabernacle? Who may live on Your holy mountain? He who walks uprightly and works righteousness and speaks the truth in his heart; he does not slander with his tongue nor does evil to his neighbor nor takes up a reproach against his friend; he despises the reprobate but honors those who fear the Lord. He keeps his oath even when it hurts, lends his money without interest, and does not accept a bribe against the innocent. He who does these things will never be shaken. (Psalm 15:1-5)

❧

Lord, I thank You for Your righteousness and for being my rock and my fortress and my deliverer. Help me to walk uprightly, work righteousness, and speak the truth in my heart.

DAY 236

LIVING TOGETHER IN UNITY

LORD, I DRAW NEAR TO YOU

Lord, You have invited me to pray for the needs of others, and since You desire what is best for them, I take this opportunity to bring these requests to You.

May we conduct ourselves in a manner worthy of the gospel of Christ, standing firm in one spirit with other believers, with one mind striving together for the faith of the gospel. (Philippians 1:27)

May our hearts be encouraged, being joined together in love, so that we may have the riches of the full assurance of understanding. (Colossians 2:2)

Take a moment to lift up the needs of your family and friends, and to offer up any additional burdens for others that the Lord brings to mind.

THANK YOU, LORD, FOR WHAT YOU HAVE DONE

246

Be exalted, O God, above the heavens; let Your glory be over all the earth. For Your mercy reaches to the heavens, and Your faithfulness reaches to the clouds. (Psalm 57:5,10)

The Lord appoints the number of the stars and calls them each by name. (Psalm 147:4)

LORD, I LISTEN TO YOUR WORDS OF TRUTH

Let those who love the Lord hate evil. He preserves the souls of His saints and delivers them from the hand of the wicked. Light is sown for the righteous and gladness for the upright in heart. (Psalm 97:10-11)

LORD, I RESPOND TO YOUR INSTRUCTION

How good and pleasant it is when brothers live together in unity! (Psalm 133:1)

May those who hope in You not be ashamed because of me, O Lord God of hosts; may those who seek You not be dishonored because of me, O God of Israel. (Psalm 69:6)

Lord, I thank You that You are exalted above the heavens and intimately involved with Your creation. I thank You that You preserve the souls of Your saints. I will seek unity and mutual edification with other believers.

DAY 237

PUTTING JESUS FIRST

LORD, I DRAW NEAR TO YOU

Lord, I want Your Word to be deeply implanted in me so that I will know the truth and be able to express it in the way I live.

For those who revere Your name, the Sun of righteousness will rise with healing in His wings. And they will go out and leap like calves released from the stall. (Malachi 4:2)

Take a moment to affirm the truth of these words from Scripture and ask God to make them a growing reality in your life.

THANK YOU, LORD, FOR WHAT YOU HAVE DONE

I will enter the Lord's gates with thanksgiving and His courts with praise; I will give thanks to Him and bless His name. For the Lord is good and His lovingkindness endures forever; His faithfulness continues through all generations. (Psalm 100:4-5)

Joshua said to Israel, "Now I am about to go the way of all the earth. You know with all your hearts and souls that not one of all the good promises the Lord your God gave you has failed. Every promise has been fulfilled; not one has failed." (Joshua 23:14)

247

LORD, I LISTEN TO YOUR WORDS OF TRUTH

If anyone comes to You and does not hate his father and mother, his wife and children, his brothers and sisters—yes, even his own life—he cannot be Your disciple. And whoever does not carry his cross and follow You cannot be Your disciple. (Luke 14:26-27)

LORD, I RESPOND TO YOUR INSTRUCTION

I will not be like the man who did not make God his strength but trusted in the abundance of his wealth and strengthened himself in his evil desires. (Psalm 52:7)

Lord, I thank You for Your goodness, lovingkindness, and faithfulness and for fulfilling Your good promises to Your people. I will put Jesus first in my life and make You my strength.

DAY 238

LABORING IN GOD'S STRENGTH

LORD, I DRAW NEAR TO YOU

O Lord, I am deeply grateful for Your wonderful acts, for Your abundant promises, and for the gift of my relationship with You through the merits of Christ.

Oh give thanks to the Lord, call upon His name;
Make His deeds known among the nations.
Sing to Him, sing praises to Him;
Tell of all His wonders.
Glory in His holy name;
Let the hearts of those who seek the Lord rejoice. (Psalm 105:1-3)

Take a moment to express your gratitude for the many blessings that you have received from the Lord.

THANK YOU, LORD, FOR WHAT YOU HAVE DONE

248

Your Word is settled in heaven forever, O Lord. Your faithfulness continues through all generations; You established the earth, and it stands. They continue to this day according to Your ordinances, for all things serve You. (Psalm 119:89-91)

Blessed is the Lord, who has not left His people without a kinsman-redeemer. (Ruth 4:14)

LORD, I LISTEN TO YOUR WORDS OF TRUTH

A natural man does not receive the things of the Spirit, for they are foolishness to him, and he cannot understand them, because they are spiritually discerned. "For who has known the mind of the Lord that he may instruct Him?" But we have the mind of Christ. (1 Corinthians 2:14,16)

LORD, I RESPOND TO YOUR INSTRUCTION

Unless the Lord builds the house, its builders labor in vain. Unless the Lord guards the city, the watchmen stay awake in vain. (Psalm 127:1)

Lord, I thank You for the faithfulness of Your Word and for Your Holy Spirit Who illuminates my mind. Help me to labor in Your strength.

DAY 239

RECEIVING GOD'S GRACE

❧

LORD, I DRAW NEAR TO YOU

Lord, I give thanks for Your greatness, Your goodness, and Your love, and I now draw near to enjoy Your presence.

The Lord is the true God;
He is the living God and the everlasting King.
At His wrath, the earth trembles,
And the nations cannot endure His indignation. (Jeremiah 10:10)

Take a moment to consider God's awesome majesty and thank Him that He loves you and wants an intimate relationship with you.

THANK YOU, LORD, FOR WHAT YOU HAVE DONE

The Lord longs to be gracious and rises to show compassion. For the Lord is a God of justice; blessed are all those who wait for Him! (Isaiah 30:18)

249
❧

LORD, I LISTEN TO YOUR WORDS OF TRUTH

May the God of my Lord Jesus Christ, the Father of glory, give me a spirit of wisdom and of revelation in the full knowledge of Him, and may the eyes of my heart be enlightened, in order that I may know what is the hope of His calling, what are the riches of His glorious inheritance in the saints, and what is the incomparable greatness of His power toward us who believe. (Ephesians 1:17-19)

LORD, I RESPOND TO YOUR INSTRUCTION

There is neither Jew nor Greek; there is neither slave nor free; there is neither male nor female, for we are all one in Christ Jesus. (Galatians 3:28)

❧

Lord, I thank You that You delight in showing grace and compassion and for giving me a spirit of wisdom and revelation in the knowledge of You. I will treat others with fairness and dignity.

DAY 240

LIVING A HOLY LIFE

LORD, I DRAW NEAR TO YOU

I am grateful to You, O God, for the blessing of Your forgiveness. I thank You that in Christ, You set me free from the guilt of the past and give me hope for the future.

May I produce fruit worthy of repentance. (Matthew 3:8)

Take a moment to ask the Spirit to search your heart and reveal any areas of unconfessed sin. Acknowledge these to the Lord and thank Him for His forgiveness.

THANK YOU, LORD, FOR WHAT YOU HAVE DONE

My soul magnifies the Lord and my spirit rejoices in God my Savior, for the Mighty One has done great things for me, and holy is His name. His mercy is on those who fear Him, from generation to generation. (Luke 1:46-47, 49-50)

I will praise You forever for what You have done; I will hope in Your name, for it is good. I will praise You in the presence of Your saints. (Psalm 52:9)

LORD, I LISTEN TO YOUR WORDS OF TRUTH

I know that I abide in Christ, and He in me, because He has given me of His Spirit. (1 John 4:13)

LORD, I RESPOND TO YOUR INSTRUCTION

This is the will of God, my sanctification, that I abstain from immorality and learn to possess my own vessel in sanctification and honor. For God did not call me to be impure, but to live a holy life. (1 Thessalonians 4:3-4,7)

If someone is caught in a trespass, we who are spiritual should restore him in a spirit of gentleness, considering ourselves, lest we also be tempted. (Galatians 6:1)

Lord, I thank You for the great things You have done for me and for Your mercy on those who fear You. I thank You for giving me Your Holy Spirit. Help me to walk in purity and not succumb to temptation.

DAY 241

WEIGHING MY MOTIVES

LORD, I DRAW NEAR TO YOU

I praise You, Lord, that You are intimately acquainted with my ways and that You always love me and have my best interests at heart.

Teach me to number my days,
That I may gain a heart of wisdom. (Psalm 90:12)

May I let my eyes look straight ahead,
And fix my gaze straight before me.
May I ponder the path of my feet
So that all my ways will be established.
May I not turn to the right or to the left
But keep my foot from evil. (Proverbs 4:25-27)

Take a moment to offer this day to the Lord and ask Him for the grace to grow in your knowledge and love for Him.

THANK YOU, LORD, FOR WHAT YOU HAVE DONE

251

In Christ are hidden all the treasures of wisdom and knowledge. (Colossians 2:3)

The Lord gave the knowledge of the mysteries of the kingdom of God to His disciples, but to others He spoke in parables, that "seeing they may not see and hearing they may not understand." (Luke 8:10)

LORD, I LISTEN TO YOUR WORDS OF TRUTH

The righteous shall rejoice in the Lord and trust in Him, and all the upright in heart will glory. (Psalm 64:10)

LORD, I RESPOND TO YOUR INSTRUCTION

He who trusts in his riches will fall, but the righteous will flourish like a green leaf. (Proverbs 11:28)

All a man's ways are pure in his own eyes, but the Lord weighs the motives. (Proverbs 16:2)

Lord, I thank You for the treasures of wisdom and knowledge that are in Christ and for His revelation of the mysteries of Your kingdom. I thank You that the upright in heart will glory. I will trust in You and not in my own resources.

DAY 242
REMEMBERING GOD'S BENEFITS

LORD, I DRAW NEAR TO YOU

As I approach Your throne of grace today, I am grateful that You care about the things that concern me and that You want me to offer them up to You.

This is the will of God, my sanctification, that I abstain from immorality and learn to possess my own vessel in sanctification and honor. For God did not call me to be impure, but to live a holy life. (1 Thessalonians 4:3-4,7)

Take a moment to share your personal needs with God, including your physical, emotional, relational, and spiritual concerns.

THANK YOU, LORD, FOR WHAT YOU HAVE DONE

Hallelujah! Salvation and glory and power belong to our God, because His judgments are true and righteous. (Revelation 19:1-2)

The mystery that has been kept hidden for ages and generations is now disclosed to the saints. To them God has chosen to make known among the Gentiles the glorious riches of this mystery, which is Christ in you, the hope of glory. (Colossians 1:26-27)

LORD, I LISTEN TO YOUR WORDS OF TRUTH

Bless the Lord, O my soul, and forget not all His benefits; Who forgives all your iniquities and heals all your diseases; Who redeems your life from the pit and crowns you with love and compassion; Who satisfies your desires with good things, so that your youth is renewed like the eagle's. (Psalm 103:2-5)

LORD, I RESPOND TO YOUR INSTRUCTION

I have been born again, not of perishable seed, but of imperishable, through the living and abiding Word of God. Therefore, I will put away all malice and all guile and hypocrisy and envy and all slander. (1 Peter 1:23; 2:1)

Lord, I thank You that salvation, glory, and power belong to You and that You have revealed the mystery of Christ to Your people. I thank You for Your many benefits. Help me to put away the things that displease You.

DAY 243

FEARING GOD MORE THAN MEN

LORD, I DRAW NEAR TO YOU

Lord, You have invited me to pray for the needs of others, and since You desire what is best for them, I take this opportunity to bring these requests to You.

We should devote ourselves to prayer, being watchful in it with thanksgiving. (Colossians 4:2)

We should always thank God for other believers, mentioning them in our prayers. (1 Thessalonians 1:2)

Take a moment to lift up the needs of your family and friends, and to offer up any additional burdens for others that the Lord brings to mind.

THANK YOU, LORD, FOR WHAT YOU HAVE DONE

All authority in heaven and on earth has been given to the Son of God. (Matthew 28:18)

253

Christ is the end of the law for righteousness to everyone who believes. (Romans 10:4)

LORD, I LISTEN TO YOUR WORDS OF TRUTH

I will fear God and give Him glory, because the hour of His judgment has come. I will worship Him Who made the heavens and the earth, the sea and the springs of water. (Revelation 14:7)

LORD, I RESPOND TO YOUR INSTRUCTION

As one who knows righteousness, who has Your law in my heart, I will not fear the reproach of men or be terrified by their revilings. (Isaiah 51:7)

I will fear God and keep His commandments, for this applies to every person. (Ecclesiastes 12:13)

Lord, I thank You that all authority rests in Christ and that He provides righteousness to all who trust in Him. I thank You that You will judge the world with perfect justice. I will fear You more than men and keep Your commandments.

DAY 244

PUTTING AWAY FALSEHOOD

LORD, I DRAW NEAR TO YOU

Lord, I want Your Word to be deeply implanted in me so that I will know the truth and be able to express it in the way I live.

God will keep me strong to the end, so that I will be blameless on the day of our Lord Jesus Christ. God is faithful, through Whom I was called into fellowship with His Son, Jesus Christ our Lord. (1 Corinthians 1:8-9)

Take a moment to affirm the truth of these words from Scripture and ask God to make them a growing reality in your life.

THANK YOU, LORD, FOR WHAT YOU HAVE DONE

You are the Lord, and there is no Savior besides You. From ancient days You are He, and no one can deliver out of Your hand; You act, and who can reverse it? (Isaiah 43:11,13)

Christ died and returned to life, that He might be the Lord of both the dead and the living. (Romans 14:9)

LORD, I LISTEN TO YOUR WORDS OF TRUTH

I am not in the flesh but in the Spirit, since the Spirit of God lives in me. And if anyone does not have the Spirit of Christ, he does not belong to Him. (Romans 8:9)

LORD, I RESPOND TO YOUR INSTRUCTION

I will put away perversity from my mouth and keep corrupt talk far from my lips. (Proverbs 4:24)

Each of us must put off falsehood and speak truthfully to his neighbor, for we are members of one another. (Ephesians 4:25)

Lord, I thank You that You are the only Savior and Lord of both the dead and the living. I thank You that Your Spirit lives in me. Help me to put away falsehood and speak in truth.

DAY 245

RECEIVING THE SPIRIT OF ADOPTION

LORD, I DRAW NEAR TO YOU

O Lord, I am deeply grateful for Your wonderful acts, for Your abundant promises, and for the gift of my relationship with You through the merits of Christ.

Praise the Lord!
I will thank the Lord with all my heart
In the council of the upright and in the assembly.
Great are the works of the Lord;
They are pondered by all who delight in them.
Splendid and majestic is His work,
And His righteousness endures forever.
He has caused His wonderful acts to be remembered;
The Lord is gracious and compassionate. (Psalm 111:1-4)

Take a moment to express your gratitude for the many blessings that you have received from the Lord.

255

THANK YOU, LORD, FOR WHAT YOU HAVE DONE

Though the Lord is on high, yet He looks upon the lowly, but the proud He knows from afar. (Psalm 138:6)

Greater love has no one than this, that he lay down his life for his friends. (John 15:13)

LORD, I LISTEN TO YOUR WORDS OF TRUTH

I did not receive a spirit of slavery again to fear, but I received the Spirit of adoption by whom I cry, "Abba, Father." The Spirit Himself testifies with my spirit that I am a child of God. (Romans 8:15-16)

LORD, I RESPOND TO YOUR INSTRUCTION

Blessed are those who hunger and thirst for righteousness, for they shall be satisfied. (Matthew 5:6)

Lord, I thank You for looking upon the lowly and for laying down Your life for Your friends. I thank You that I have received the Spirit of adoption as Your child. Continually, I will seek Your righteousness and purpose to be more like Christ.

DAY 246

BEING CALLED APART FOR GOD

❧

LORD, I DRAW NEAR TO YOU

Lord, I give thanks for Your greatness, Your goodness, and Your love, and I now draw near to enjoy Your presence.

Do you not know? Have you not heard?
The everlasting God, the Lord, the Creator of the ends of the earth,
Does not grow tired or weary.
No one can fathom His understanding. (Isaiah 40:28)

You, O Lord, remain forever;
Your throne endures from generation to generation. (Lamentations 5:19)

Take a moment to consider God's awesome majesty and thank Him that He loves you and wants an intimate relationship with you.

THANK YOU, LORD, FOR WHAT YOU HAVE DONE

You are the righteous God, who searches the hearts and secret thoughts. (Psalm 7:9)

The Son of Man has authority on earth to forgive sins. (Matthew 9:6)

LORD, I LISTEN TO YOUR WORDS OF TRUTH

I have been sanctified in Christ Jesus and called to be a saint, together with all those everywhere who call on the name of our Lord Jesus Christ, their Lord and ours. (1 Corinthians 1:2)

LORD, I RESPOND TO YOUR INSTRUCTION

Reckless words pierce like a sword, but the tongue of the wise brings healing. (Proverbs 12:18)

We should let the Word of Christ dwell in us richly as we teach and admonish one another with all wisdom and as we sing psalms, hymns, and spiritual songs with gratitude in our hearts to God. (Colossians 3:16)

❧

Lord, I thank You that You search the secret thoughts and forgive our deepest sins. I thank You for calling me apart for Yourself, and I pray that my words would bring healing and nourishment to those who hear them.

DAY 247

STAYING FERVENT IN SPIRIT

◆

LORD, I DRAW NEAR TO YOU

I am grateful to You, O God, for the blessing of Your forgiveness. I thank You that in Christ, You set me free from the guilt of the past and give me hope for the future.

My little children, I write these things to you that you may not sin. But if anyone sins, we have an Advocate with the Father, Jesus Christ, the Righteous. And He is the propitiation for our sins, and not for ours only but also for the whole world. (1 John 2:1-2)

Take a moment to ask the Spirit to search your heart and reveal any areas of unconfessed sin. Acknowledge these to the Lord and thank Him for His forgiveness.

THANK YOU, LORD, FOR WHAT YOU HAVE DONE

Yours, O Lord, is the greatness and the power and the glory and the victory and the majesty, for everything in heaven and earth is Yours. Yours, O Lord, is the kingdom, and You are exalted as head over all. Both riches and honor come from You, and You are the ruler of all things. In Your hand are power and might to exalt and to give strength to all. Therefore, my God, I give You thanks and praise Your glorious name. All things come from You, and I can only give You what comes from Your hand. (1 Chronicles 29:11-14)

257

◆

LORD, I LISTEN TO YOUR WORDS OF TRUTH

He who makes me stand firm in Christ and anointed me is God, Who also sealed me and gave me the Spirit in my heart as a deposit. (2 Corinthians 1:21-22)

LORD, I RESPOND TO YOUR INSTRUCTION

I will not be lacking in zeal, but I will keep fervent in spirit, serving the Lord. (Romans 12:11)

The kingdom of God is not a matter of eating and drinking, but of righteousness and peace and joy in the Holy Spirit. (Romans 14:17)

◆

Lord, I thank You for Your immeasurable greatness, power, glory, and majesty and for making me stand firm in Christ. Help me to stay fervent in spirit, and live in righteousness, peace, and joy in the Holy Spirit.

DAY 248

USING MY TONGUE WISELY

LORD, I DRAW NEAR TO YOU

I praise You, Lord, that You are intimately acquainted with my ways and that You always love me and have my best interests at heart.

May I watch and pray so that I will not fall into temptation; the spirit is willing, but the flesh is weak. (Matthew 26:41)

Take a moment to offer this day to the Lord and ask Him for the grace to grow in your knowledge and love for Him.

THANK YOU, LORD, FOR WHAT YOU HAVE DONE

There is but one God, the Father, from Whom all things came and for Whom I live; and there is but one Lord, Jesus Christ, through Whom all things came and through Whom I live. (1 Corinthians 8:6)

The Lord told the apostles, "You will receive power when the Holy Spirit comes upon you; and you will be My witnesses in Jerusalem, and in all Judea and Samaria, and to the ends of the earth." (Acts 1:8)

LORD, I LISTEN TO YOUR WORDS OF TRUTH

I am not competent in myself to claim anything for myself, but my competence comes from God. He has made me competent as a minister of a new covenant, not of the letter, but of the Spirit; for the letter kills, but the Spirit gives life. (2 Corinthians 3:5-6)

LORD, I RESPOND TO YOUR INSTRUCTION

A gentle answer turns away wrath, but a harsh word stirs up anger. The tongue of the wise uses knowledge rightly, but the mouth of the fool pours out folly. (Proverbs 15:1-2)

Since I have God's promises, I will cleanse myself from all pollution of body and spirit, perfecting holiness in the fear of God. (2 Corinthians 7:1)

Lord, I thank You that all things come from You and through You and that You have empowered me through Your indwelling Spirit. I thank You for making me competent to minister. Help me to use my tongue wisely and to keep myself clean as I seek Your holiness.

DAY 249

LIVING BY GOD'S POWER

~

As I approach Your throne of grace today, I am grateful that You care about the things that concern me and that You want me to offer them up to You.

As I have been instructed how I ought to walk and to please God, may I follow Paul's exhortation in the Lord Jesus to do this more and more. (1 Thessalonians 4:1)

May I examine all things, hold fast to the good, and abstain from every form of evil. (1 Thessalonians 5:21-22)

Take a moment to share your personal needs with God, including your physical, emotional, relational, and spiritual concerns.

THANK YOU, LORD, FOR WHAT YOU HAVE DONE

Jesus is Your beloved Son in Whom You are well pleased. (Matthew 3:17; Mark 1:11; Luke 3:22)

259
~

The wages of sin is death, but the gift of God is eternal life in Christ Jesus our Lord. (Romans 6:23)

LORD, I LISTEN TO YOUR WORDS OF TRUTH

Christ is not weak in dealing with us, but is powerful among us. For though He was crucified in weakness, yet He lives by the power of God. For we are weak in Him, yet by the power of God we will live with Him to serve others. (2 Corinthians 13:3-4)

LORD, I RESPOND TO YOUR INSTRUCTION

We should always thank God for other believers, mentioning them in our prayers. (1 Thessalonians 1:2)

We should always pray for other believers, that our God may count us worthy of His calling and fulfill every desire for goodness and every work of faith with power. (2 Thessalonians 1:11)

~

Lord, I thank You for Your beloved Son and for His provision of the gift of eternal life. I thank You that I can live by Your power. Help me to be worthy of my calling as I pray for other believers.

DAY 250

BECOMING GOD'S CHILD THROUGH FAITH

❧

LORD, I DRAW NEAR TO YOU

Lord, You have invited me to pray for the needs of others, and since You desire what is best for them, I take this opportunity to bring these requests to You.

Concerning brotherly love, we have been taught by God to love each other, and the Lord urges us to increase more and more.
(1 Thessalonians 4:9-10)

We should encourage one another and build each other up in Christ Jesus. (1 Thessalonians 5:11)

Take a moment to lift up the needs of your family and friends, and to offer up any other burdens for others that the Lord brings to mind.

THANK YOU, LORD, FOR WHAT YOU HAVE DONE

I will exalt You, my God and King; I will bless Your name for ever and ever. Every day I will bless You, and I will praise Your name for ever and ever. Great is the Lord and most worthy of praise; His greatness is unsearchable. (Psalm 145:1-3)

Shout for joy, O heavens! Rejoice, O earth! Break out into singing, O mountains! For the Lord has comforted His people and will have compassion on His afflicted. (Isaiah 49:13)

LORD, I LISTEN TO YOUR WORDS OF TRUTH

We are all sons of God through faith in Christ Jesus, for all of us who were baptized into Christ have clothed ourselves with Christ.
(Galatians 3:26-27)

LORD, I RESPOND TO YOUR INSTRUCTION

I will be strong in the grace that is in Christ Jesus. (2 Timothy 2:1)

I will pursue peace with all men and sanctification, without which no one will see the Lord. (Hebrews 12:14)

❧

Lord, I thank You that You are most worthy of praise and that You have comforted Your people. I thank You that I have become Your child through faith in Christ Jesus. Help me to be strong in His grace and pursue peace and holiness.

DAY 251

FULFILLING GOD'S PURPOSE

~❧~

LORD, I DRAW NEAR TO YOU

Lord, I want Your Word to be deeply implanted in me so that I will know the truth and be able to express it in the way I live.

I do not lose heart; even though my outward man is perishing, yet my inner man is being renewed day by day. For this light affliction which is momentary is working for me a far more exceeding and eternal weight of glory, while I do not look at the things which are seen but at the things which are unseen. For the things which are seen are temporary, but the things which are unseen are eternal. (2 Corinthians 4:16-18)

Take a moment to affirm the truth of these words from Scripture and ask God to make them a growing reality in your life.

THANK YOU, LORD, FOR WHAT YOU HAVE DONE

The Lord Most High is awesome, the great King over all the earth! God is the King of all the earth, and I will sing His praise. God reigns over the nations; God is seated on His holy throne. (Psalm 47:2,7-8)

Was it not You who dried up the sea, the waters of the great deep; who made the depths of the sea a road so that the redeemed might cross over? (Isaiah 51:10)

LORD, I LISTEN TO YOUR WORDS OF TRUTH

Have mercy on me, O God, have mercy on me, for in You my soul takes refuge. I will take refuge in the shadow of Your wings until destruction passes by. I cry out to God Most High, to God who fulfills His purpose for me. (Psalm 57:1-2)

LORD, I RESPOND TO YOUR INSTRUCTION

I will remember those who led me, who spoke the Word of God to me. I will consider the outcome of their way of life and imitate their faith. (Hebrews 13:7)

~❧~

Lord, I thank You that You are the awesome King over all the nations and that You redeemed Your people out of the hands of their enemies. Fulfill Your purpose in me, and teach me to imitate those who walk by faith.

261
~❧~

DAY 252

BEING SEALED BY THE HOLY SPIRIT

*

LORD, I DRAW NEAR TO YOU

O Lord, I am deeply grateful for Your wonderful acts, for Your abundant promises, and for the gift of my relationship with You through the merits of Christ.

I will give thanks to the God of heaven,
For His merciful love endures forever. (Psalm 136:26)

Take a moment to express your gratitude for the many blessings that you have received from the Lord.

THANK YOU, LORD, FOR WHAT YOU HAVE DONE

I acknowledge this day and take it to my heart that the Lord is God in heaven above and on the earth below; there is no other. (Deuteronomy 4:39)

The Lord has bared His holy arm in the sight of all the nations, and all the ends of the earth will see the salvation of our God. (Isaiah 52:10)

LORD, I LISTEN TO YOUR WORDS OF TRUTH

I trusted in Christ when I heard the Word of truth, the gospel of my salvation. Having believed, I was sealed in Him with the Holy Spirit of promise, Who is a deposit guaranteeing my inheritance until the redemption of those who are God's possession, to the praise of His glory. (Ephesians 1:13-14)

LORD, I RESPOND TO YOUR INSTRUCTION

Through love and truth, iniquity is atoned for; and by the fear of the Lord, one turns aside from evil. When a man's ways are pleasing to the Lord, he makes even his enemies live at peace with him. (Proverbs 16:6-7)

We should all be of one mind and be sympathetic, loving as brothers, compassionate, and humble. (1 Peter 3:8)

*

Lord, I thank You that You are God in heaven above and on the earth below and that Your salvation will extend to the ends of the earth. I thank You that I was sealed by the Holy Spirit when I trusted in Christ. Help me to keep my ways pleasing to You that I may live in peace with others.

DAY 253

BEING IDENTIFIED WITH CHRIST

∽

LORD, I DRAW NEAR TO YOU

Lord, I give thanks for Your greatness, Your goodness, and Your love, and I now draw near to enjoy Your presence.

In the beginning was the Word, and the Word was with God, and the Word was God. He was in the beginning with God. (John 1:1-2)

Take a moment to consider God's awesome majesty and thank Him that He loves you and wants an intimate relationship with you.

THANK YOU, LORD, FOR WHAT YOU HAVE DONE

Bless the Lord, O my soul. O Lord, my God, You are very great; You are clothed with splendor and majesty. (Psalm 104:1)

The heavens are Yours; the earth also is Yours; You founded the world and all its fullness. (Psalm 89:11)

LORD, I LISTEN TO YOUR WORDS OF TRUTH

With regard to my former way of life, I am to put off my old self, which is being corrupted by its deceitful desires, and be renewed in the spirit of my mind; and I am to put on the new self, which was created according to God in righteousness and true holiness. (Ephesians 4:22-24)

LORD, I RESPOND TO YOUR INSTRUCTION

If I speak in the tongues of men and of angels, but have not love, I am only a resounding gong or a clanging cymbal. And if I have the gift of prophecy and understand all mysteries and all knowledge, and if I have all faith so as to remove mountains, but have not love, I am nothing. And if I give all my possessions to the poor, and if I deliver my body to be burned, but have not love, it profits me nothing. (1 Corinthians 13:1-3)

I will sow righteousness, reap the fruit of unfailing love, and break up my fallow ground; for it is time to seek the Lord, until He comes and rains righteousness on me. (Hosea 10:12)

∽

Lord, I thank You that You are clothed with splendor and majesty and that You are sovereign over all things. Help me to live consistently with my new identity in Christ, displaying His love and righteousness.

263

DAY 254

PROCLAIMING THE MYSTERY
OF CHRIST

❧

LORD, I DRAW NEAR TO YOU

I am grateful to You, O God, for the blessing of Your forgiveness. I thank You that in Christ, You set me free from the guilt of the past and give me hope for the future.

I know that You are a gracious and compassionate God, slow to anger and abounding in lovingkindness, a God who relents from sending calamity. (Jonah 4:2)

Take a moment to ask the Spirit to search your heart and reveal any areas of unconfessed sin. Acknowledge these to the Lord and thank Him for His forgiveness.

THANK YOU, LORD, FOR WHAT YOU HAVE DONE

264

The earth is the Lord's, and everything in it, the world and all who dwell in it. For He founded it upon the seas and established it upon the waters. (Psalm 24:1-2)

LORD, I LISTEN TO YOUR WORDS OF TRUTH

Since I died with Christ to the basic principles of this world, I should not submit to its regulations as though I still belonged to it. (Colossians 2:20)

LORD, I RESPOND TO YOUR INSTRUCTION

All things are for our sakes, so that the grace that is reaching more and more people may cause thanksgiving to abound to the glory of God. (2 Corinthians 4:15)

I pray that God may open to me a door for the Word, so that I may speak the mystery of Christ and proclaim it clearly, as I ought to speak. (Colossians 4:3-4)

❧

Lord, I thank You that You are my Redeemer and that all things belong to You. I thank You that in Christ I am no longer bound by the ways of this world. Help me to communicate the mystery of Christ to those in my sphere of influence.

DAY 255

HUMBLING MYSELF BEFORE GOD

LORD, I DRAW NEAR TO YOU

I praise You, Lord, that You are intimately acquainted with my ways and that You always love me and have my best interests at heart.

May I not be like those rocky places on whom seed was thrown, who hear the Word and at once receive it with joy, but since they have no root, last only a short time; when affliction or persecution comes because of the Word, they quickly fall away. And may I not be like those among the thorns on whom seed was sown, who hear the Word, but the worries of this world, the deceitfulness of riches and pleasures, and the desires for other things come in and choke the Word, making it immature and unfruitful. Instead, may I be like the good soil on whom seed was sown, who with a noble and good heart hear the Word, understand and accept it, and with perseverance bear fruit, yielding thirty, sixty, or a hundred times what was sown. (Matthew 13:20-23; Mark 4:16-20; Luke 8:13-15)

Take a moment to offer this day to the Lord and ask Him for the grace to grow in your knowledge and love for Him.

265

THANK YOU, LORD, FOR WHAT YOU HAVE DONE

The Lord has said, "If My people who are called by My name will humble themselves and pray and seek My face and turn from their wicked ways, then I will hear from heaven and will forgive their sin and heal their land." (2 Chronicles 7:14)

LORD, I LISTEN TO YOUR WORDS OF TRUTH

I have been chosen according to the foreknowledge of God the Father, in sanctification of the Spirit, for obedience to Jesus Christ and sprinkling of His blood; grace and peace are mine in abundance. (1 Peter 1:2)

LORD, I RESPOND TO YOUR INSTRUCTION

From now on I will regard no one only according to the flesh. (2 Corinthians 5:16)

Lord, I thank You for Your sovereign majesty and for Your willingness to forgive and restore. Help me to see people as You see them.

DAY 256

SEEKING TRUTH AND UNDERSTANDING

LORD, I DRAW NEAR TO YOU

As I approach Your throne of grace today, I am grateful that You care about the things that concern me and that You want me to offer them up to You.

May I keep the pattern of sound teaching that I have heard, in faith and love which are in Christ Jesus. (2 Timothy 1:13)

Take a moment to share your personal needs with God, including your physical, emotional, relational, and spiritual concerns.

THANK YOU, LORD, FOR WHAT YOU HAVE DONE

The Son is the radiance of God's glory and the exact representation of His being, upholding all things by His powerful Word. After He cleansed our sins, He sat down at the right hand of the Majesty on high, having become as much superior to angels as the name He has inherited is more excellent than theirs. (Hebrews 1:3-4)

The gospel of the kingdom will be preached in the whole world as a witness to all the nations, and then the end will come. (Matthew 24:14)

LORD, I LISTEN TO YOUR WORDS OF TRUTH

How great is the love the Father has lavished on me, that I should be called a child of God—and I am! Therefore, the world does not know me, because it did not know Him. (1 John 3:1)

LORD, I RESPOND TO YOUR INSTRUCTION

Surely You desire truth in the inner parts, and in the hidden part You make me know wisdom. (Psalm 51:6)

The entrance of Your words gives light; it gives understanding to the simple. (Psalm 119:130)

Lord, I thank You that Your Son is the radiance of Your glory and that He cleansed my sins. I thank You for the greatness of the love that You have lavished on me. Continually, I will seek truth and understanding in Your words.

DAY 257

DEPENDING ON GOD

LORD, I DRAW NEAR TO YOU

Lord, You have invited me to pray for the needs of others, and since You desire what is best for them, I take this opportunity to bring these requests to You.

We ought always to thank God for other believers and pray that their faith would grow more and more, and that the love each of them has toward one another would increase. (2 Thessalonians 1:3)

May the Lord direct our hearts into the love of God and into the patience of Christ. (2 Thessalonians 3:5)

Take a moment to lift up the needs of your family and friends, and to offer up any additional burdens for others that the Lord brings to mind.

THANK YOU, LORD, FOR WHAT YOU HAVE DONE

The Lord will be gracious to whom He will be gracious, and He will have compassion on whom He will have compassion. (Exodus 33:19)

Jesus had compassion on the crowds, because they were like sheep without a shepherd. So he began to teach them many things. (Mark 6:34)

LORD, I LISTEN TO YOUR WORDS OF TRUTH

I will not depend on human strength, but on the Lord my God for help and deliverance. (2 Chronicles 16:7-8,12)

LORD, I RESPOND TO YOUR INSTRUCTION

The brother in humble circumstances should glory in his high position, and the one who is rich should glory in his humiliation, because he will pass away like a flower of the field. (James 1:9-10)

Better a meal of vegetables where there is love than a fattened calf with hatred. (Proverbs 15:17)

Lord, I thank You for Your grace and compassion and for the way Your compassion was revealed in the ministry of Your Son. I thank You that I can depend on You for help and deliverance. I will walk in humility and avoid strife.

DAY 258

PRESERVING SOUND WISDOM

❧

LORD, I DRAW NEAR TO YOU

Lord, I want Your Word to be deeply implanted in me so that I will know the truth and be able to express it in the way I live.

Because I am a son, God has sent the Spirit of His Son into my heart, crying, "Abba, Father." So I am no longer a slave, but a son; and if a son, then an heir through God. (Galatians 4:6-7)

Take a moment to affirm the truth of these words from Scripture and ask God to make them a growing reality in your life.

THANK YOU, LORD, FOR WHAT YOU HAVE DONE

You are the great, the mighty, and the awesome God, who keeps His covenant of lovingkindness. (Nehemiah 9:32)

The Son of Man came to seek and to save that which was lost. (Luke 19:10)

LORD, I LISTEN TO YOUR WORDS OF TRUTH

He who dwells in the shelter of the Most High will rest in the shadow of the Almighty. I will say of the Lord, "He is my refuge and my fortress, my God, in Whom I trust." (Psalm 91:1-2)

LORD, I RESPOND TO YOUR INSTRUCTION

I will preserve sound wisdom and discretion, not letting them out of my sight; they will be life to my soul. (Proverbs 3:21-22)

The fruit of the righteous is a tree of life, and he who wins souls is wise. (Proverbs 11:30)

❧

Lord, I thank You that You are mighty and awesome and that Your Son came to seek and to save the lost. I thank You that You are my refuge and my fortress in whom I trust. Help me to preserve wisdom and discretion and lead others to the knowledge of Christ.

DAY 259

CASTING MY CARES ON GOD

LORD, I DRAW NEAR TO YOU

O Lord, I am deeply grateful for Your wonderful acts, for Your abundant promises, and for the gift of my relationship with You through the merits of Christ.

You are my God, and I will give thanks to You;
You are my God, and I will exalt You.
I will give thanks to the Lord, for He is good;
His loyal love endures forever. (Psalm 118:28-29)

Take a moment to express your gratitude for the many blessings that you have received from the Lord.

THANK YOU, LORD, FOR WHAT YOU HAVE DONE

The Lord reigns; He is clothed with majesty; the Lord is robed in majesty and is armed with strength. Indeed, the world is firmly established; it cannot be moved. Your throne is established from of old; You are from everlasting. Your testimonies stand firm; holiness adorns Your house, O Lord, forever. (Psalm 93:1-2,5)

269

LORD, I LISTEN TO YOUR WORDS OF TRUTH

I will seek the Lord and His strength; I will seek His face continually. I will remember the wonders He has done, His miracles, and the judgments of His mouth. (Psalm 105:4-5)

LORD, I RESPOND TO YOUR INSTRUCTION

I will humble myself under the mighty hand of God, that He may exalt me in due time, casting all my anxiety upon Him, because He cares for me. (1 Peter 5:6-7)

I will love my enemies and pray for those who persecute me. (Matthew 5:44)

Lord, I thank You that You are robed in eternal majesty and for the wonders You have done. I will humble myself under Your mighty hand and cast all my cares upon You.

DAY 260

BEING DELIVERED FROM THE EVIL ONE

LORD, I DRAW NEAR TO YOU

Lord, I give thanks for Your greatness, Your goodness, and Your love, and I now draw near to enjoy Your presence.

I know that You can do all things
And that no purpose of Yours can be thwarted. (Job 42:2)

Take a moment to consider God's awesome majesty and thank Him that He loves you and wants an intimate relationship with you.

THANK YOU, LORD, FOR WHAT YOU HAVE DONE

The eyes of the Lord are everywhere, keeping watch on the evil and the good. (Proverbs 15:3)

270

The Lord said, "Behold, I stand at the door and knock. If anyone hears My voice and opens the door, I will come in to him and dine with him, and he with Me. To him who overcomes, I will give the right to sit with Me on My throne, just as I overcame and sat down with My Father on His throne." (Revelation 3:20-21)

LORD, I LISTEN TO YOUR WORDS OF TRUTH

I look to You for my daily bread, to forgive me my debts as I also have forgiven my debtors, and to lead me not into temptation, but to deliver me from the evil one. For Yours is the kingdom and the power and the glory forever. (Matthew 6:11-13)

LORD, I RESPOND TO YOUR INSTRUCTION

Woe to those who call evil good and good evil, who put darkness for light and light for darkness, who put bitter for sweet and sweet for bitter. (Isaiah 5:20)

He who trusts in his own heart is a fool, but he who walks in wisdom will be delivered. (Proverbs 28:26)

Lord, I thank You that You know all things and that You invite me into the joy of Your presence through Jesus Christ Your Son. I pray for Your provision and protection. I will not trust in my own heart but walk in wisdom.

DAY 261

DISCERNING WHAT IS GOOD

LORD, I DRAW NEAR TO YOU

I am grateful to You, O God, for the blessing of Your forgiveness. I thank You that in Christ, You set me free from the guilt of the past and give me hope for the future.

I know, O Lord, that a man's way is not his own;
It is not in a man who walks to direct his steps.
O Lord, correct me, but with justice—
Not in Your anger, lest You reduce me to nothing. (Jeremiah 10:23-24)

Take a moment to ask the Spirit to search your heart and reveal any areas of unconfessed sin. Acknowledge these to the Lord and thank Him for His forgiveness.

THANK YOU, LORD, FOR WHAT YOU HAVE DONE

You have sworn by Yourself; the Word has gone out of Your mouth in righteousness and will not return. Every knee will bow before You, and every tongue will acknowledge You. (Isaiah 45:23)

271

A great multitude, which no one could number, from all nations and tribes and peoples and languages will stand before the throne and before the Lamb, clothed with white robes with palm branches in their hands, and will cry out with a loud voice, "Salvation belongs to our God, who sits on the throne, and to the Lamb!" (Revelation 7:9-10)

LORD, I LISTEN TO YOUR WORDS OF TRUTH

Lord Jesus, I have nowhere else to go; You have the words of eternal life. I believe and know that You are the Holy One of God. (John 6:68-69)

LORD, I RESPOND TO YOUR INSTRUCTION

In my obedience, I want to be wise about what is good and innocent about what is evil. (Romans 16:19)

Lord, I thank You that every knee will bow before You and that all will acknowledge that salvation belongs to You and to the Lamb. I thank You that the Lord Jesus has the words of eternal life. Renew me in Your truth so I will discern what is good and not succumb to evil.

DAY 262

CHOOSING NOT TO JUDGE

LORD, I DRAW NEAR TO YOU

I praise You, Lord, that You are intimately acquainted with my ways and that You always love me and have my best interests at heart.

May I receive the words of wisdom
And treasure her commands within me,
Turning my ear to wisdom
And applying my heart to understanding. (Proverbs 2:1-2)

Take a moment to offer this day to the Lord and ask Him for the grace to grow in your knowledge and love for Him.

THANK YOU, LORD, FOR WHAT YOU HAVE DONE

You are the Lord, the God of all mankind. Nothing is too difficult for You. (Jeremiah 32:27)

272

The Lord confirmed that Abraham would surely become a great and powerful nation, and all nations on earth would be blessed through him. (Genesis 18:18)

LORD, I LISTEN TO YOUR WORDS OF TRUTH

You are the light of the world. He who follows You will not walk in the darkness but will have the light of life. (John 8:12)

LORD, I RESPOND TO YOUR INSTRUCTION

I will not judge, so that I will not be judged. For in the same way I judge others, I will be judged; and with the measure I use, it will be measured to me. (Matthew 7:1-2)

I will not judge my brother or regard him with contempt. Instead of judging him, I will resolve not to put a stumbling block or obstacle in my brother's way. (Romans 14:10,13)

Lord, I thank You that nothing is too difficult for You and that You always fulfill Your promises. I thank You that Christ is the light of the world. I will purpose not to regard others with contempt but to treat them with kindness instead.

DAY 263

ABOUNDING IN LOVE FOR OTHERS

❧

LORD, I DRAW NEAR TO YOU

As I approach Your throne of grace today, I am grateful that You care about the things that concern me and that You want me to offer them up to You.

May I not boast about tomorrow,
For I do not know what a day may bring forth. (Proverbs 27:1)

Take a moment to share your personal needs with God, including your physical, emotional, relational, and spiritual concerns.

THANK YOU, LORD, FOR WHAT YOU HAVE DONE

To the King eternal, immortal, invisible, the only God, be honor and glory forever and ever. (1 Timothy 1:17)

O Lord, You are my God; I will exalt You and praise Your name, for You have done wonderful things, things planned long ago in perfect faithfulness. (Isaiah 25:1)

273
❧

LORD, I LISTEN TO YOUR WORDS OF TRUTH

He who believes in You, as the Scripture has said, rivers of living water will flow from within him, because Your Spirit indwells him. (John 7:38-39)

LORD, I RESPOND TO YOUR INSTRUCTION

Whoever is wise and understanding will show it by his good conduct and works done in the humility that comes from wisdom. If I harbor bitter envy and selfish ambition in my heart, I should not boast and lie against the truth. This wisdom does not come down from above, but is earthly, natural, demonic. For where there is envy and selfish ambition, there is disorder and every evil practice. (James 3:13-16)

May the Lord make me increase and abound in my love for believers and for unbelievers. (1 Thessalonians 3:12)

❧

Lord, I thank You that You are the King eternal, immortal, and invisible and that You have done wonderful things. I thank You for the gift of Your indwelling Holy Spirit. I will submit my plans to You and seek to abound in my love for others.

DAY 264

PURIFYING MY SOUL

LORD, I DRAW NEAR TO YOU

Lord, You have invited me to pray for the needs of others, and since You desire what is best for them, I take this opportunity to bring these requests to You.

We should always pray for other believers, that our God may count them worthy of His calling and fulfill every desire for goodness and every work of faith with power. (2 Thessalonians 1:11)

Take a moment to lift up the needs of your family and friends, and to offer up any additional burdens for others that the Lord brings to mind.

THANK YOU, LORD, FOR WHAT YOU HAVE DONE

The Lord my God is God of gods and Lord of lords, the great God, mighty and awesome, Who shows no partiality and accepts no bribes. He executes justice for the fatherless and the widow and loves the alien, giving him food and clothing. (Deuteronomy 10:17-18)

274

The Lord watches over the strangers; He sustains the orphan and the widow, but He thwarts the way of the wicked. (Psalm 146:9)

LORD, I LISTEN TO YOUR WORDS OF TRUTH

Lord Jesus, he who believes in You does not believe in You only, but in the One who sent You. And he who beholds You beholds the One who sent You. (John 12:44-45)

LORD, I RESPOND TO YOUR INSTRUCTION

Our fathers disciplined us for a little while as they thought best, but God disciplines us for our good, that we may share in His holiness. No discipline seems pleasant at the time, but painful; later on, however, it produces the peaceable fruit of righteousness for those who have been trained by it. (Hebrews 12:10-11)

In obedience to the truth I will purify my soul for a sincere love of the brethren, and I will love others fervently from the heart. (1 Peter 1:22)

Lord, I thank You for Your power and for Your passion for justice. Teach me through Your discipline to demonstrate the peaceable fruit of righteousness and purify my soul to love others with sincerity.

DAY 265

WALKING HONESTLY BEFORE MEN

~&~

LORD, I DRAW NEAR TO YOU

Lord, I want Your Word to be deeply implanted in me so that I will know the truth and be able to express it in the way I live.

I have been called by God my Savior, and Christ Jesus is my hope. (1 Timothy 1:1)

The grace of my Lord was poured out on me abundantly, along with the faith and love that are in Christ Jesus. (1 Timothy 1:14)

Take a moment to affirm the truth of these words from Scripture and ask God to make them a growing reality in your life.

THANK YOU, LORD, FOR WHAT YOU HAVE DONE

To God belong wisdom and power; counsel and understanding are His. (Job 12:13)

275
~&~

The Lord guides the humble in what is right and teaches the humble His way. (Psalm 25:9)

LORD, I LISTEN TO YOUR WORDS OF TRUTH

He who receives whomever You send receives You, and whoever receives You receives the One who sent You. (John 13:20)

LORD, I RESPOND TO YOUR INSTRUCTION

I will have accurate and honest standards in my business practices. (Deuteronomy 25:15)

I want to be a faithful person who fears God. (Nehemiah 7:2)

~&~

Lord, I thank You that wisdom, power, counsel, and understanding belong to You and that You teach Your ways to the humble. I thank You that those who receive Jesus Christ receive You. Help me to be an honest and faithful person before You and others.

DAY 266

VIEWING MYSELF PROPERLY

LORD, I DRAW NEAR TO YOU

O Lord, I am deeply grateful for Your wonderful acts, for Your abundant promises, and for the gift of my relationship with You through the merits of Christ.

It is God the Lord
Who created the heavens and stretched them out,
Who spread out the earth and all that comes out of it,
Who gives breath to its people,
And spirit to those who walk upon it. (Isaiah 42:5)

Take a moment to express your gratitude for the many blessings that you have received from the Lord.

THANK YOU, LORD, FOR WHAT YOU HAVE DONE

Once God has spoken; twice I have heard this: that power belongs to God, and that You, O Lord, are loving. For You reward each person according to what he has done. (Psalm 62:11-12)

Jesus performed the first of His miraculous signs in Cana of Galilee and manifested His glory, and His disciples believed in Him. (John 2:11)

LORD, I LISTEN TO YOUR WORDS OF TRUTH

I will not think of myself more highly than I ought to think, but I will think soberly, in accordance with the measure of faith God has given me. (Romans 12:3)

LORD, I RESPOND TO YOUR INSTRUCTION

The fear of the Lord is to hate evil; wisdom hates pride and arrogance and the evil way and the perverse mouth. (Proverbs 8:13)

He who oppresses the poor reproaches his Maker, but whoever is kind to the needy honors Him. (Proverbs 14:31)

Lord, I thank You for Your power and love and for the glorious ministry of Jesus Christ. Give me a proper view of myself, so I will not capitulate to pride but show kindness to the needy.

276

DAY 267

GIVING THANKS FOR GOD'S GOODNESS

❧

LORD, I DRAW NEAR TO YOU

Lord, I give thanks for Your greatness, Your goodness, and Your love, and I now draw near to enjoy Your presence.

The earth is the Lord's, and everything in it,
The world and all who dwell in it.
For He founded it upon the seas
And established it upon the waters. (Psalm 24:1-2)

Take a moment to consider God's awesome majesty and thank Him that He loves you and wants an intimate relationship with you.

THANK YOU, LORD, FOR WHAT YOU HAVE DONE

I will give thanks to the Lord, for He is good; His lovingkindness endures forever. (Psalm 118:1)

277
❧

LORD, I LISTEN TO YOUR WORDS OF TRUTH

Knowing that a man is not justified by the works of the law, but through faith in Christ Jesus, I have believed in Christ Jesus, that I may be justified through faith in Christ and not by the works of the law; for by the works of the law, no flesh will be justified. (Galatians 2:16)

LORD, I RESPOND TO YOUR INSTRUCTION

I will not lay up for myself treasures on earth, where moth and rust destroy and where thieves break in and steal. But I will lay up for myself treasures in heaven, where moth and rust do not destroy and where thieves do not break in and steal. For where my treasure is, there my heart will be also. (Matthew 6:19-21; Luke 12:34)

He who is generous will be blessed, for he shares his food with the poor. (Proverbs 22:9)

❧

Lord, I thank You for Your goodness and lovingkindness and that I have been made acceptable in Your sight through faith in Christ. I will lay up lasting treasure in heaven by being generous to others.

DAY 268

BEING ROOTED AND ESTABLISHED IN CHRIST

LORD, I DRAW NEAR TO YOU

I am grateful to You, O God, for the blessing of Your forgiveness. I thank You that in Christ, You set me free from the guilt of the past and give me hope for the future.

The refining pot is for silver and the furnace for gold,
But the Lord tests the hearts. (Proverbs 17:3)

Take a moment to ask the Spirit to search your heart and reveal any areas of unconfessed sin. Acknowledge these to the Lord and thank Him for His forgiveness.

THANK YOU, LORD, FOR WHAT YOU HAVE DONE

How precious are Your thoughts to me, O God! How vast is the sum of them! If I should count them, they would outnumber the grains of sand. When I awake, I am still with You. (Psalm 139:17-18)

Never did a man speak the way Jesus did. (John 7:46)

LORD, I LISTEN TO YOUR WORDS OF TRUTH

Just as I received Christ Jesus the Lord, so I will walk in Him, rooted and built up in Him, and established in the faith, as I was taught, and abounding in thanksgiving. (Colossians 2:6-7)

LORD, I RESPOND TO YOUR INSTRUCTION

I will have nothing to do with the fruitless deeds of darkness, but rather I will expose them. (Ephesians 5:11)

I will put away all filthiness and the overflow of wickedness, and in meekness I will accept the Word planted in me, which is able to save my soul. (James 1:21)

Lord, I thank You for the preciousness of Your thoughts and for the authoritative words of Your Son. I pray that I would be rooted and established in Christ Jesus. Help me to put away the fruitless deeds of darkness and humbly walk in Your light.

DAY 269

DOING THE GOOD THAT IS IN MY POWER

LORD, I DRAW NEAR TO YOU

I praise You, Lord, that You are intimately acquainted with my ways and that You always love me and have my best interests at heart.

May I know God and serve Him with a whole heart and with a willing mind; for the Lord searches all hearts and understands every motive behind the thoughts. (1 Chronicles 28:9)

Take a moment to offer this day to the Lord and ask Him for the grace to grow in your knowledge and love for Him.

THANK YOU, LORD, FOR WHAT YOU HAVE DONE

"My thoughts are not your thoughts, neither are your ways My ways," declares the Lord. "As the heavens are higher than the earth, so are My ways higher than your ways, and My thoughts than your thoughts." (Isaiah 55:8-9)

279

It is the Spirit who gives life; the flesh counts for nothing. The words Jesus spoke are spirit and are life. (John 6:63)

LORD, I LISTEN TO YOUR WORDS OF TRUTH

I am not ashamed, because I know Whom I have believed and am convinced that He is able to guard what I have entrusted to Him until that day. (2 Timothy 1:12)

LORD, I RESPOND TO YOUR INSTRUCTION

I will not worry about tomorrow, for tomorrow will worry about itself. Each day has enough trouble of its own. (Matthew 6:34)

I will not withhold good from those to whom it is due, when it is in my power to act. (Proverbs 3:27)

Lord, I thank You for the greatness of Your thoughts and ways and for Your Spirit who gives life. I thank You that Christ will guard and protect me until the day I see Him. I will not be anxious about tomorrow, but I will do good to others as it is in my power to do.

DAY 270

REMAINING FAITHFUL

~

LORD, I DRAW NEAR TO YOU

As I approach Your throne of grace today, I am grateful that You care about the things that concern me and that You want me to offer them up to You.

May I not love the world or the things in the world. If anyone loves the world, the love of the Father is not in him. For all that is in the world — the lust of the flesh, the lust of the eyes, and the pride of life — is not of the Father but of the world. And the world and its lusts are passing away, but the one who does the will of God abides forever. (1 John 2:15-17)

Take a moment to share your personal needs with God, including your physical, emotional, relational, and spiritual concerns.

THANK YOU, LORD, FOR WHAT YOU HAVE DONE

I know that You are a gracious and compassionate God, slow to anger and abounding in lovingkindness, a God who relents from sending calamity. (Jonah 4:2)

The Son of Man did not come to be served, but to serve, and to give His life as a ransom for many. (Mark 10:45)

LORD, I LISTEN TO YOUR WORDS OF TRUTH

This is a trustworthy saying: If we died with Him, we will also live with Him; if we endure, we will also reign with Him. If we deny Him, He will also deny us; if we are faithless, He will remain faithful, for He cannot deny Himself. (2 Timothy 2:11-13)

LORD, I RESPOND TO YOUR INSTRUCTION

A talebearer reveals secrets, but he who is trustworthy conceals a matter. (Proverbs 11:13)

In a multitude of words, transgression does not cease, but he who restrains his lips is wise. (Proverbs 10:19)

~

Lord, I thank You for Your grace and compassion and for the display of Your grace and compassion in the ministry of Jesus. I thank You for the faithfulness of Your promises. Help me to be trustworthy and control my speech wisely.

DAY 271

BECOMING RICH TOWARD GOD

❦

LORD, I DRAW NEAR TO YOU

Lord, You have invited me to pray for the needs of others, and since You desire what is best for them, I take this opportunity to bring these requests to You.

We should offer petitions, prayers, intercessions, and thanksgivings on behalf of all men, for kings and all those who are in authority, that we may live peaceful and quiet lives in all godliness and reverence. This is good and acceptable in the sight of God our Savior, who desires all men to be saved and to come to the knowledge of the truth. (1 Timothy 2:1-4)

Take a moment to lift up the needs of your family and friends, and to offer up any additional burdens for others that the Lord brings to mind.

THANK YOU, LORD, FOR WHAT YOU HAVE DONE

In Christ are hidden all the treasures of wisdom and knowledge. (Colossians 2:3)

Jesus did all things well. He made the deaf hear and the mute speak. (Mark 7:37)

LORD, I LISTEN TO YOUR WORDS OF TRUTH

I will draw near to God with a sincere heart in full assurance of faith, having my heart sprinkled to cleanse me from an evil conscience and my body washed with pure water. (Hebrews 10:22)

LORD, I RESPOND TO YOUR INSTRUCTION

I do not want to lay up treasure for myself without being rich toward God. (Luke 12:21)

He who is kind to the poor lends to the Lord, and He will reward him for what he has done. (Proverbs 19:17)

❦

Lord, I thank You that all the treasures of wisdom and knowledge are hidden in Jesus who did all things well. I thank You that I can draw near to You in full assurance of faith. I desire to be rich toward You and generous to those who are in need.

281
❦

DAY 272
ASKING ACCORDING TO GOD'S WILL

LORD, I DRAW NEAR TO YOU

Lord, I want Your Word to be deeply implanted in me so that I will know the truth and be able to express it in the way I live.

The Lord is seated on His throne with all the host of heaven standing by Him on His right and on His left. (1 Kings 22:19)

O Lord, God of Israel, enthroned between the cherubim, You alone are God over all the kingdoms of the earth. You have made heaven and earth. (2 Kings 19:15)

Take a moment to affirm the truth of these words from Scripture and ask God to make them a growing reality in your life.

THANK YOU, LORD, FOR WHAT YOU HAVE DONE

282

God is light; in Him there is no darkness at all. (1 John 1:5)

Clearly no one is justified before God by the law, for "The righteous will live by faith." (Galatians 3:11)

LORD, I LISTEN TO YOUR WORDS OF TRUTH

This is the confidence I have in the Son of God, that if I ask anything according to His will, He hears me. And if I know that He hears me, whatever I ask, I know that I have the requests that I have asked from Him. (1 John 5:14-15)

LORD, I RESPOND TO YOUR INSTRUCTION

Lying lips are hateful to the Lord, but He delights in those who deal faithfully. (Proverbs 12:22)

A rod of pride is in the mouth of a fool, but the lips of the wise will preserve them. (Proverbs 14:3)

Lord, I thank You that there is no darkness in You and that You have justified me by faith in the Lord Jesus. I thank You for the confidence that You hear my requests and answer me. Help me to deal faithfully and wisely with my tongue.

DAY 273

LEARNING TO BE CONTENT

LORD, I DRAW NEAR TO YOU

O Lord, I am deeply grateful for Your wonderful acts, for Your abundant promises, and for the gift of my relationship with You through the merits of Christ.

Blessed be the Lord,
For He has heard the voice of my prayers.
The Lord is my strength and my shield;
My heart trusts in Him, and I am helped.
My heart greatly rejoices,
And I will give thanks to Him in song. (Psalm 28:6-7)

Take a moment to express your gratitude for the many blessings that you have received from the Lord.

THANK YOU, LORD, FOR WHAT YOU HAVE DONE

All things are possible with God. (Matthew 19:26; Mark 10:27)

283

Christ redeemed us from the curse of the law by becoming a curse for us, for it is written: "Cursed is everyone who hangs on a tree." (Galatians 3:13)

LORD, I LISTEN TO YOUR WORDS OF TRUTH

By Your grace I will not forsake You, the fountain of living waters, to dig my own cisterns, broken cisterns that can hold no water. (Jeremiah 2:13)

LORD, I RESPOND TO YOUR INSTRUCTION

Godliness with contentment is great gain. For I brought nothing into the world, and I can take nothing out of it. But if I have food and clothing, with these I will be content. (1 Timothy 6:6-8)

A generous man will prosper, and he who waters will himself be refreshed. (Proverbs 11:25)

Lord, I thank You that all things are possible with You and that Christ redeemed me from the curse of the law. I pray that I would never forsake You to seek significance and security in worldly things. Teach me the secret of contentment and to be charitable and generous with others.

DAY 274

PARTAKING IN THE PROMISE
OF CHRIST

LORD, I DRAW NEAR TO YOU

Lord, I give thanks for Your greatness, Your goodness, and Your love, and I now draw near to enjoy Your presence.

You are He; You are the first,
And You are also the last. (Isaiah 48:12)

Take a moment to consider God's awesome majesty and thank Him that He loves you and wants an intimate relationship with you.

THANK YOU, LORD, FOR WHAT YOU HAVE DONE

The Most High is sovereign over the kingdoms of men and gives them to whomever He wishes and sets over them the lowliest of men. (Daniel 4:17)

Through the gospel, the Gentiles are fellow heirs with Israel, fellow members of the same body, and fellow partakers of the promise in Christ Jesus. (Ephesians 3:6)

LORD, I LISTEN TO YOUR WORDS OF TRUTH

The kingdom of heaven is like treasure hidden in a field, which a man found and hid; and from his joy, he went and sold all he had and bought that field. Again, the kingdom of heaven is like a merchant looking for fine pearls; and finding one pearl of great value, he went away and sold all that he had and bought it. (Matthew 13:44-46)

LORD, I RESPOND TO YOUR INSTRUCTION

The tongue has the power of death and life, and those who love it will eat its fruit. (Proverbs 18:21)

Lord, I thank You that Your dominion extends to all times and places and that I have become a partaker of the promise in Christ Jesus. I will treasure Your kingdom above all things. Help me to be truthful and loving in my words to others.

DAY 275

BECOMING A WISE AND FAITHFUL SERVANT

~❧~

LORD, I DRAW NEAR TO YOU

I am grateful to You, O God, for the blessing of Your forgiveness. I thank You that in Christ, You set me free from the guilt of the past and give me hope for the future.

The ways of a man are before the eyes of the Lord,
And He examines all his paths. (Proverbs 5:21)

All a man's ways are pure in his own eyes,
But the Lord weighs the motives. (Proverbs 16:2)

Take a moment to ask the Spirit to search your heart and reveal any areas of unconfessed sin. Acknowledge these to the Lord and thank Him for His forgiveness.

THANK YOU, LORD, FOR WHAT YOU HAVE DONE

Heaven and earth will pass away, but the words of the Lord Jesus will never pass away. (Matthew 24:35; Luke 21:33)

God's grace was given to us in Christ Jesus before the beginning of time and has now been revealed through the appearing of our Savior, Christ Jesus, Who abolished death and brought life and immortality to light through the gospel. (2 Timothy 1:9-10)

LORD, I LISTEN TO YOUR WORDS OF TRUTH

Who is the faithful and wise servant, whom the master has put in charge of his household to give them their food at the proper time? Blessed is that servant whom his master finds so doing when he comes. (Matthew 24:45-46)

LORD, I RESPOND TO YOUR INSTRUCTION

Everyone should be quick to hear, slow to speak, and slow to anger, for the anger of man does not produce the righteousness of God. (James 1:19-20)

~❧~

Lord, I thank You that Your words will never pass away and that Christ Jesus abolished death and brought life and immortality. Help me to be a wise and faithful servant, quick to hear, slow to speak, and slow to anger.

DAY 276

PRACTICING THE ROLE OF A SERVANT

❧

LORD, I DRAW NEAR TO YOU

I praise You, Lord, that You are intimately acquainted with my ways and that You always love me and have my best interests at heart.

Since I live in the Spirit, may I also walk in the Spirit. (Galatians 5:25)

May God fill me with the knowledge of His will through all spiritual wisdom and understanding, so that I may walk worthy of the Lord and please Him in every way, bearing fruit in every good work, and growing in the knowledge of God; strengthened with all power according to His glorious might, so that I may have great endurance and patience with joy. (Colossians 1:9-11)

Take a moment to offer this day to the Lord and ask Him for the grace to grow in your knowledge and love for Him.

286

THANK YOU, LORD, FOR WHAT YOU HAVE DONE

God is the Rock; His work is perfect, for all His ways are just. A God of faithfulness and without injustice, upright and just is He. (Deuteronomy 32:4)

Christ died for our sins according to the Scriptures; He was buried, and He was raised on the third day according to the Scriptures. (1 Corinthians 15:3-4)

LORD, I LISTEN TO YOUR WORDS OF TRUTH

If anyone wants to be first, he must be the last of all and the servant of all. (Mark 9:35)

LORD, I RESPOND TO YOUR INSTRUCTION

It is better to be of a humble spirit with the lowly than to divide the spoil with the proud. (Proverbs 16:19)

❧

Lord, I thank You that Your work is perfect and just and that Christ died for my sins and was raised from the dead. Teach me to be a servant of others, walking with a humble spirit.

DAY 277

FINDING MY LIFE

～❦

LORD, I DRAW NEAR TO YOU

As I approach Your throne of grace today, I am grateful that You care about the things that concern me and that You want me to offer them up to You.

My eyes are upon You, O God the Lord;
In You I take refuge; You will not leave my soul destitute. (Psalm 141:8)

Even when I am old and gray, do not forsake me, O God,
Until I declare Your strength to the next generation,
Your power to all who are to come. (Psalm 71:18)

Take a moment to share your personal needs with God, including your physical, emotional, relational, and spiritual concerns.

THANK YOU, LORD, FOR WHAT YOU HAVE DONE

In Your majesty, You dwell in the likeness of a throne of sapphire
above the expanse that is over the cherubim. (Ezekiel 10:1)

287
～❦

The heavens will vanish like smoke; the earth will wear out like a
garment, and its inhabitants will die in the same way. But Your salvation
will last forever, and Your righteousness will never fail. (Isaiah 51:6)

LORD, I LISTEN TO YOUR WORDS OF TRUTH

Whoever seeks to keep his life will lose it, and whoever loses his life
will preserve it. (Luke 17:33)

LORD, I RESPOND TO YOUR INSTRUCTION

In my anger I will not sin; I will not let the sun go down while I am still
angry, and I will not give the devil a foothold. (Ephesians 4:26-27)

Starting a quarrel is like breaching a dam, so I will stop a quarrel
before it breaks out. (Proverbs 17:14)

～❦

Lord, I thank You for Your exquisite majesty and for Your salvation that will last forever. I pray that I would find my life by losing it for the sake of Your Son. Help me to avoid quarreling whenever possible and to resolve conflicts quickly before the enemy can get a foothold.

DAY 278

SEEKING A CONTRITE SPIRIT

❧

LORD, I DRAW NEAR TO YOU

Lord, You have invited me to pray for the needs of others, and since You desire what is best for them, I take this opportunity to bring these requests to You.

We should ask that the name of our Lord Jesus may be glorified in others, and they in Him, according to the grace of our God and the Lord Jesus Christ. (2 Thessalonians 1:12)

May I remind others to be subject to rulers and authorities, to be obedient, to be ready for every good work, to slander no one, to be peaceable and gentle, and to show true humility toward all men. (Titus 3:1-2)

Take a moment to lift up the needs of your family and friends, and to offer up any additional burdens for others that the Lord brings to mind.

THANK YOU, LORD, FOR WHAT YOU HAVE DONE

The Word that goes forth from Your mouth will not return to You empty but will accomplish what You desire and achieve the purpose for which You sent it. (Isaiah 55:11)

Faith comes from hearing, and hearing by the Word of Christ. (Romans 10:17)

LORD, I LISTEN TO YOUR WORDS OF TRUTH

I will be strong in the Lord and in His mighty power. I will put on the full armor of God, so that I will be able to stand against the schemes of the devil. (Ephesians 6:10-11)

LORD, I RESPOND TO YOUR INSTRUCTION

This is the one You esteem: he who is humble and contrite of spirit, and who trembles at Your Word. (Isaiah 66:2)

❧

Lord, I thank You that Your Word always accomplishes Your purposes and that faith comes from hearing Your Word. Help me to respond to Your Word in humility with a contrite spirit.

DAY 279

SEEKING GOD'S FAVOR

~∾

LORD, I DRAW NEAR TO YOU

Lord, I want Your Word to be deeply implanted in me so that I will know the truth and be able to express it in the way I live.

Where does wisdom come from?
Where does understanding dwell?
It is hidden from the eyes of every living thing
And concealed from the birds of the air.
Destruction and death say,
"Only a rumor of it has reached our ears."
God understands its way,
And He knows its place.
For He looks to the ends of the earth
And sees everything under the heavens. (Job 28:20-24)

Take a moment to affirm the truth of these words from Scripture and ask God to make them a growing reality in your life.

289
~∾

THANK YOU, LORD, FOR WHAT YOU HAVE DONE

Many are the plans in a man's heart, but it is the counsel of the Lord that will stand. (Proverbs 19:21)

God's judgment against those who judge others and practice the same things themselves is based on truth. (Romans 2:1-2)

LORD, I LISTEN TO YOUR WORDS OF TRUTH

In my distress I will seek the favor of the Lord my God, and humble myself greatly before the God of my fathers, for I know that the Lord is God. (2 Chronicles 33:12-13)

LORD, I RESPOND TO YOUR INSTRUCTION

I will be diligent to present myself approved to God, a workman who does not need to be ashamed and who correctly handles the Word of truth. (2 Timothy 2:15)

~∾

Lord, I thank You that Your counsel always stands and that Your judgments are based on truth. I will seek Your favor. Help me to handle Your Word of truth wisely.

DAY 280

TURNING AWAY FROM MY OWN RIGHTEOUSNESS

~&

LORD, I DRAW NEAR TO YOU

O Lord, I am deeply grateful for Your wonderful acts, for Your abundant promises, and for the gift of my relationship with You through the merits of Christ.

You who fear the Lord, praise Him!
All you descendants of Jacob, glorify Him!
Stand in awe of Him, all you descendants of Israel!
For He has not despised or disdained the suffering of the afflicted one;
Nor has He hidden His face from him,
But has listened to his cry for help. (Psalm 22:23-24)

Take a moment to express your gratitude for the many blessings that you have received from the Lord.

THANK YOU, LORD, FOR WHAT YOU HAVE DONE

Whatever the Lord pleases He does, in the heavens and on the earth, in the seas and all their depths. (Psalm 135:6)

The wolf and the lamb will feed together, and the lion will eat straw like the ox, and dust will be the serpent's food. They will neither harm nor destroy in all Your holy mountain. (Isaiah 65:25)

LORD, I LISTEN TO YOUR WORDS OF TRUTH

Blessed are those whose ways are blameless, who walk in the law of the Lord. Blessed are those who keep His testimonies and seek Him with all their heart. (Psalm 119:1-2)

LORD, I RESPOND TO YOUR INSTRUCTION

You have called the humble of the earth who have upheld Your justice to seek the Lord, to seek righteousness, and to seek humility. (Zephaniah 2:3)

~&

Lord, I thank You that nothing can thwart Your purposes and that You will fulfill Your promise to restore all things. I will seek You with all my heart. Help me to practice humility instead of self-righteousness.

DAY 281

HEARING AND DOING

~

LORD, I DRAW NEAR TO YOU

Lord, I give thanks for Your greatness, Your goodness, and Your love, and I now draw near to enjoy Your presence.

Awake, harp and lyre!
I will awaken the dawn.
I will praise You, O Lord, among the peoples;
I will sing of You among the nations.
Your merciful love is higher than the heavens,
And Your truth reaches to the skies. (Psalm 108:2-4)

Take a moment to consider God's awesome majesty and thank Him that He loves you and wants an intimate relationship with you.

THANK YOU, LORD, FOR WHAT YOU HAVE DONE

God fashions the hearts of all and understands all their works. (Psalm 33:15)

God does not show favoritism but accepts those from every nation who fear Him and do what is right. (Acts 10:34-35)

291
~

LORD, I LISTEN TO YOUR WORDS OF TRUTH

Everyone who hears Your words and does them is like a wise man who built his house on the rock. (Matthew 7:24)

LORD, I RESPOND TO YOUR INSTRUCTION

I will be self-controlled and alert; my adversary the devil prowls around like a roaring lion looking for someone to devour. But I will resist him, standing firm in the faith, knowing that my brothers throughout the world are undergoing the same kind of sufferings. (1 Peter 5:8-9)

I will not repay evil for evil to anyone, but I will pursue what is good for others. (1 Thessalonians 5:15)

~

Lord, I thank You that You know each heart and that You accept all who truly seek You. Help me not only to hear Your words but to do them. I will resist the devil, stand firm in faith, and I will pursue what is good for others.

DAY 282

WALKING BLAMELESS BEFORE GOD

꙳

LORD, I DRAW NEAR TO YOU

I am grateful to You, O God, for the blessing of Your forgiveness. I thank You that in Christ, You set me free from the guilt of the past and give me hope for the future.

Blessed is the man You discipline, O Lord,
The man You teach from Your Word. (Psalm 94:12)

Take a moment to ask the Spirit to search your heart and reveal any areas of unconfessed sin. Acknowledge these to the Lord and thank Him for His forgiveness.

THANK YOU, LORD, FOR WHAT YOU HAVE DONE

The Lord is in His holy temple; the Lord is on His heavenly throne. He observes the sons of men; His eyes examine them. (Psalm 11:4)

292

The Father granted the Son authority over all people that He might give eternal life to as many as He has given Him. (John 17:2)

LORD, I LISTEN TO YOUR WORDS OF TRUTH

The Lord takes pleasure in those who fear Him, who put their hope in His unfailing love. (Psalm 147:11)

LORD, I RESPOND TO YOUR INSTRUCTION

Instruct a wise man, and he will be wiser still; teach a righteous man, and he will increase in learning. (Proverbs 9:9)

I should not say, "Today or tomorrow I will go to this or that city, spend a year there, carry on business, and make a profit." For I do not even know what my life will be tomorrow. I am a vapor that appears for a little while and then vanishes away. Instead, I ought to say, "If the Lord wills, I will live and do this or that." Otherwise, I boast in my arrogance, and all such boasting is evil. (James 4:13-16)

꙳

Lord, I thank You that You rule in sovereign majesty and that Your Son has given us eternal life. Teach me to walk blameless as I put my hope in Your unfailing love. Help me to grow in wisdom and increase in learning.

DAY 283

FULFILLING MY CALLING

~

LORD, I DRAW NEAR TO YOU

I praise You, Lord, that You are intimately acquainted with my ways and that You always love me and have my best interests at heart.

You are God Almighty; may I walk before You and be blameless. (Genesis 17:1)

May I love my enemies, do good to them, and lend to them, expecting nothing in return. Then my reward will be great, and I will be a child of the Most High; for He is kind to the ungrateful and evil. May I be merciful just as my Father is merciful. (Luke 6:35-36)

Take a moment to offer this day to the Lord and ask Him for the grace to grow in your knowledge and love for Him.

THANK YOU, LORD, FOR WHAT YOU HAVE DONE

God is wise in heart and mighty in strength. Who has resisted Him without harm? (Job 9:4)

293
~

He who hates Jesus hates His Father as well. (John 15:23)

LORD, I LISTEN TO YOUR WORDS OF TRUTH

I will judge nothing before the time, until the Lord comes, who will bring to light what is hidden in darkness and will expose the motives of men's hearts; and then each one's praise will come from God. (1 Corinthians 4:5)

LORD, I RESPOND TO YOUR INSTRUCTION

I will be strong and courageous, and act. I will not be afraid or discouraged, for the Lord God is with me. He will not fail me or forsake me. (1 Chronicles 28:20)

What is my hope or joy or crown of rejoicing in the presence of the Lord Jesus at His coming? My glory and joy are the people in whose lives I have been privileged to have a ministry. (1 Thessalonians 2:19-20)

~

Lord, I thank You for Your wisdom and might and for the person and work of Your beloved Son. I will not presume to judge the motives of others. Help me to fix my hope in You as I fulfill my calling.

DAY 284

BECOMING SALT AND LIGHT

⤮

LORD, I DRAW NEAR TO YOU

As I approach Your throne of grace today, I am grateful that You care about the things that concern me and that You want me to offer them up to You.

I cry out to God Most High,
To God who fulfills His purpose for me. (Psalm 57:2)

Take a moment to share your personal needs with God, including your physical, emotional, relational, and spiritual concerns.

THANK YOU, LORD, FOR WHAT YOU HAVE DONE

He Who is the Glory of Israel does not lie or change His mind, for He is not a man, that He should change His mind. (1 Samuel 15:29)

Jesus told His disciples, "I came from the Father and entered the world; now I am leaving the world and going back to the Father." (John 16:28)

LORD, I LISTEN TO YOUR WORDS OF TRUTH

I am the salt of the earth, but if the salt loses its flavor, how can it be made salty again? It is no longer good for anything, except to be thrown out and trampled underfoot by men. I am the light of the world. A city set on a hill cannot be hidden. Neither do people light a lamp and put it under a basket, but on a lampstand, and it gives light to all who are in the house. In the same way, I must let my light shine before men, that they may see my good deeds and praise my Father in heaven. (Matthew 5:13-16)

LORD, I RESPOND TO YOUR INSTRUCTION

Pride breeds nothing but strife, but wisdom is found in those who take advice. (Proverbs 13:10)

I will listen to counsel and accept instruction, that I may be wise in my latter days. (Proverbs 19:20)

⤮

Lord, I thank You that You never lie or change Your mind and that Jesus perfectly fulfilled Your timeless plan. Help me to become salt and light to those who know me, and to be wise enough to take advice and accept instruction.

DAY 285

REJOICING IN OPPORTUNITY

~&

LORD, I DRAW NEAR TO YOU

Lord, You have invited me to pray for the needs of others, and since You desire what is best for them, I take this opportunity to bring these requests to You.

I pray that the sharing of my faith may become effective through the knowledge of every good thing which is in me for Christ's sake. (Philemon 6)

May I have mercy on those who are doubting. (Jude 22)

Take a moment to lift up the needs of your family and friends, and to offer up any additional burdens for others that the Lord brings to mind.

THANK YOU, LORD, FOR WHAT YOU HAVE DONE

Long ago You ordained Your plan, and now You are bringing it to pass. (2 Kings 19:25; Isaiah 37:26)

The Lord Jesus was taken up to heaven, after He gave instructions through the Holy Spirit to the apostles He had chosen. (Acts 1:2)

295
~&

LORD, I LISTEN TO YOUR WORDS OF TRUTH

Since God has made me adequate as a minister of the new covenant, as I have received mercy, I do not lose heart. (2 Corinthians 3:6; 4:1)

LORD, I RESPOND TO YOUR INSTRUCTION

This is the day the Lord has made; I will rejoice and be glad in it. (Psalm 118:24)

I want the Lord to establish my heart as blameless and holy before our God and Father at the coming of our Lord Jesus with all His saints. (1 Thessalonians 3:13)

~&

Lord, I thank You for Your eternal plan and for Jesus who brought it to pass. I thank You that You have given me the power to fulfill Your purpose for my life. I will rejoice in the opportunities You have given me and prepare myself for the day when I will see Christ.

DAY 286

BECOMING A PEACEMAKER

LORD, I DRAW NEAR TO YOU

Lord, I want Your Word to be deeply implanted in me so that I will know the truth and be able to express it in the way I live.

O Sovereign Lord, You are God! Your words are true, and You have promised good things to Your servant. (2 Samuel 7:28)

Rejoice in the Lord, O you righteous;
Praise is becoming to the upright. (Psalm 33:1)

Take a moment to affirm the truth of these words from Scripture and ask God to make them a growing reality in your life.

THANK YOU, LORD, FOR WHAT YOU HAVE DONE

God alone stretches out the heavens and treads on the waves of the sea. (Job 9:8)

The day is Yours; the night also is Yours; You established the sun and moon. It was You who set all the boundaries of the earth; You made both summer and winter. (Psalm 74:16-17)

LORD, I LISTEN TO YOUR WORDS OF TRUTH

Through the Spirit, by faith, I eagerly await the righteousness for which I hope. (Galatians 5:5)

LORD, I RESPOND TO YOUR INSTRUCTION

Better a little with the fear of the Lord than great wealth with turmoil. (Proverbs 15:16)

In my faith in our glorious Lord Jesus Christ, I will not show partiality to some people above others. (James 2:1)

Lord, I thank You for Your creation and for Your authority over the heavens and the earth. I thank You for the hope of righteousness through Your Spirit, and I ask that my faith in Christ would make me a peacemaker.

DAY 287

PERSERVERING UNDER TRIAL

LORD, I DRAW NEAR TO YOU

O Lord, I am deeply grateful for Your wonderful acts, for Your abundant promises, and for the gift of my relationship with You through the merits of Christ.

The heavens declare the glory of God,
And the skies proclaim the work of His hands.
Day after day they pour forth speech;
Night after night they reveal knowledge. (Psalm 19:2)
O Lord my God,
I cried to You for help and You healed me. (Psalm 30:1-2)

Take a moment to express your gratitude for the many blessings that you have received from the Lord.

THANK YOU, LORD, FOR WHAT YOU HAVE DONE

297

Your throne, O God, is forever and ever; a scepter of righteousness is the scepter of Your kingdom. (Psalm 45:6)

Heaven is Your throne, and the earth is Your footstool. Your hand made all these things, and so they came into being. (Isaiah 66:1-2)

LORD, I LISTEN TO YOUR WORDS OF TRUTH

I have set my hope on the living God, Who is the Savior of all men, especially of those who believe. (1 Timothy 4:10)

LORD, I RESPOND TO YOUR INSTRUCTION

I desire to be diligent to realize the full assurance of hope to the end. I do not want to become sluggish but to imitate those who through faith and patience inherit the promises. (Hebrews 6:11-12)

Blessed is the man who perseveres under trial, because when he has been approved, he will receive the crown of life that God has promised to those who love Him. (James 1:12)

Lord, I thank You that You reign in righteousness and that all things came into being through You. I have fixed my hope in Your character and promises, and I will persevere under trial and realize the full assurance of hope to the end.

DAY 288

SEEKING THE CITY THAT IS TO COME

LORD, I DRAW NEAR TO YOU

Lord, I give thanks for Your greatness, Your goodness, and Your love, and I now draw near to enjoy Your presence.

Great is the Lord, and most worthy of praise
In the city of our God, His holy mountain.
We have meditated on Your unfailing love, O God,
In the midst of Your temple.
As is Your name, O God,
So is Your praise to the ends of the earth;
Your right hand is filled with righteousness. (Psalm 48:1,9-10)

O come, let us worship and bow down,
Let us kneel before the Lord our Maker. (Psalm 95:6)

Take a moment to consider God's awesome majesty and thank Him that He loves you and wants an intimate relationship with you.

298

THANK YOU, LORD, FOR WHAT YOU HAVE DONE

Great is our Lord and mighty in power; His understanding is infinite. (Psalm 147:5)

Through Christ all things were made, and without Him nothing was made that has been made. In Him was life, and the life was the light of men. (John 1:3-4)

LORD, I LISTEN TO YOUR WORDS OF TRUTH

Here I do not have an enduring city, but I am seeking the city that is to come. (Hebrews 13:14)

LORD, I RESPOND TO YOUR INSTRUCTION

He who loves money will not be satisfied with money; nor he who loves abundance, with its increase. (Ecclesiastes 5:10)

I will covet no one's money or possessions. (Acts 20:33)

Lord, I thank You for Your infinite power and understanding and for the authority of Christ through Whom all things were created. I will seek the city that is to come and not succumb to greed and covetousness.

DAY 289

HONORING MY FATHER
AND MOTHER

❧

LORD, I DRAW NEAR TO YOU

I am grateful to You, O God, for the blessing of Your forgiveness. I thank You that in Christ, You set me free from the guilt of the past and give me hope for the future.

Who can discern his errors?
Cleanse me from hidden faults.
Keep Your servant also from presumptuous sins;
Let them not rule over me. (Psalm 19:13)

Take a moment to ask the Spirit to search your heart and reveal any areas of unconfessed sin. Acknowledge these to the Lord and thank Him for His forgiveness.

THANK YOU, LORD, FOR WHAT YOU HAVE DONE

You declare the end from the beginning, and from ancient times things that have not yet been done, saying, "My purpose will stand, and I will do all My pleasure." (Isaiah 46:10)

God gives life to the dead and calls into being things that do not exist. (Romans 4:17)

299
❧

LORD, I LISTEN TO YOUR WORDS OF TRUTH

Blessed is the one You choose and bring near to live in Your courts. We will be satisfied with the goodness of Your house, of Your holy temple. (Psalm 65:4)

LORD, I RESPOND TO YOUR INSTRUCTION

I will honor my father and my mother. (Exodus 20:12; Deuteronomy 5:16)

The father of the righteous will greatly rejoice, and he who begets a wise son will be glad in him. May my father and mother be glad; may she who gave me birth rejoice. (Proverbs 23:24-25)

❧

Lord, I thank You that Your purpose will stand and that You speak all things into being. I will be satisfied with Your goodness, and will honor my parents in the way that I live.

DAY 290

LETTING GOD'S PEACE RULE
IN MY HEART

❧

LORD, I DRAW NEAR TO YOU

I praise You, Lord, that You are intimately acquainted with my ways and that You always love me and have my best interests at heart.

May my love abound more and more in full knowledge and depth of insight, so that I may be able to approve the things that are excellent, in order to be sincere and blameless until the day of Christ—having been filled with the fruit of righteousness that comes through Jesus Christ, to the glory and praise of God. (Philippians 1:9-11)

Take a moment to offer this day to the Lord and ask Him for the grace to grow in your knowledge and love for Him.

THANK YOU, LORD, FOR WHAT YOU HAVE DONE

To the only God our Savior, through Jesus Christ our Lord, be glory, majesty, dominion, and authority, before all ages and now and forever. Amen. (Jude 25)

LORD, I LISTEN TO YOUR WORDS OF TRUTH

I have been set apart for the gospel of God—I am among those who are called to belong to Jesus Christ. (Romans 1:1,6)

LORD, I RESPOND TO YOUR INSTRUCTION

I will not love the world or the things in the world. If anyone loves the world, the love of the Father is not in him. For all that is in the world—the lust of the flesh, the lust of the eyes, and the pride of life—is not of the Father but of the world. And the world and its lusts are passing away, but the one who does the will of God abides forever. (1 John 2:15-17)

I will let the peace of Christ rule in my heart, to which I was called as a member of one body, and I will be thankful. (Colossians 3:15)

❧

Lord, I thank You that all glory, majesty, dominion, and authority belong to You. I will not love the things of the world but will do the will of God and let the peace of Christ rule in my heart.

DAY 291

LIVING UPRIGHTLY IN MY GENERATION

꙳

LORD, I DRAW NEAR TO YOU

As I approach Your throne of grace today, I am grateful that You care about the things that concern me and that You want me to offer them up to You.

Hear, O Lord, and be merciful to me;
O Lord, be my helper.
You turned my mourning into dancing;
You removed my sackcloth and clothed me with gladness,
That my heart may sing praise to You and not be silent.
O Lord my God, I will give thanks to You forever. (Psalm 30:10-12)

Take a moment to share your personal needs with God, including your physical, emotional, relational, and spiritual concerns.

THANK YOU, LORD, FOR WHAT YOU HAVE DONE

301
꙳

O Lord, God of heaven, You are the great and awesome God, keeping Your covenant of loyal love with those who love You and who obey Your commands. (Nehemiah 1:5)

The Lord said, "In My Father's house are many dwellings; if it were not so, I would have told you. I am going there to prepare a place for you. And if I go and prepare a place for you, I will come again and receive you to Myself, that you also may be where I am." (John 14:2-3)

LORD, I LISTEN TO YOUR WORDS OF TRUTH

I have been called, having been loved by God the Father and kept by Jesus Christ. (Jude 1)

LORD, I RESPOND TO YOUR INSTRUCTION

I desire to be righteous before You in my generation. (Genesis 7:1)

꙳

Lord, I thank You that You keep Your covenant of loyal love and that Jesus is preparing a dwelling place for those who know Him. I thank You for calling and loving me. Help me to be upright in my generation.

DAY 292

DOING RIGHT IN THE SIGHT OF GOD

❧

LORD, I DRAW NEAR TO YOU

Lord, You have invited me to pray for the needs of others, and since You desire what is best for them, I take this opportunity to bring these requests to You.

May I remember those in prison as though bound with them, and those who are mistreated, since I myself am also in the body. (Hebrews 13:3)

Take a moment to lift up the needs of your family and friends, and to offer up any additional burdens for others that the Lord brings to mind.

THANK YOU, LORD, FOR WHAT YOU HAVE DONE

The law of the Lord is perfect, restoring the soul. The testimony of the Lord is sure, making wise the simple. The precepts of the Lord are right, rejoicing the heart. The commandment of the Lord is pure, enlightening the eyes. The fear of the Lord is clean, enduring forever. The judgments of the Lord are true and altogether righteous. They are more desirable than gold, than much pure gold; they are sweeter than honey, than honey from the comb. Moreover, by them is Your servant warned; in keeping them there is great reward. (Psalm 19:7-11)

All that belongs to the Father is Mine. Therefore I said that He will take from what is Mine and make it known to you." (John 16:15)

LORD, I LISTEN TO YOUR WORDS OF TRUTH

The Lord is close to the brokenhearted and saves those who are crushed in spirit. (Psalm 34:18)

LORD, I RESPOND TO YOUR INSTRUCTION

Like Josiah, I desire to do what is right in the sight of the Lord, walking in the ways of David and not turning aside to the right or to the left. (2 Chronicles 34:1-2)

❧

Lord, I thank You for Your life-giving words and for Your Holy Spirit who illuminates them. I thank You for Your compassion and mercy. I will seek to do what is right in Your sight.

DAY 293

DECLARING GOD'S LOVINGKINDNESS

∾

LORD, I DRAW NEAR TO YOU

Lord, I want Your Word to be deeply implanted in me so that I will know the truth and be able to express it in the way I live.

I will bless the Lord at all times;
His praise will always be in my mouth.
My soul will make its boast in the Lord;
The humble will hear and be glad.
O magnify the Lord with me,
And let us exalt His name together. (Psalm 34:1-3)

Take a moment to affirm the truth of these words from Scripture and ask God to make them a growing reality in your life.

THANK YOU, LORD, FOR WHAT YOU HAVE DONE

It is good to give thanks to the Lord and to sing praises to Your name, O Most High, to declare Your lovingkindness in the morning and Your faithfulness at night. (Psalm 92:1-2)

Through Jesus the forgiveness of sins is proclaimed, that through Him everyone who believes is justified from all things from which they could not be justified by the law of Moses. (Acts 13:38-39)

LORD, I LISTEN TO YOUR WORDS OF TRUTH

The sacrifices of God are a broken spirit; a broken and contrite heart, O God, You will not despise. (Psalm 51:17)

LORD, I RESPOND TO YOUR INSTRUCTION

A fool shows his annoyance at once, but a prudent man overlooks an insult. (Proverbs 12:16)

I will not be quickly provoked in my spirit, for anger rests in the bosom of fools. (Ecclesiastes 7:9)

∾

Lord, I thank You for Your lovingkindness and faithfulness and for the forgiveness of sins that is granted through Jesus Christ. I will humble myself before You, and keep myself from anger.

303
∾

DAY 294

CALLING ON GOD IN PRAYER

❧

LORD, I DRAW NEAR TO YOU

O Lord, I am deeply grateful for Your wonderful acts, for Your abundant promises, and for the gift of my relationship with You through the merits of Christ.

Surely God is my helper;
The Lord is the sustainer of my soul. (Psalm 54:4)

Take a moment to express your gratitude for the many blessings that you have received from the Lord.

THANK YOU, LORD, FOR WHAT YOU HAVE DONE

Your merciful love is higher than the heavens, and Your truth reaches to the skies. (Psalm 108:4)

If by the trespass of the one man, death reigned through that one man, much more will those who receive the abundance of grace and of the gift of righteousness reign in life through the one Man, Jesus Christ. Consequently, just as the result of one trespass was condemnation for all men, so also the result of one act of righteousness was justification that brings life for all men. For just as through the disobedience of the one man the many were made sinners, so also through the obedience of the one Man the many will be made righteous. (Romans 5:17-19)

LORD, I LISTEN TO YOUR WORDS OF TRUTH

I love the Lord, because He has heard my voice and my supplications. Because He turned His ear to me, I will call on Him as long as I live. (Psalm 116:1-2)

LORD, I RESPOND TO YOUR INSTRUCTION

Your Word is a lamp to my feet and a light to my path. I have inclined my heart to perform Your statutes to the very end. (Psalm 119:105, 112)

❧

Lord, I thank You for Your merciful love and truth and for the abundance of grace that came through Jesus Christ. I thank You for hearing my prayers. Help me to walk in the light of Your Word.

DAY 295

ASKING AND RECEIVING

LORD, I DRAW NEAR TO YOU

Lord, I give thanks for Your greatness, Your goodness, and Your love, and I now draw near to enjoy Your presence.

The Lord God of hosts—
He Who touches the earth and it melts,
And all who live in it mourn;
He Who builds His staircase in the heavens
And founded the expanse over the earth;
He Who calls for the waters of the sea
And pours them out over the face of the earth—
The Lord is His name. (Amos 9:5-6)

Take a moment to consider God's awesome majesty and thank Him that He loves you and wants an intimate relationship with you.

THANK YOU, LORD, FOR WHAT YOU HAVE DONE

305

The Lord of hosts will be exalted in judgment, and the holy God will show Himself holy in righteousness. (Isaiah 5:16)

God is able to do immeasurably more than all that we ask or think, according to His power that is at work within us. To Him be glory in the church and in Christ Jesus throughout all generations, for ever and ever. (Ephesians 3:20-21)

LORD, I LISTEN TO YOUR WORDS OF TRUTH

Let the wicked forsake his way and the unrighteous man his thoughts; let him return to the Lord, and He will have mercy on him, and to our God, for He will abundantly pardon. (Isaiah 55:7)

LORD, I RESPOND TO YOUR INSTRUCTION

I will train up each child according to His way; even when he is old he will not depart from it. (Proverbs 22:6)

Lord, I thank You that You are exalted in judgment and holy in righteousness and that You are able to do so much more than I can ask or think. I will forsake anything that is displeasing to You. Help me to instruct others in Your ways.

DAY 296

BEING STRONG AND COURAGEOUS

❧

LORD, I DRAW NEAR TO YOU

I am grateful to You, O God, for the blessing of Your forgiveness. I thank You that in Christ, You set me free from the guilt of the past and give me hope for the future.

Have mercy on me, O God,
According to Your loyal love;
According to the greatness of Your compassion
Blot out my transgressions.
Wash me completely from my iniquity
And cleanse me from my sin.
For I know my transgressions,
And my sin is ever before me.
Against You, You only, have I sinned
And done what is evil in Your sight,
So that You are justified when You speak
And blameless when You judge. (Psalm 51:1-4)

Take a moment to ask the Spirit to search your heart and reveal any areas of unconfessed sin. Acknowledge these to the Lord and thank Him for His forgiveness.

THANK YOU, LORD, FOR WHAT YOU HAVE DONE

The Lord is our judge, the Lord is our lawgiver, the Lord is our king; it is He who will save us. (Isaiah 33:22)

LORD, I LISTEN TO YOUR WORDS OF TRUTH

Whoever believes in the Son has eternal life, but whoever rejects the Son will not see life, for the wrath of God remains on him. (John 3:36)

LORD, I RESPOND TO YOUR INSTRUCTION

I will be strong and courageous; I will not be afraid or discouraged, for the Lord my God will be with me wherever I go. (Joshua 1:9)

❧

Lord, I thank You that You are my King and that eternal life rests in Your Son. I will be strong and courageous, because You are with me wherever I go.

DAY 297

RESTING IN THE HOPE
OF ETERNAL LIFE

LORD, I DRAW NEAR TO YOU

I praise You, Lord, that You are intimately acquainted with my ways and that You always love me and have my best interests at heart.

May I not work for the food that perishes, but for the food that endures to eternal life, which the Son of Man gives me, for God the Father has set His seal on Him. (John 6:27)

Take a moment to offer this day to the Lord and ask Him for the grace to grow in your knowledge and love for Him.

THANK YOU, LORD, FOR WHAT YOU HAVE DONE

The Lord is good, a refuge in times of trouble; He knows those who trust in Him. (Nahum 1:7)

The faith of those chosen of God and the knowledge of the truth, which is according to godliness, is a faith and knowledge resting in the hope of eternal life, which God, Who does not lie, promised before the beginning of time. At the appointed time, He manifested His Word through the preaching entrusted to the apostles by the command of God our Savior. (Titus 1:1-3)

307

LORD, I LISTEN TO YOUR WORDS OF TRUTH

God did not appoint me to suffer wrath but to obtain salvation through my Lord Jesus Christ. He died for me, so that, whether I am awake or asleep, I may live together with Him. (1 Thessalonians 5:9-10)

LORD, I RESPOND TO YOUR INSTRUCTION

O Lord, I hope for Your salvation, and I follow Your commands. My soul keeps Your testimonies, for I love them greatly. I keep Your precepts and Your testimonies, for all my ways are known to You. (Psalm 119:166-168)

Lord, I thank You that You are a refuge in times of trouble and that You have called me to faith and hope in Jesus Christ. I thank You for His gift of salvation. I will hope in Your promises.

DAY 298

CLINGING TO THE GOD
OF ALL COMFORT

LORD, I DRAW NEAR TO YOU

As I approach Your throne of grace today, I am grateful that You care about the things that concern me and that You want me to offer them up to You.

May I be strong and courageous, being careful to obey Your Word; may I not turn from it to the right or to the left, that I may act wisely wherever I go. (Joshua 1:7)

Take a moment to share your personal needs with God, including your physical, emotional, relational, and spiritual concerns.

THANK YOU, LORD, FOR WHAT YOU HAVE DONE

Blessed be the God and Father of our Lord Jesus Christ, the Father of mercies and the God of all comfort. (2 Corinthians 1:3)

Christ had to be made like His brothers in every way, in order that He might become a merciful and faithful high priest in things pertaining to God, to make propitiation for the sins of the people. Because He Himself suffered when He was tempted, He is able to help those who are being tempted. (Hebrews 2:17-18)

LORD, I LISTEN TO YOUR WORDS OF TRUTH

From the beginning, God chose me for salvation through sanctification by the Spirit and through belief in the truth. He called me to this through the gospel, that I might obtain the glory of my Lord Jesus Christ. (2 Thessalonians 2:13-14)

LORD, I RESPOND TO YOUR INSTRUCTION

I do not want to grow weary in doing what is right. (2 Thessalonians 3:13)

Lord, I thank You that You are the Father of mercies and the God of all comfort and that Christ helps me when I am being tempted. I thank You for calling me into a relationship with You. I will not grow weary in doing what is right.

DAY 299

NOURISHING OTHERS
IN THE FAITH

❧

LORD, I DRAW NEAR TO YOU

Lord, You have invited me to pray for the needs of others, and since You desire what is best for them, I take this opportunity to bring these requests to You.

We must encourage one another daily, as long as it is still called "Today," lest any of us be hardened by the deceitfulness of sin. (Hebrews 3:13)

Take a moment to lift up the needs of your family and friends, and to offer up any additional burdens for others that the Lord brings to mind.

THANK YOU, LORD, FOR WHAT YOU HAVE DONE

The Lord of hosts is wonderful in counsel and great in wisdom. (Isaiah 28:29)

Jesus as our high priest meets our needs. (Hebrews 7:26)

309
❧

LORD, I LISTEN TO YOUR WORDS OF TRUTH

Those whom You love You rebuke and discipline. Therefore I will be zealous and repent. (Revelation 3:19)

LORD, I RESPOND TO YOUR INSTRUCTION

In Christ Jesus, God's whole building is joined together and growing into a holy temple in the Lord, in Whom we also are being built together into a dwelling of God in the Spirit. (Ephesians 2:21-22)

Grace has been given to each one of us according to the measure of the gift of Christ. And He gave some to be apostles, some to be prophets, some to be evangelists, and some to be pastors and teachers, for the equipping of the saints for the work of ministry, for the building up of the body of Christ. (Ephesians 4:7,11-12)

❧

Lord, I thank You for Your wonderful counsel and wisdom and for the perfection of Jesus, my high priest. I thank You for loving me enough to correct me. I will seek to nourish others in the faith through the spiritual gifts You have given to me.

DAY 300

SUFFERING FOR THE SAKE OF CHRIST

LORD, I DRAW NEAR TO YOU

Lord, I want Your Word to be deeply implanted in me so that I will know the truth and be able to express it in the way I live.

I have tasted and seen that the Lord is good;
Blessed is the man who takes refuge in Him! (Psalm 34:8)

Take a moment to affirm the truth of these words from Scripture and ask God to make them a growing reality in your life.

THANK YOU, LORD, FOR WHAT YOU HAVE DONE

I will give thanks to the God of heaven, for His merciful love endures forever. (Psalm 136:26)

By the will of God, I have been sanctified through the offering of the body of Jesus Christ once for all. And every priest stands daily ministering and offering again and again the same sacrifices, which can never take away sins. But when this Priest had offered for all time one sacrifice for sins, He sat down at the right hand of God, waiting from that time for His enemies to be made a footstool for His feet. For by one offering, He has made perfect forever those who are being sanctified. (Hebrews 10:10-14)

LORD, I LISTEN TO YOUR WORDS OF TRUTH

The secret things belong to the Lord our God, but the things revealed belong to us and to our children forever, that we may observe Your words. (Deuteronomy 29:29)

LORD, I RESPOND TO YOUR INSTRUCTION

Who is going to harm me if I am eager to do good? But even if I should suffer for what is right, I am blessed, and I will not fear what they fear or be intimidated. (1 Peter 3:13-14)

Lord, I thank You for Your merciful love and for the perfect offering of Christ as a sacrifice for sins. I thank You for the things You have revealed in Your Word. I will persevere and be willing to suffer for the sake of Christ.

DAY 301

WALKING IN GOD'S WAYS

❧

LORD, I DRAW NEAR TO YOU

O Lord, I am deeply grateful for Your wonderful acts, for Your abundant promises, and for the gift of my relationship with You through the merits of Christ.

I will sing of Your strength,
Yes, I will sing of Your mercy in the morning,
For You have been my stronghold,
My refuge in times of trouble.
To You, O my Strength, I will sing praises,
For God is my fortress, my loving God. (Psalm 59:16-17)

Take a moment to express your gratitude for the many blessings that you have received from the Lord.

THANK YOU, LORD, FOR WHAT YOU HAVE DONE

Your testimonies, which You have commanded, are righteous and trustworthy. Your righteousness is everlasting, and Your law is truth. (Psalm 119:138,142)

LORD, I LISTEN TO YOUR WORDS OF TRUTH

Thus says the Lord, my Redeemer, the Holy One of Israel: "I am the Lord your God, Who teaches you to profit, Who leads you in the way you should go." (Isaiah 48:17)

LORD, I RESPOND TO YOUR INSTRUCTION

I will commit my works to the Lord, and my plans will be established. (Proverbs 16:3)

The Lord is far from the wicked, but He hears the prayer of the righteous. (Proverbs 15:29)

❧

Lord, I thank You for the trustworthiness of Your words and for Your great and awesome deeds. I thank You for leading me in the way I should go. I will commit my works to You and walk in Your ways.

DAY 302

SEEKING GOD WITH ALL MY HEART

❧

LORD, I DRAW NEAR TO YOU

Lord, I give thanks for Your greatness, Your goodness, and Your love, and I now draw near to enjoy Your presence.

The Lord reigns; He is clothed with majesty;
The Lord is robed in majesty and is armed with strength.
Indeed, the world is firmly established; it cannot be moved.
Your throne is established from of old;
You are from everlasting.
Your testimonies stand firm;
Holiness adorns Your house,
O Lord, forever. (Psalm 93:1-2,5)

Take a moment to consider God's awesome majesty and thank Him that He loves you and wants an intimate relationship with you.

THANK YOU, LORD, FOR WHAT YOU HAVE DONE

Righteousness and justice are the foundation of Your throne;
lovingkindness and truth go before You. (Psalm 89:14)

The Lord is our praise, and He is our God, Who performed for the children of Israel those great and awesome wonders which they saw with their own eyes. (Deuteronomy 10:21)

LORD, I LISTEN TO YOUR WORDS OF TRUTH

I will call upon You and come and pray to You, and You will listen to me. I will seek You and find You when I search for You with all my heart. (Jeremiah 29:12-13)

LORD, I RESPOND TO YOUR INSTRUCTION

Like Hezekiah, I want to do what is good and right and true before the Lord my God by seeking Him with all my heart. (2 Chronicles 31:20-21)

The Lord rewards every man for his righteousness and faithfulness. (1 Samuel 26:23)

❧

Lord, I thank You that Your throne is founded on righteousness and justice and that You have performed wonders for Your people. I will continue to search for You with all my heart and to do what is right in Your sight.

DAY 303

MANIFESTING GOD'S GIFTS

❧

LORD, I DRAW NEAR TO YOU

I am grateful to You, O God, for the blessing of Your forgiveness. I thank You that in Christ, You set me free from the guilt of the past and give me hope for the future.

Does God not see my ways
And count all my steps? (Job 31:4)

If I claim to be without sin, I deceive myself, and the truth is not in me. If I confess my sins, He is faithful and just and will forgive me my sins and purify me from all unrighteousness. If I claim I have not sinned, I make Him a liar and His Word is not in me. (1 John 1:8-10)

Take a moment to ask the Spirit to search your heart and reveal any areas of unconfessed sin. Acknowledge these to the Lord and thank Him for His forgiveness.

THANK YOU, LORD, FOR WHAT YOU HAVE DONE

313
❧

The Lord is upright; He is my Rock, and there is no unrighteousness in Him. (Psalm 92:15)

You are the Lord our God, who brought Your people out of Egypt so that they would no longer be their slaves; You broke the bars of their yoke and enabled them to walk with heads held high. (Leviticus 26:13)

LORD, I LISTEN TO YOUR WORDS OF TRUTH

I will not be afraid of those who kill the body and after that can do no more. But I will fear the One who, after killing, has authority to cast into hell. (Luke 12:4-5)

LORD, I RESPOND TO YOUR INSTRUCTION

Just as we have many members in one body, but all the members do not have the same function, so we who are many are one body in Christ and individually members of one another. And we have different gifts, according to the grace given to us. (Romans 12:4-6)

❧

Lord, I thank You that You have delivered Your people from their slavery to sin and death. I will revere You more than people and use the gifts You have given to me to uplift other members of Your body.

DAY 304

COMPREHENDING THE DEPTH OF GOD'S LOVE

❧

LORD, I DRAW NEAR TO YOU

I praise You, Lord, that You are intimately acquainted with my ways and that You always love me and have my best interests at heart.

Teach me to do Your will,
For You are my God;
May Your good Spirit lead me on level ground. (Psalm 143:10)

Take a moment to offer this day to the Lord and ask Him for the grace to grow in your knowledge and love for Him.

THANK YOU, LORD, FOR WHAT YOU HAVE DONE

The eyes of the Lord move to and fro throughout the whole earth to strengthen those whose hearts are fully committed to Him. (2 Chronicles 16:9)

LORD, I LISTEN TO YOUR WORDS OF TRUTH

May God grant me, according to the riches of His glory, to be strengthened with power through His Spirit in my inner being, so that Christ may dwell in my heart through faith. And may I, being rooted and grounded in love, be able to comprehend with all the saints what is the width and length and height and depth of the love of Christ, and to know this love that surpasses knowledge, that I may be filled to all the fullness of God. (Ephesians 3:16-19)

LORD, I RESPOND TO YOUR INSTRUCTION

I have sought You with my whole heart; do not let me stray from Your commands. (Psalm 119:10)

Blessed is everyone who fears the Lord, who walks in His ways. (Psalm 128:1)

❧

Lord, I thank You for strengthening the hearts of those who are committed to You. Help me to gain a deeper understanding of the love of Christ, as I seek You with my whole heart and walk in Your ways.

DAY 305

TAKING UP MY CROSS

—❧—

LORD, I DRAW NEAR TO YOU

As I approach Your throne of grace today, I am grateful that You care about the things that concern me and that You want me to offer them up to You.

May I be above reproach, blameless as a steward of God, not self-willed, not quick-tempered, not given to wine, not violent, not fond of dishonest gain, but hospitable, a lover of what is good, sensible, just, holy, and self-controlled. (Titus 1:6-8)

Take a moment to share your personal needs with God, including your physical, emotional, relational, and spiritual concerns.

THANK YOU, LORD, FOR WHAT YOU HAVE DONE

As for God, His way is perfect; the Word of the Lord is proven. He is a shield to all who take refuge in Him. For who is God besides the Lord? And who is the Rock except our God? (Psalm 18:30-31)

You save the humble but bring low those whose eyes are haughty. (Psalm 18:27)

315
—❧—

LORD, I LISTEN TO YOUR WORDS OF TRUTH

If anyone wishes to come after You, he must deny himself and take up his cross and follow You. For whoever wants to save his life will lose it, but whoever loses his life for Your sake and the gospel's will find it. For what is a man profited if he gains the whole world, yet forfeits his soul? Or what will a man give in exchange for his soul? (Matthew 16:24-26; Mark 8:34-37; Luke 9:23-25)

LORD, I RESPOND TO YOUR INSTRUCTION

May the God Who gives endurance and encouragement grant us to be of the same mind toward one another according to Christ Jesus, so that with one accord and one mouth we may glorify the God and Father of our Lord Jesus Christ. (Romans 15:5-6)

—❧—

Lord, I thank You that Your way is perfect and that You save the humble. I pray that I would save my life by losing it for the sake of Christ. Help me to be of one mind with other believers.

DAY 306

HONORING GOD WITH MY FIRSTFRUITS

LORD, I DRAW NEAR TO YOU

Lord, You have invited me to pray for the needs of others, and since You desire what is best for them, I take this opportunity to bring these requests to You.

May the God of peace Himself sanctify us completely, and may our whole spirit, soul, and body will be preserved blameless at the coming of our Lord Jesus Christ. He who calls us is faithful, who also will do it. (1 Thessalonians 5:23-24)

Take a moment to lift up the needs of your family and friends, and to offer up any additional burdens for others that the Lord brings to mind.

THANK YOU, LORD, FOR WHAT YOU HAVE DONE

I will give thanks to the Lord according to His righteousness and will sing praise to the name of the Lord Most High. (Psalm 7:17)

As the earth brings forth its sprouts and as a garden causes that which is sown to spring up, so the Lord God will make righteousness and praise spring up before all nations. (Isaiah 61:11)

LORD, I LISTEN TO YOUR WORDS OF TRUTH

Through Jesus, I will continually offer to God a sacrifice of praise, that is, the fruit of my lips that give thanks to His name. (Hebrews 13:15)

LORD, I RESPOND TO YOUR INSTRUCTION

Riches do not profit in the day of wrath, but righteousness delivers from death. (Proverbs 11:4)

I will honor the Lord with my wealth and with the firstfruits of all my increase. (Proverbs 3:9)

Lord, I thank You for Your perfect character and for Your intention to extend Your righteousness throughout the earth. I will take pleasure in You above all things and honor You with the resources You have entrusted to me.

DAY 307

CELEBRATING CHRIST IN ME

❧

LORD, I DRAW NEAR TO YOU

Lord, I want Your Word to be deeply implanted in me so that I will know the truth and be able to express it in the way I live.

O God, You are my God;
Earnestly I seek You;
My soul thirsts for You;
My body longs for You,
In a dry and weary land
Where there is no water. (Psalm 63:1)

Take a moment to affirm the truth of these words from Scripture and ask God to make them a growing reality in your life.

THANK YOU, LORD, FOR WHAT YOU HAVE DONE

Let me fall into the hands of the Lord, for His mercies are very great; but do not let me fall into the hands of men. (1 Chronicles 21:13)

I will sing to the Lord and give praise to the Lord, for He has rescued the life of the needy from the hands of evildoers. (Jeremiah 20:13)

317
❧

LORD, I LISTEN TO YOUR WORDS OF TRUTH

Lord Jesus, You are in Your Father, and I am in You, and You are in me. (John 14:20)

LORD, I RESPOND TO YOUR INSTRUCTION

Cursed is the one who trusts in man, who depends on flesh for his strength and whose heart turns away from the Lord. But blessed is the man who trusts in the Lord, whose confidence is in Him. (Jeremiah 17:5,7)

The fear of man brings a snare, but he who trusts in the Lord is set on high. (Proverbs 29:25)

❧

Lord, I thank You for the greatness of Your mercies and for rescuing the life of the needy. I thank You that I am in Christ and Christ is in me. I will trust in You and not put my hope in people.

DAY 308

RECEIVING THE COMFORT OF THE HOLY SPIRIT

⤫

LORD, I DRAW NEAR TO YOU

O Lord, I am deeply grateful for Your wonderful acts, for Your abundant promises, and for the gift of my relationship with You through the merits of Christ.

I will give thanks to the Lord, for He is good;
His lovingkindness endures forever. (Psalm 118:1)

Take a moment to express your gratitude for the many blessings that you have received from the Lord.

THANK YOU, LORD, FOR WHAT YOU HAVE DONE

O Lord, God of Israel, there is no God like You in heaven above or on earth below; You keep Your covenant and mercy with Your servants who walk before You with all their heart. (1 Kings 8:23; 2 Chronicles 6:14)

318

You promised to restore the children of Israel and Judah, saying, "They shall be My people, and I will be their God. And I will give them one heart and one way, so that they will always fear Me for their own good and the good of their children after them." (Jeremiah 32:38-39)

LORD, I LISTEN TO YOUR WORDS OF TRUTH

It is for my good that You returned to the Father, because You have sent the Counselor, the Holy Spirit, to me. (John 16:7)

LORD, I RESPOND TO YOUR INSTRUCTION

The name of the Lord is a strong tower; the righteous run to it and are safe. (Proverbs 18:10)

I will stop trusting in man, whose breath is in his nostrils. For in what should he be esteemed? (Isaiah 2:22)

⤫

Lord, I thank You that You are utterly unique and that You are faithful to Your promises. I thank You for the Holy Spirit Who lives in me and comforts me. I will trust in You my strong tower.

DAY 309

CONCERNING MYSELF WITH THE THINGS OF GOD

LORD, I DRAW NEAR TO YOU

Lord, I give thanks for Your greatness, Your goodness, and Your love, and I now draw near to enjoy Your presence.

Your name, O Lord, endures forever,
Your renown, O Lord, through all generations. (Psalm 135:13)

Take a moment to consider God's awesome majesty and thank Him that He loves you and wants an intimate relationship with you.

THANK YOU, LORD, FOR WHAT YOU HAVE DONE

You must be treated as holy by those who come near You, and before all people, You will be honored. (Leviticus 10:3)

For those who revere Your name, the Sun of righteousness will rise with healing in His wings. And they will go out and leap like calves released from the stall. (Malachi 4:2)

319

LORD, I LISTEN TO YOUR WORDS OF TRUTH

We are an epistle from Christ, written not with ink, but with the Spirit of the living God, not on tablets of stone, but on tablets of human hearts. (2 Corinthians 3:3)

LORD, I RESPOND TO YOUR INSTRUCTION

I will not fear those who kill the body but cannot kill the soul, but rather, I will fear the One Who is able to destroy both soul and body in hell. (Matthew 10:28)

I want to be more concerned about the things of God than the things of men. (Mark 8:33)

Lord, I thank You for Your unblemished holiness and for Your promise to perfect those who revere Your name. I thank You for the Spirit of the living God Who resides in my heart. I will revere You more than men.

DAY 310

STIRRING OTHERS TOWARD LOVE AND GOOD WORKS

❧

LORD, I DRAW NEAR TO YOU

I am grateful to You, O God, for the blessing of Your forgiveness. I thank You that in Christ, You set me free from the guilt of the past and give me hope for the future.

No temptation has overtaken me except what is common to man. And God is faithful, Who will not let me be tempted beyond what I am able, but with the temptation will also provide a way out, so that I may be able to endure it. (1 Corinthians 10:13)

Take a moment to ask the Spirit to search your heart and reveal any areas of unconfessed sin. Acknowledge these to the Lord and thank Him for His forgiveness.

THANK YOU, LORD, FOR WHAT YOU HAVE DONE

320
❧

The Lord Jesus, Who is holy and true, holds the key of David. What He opens no one can shut, and what He shuts no one can open. (Revelation 3:7)

Where Jesus went, the blind received sight, the lame walked, the lepers were cured, the deaf heard, the dead were raised up, and the good news was preached to the poor. (Matthew 11:5)

LORD, I LISTEN TO YOUR WORDS OF TRUTH

If I belong to Christ, then I am Abraham's seed and an heir according to the promise. (Galatians 3:29)

LORD, I RESPOND TO YOUR INSTRUCTION

We must encourage one another daily, as long as it is still called "Today," lest any of us be hardened by the deceitfulness of sin. (Hebrews 3:13)

We should consider how to stir up one another toward love and good works. (Hebrews 10:24)

❧

Lord, I thank You for the authority and for the servanthood of the Lord Jesus Christ. I thank You that I belong to Him. I will encourage others and stir them toward love and good works.

DAY 311

GUARDING MY CONSCIENCE

LORD, I DRAW NEAR TO YOU

I praise You, Lord, that You are intimately acquainted with my ways and that You always love me and have my best interests at heart.

May I have no other gods before You nor make for myself an idol in any form, because You are a jealous God, punishing the children for the sin of the fathers to the third and fourth generation of those who hate You, but showing love to a thousand of those who love You and keep Your commandments. (Exodus 20:3-6)

Take a moment to offer this day to the Lord and ask Him for the grace to grow in your knowledge and love for Him.

THANK YOU, LORD, FOR WHAT YOU HAVE DONE

Jesus preached the gospel of the kingdom of God, and said, "The time is fulfilled, and the kingdom of God is at hand. Repent and believe the good news." (Mark 1:14-15)

LORD, I LISTEN TO YOUR WORDS OF TRUTH

It is for freedom that Christ has set me free. I should stand firm, therefore, and not let myself be burdened again by a yoke of slavery. (Galatians 5:1)

LORD, I RESPOND TO YOUR INSTRUCTION

I was once darkness, but now I am light in the Lord. I will walk as a child of light (for the fruit of the light consists in all goodness and righteousness and truth), learning what is pleasing to the Lord. (Ephesians 5:8-10)

I want my conscience to testify that I have conducted myself in the world in the holiness and sincerity that are from God, not in fleshly wisdom but in the grace of God, especially in my relations with others. (2 Corinthians 1:12)

Lord, I thank You that there is no one like You and that You sent Jesus into the world so that we could enter into a relationship with You. I thank You for setting me free from the burden of my sins. Help me to walk as a child of light and conduct my affairs in holiness and sincerity.

DAY 312

DOING ALL TO HONOR CHRIST

LORD, I DRAW NEAR TO YOU

As I approach Your throne of grace today, I am grateful that You care about the things that concern me and that You want me to offer them up to You.

May I not throw away my confidence; it will be richly rewarded. Let me persevere so that when I have done the will of God, I will receive what He has promised. (Hebrews 10:35-36)

Above all, give me a fervent love for others, because love covers a multitude of sins. (1 Peter 4:8)

Take a moment to share your personal needs with God, including your physical, emotional, relational, and spiritual concerns.

THANK YOU, LORD, FOR WHAT YOU HAVE DONE

You know me, O Lord; You see me and test my thoughts about You. (Jeremiah 12:3)

If anyone is ashamed of You and Your words in this adulterous and sinful generation, the Son of Man will be ashamed of him when He comes in the glory of His Father with the holy angels. (Mark 8:38)

LORD, I LISTEN TO YOUR WORDS OF TRUTH

To me, to live is Christ and to die is gain. (Philippians 1:21)

LORD, I RESPOND TO YOUR INSTRUCTION

I do not want to love praise from men more than praise from God. (John 12:43)

Whatever I do, I should do all to the glory of God. (1 Corinthians 10:31)

Lord, I thank You that You know me and I am not ashamed of Jesus Christ or of His words. For me, to live is Christ and to die is gain, and I will do all things for Your honor and glory.

DAY 313

STRIVING TOGETHER FOR THE GOSPEL

LORD, I DRAW NEAR TO YOU

Lord, You have invited me to pray for the needs of others, and since You desire what is best for them, I take this opportunity to bring these requests to You.

May the God who gives endurance and encouragement grant us to be of the same mind toward one another according to Christ Jesus, so that with one accord and one mouth we may glorify the God and Father of our Lord Jesus Christ. (Romans 15:5-6)

Take a moment to lift up the needs of your family and friends, and to offer up any additional burdens for others that the Lord brings to mind.

THANK YOU, LORD, FOR WHAT YOU HAVE DONE

In his heart a man plans his way, but the Lord determines his steps. (Proverbs 16:9)

The Son of Man knew that He must suffer many things and be rejected by the elders, chief priests, and scribes, and be killed and be raised on the third day. (Luke 9:22)

LORD, I LISTEN TO YOUR WORDS OF TRUTH

I have been made complete in Christ, who is the head over all rule and authority. (Colossians 2:10)

LORD, I RESPOND TO YOUR INSTRUCTION

I will conduct myself in a manner worthy of the gospel of Christ, standing firm in one spirit with other believers, with one mind striving together for the faith of the gospel. (Philippians 1:27)

As I have been instructed how I ought to walk and to please God, I want to follow Paul's exhortation in the Lord Jesus to do this more and more. (1 Thessalonians 4:1)

Lord, I thank You that You determine my steps and that Your Son suffered rejection and death on my behalf. I thank You for making me complete in Christ. I will conduct myself in a manner that is pleasing and honoring to You and strive together with other believers for the faith of the gospel.

DAY 314

EXTOLLING MY ETERNAL GOD

❧

Lord, I want Your Word to be deeply implanted in me so that I will know the truth and be able to express it in the way I live.

Make a joyful shout to God, all the earth!
Sing the glory of His name;
Make His praise glorious.
Say to God, "How awesome are Your works!
Through the greatness of Your power
Your enemies submit themselves to You.
All the earth will worship You
And sing praises to You;
They will sing praise to Your name." (Psalm 66:1-4)

Take a moment to affirm the truth of these words from Scripture and ask God to make them a growing reality in your life.

THANK YOU, LORD, FOR WHAT YOU HAVE DONE

My days are like a lengthened shadow, and I wither away like grass. But You, O Lord, will endure forever, and the remembrance of Your name to all generations. (Psalm 102:11-12)

Blessed is the King who comes in the name of the Lord! Peace in heaven and glory in the highest! (Luke 19:38)

LORD, I LISTEN TO YOUR WORDS OF TRUTH

I am from God and am an overcomer, because He who is in me is greater than he who is in the world. (1 John 4:4)

LORD, I RESPOND TO YOUR INSTRUCTION

I will not be ashamed to testify about our Lord, but I will join with others in suffering for the gospel according to the power of God. (2 Timothy 1:8)

❧

Lord, I thank You that You are eternal and that Christ has come in Your name. I thank You for dwelling in me. Help me never to be ashamed of Jesus Christ but to be willing to suffer for the gospel according to Your power.

DAY 315

PARTICIPATING IN GOD'S GREAT COMMISSION

~❧~

LORD, I DRAW NEAR TO YOU

O Lord, I am deeply grateful for Your wonderful acts, for Your abundant promises, and for the gift of my relationship with You through the merits of Christ.

Even to my old age, You are the same,
And even to my gray hairs You will carry me.
You have made me, and You will bear me;
You will sustain me and You will deliver me. (Isaiah 46:4)

Take a moment to express your gratitude for the many blessings that you have received from the Lord.

THANK YOU, LORD, FOR WHAT YOU HAVE DONE

I will ascribe to the Lord glory and strength. I will ascribe to the Lord the glory due His name and worship the Lord in the beauty of holiness. (Psalm 29:1-2)

Christ was in the world, and the world was made through Him, and the world did not know Him. He came to His own, but His own did not receive Him. (John 1:10-11)

325

LORD, I LISTEN TO YOUR WORDS OF TRUTH

In the morning, O Lord, You will hear my voice; in the morning I will set my prayers before You and I will look to You. (Psalm 5:3)

LORD, I RESPOND TO YOUR INSTRUCTION

As the Father sent the Son into the world, He also has sent us into the world. And He has prayed for those who will believe in Him through our message. (John 17:18,20)

~❧~

Lord, I thank You for Your glory and strength and for Christ's willingness to experience rejection and to bring salvation. I thank You that You hear my prayers. From this day forward, I choose to participate in Your Great Commission to share the message of Christ with others.

DAY 316

IMITATING THE LOVE OF CHRIST

LORD, I DRAW NEAR TO YOU

Lord, I give thanks for Your greatness, Your goodness, and Your love, and I now draw near to enjoy Your presence.

I praise, exalt, and honor the King of heaven,
For all His works are true, and all His ways are just,
And He is able to humble those who walk in pride. (Daniel 4:37)

Take a moment to consider God's awesome majesty and thank Him that He loves you and wants an intimate relationship with you.

THANK YOU, LORD, FOR WHAT YOU HAVE DONE

Will God indeed dwell on earth? Heaven and the highest heaven cannot contain You. (1 Kings 8:27)

The Lord said, "Destroy this temple, and I will raise it again in three days." But He was speaking of the temple of His body. After He was raised from the dead, His disciples remembered that He had said this to them, and they believed the Scripture and the words that Jesus had spoken. (John 2:19,21-22)

LORD, I LISTEN TO YOUR WORDS OF TRUTH

You preserve my life, and I am devoted to You. You are my God; You will save Your servant who trusts in You. (Psalm 86:2)

LORD, I RESPOND TO YOUR INSTRUCTION

I will be an imitator of God as a beloved child, and I will walk in love, just as Christ loved me and gave Himself up for me as a fragrant offering and sacrifice to God. (Ephesians 5:1-2)

The goal of our instruction is love, which comes from a pure heart and a good conscience and a sincere faith. (1 Timothy 1:5)

Lord, I thank You that You transcend the created heavens and earth and that You raised Your Son from the dead. I thank You for preserving my life. Help me to imitate the sacrificial love of Christ in my relationships with others.

DAY 317

PRODUCING FRUIT PLEASING TO GOD

❧

LORD, I DRAW NEAR TO YOU

I am grateful to You, O God, for the blessing of Your forgiveness. I thank You that in Christ, You set me free from the guilt of the past and give me hope for the future.

What is man that You should magnify him,
That you should set Your heart on him,
That You examine him every morning
And test him every moment? (Job 7:17-18)

Take a moment to ask the Spirit to search your heart and reveal any areas of unconfessed sin. Acknowledge these to the Lord and thank Him for His forgiveness.

THANK YOU, LORD, FOR WHAT YOU HAVE DONE

Just as the Father raises the dead and gives them life, even so the Son gives life to whom He wishes. (John 5:21)

327
❧

LORD, I LISTEN TO YOUR WORDS OF TRUTH

I lift up my eyes to You, to You Who dwell in heaven. As the eyes of servants look to the hand of their master, as the eyes of a maid look to the hand of her mistress, so my eyes look to the Lord my God, until He shows me His mercy. (Psalm 123:1-2)

LORD, I RESPOND TO YOUR INSTRUCTION

I will not love with words or tongue, but in deed and in truth. By this I will know that I am of the truth and will assure my heart before Him; for if my heart condemns me, God is greater than my heart, and knows all things. If my heart does not condemn me, I have confidence before God and receive from Him whatever I ask, because I keep His commandments and do the things that are pleasing in His sight. (1 John 3:18-22)

❧

Lord, I thank You for protecting Your saints and for giving them life through Your Son. I pray that the unselfish actions of my love will produce fruit for others that is pleasing to You.

DAY 318

EMBRACING WISDOM

LORD, I DRAW NEAR TO YOU

I praise You, Lord, that You are intimately acquainted with my ways and that You always love me and have my best interests at heart.

Search me, O God, and know my heart;
Try me and know my anxious thoughts,
And see if there is any wicked way in me,
And lead me in the way everlasting. (Psalm 139:23-24)

Take a moment to offer this day to the Lord and ask Him for the grace to grow in your knowledge and love for Him.

THANK YOU, LORD, FOR WHAT YOU HAVE DONE

The Lord brings death and makes alive; He brings down to the grave and raises up. The Lord sends poverty and wealth; He humbles and He exalts. He raises the poor from the dust and lifts the needy from the ash heap, to seat them with princes and make them inherit a throne of honor. For the foundations of the earth are the Lord's, and He has set the world upon them. (1 Samuel 2:6-8)

When Judas went out to betray Him, Jesus said, "Now is the Son of Man glorified, and God is glorified in Him. If God is glorified in Him, God will glorify the Son in Himself and will glorify Him immediately." (John 13:31-32)

LORD, I LISTEN TO YOUR WORDS OF TRUTH

My eyes are upon You, O God the Lord; in You I take refuge; You will not leave my soul destitute. (Psalm 141:8)

LORD, I RESPOND TO YOUR INSTRUCTION

Wisdom is foremost; therefore I will get wisdom, and though it costs all I have, I will get understanding. I will esteem her, and she will exalt me; I will embrace her, and she will honor me. (Proverbs 4:7-8)

Lord, I thank You for Your absolute authority and for glorifying Yourself in the redemptive work of Your Son. I thank You that I can take refuge in You. Help me to embrace wisdom.

328

DAY 319

FINDING MY PORTION IN THE LAND
❧

LORD, I DRAW NEAR TO YOU

As I approach Your throne of grace today, I am grateful that You care about the things that concern me and that You want me to offer them up to You.

May I live as one who is free, but without using my freedom as a cloak for evil, but as a servant of God. (1 Peter 2:16)

Take a moment to share your personal needs with God, including your physical, emotional, relational, and spiritual concerns.

THANK YOU, LORD, FOR WHAT YOU HAVE DONE

The Lord Jesus is the first and the last, and the Living One; He was dead, and behold He is alive forevermore and holds the keys of death and of Hades. (Revelation 1:17-18)

Jesus told His opponents, "You are from below; I am from above. You are of this world; I am not of this world. I told you, therefore, that you would die in your sins, for if you do not believe that I AM, you will die in your sins." (John 8:23-24)

329
❧

LORD, I LISTEN TO YOUR WORDS OF TRUTH

I cry out to You, O Lord, and say, "You are my refuge, my portion in the land of the living." (Psalm 142:5)

LORD, I RESPOND TO YOUR INSTRUCTION

I will not take vengeance or bear a grudge against others, but I will love my neighbor as myself. (Leviticus 19:18)

Whatever I want others to do to me, I will also do to them, for this is the law and the prophets. (Matthew 7:12)

❧

Lord, I thank You for the supremacy of the Lord Jesus and for His eternal being. I thank You for being my portion in the land of the living. Help me to love others by treating them as I would wish to be treated.

DAY 320

APPLYING MY HEART TO UNDERSTANDING

❧

LORD, I DRAW NEAR TO YOU

Lord, You have invited me to pray for the needs of others, and since You desire what is best for them, I take this opportunity to bring these requests to You.

You have shown me what is good;
And what does the Lord require of me
But to act justly and to love mercy
And to walk humbly with my God. (Micah 6:8)

Take a moment to lift up the needs of your family and friends, and to offer up any additional burdens for others that the Lord brings to mind.

THANK YOU, LORD, FOR WHAT YOU HAVE DONE

The Lord God is the Alpha and the Omega, Who is, and Who was, and Who is to come, the Almighty. (Revelation 1:8)

Jesus said, "My Father loves Me because I lay down My life that I may take it up again. No one takes it from Me, but I lay it down of My own accord. I have authority to lay it down and authority to take it up again. This command I received from My Father." (John 10:17-18)

LORD, I LISTEN TO YOUR WORDS OF TRUTH

Every word of God is tested; He is a shield to those who take refuge in Him. (Proverbs 30:5)

LORD, I RESPOND TO YOUR INSTRUCTION

I will receive the words of wisdom and treasure her commands within me, turning my ear to wisdom and applying my heart to understanding. If I cry for discernment and lift up my voice for understanding, if I seek her as silver and search for her as for hidden treasures, then I will understand the fear of the Lord and find the knowledge of God. (Proverbs 2:1-5)

❧

Lord, I thank You that You are the Alpha and the Omega and that Jesus received all authority over life and death from You. I thank You for Your constant protection. I will apply my heart to understanding.

DAY 321

WALKING IN PERFECT PEACE

LORD, I DRAW NEAR TO YOU

Lord, I want Your Word to be deeply implanted in me so that I will know the truth and be able to express it in the way I live.

My soul will rejoice in the Lord
And delight in His salvation. (Psalm 35:9)

I will praise the name of God in song
And magnify Him with thanksgiving. (Psalm 69:30)

Take a moment to affirm the truth of these words from Scripture and ask God to make them a growing reality in your life.

THANK YOU, LORD, FOR WHAT YOU HAVE DONE

Jesus proved through His works that the Father is in Him, and that He is in the Father. (John 10:38)

All these testified that Jesus is the Son of God: John the Baptist, the works that Jesus did, the Father, and the Scriptures. (John 5:31-39)

331

LORD, I LISTEN TO YOUR WORDS OF TRUTH

You will keep in perfect peace him whose mind is stayed on You, because he trusts in You. (Isaiah 26:3)

LORD, I RESPOND TO YOUR INSTRUCTION

The fear of the Lord is a fountain of life, to turn one away from the snares of death. (Proverbs 14:27)

I will let the fear of the Lord be upon me, and I will be careful in what I do, for with the Lord my God there is no injustice or partiality or bribery. (2 Chronicles 19:7)

Lord, I thank You that You authenticated the person and work of Your Son. I thank You for the peace I find when I trust in You. I will treat You with awe and avoid injustice.

DAY 322

LOVING GOD WITH ALL MY HEART

LORD, I DRAW NEAR TO YOU

O Lord, I am deeply grateful for Your wonderful acts, for Your abundant promises, and for the gift of my relationship with You through the merits of Christ.

If I have been united with Christ in the likeness of His death, I will certainly also be united with Him in the likeness of His resurrection. (Romans 6:5)

Take a moment to express your gratitude for the many blessings that you have received from the Lord.

THANK YOU, LORD, FOR WHAT YOU HAVE DONE

Jesus knew that the Father had given all things into His hands and that He had come from God and was returning to God. (John 13:3)

He who comes from above is above all; he who is from the earth belongs to the earth, and speaks as one from the earth. He who comes from heaven is above all. He whom God has sent speaks the words of God, for He has been given the Spirit without limit. (John 3:31,34)

LORD, I LISTEN TO YOUR WORDS OF TRUTH

O Lord, the hope of Israel, all who forsake You will be put to shame. Those who depart from You will be written in the dust because they have forsaken the Lord, the fountain of living water. (Jeremiah 17:13)

LORD, I RESPOND TO YOUR INSTRUCTION

"You shall love the Lord your God with all your heart and with all your soul and with all your mind." This is the first and great commandment. And the second is like it: "You shall love your neighbor as yourself." All the law and the prophets hang on these two commandments. (Matthew 22:37-40)

Lord, I thank You that Jesus came from heaven and that You gave all things into His hands. I will never forsake You, and I will love You with all my heart, soul, and mind and love my neighbor as myself.

DAY 323

PRACTICING JUSTICE, RIGHTEOUSNESS, AND INTEGRITY

~

LORD, I DRAW NEAR TO YOU

Lord, I give thanks for Your greatness, Your goodness, and Your love, and I now draw near to enjoy Your presence.

Through Christ all things were made, and without Him nothing was made that has been made. In Him was life, and the life was the light of men. (John 1:3-4)

The Lord Jesus, Who is holy and true, holds the key of David. What He opens no one can shut, and what He shuts no one can open. (Revelation 3:7)

Take a moment to consider God's awesome majesty and thank Him that He loves you and wants an intimate relationship with you.

THANK YOU, LORD, FOR WHAT YOU HAVE DONE

Before Abraham was born, Jesus Christ always exists. (John 8:58)

From Christ's fullness we have all received, and grace upon grace. For the law was given through Moses; grace and truth came through Jesus Christ. (John 1:16-17)

LORD, I LISTEN TO YOUR WORDS OF TRUTH

What we must do to work the works of God is to believe in Him Whom He has sent. (John 6:28-29)

LORD, I RESPOND TO YOUR INSTRUCTION

Blessed are they who maintain justice, who do righteousness at all times. (Psalm 106:3)

He who walks in integrity walks securely, but he who perverts his way will be found out. (Proverbs 10:9)

~

Lord, I thank You for the eternity of Jesus Christ and for the fullness, grace, and truth that we have received from Him. I believe in Him Whom You have sent, and I will practice justice, righteousness, and integrity.

DAY 324

TAKING MY THOUGHTS CAPTIVE

LORD, I DRAW NEAR TO YOU

I am grateful to You, O God, for the blessing of Your forgiveness. I thank You that in Christ, You set me free from the guilt of the past and give me hope for the future.

Remember, O Lord, Your compassions and Your mercies,
For they are from of old.
Do not remember the sins of my youth or my transgressions;
According to Your loyal love remember me,
For Your goodness' sake, O Lord. (Psalm 25:6-7)

Take a moment to ask the Spirit to search your heart and reveal any areas of unconfessed sin. Acknowledge these to the Lord and thank Him for His forgiveness.

THANK YOU, LORD, FOR WHAT YOU HAVE DONE

334

God raised Jesus from the dead, freeing Him from the agony of death, because it was impossible for Him to be held by it. (Acts 2:24)

LORD, I LISTEN TO YOUR WORDS OF TRUTH

I will not let my heart be troubled. I will trust in God and trust also in Christ. (John 14:1)

LORD, I RESPOND TO YOUR INSTRUCTION

Whoever is wise understands these things; whoever is discerning knows them. The ways of the Lord are right; the righteous will walk in them, but transgressors will stumble in them. (Hosea 14:9)

Though I walk in the flesh, I do not war according to the flesh. The weapons of my warfare are not fleshly, but divinely powerful to overthrow strongholds, casting down arguments and every pretension that sets itself up against the knowledge of God, and taking every thought captive to the obedience of Christ. (2 Corinthians 10:3-5)

Lord, I thank You that You have conquered sin and death through Your Son. I thank You that I can find comfort by trusting in Christ. Teach me to seek wisdom and to use my spiritual weapons effectively.

DAY 325

FINDING MY LIFE IN CHRIST

LORD, I DRAW NEAR TO YOU

I praise You, Lord, that You are intimately acquainted with my ways and that You always love me and have my best interests at heart.

O Lord my God, may I fear you, walk in all Your ways, love You, and serve You with all my heart and with all my soul. (Deuteronomy 10:12)

Take a moment to offer this day to the Lord and ask Him for the grace to grow in your knowledge and love for Him.

THANK YOU, LORD, FOR WHAT YOU HAVE DONE

I will regard the Lord of hosts as holy; He shall be my fear, and He shall be my dread. (Isaiah 8:13)

Jesus is the stone which was rejected by the builders, but which has become the chief cornerstone. Salvation is found in no one else, for there is no other name under heaven given to men by which we must be saved. (Acts 4:11-12)

335

LORD, I LISTEN TO YOUR WORDS OF TRUTH

I believe that Jesus is the Christ, the Son of God, and by believing, I have life in His name. (John 20:31)

LORD, I RESPOND TO YOUR INSTRUCTION

He who walks in uprightness fears the Lord, but he who is devious in his ways despises Him. (Proverbs 14:2)

A man will be satisfied with good from the fruit of his mouth, and the deeds of a man's hands will return to him. (Proverbs 12:14)

Lord, I thank You that You are my fear and that Jesus is the way You have provided for salvation. I thank You that by believing in Christ Jesus, I have life in His name. I choose this day to walk uprightly in all that I say and do.

DAY 326
COVERING A MULTITUDE OF SINS

LORD, I DRAW NEAR TO YOU

As I approach Your throne of grace today, I am grateful that You care about the things that concern me and that You want me to offer them up to You.

May I not say when I am tempted, "I am being tempted by God"; for God cannot be tempted by evil, nor does He tempt anyone. But each one is tempted when he is drawn away and enticed by his own lust. Then, after lust has conceived, it gives birth to sin; and sin, when it is full grown, gives birth to death. (James 1:13-15)

Take a moment to share your personal needs with God, including your physical, emotional, relational, and spiritual concerns.

THANK YOU, LORD, FOR WHAT YOU HAVE DONE

Holy, Holy, Holy is the Lord of hosts; the whole earth is full of His glory. (Isaiah 6:3)

Our Lord Jesus Christ gave Himself for our sins to rescue us from the present evil age, according to the will of our God and Father, to Whom be glory for ever and ever. (Galatians 1:3-5)

LORD, I LISTEN TO YOUR WORDS OF TRUTH

Like Abraham, I will not waver through unbelief regarding the promise of God, but I want to be strengthened in my faith and give glory to God, being fully persuaded that God is able to do what He has promised. (Romans 4:20-21)

LORD, I RESPOND TO YOUR INSTRUCTION

Above all, I will have a fervent love for others, because love covers a multitude of sins. (1 Peter 4:8)

If I forgive men for their transgressions, my Heavenly Father will also forgive me. (Matthew 6:14)

Lord, I thank You that the whole earth is full of Your glory and that Jesus Christ gave Himself for my sins. I thank You that You are able to do what You promise. I will not harbor any unforgiveness and will have a heartfelt love for others.

DAY 327

SOWING IN PEACE

LORD, I DRAW NEAR TO YOU

Lord, You have invited me to pray for the needs of others, and since You desire what is best for them, I take this opportunity to bring these requests to You.

Love the Lord, all you His saints!
The Lord preserves the faithful,
And fully repays the proud doer.
Be of good courage and He will strengthen your heart,
All you who hope in the Lord. (Psalm 31:23-24)

Take a moment to lift up the needs of your family and friends, and to offer up any additional burdens for others that the Lord brings to mind.

THANK YOU, LORD, FOR WHAT YOU HAVE DONE

I know that You alone, Whose name is the Lord, are the Most High over all the earth. (Psalm 83:18)

God placed all things under Christ's feet and gave Him to be head over all things to the church, which is His body, the fullness of Him Who fills all in all. (Ephesians 1:22-23)

337

LORD, I LISTEN TO YOUR WORDS OF TRUTH

Since I live in the Spirit, I will also walk in the Spirit. (Galatians 5:25)

LORD, I RESPOND TO YOUR INSTRUCTION

The wisdom that comes from above is first pure, then peaceable, gentle, submissive, full of mercy and good fruits, without partiality and hypocrisy. And the fruit of righteousness is sown in peace by those who make peace. (James 3:17-18)

I will examine all things, hold fast to the good, and abstain from every form of evil. (1 Thessalonians 5:21-22)

Lord, I thank You that You are Most High over all the earth and that You placed all things under Your Son's feet. Help me to walk in the power of Your Spirit, as I seek the wisdom that comes from You and sow in peace in order to harvest the peaceable fruit of righteousness.

DAY 328

GAINING HONOR THROUGH HUMILITY

❧

LORD, I DRAW NEAR TO YOU

Lord, I want Your Word to be deeply implanted in me so that I will know the truth and be able to express it in the way I live.

How lovely are Your dwellings,
O Lord of hosts!
My soul longs and even faints for the courts of the Lord;
My heart and my flesh cry out for the living God. (Psalm 84:1-2)

Take a moment to affirm the truth of these words from Scripture and ask God to make them a growing reality in your life.

THANK YOU, LORD, FOR WHAT YOU HAVE DONE

O Lord, our Lord, how majestic is Your name in all the earth! You have set Your glory above the heavens! (Psalm 8:1)

The wrath of God is revealed from heaven against all the godlessness and unrighteousness of men who suppress the truth by their unrighteousness, since what may be known about God is manifest in them, because God has manifested it to them. (Romans 1:18-19)

LORD, I LISTEN TO YOUR WORDS OF TRUTH

Having begun in the Spirit, I will not seek to be perfected by the flesh. (Galatians 3:3)

LORD, I RESPOND TO YOUR INSTRUCTION

A man's pride brings him low, but the humble of spirit will gain honor. (Proverbs 29:23)

Pride goes before destruction, and a haughty spirit before a fall. (Proverbs 16:18)

❧

Lord, I thank You for the glory of the heavens and for manifesting Yourself in this way to all people. I thank You for Your Holy Spirit Who empowers me. Protect me from operating in a haughty spirit so I may gain honor in Your sight.

DAY 329
LOVING MY ENEMIES

❦

LORD, I DRAW NEAR TO YOU

O Lord, I am deeply grateful for Your wonderful acts, for Your abundant promises, and for the gift of my relationship with You through the merits of Christ.

Thanks be to God, Who gives us the victory through our Lord Jesus Christ. Therefore let us be steadfast, immovable, abounding in the work of the Lord, knowing that our labor in the Lord is not in vain. (1 Corinthians 15:57-58)

Take a moment to express your gratitude for the many blessings that you have received from the Lord.

THANK YOU, LORD, FOR WHAT YOU HAVE DONE

Your righteousness, O God, reaches to the heavens, You who have done great things. O God, who is like You? (Psalm 71:19)

339

❦

We know that whatever the law says, it says to those who are under the law, that every mouth may be silenced, and the whole world held accountable to God; because no one will be justified in His sight by the works of the law, for through the law comes the knowledge of sin. (Romans 3:19-20)

LORD, I LISTEN TO YOUR WORDS OF TRUTH

I can say with confidence, "The Lord is my helper; I will not be afraid. What can man do to me?" (Hebrews 13:6)

LORD, I RESPOND TO YOUR INSTRUCTION

I will love my enemies, do good to them, and lend to them, expecting nothing in return. Then my reward will be great, and I will be a child of the Most High; for He is kind to the ungrateful and evil. I will be merciful just as my Father is merciful. (Luke 6:35-36)

❦

Lord, I thank You for Your unbounded righteousness and for Your law that reveals Your utter perfection. I put all my confidence in You, and will be merciful and forgiving to others, just as You have been for me.

DAY 330

KEEPING MY HEART AT PEACE

❧

LORD, I DRAW NEAR TO YOU

Lord, I give thanks for Your greatness, Your goodness, and Your love, and I now draw near to enjoy Your presence.

Praise the Lord!
Give thanks to the Lord, for He is good;
For His loving mercy endures forever.
Who can express the mighty acts of the Lord
Or fully declare His praise? (Psalm 106:1-2)

You endowed the heart with wisdom
And gave understanding to the mind. (Job 38:36)

Take a moment to consider God's awesome majesty and thank Him that He loves you and wants an intimate relationship with you.

THANK YOU, LORD, FOR WHAT YOU HAVE DONE

340
❧

O Sovereign Lord, You are God! Your words are true, and You have promised good things to Your servant. (2 Samuel 7:28)

God will impute righteousness to us who believe in Him Who raised Jesus our Lord from the dead, Who was delivered over to death because of our sins and was raised because of our justification. (Romans 4:24-25)

LORD, I LISTEN TO YOUR WORDS OF TRUTH

Through faith I am guarded by the power of God for salvation that is ready to be revealed in the last time. (1 Peter 1:5)

LORD, I RESPOND TO YOUR INSTRUCTION

A heart at peace gives life to the body, but envy is rottenness to the bones. (Proverbs 14:30)

The words of a gossip are like choice morsels; they go down into the innermost parts of the body. (Proverbs 18:8)

❧

Lord, I thank You for the greatness of Your promises and for the righteousness You have given to me in Christ. I thank You for the salvation that will be fully revealed at His coming. Help me to give life to my body by keeping my heart at peace.

DAY 331

DEALING HONESTLY AND JUSTLY

LORD, I DRAW NEAR TO YOU

I am grateful to You, O God, for the blessing of Your forgiveness. I thank You that in Christ, You set me free from the guilt of the past and give me hope for the future.

O God, You know my foolishness,
And my guilt is not hidden from You.
May those who hope in You not be ashamed because of me, O Lord God of hosts. (Psalm 69:5-6)

Take a moment to ask the Spirit to search your heart and reveal any areas of unconfessed sin. Acknowledge these to the Lord and thank Him for His forgiveness.

THANK YOU, LORD, FOR WHAT YOU HAVE DONE

I will arise and bless the Lord, my God, Who is from everlasting to everlasting. Blessed be Your glorious name, which is exalted above all blessing and praise! (Nehemiah 9:5)

The earnest expectation of the creation eagerly waits for the revealing of the sons of God. (Romans 8:19)

341

LORD, I LISTEN TO YOUR WORDS OF TRUTH

I will not forget the covenant You have made with me, nor will I worship other gods. But I will fear the Lord my God; it is He Who will deliver me from the hand of all my enemies. (2 Kings 17:38-39)

LORD, I RESPOND TO YOUR INSTRUCTION

I will not be dishonest in judgment, in measurement of weight or quantity. I will be honest and just in my business affairs. (Leviticus 19:35-36)

I will not follow the crowd in doing wrong. (Exodus 23:2)

Lord, I thank You that Your glorious name is exalted above all blessing and praise and that all creation awaits the time of resurrection. I thank You for delivering me from the hand of all my enemies. Help me to demonstrate integrity and justice in my dealings with others.

DAY 332

DEPARTING FROM EVIL

❧

LORD, I DRAW NEAR TO YOU

I praise You, Lord, that You are intimately acquainted with my ways and that You always love me and have my best interests at heart.

Blessed are the poor in spirit, for theirs is the kingdom of heaven.
Blessed are those who mourn, for they will be comforted.
Blessed are the meek, for they will inherit the earth.
Blessed are those who hunger and thirst for righteousness, for they shall be satisfied.
Blessed are the merciful, for they shall obtain mercy. (Matthew 5:3-7)

Take a moment to offer this day to the Lord and ask Him for the grace to grow in your knowledge and love for Him.

THANK YOU, LORD, FOR WHAT YOU HAVE DONE

There is no one holy like the Lord; there is no one besides You; nor is there any Rock like our God. (1 Samuel 2:2)

God will have mercy on whom He has mercy, and He will have compassion on whom He has compassion. It does not depend on human desire or effort, but on God's mercy. (Romans 9:15-16)

LORD, I LISTEN TO YOUR WORDS OF TRUTH

I shall consecrate myself and be holy, because You are the Lord my God. I shall keep Your statutes and practice them; You are the Lord Who sanctifies me. (Leviticus 20:7-8)

LORD, I RESPOND TO YOUR INSTRUCTION

A wise man fears and departs from evil, but a fool is arrogant and bold. A quick-tempered man acts foolishly, and a man of evil plots is hated. (Proverbs 14:16-17)

It is not good for a person to be without knowledge, and he who hastens with his feet sins. (Proverbs 19:2)

❧

Lord, I thank You for Your matchless holiness and for Your mercy and compassion toward Your people. I thank You that You are the Lord who sanctifies me. I will depart from evil and pursue wisdom and knowledge.

DAY 333

ABANDONING STRIFE
AND ANGER

❧

LORD, I DRAW NEAR TO YOU

As I approach Your throne of grace today, I am grateful that You care about the things that concern me and that You want me to offer them up to You.

May I fight the good fight, finish the race, and keep the faith, so that there will be laid up for me the crown of righteousness, which the Lord, the righteous Judge, will award to me on that day; and not only to me, but also to all who have longed for His appearing. (2 Timothy 4:7-8)

Take a moment to share your personal needs with God, including your physical, emotional, relational, and spiritual concerns.

THANK YOU, LORD, FOR WHAT YOU HAVE DONE

You revealed Yourself to Moses as "I AM WHO I AM." (Exodus 3:14)

There is one body and one Spirit, just as we were called in one hope of our calling; one Lord, one faith, one baptism, one God and Father of all, Who is over all and through all and in all. (Ephesians 4:4-6)

343
❧

LORD, I LISTEN TO YOUR WORDS OF TRUTH

I will fear the Lord and serve Him in truth with all my heart, for I consider what great things He has done for me. (1 Samuel 12:24)

LORD, I RESPOND TO YOUR INSTRUCTION

Better is a dry crust with quietness than a house full of feasting with strife. (Proverbs 17:1)

A man of great wrath must pay the penalty; if you rescue him, you will have to do it again. (Proverbs 19:19)

❧

Lord, I thank You that You are the everlasting God and that You are over all, through all, and in all. I thank You for the great things You have done for me. Help me not to give in to strife and anger.

DAY 334

PRACTICING VIRTUE

❧

LORD, I DRAW NEAR TO YOU

Lord, You have invited me to pray for the needs of others, and since You desire what is best for them, I take this opportunity to bring these requests to You.

Save Your people and bless Your inheritance;
Be their shepherd and carry them forever. (Psalm 28:9)

Take a moment to lift up the needs of your family and friends, and to offer up any additional burdens for others that the Lord brings to mind.

THANK YOU, LORD, FOR WHAT YOU HAVE DONE

Surely the Lord's hand is not too short to save, nor His ear too dull to hear. But our iniquities have separated us from our God; our sins have hidden His face from us, so that He will not hear. Yet the Lord saw that there was no one to intervene; so His own arm worked salvation for Him, and His righteousness sustained Him. He put on righteousness as His breastplate, and the helmet of salvation on His head; He put on the garments of vengeance and wrapped Himself in zeal as a cloak. From the West, men will fear the name of the Lord, and from the rising of the sun, they will revere His glory. For He will come like a flood that the breath of the Lord drives along. (Isaiah 59:1-2,16-19)

LORD, I LISTEN TO YOUR WORDS OF TRUTH

I want to remove the places of idolatry from my life, and like Asa, I want my heart to be fully committed to God all my days. (2 Chronicles 15:17)

LORD, I RESPOND TO YOUR INSTRUCTION

I will put away all bitterness and anger and wrath and shouting and slander, along with all malice. And I will be kind and compassionate to others, forgiving them just as God in Christ also forgave me. (Ephesians 4:31-32)

❧

Lord, I thank You that You sent Your Son into the world and that He purchased our salvation. I will be fully committed to You all my days, and I will put away slander, wrath, and abusive speech but instead practice the virtues of kindness, compassion, and forgiveness.

DAY 335

REMEMBERING THE ROCK
OF MY REFUGE

❧

LORD, I DRAW NEAR TO YOU

Lord, I want Your Word to be deeply implanted in me so that I will know the truth and be able to express it in the way I live.

Walking in the way of Your laws,
O Lord, I wait for You;
Your name and Your memory are the desire of my soul. (Isaiah 26:8)

The Lord longs to be gracious and rises to show compassion.
For the Lord is a God of justice;
Blessed are all those who wait for Him! (Isaiah 30:18)

Take a moment to affirm the truth of these words from Scripture and ask God to make them a growing reality in your life.

THANK YOU, LORD, FOR WHAT YOU HAVE DONE

345
❧

Jesus is the way and the truth and the life. No one comes to the Father except through Him. (John 14:6)

The angel said to the shepherds, "Do not be afraid. I bring you good news of great joy that will be for all the people. For today in the city of David a Savior has been born to you, Who is Christ the Lord." (Luke 2:10-11)

LORD, I LISTEN TO YOUR WORDS OF TRUTH

I will not forget the God of my salvation; I will remember the Rock of my refuge. (Isaiah 17:10)

LORD, I RESPOND TO YOUR INSTRUCTION

I will learn to do good, seek justice, remove the oppressor, defend the orphan, and plead for the widow. (Isaiah 1:17)

I will not forget to do good and to share with others, for with such sacrifices God is well pleased. (Hebrews 13:16)

❧

Lord, I thank You for the good news that I can joyfully come to You through Christ Jesus. I thank You that You are the Rock of my refuge. I will do good and share with those who are in need.

DAY 336

KEEPING MY FEET ON GOD'S PATH

LORD, I DRAW NEAR TO YOU

O Lord, I am deeply grateful for Your wonderful acts, for Your abundant promises, and for the gift of my relationship with You through the merits of Christ.

Thanks be to God, Who always leads us in triumph in Christ and through us spreads everywhere the fragrance of the knowledge of Him. (2 Corinthians 2:14)

Take a moment to express your gratitude for the many blessings that you have received from the Lord.

THANK YOU, LORD, FOR WHAT YOU HAVE DONE

The Lord is the Spirit, and where the Spirit of the Lord is, there is freedom. (2 Corinthians 3:17)

346

When He was asked by the Pharisees when the kingdom of God would come, Jesus replied, "The kingdom of God does not come with observation, nor will people say, 'Here it is,' or 'There it is,' for behold, the kingdom of God is within you." (Luke 17:20-21)

LORD, I LISTEN TO YOUR WORDS OF TRUTH

Many who are first will be last, and the last first. (Matthew 19:30; Mark 10:31)

LORD, I RESPOND TO YOUR INSTRUCTION

Trouble and anguish have come upon me, but Your commands are my delight. (Psalm 119:143)

You know the way that I take; when You have tested me, I shall come forth as gold. My feet have held fast to Your steps; I have kept to Your way without turning aside. (Job 23:10-11)

Lord, I thank You for the freedom that comes from Your Spirit and for the reality of Your kingdom. I thank You that Your Word challenges our false assumptions. I will hold fast to Your steps and delight in Your commands.

DAY 337

MAKING NO PROVISION FOR THE FLESH

❧

LORD, I DRAW NEAR TO YOU

Lord, I give thanks for Your greatness, Your goodness, and Your love, and I now draw near to enjoy Your presence.

Your throne, O God, is forever and ever;
A scepter of righteousness is the scepter of Your kingdom.
You love righteousness and hate wickedness;
Therefore God, Your God, has anointed You
With the oil of gladness more than your companions. (Psalm 45:6-7)

Take a moment to consider God's awesome majesty and thank Him that He loves you and wants an intimate relationship with you.

THANK YOU, LORD, FOR WHAT YOU HAVE DONE

The Lord does not see as man sees. Man looks at the outward appearance, but the Lord looks at the heart. (1 Samuel 16:7)

Jesus knew all men, and had no need for anyone's testimony about man, for He knew what was in man. (John 2:24-25)

347
❧

LORD, I LISTEN TO YOUR WORDS OF TRUTH

Christ must increase; I must decrease. (John 3:30)

LORD, I RESPOND TO YOUR INSTRUCTION

The thoughts of the righteous are just, but the advice of the wicked is deceitful. (Proverbs 12:5)

I will walk properly as in the daytime, not in revellings and drunkenness, not in promiscuity and debauchery, not in strife and jealousy. Rather, I will put on the Lord Jesus Christ and make no provision to gratify the lusts of the flesh. (Romans 13:13-14)

❧

Lord, I thank You that You look at the heart and not at outward appearances. I pray that Christ would increase in my life. I will live in His power and turn away from the lusts of the flesh.

DAY 338

ACCOMPLISHING GOD'S WORK

LORD, I DRAW NEAR TO YOU

I am grateful to You, O God, for the blessing of Your forgiveness. I thank You that in Christ, You set me free from the guilt of the past and give me hope for the future.

Create in me a clean heart, O God,
And renew a steadfast spirit within me.
Do not cast me from Your presence
Or take Your Holy Spirit from me.
Restore to me the joy of Your salvation
And uphold me with a willing spirit.
Then I will teach transgressors Your ways,
And sinners will be converted to You. (Psalm 51:10-13)

Take a moment to ask the Spirit to search your heart and reveal any areas of unconfessed sin. Acknowledge these to the Lord and thank Him for His forgiveness.

THANK YOU, LORD, FOR WHAT YOU HAVE DONE

I know that You can do all things and that no purpose of Yours can be thwarted. (Job 42:2)

While Jesus was in the world, He was the light of the world. For judgment He came into this world, that those who do not see may see, and that those who see may become blind. (John 9:5,39)

LORD, I LISTEN TO YOUR WORDS OF TRUTH

Like Jesus, my food is to do the will of Him Who sent me and to accomplish His work. (John 4:34)

LORD, I RESPOND TO YOUR INSTRUCTION

I will be hospitable to others without grumbling. (1 Peter 4:9)

I will remember those in prison as though bound with them, and those who are mistreated, since I myself am also in the body. (Hebrews 13:3)

Lord, I thank You that none of Your purposes can be thwarted and that Jesus has illuminated our darkness. I choose to do Your will and accomplish Your work, and I will be gracious and sympathetic to others.

DAY 339

BEING FOUND FAITHFUL

~❧~

I praise You, Lord, that You are intimately acquainted with my ways and that You always love me and have my best interests at heart.

Blessed are the pure in heart, for they shall see God. Blessed are the peacemakers, for they shall be called sons of God. (Matthew 5:8-9)

Take a moment to offer this day to the Lord and ask Him for the grace to grow in your knowledge and love for Him.

Lord, You have been our dwelling place throughout all generations. Before the mountains were born or You brought forth the earth and the world, from everlasting to everlasting, You are God. You turn men back into dust, and say, "Return, O children of men." For a thousand years in Your sight are like yesterday when it passes by or like a watch in the night. (Psalm 90:1-4)

349
~❧

Multitudes who sleep in the dust of the earth will awake, some to everlasting life, others to shame and everlasting contempt. Those who are wise will shine like the brightness of the heavens, and those who lead many to righteousness like the stars for ever and ever. (Daniel 12:2-3)

As a servant of Christ and a steward of His possessions, it is required that I be found faithful. (1 Corinthians 4:1-2)

There is a time for everything, and a season for every activity under heaven. (Ecclesiastes 3:1)

Whoever is wise will consider the lovingkindness of the Lord. (Psalm 107:43)

~❧~

Lord, I thank You that You are everlasting and that You promise to raise me from the dead so that I can live with You forever. I pray that I will be a faithful steward of Your possessions and walk in wisdom by doing the right thing at the right time in the right way.

DAY 340

TRUSTING GOD'S CHARACTER

LORD, I DRAW NEAR TO YOU

As I approach Your throne of grace today, I am grateful that You care about the things that concern me and that You want me to offer them up to You.

May I obey those who are in authority over me in all things, not with external service as a pleaser of men, but with sincerity of heart, fearing the Lord. Whatever I do, may I work at it with all my heart, as to the Lord and not to men, knowing that I will receive the reward of the inheritance from the Lord. It is the Lord Christ I am serving. (Colossians 3:22-24)

Take a moment to share your personal needs with God, including your physical, emotional, relational, and spiritual concerns.

THANK YOU, LORD, FOR WHAT YOU HAVE DONE

You are the righteous God, Who searches the hearts and secret thoughts. (Psalm 7:9)

The Son of Man is going to come in the glory of His Father with His angels, and then He will reward each person according to his works. (Matthew 16:27)

LORD, I LISTEN TO YOUR WORDS OF TRUTH

I want to follow Abraham's example of willingness to offer all that I have to You, holding nothing back and trusting in Your character and in Your promises. (Genesis 22:2-11)

LORD, I RESPOND TO YOUR INSTRUCTION

A simple man believes everything, but a prudent man considers his steps. (Proverbs 14:15)

I will not spread false reports, nor will I help a wicked man by being a malicious witness. (Exodus 23:1)

Lord, I am thankful that You search our hearts and secret thoughts and that the Son of Man will reward each person according to his works. I trust wholly in Your character and in Your promises. I will consider my steps and speak the truth.

DAY 341

WALKING IN OBEDIENCE

❧

L O R D ,   I   D R A W   N E A R   T O   Y O U

Lord, You have invited me to pray for the needs of others, and since You desire what is best for them, I take this opportunity to bring these requests to You.

Far be it from me that I should sin against the Lord by ceasing to pray for others. (1 Samuel 12:23)

Oh, that they would always have such a heart to fear Me and keep all My commandments, so that it might be well with them and with their children forever! (Deuteronomy 5:29)

Take a moment to lift up the needs of your family and friends, and to offer up any additional burdens for others that the Lord brings to mind.

T H A N K   Y O U ,   L O R D ,   F O R   W H A T   Y O U   H A V E   D O N E

All a man's ways are right in his own eyes, but the Lord weighs the hearts. (Proverbs 21:2)

351
❧

Nothing is hidden that will not be revealed, and nothing is secret that will not be known and come out into the open. (Luke 8:17)

L O R D ,   I   L I S T E N   T O   Y O U R   W O R D S   O F   T R U T H

Has the Lord as much delight in burnt offerings and sacrifices as in obeying the voice of the Lord? To obey is better than sacrifice, and to heed is better than the fat of rams. For rebellion is like the sin of divination, and stubbornness is as iniquity and idolatry. (1 Samuel 15:22-23)

L O R D ,   I   R E S P O N D   T O   Y O U R   I N S T R U C T I O N

I will not make friends with a hot-tempered man or associate with one easily angered, lest I learn his ways and set a snare for my soul. (Proverbs 22:24-25)

I will not become conceited, provoking others and envying others. (Galatians 5:26)

❧

Lord, I thank You that You weigh the hearts and that all things will be revealed by the light of Christ. Help me to be obedient rather than stubborn or rebellious and not to be hot-tempered or conceited.

DAY 342

HIDING MYSELF FROM EVIL

Lord, I want Your Word to be deeply implanted in me so that I will know the truth and be able to express it in the way I live.

Behold, He who forms the mountains and creates the wind,
And reveals His thoughts to man,
He Who turns dawn to darkness,
And treads the high places of the earth—
The Lord God of hosts is His name. (Amos 4:13)

Take a moment to affirm the truth of these words from Scripture and ask God to make them a growing reality in your life.

Before You formed me in the womb, You knew me; before I was born, You set me apart. (Jeremiah 1:5)

352

Because Jesus lives forever, He has a permanent priesthood. Therefore He is also able to save completely those who come to God through Him, since He always lives to intercede for them. (Hebrews 7:24-25)

Like Josiah, I want to do what is right in the sight of the Lord and walk in all the ways of David, not turning aside to the right or to the left. (2 Kings 22:1-2)

A prudent man sees evil and hides himself, but the simple keep going and suffer for it. (Proverbs 22:3; 27:12)

A fool has no delight in understanding, but only in airing his own opinions. (Proverbs 18:2)

Lord, I thank You that You knew me before I was born and that You are able to save completely those who come to You through Jesus Christ. Help me to do what is right in Your sight, to be prudent enough to avoid evil, and to gain understanding.

DAY 343

CULTIVATING MY HEART

⤳

LORD, I DRAW NEAR TO YOU

O Lord, I am deeply grateful for Your wonderful acts, for Your abundant promises, and for the gift of my relationship with You through the merits of Christ.

I will not forget the God of my salvation;
I will remember the Rock of my refuge. (Isaiah 17:10)

Take a moment to express your gratitude for the many blessings that you have received from the Lord.

THANK YOU, LORD, FOR WHAT YOU HAVE DONE

The god of this age has blinded the minds of unbelievers, so that they cannot see the light of the gospel of the glory of Christ, Who is the image of God. (2 Corinthians 4:4)

LORD, I LISTEN TO YOUR WORDS OF TRUTH

353
⤳

I do not want to be like those rocky places on whom seed was thrown, who hear the Word and at once receive it with joy, but since they have no root, last only a short time; when affliction or persecution comes because of the Word, they quickly fall away. Nor do I want to be like those among the thorns on whom seed was sown, who hear the Word, but the worries of this world, the deceitfulness of riches and pleasures, and the desires for other things come in and choke the Word, making it immature and unfruitful. Instead, I want to be like the good soil on whom seed was sown, who with a noble and good heart hear the Word, understand and accept it, and with perseverance bear fruit, yielding thirty, sixty, or a hundred times what was sown. (Matthew 13:20-23; Mark 4:16-20; Luke 8:13-15)

LORD, I RESPOND TO YOUR INSTRUCTION

He who justifies the wicked, and he who condemns the just; both of them are detestable to the Lord. (Proverbs 17:15)

⤳

Lord, I thank You for removing my blindness so I can see the light of Christ. I pray that Your Word in me would bear fruit and not be choked by the distractions of this world.

DAY 344

DEALING FAITHFULLY WITH OTHERS

L O R D , I D R A W N E A R T O Y O U

Lord, I give thanks for Your greatness, Your goodness, and Your love, and I now draw near to enjoy Your presence.

I will regard the Lord of hosts as holy;
He shall be my fear,
And He shall be my dread. (Isaiah 8:13)

You are the stability of our times,
A wealth of salvation, wisdom, and knowledge;
The fear of the Lord is the key to this treasure. (Isaiah 33:6)

Take a moment to consider God's awesome majesty and thank Him that He loves you and wants an intimate relationship with you.

T H A N K Y O U , L O R D , F O R W H A T Y O U H A V E D O N E

I will give thanks to the Lord, for He is good; His love endures forever. (1 Chronicles 16:34)

Jesus did not ask that the Father should take us out of the world, but that He protect us from the evil one. He prayed, "Father, I desire those You have given Me to be with Me where I am, that they may behold My glory, the glory You have given Me because You loved Me before the foundation of the world." (John 17:15,24)

L O R D , I L I S T E N T O Y O U R W O R D S O F T R U T H

When I have done all the things which are commanded me, I should realize that I am an unworthy servant; I have only done what I ought to have done. (Luke 17:10)

L O R D , I R E S P O N D T O Y O U R I N S T R U C T I O N

Since she is a companion and a wife by covenant, a husband should not deal treacherously against the wife of his youth. The Lord God of hosts seeks a godly offspring and hates divorce; therefore we must take heed to our spirit and not deal treacherously. (Malachi 2:14-16)

Lord, I thank You that Your love endures forever and that I will be with Jesus and behold His glory. Help me to be a faithful servant to You and faithful in my relationships with others.

DAY 345

ABANDONING PRIDE AND ARROGANCE

~&

LORD, I DRAW NEAR TO YOU

I am grateful to You, O God, for the blessing of Your forgiveness. I thank You that in Christ, You set me free from the guilt of the past and give me hope for the future.

I have blotted out your transgressions like a thick cloud,
And your sins like the morning mist.
Return to Me, for I have redeemed you. (Isaiah 44:22)

Take a moment to ask the Spirit to search your heart and reveal any areas of unconfessed sin. Acknowledge these to the Lord and thank Him for His forgiveness.

THANK YOU, LORD, FOR WHAT YOU HAVE DONE

Lovingkindness and truth have met together; righteousness and peace have kissed each other. Truth shall spring forth from the earth, and righteousness looks down from heaven. (Psalm 85:10-11)

The Lord prayed, "I glorified You on the earth by completing the work You gave Me to do. And now, Father, glorify Me in Your presence with the glory I had with You before the world began." (John 17:4-5)

LORD, I LISTEN TO YOUR WORDS OF TRUTH

I must do the work of Him Who sent me while it is day; night is coming, when no one can work. (John 9:4)

LORD, I RESPOND TO YOUR INSTRUCTION

Haughty eyes and a proud heart, the lamp of the wicked, are sin. (Proverbs 21:4)

The proud looks of man will be humbled, and the loftiness of men brought low; the Lord alone will be exalted. (Isaiah 2:11)

Let him who boasts, boast in the Lord. (1 Corinthians 1:31)

~&

Lord, I thank You for Your lovingkindness and truth and for the complete and perfect work that Jesus accomplished in His earthly ministry. Help me to accomplish the work You have sent me to do and avoid the folly of pride and arrogance.

355
~&

DAY 346

IMPARTING GRACE THROUGH MY WORDS

LORD, I DRAW NEAR TO YOU

I praise You, Lord, that You are intimately acquainted with my ways and that You always love me and have my best interests at heart.

May I be righteous before God, walking blamelessly in all the commandments and ordinances of the Lord. (Luke 1:6)

Take a moment to offer this day to the Lord and ask Him for the grace to grow in your knowledge and love for Him.

THANK YOU, LORD, FOR WHAT YOU HAVE DONE

You, Lord, are good and ready to forgive and abundant in mercy to all who call upon You. (Psalm 86:5)

Peter told the council, "The God of our fathers raised up Jesus Whom you had killed by hanging Him on a tree. God exalted Him to His own right hand as Prince and Savior, that He might give repentance and forgiveness of sins to Israel." (Acts 5:30-31)

LORD, I LISTEN TO YOUR WORDS OF TRUTH

If anyone loves You, he will keep Your Word; and Your Father will love him, and You and Your Father will come to him and make Your home with him. (John 14:23)

LORD, I RESPOND TO YOUR INSTRUCTION

The fear of the Lord is the instruction for wisdom, and humility comes before honor. (Proverbs 15:33)

I will not let any corrupt word come out of my mouth, but only what is helpful for building others up according to their needs, that it may impart grace to those who hear. (Ephesians 4:29)

Lord, I thank You for the abundance of Your mercy and for Your great gift of forgiveness through the resurrected Christ. As I continually seek to love You more, help me to be humble and build others up with my words.

DAY 347

REAPING ETERNAL LIFE

❧

LORD, I DRAW NEAR TO YOU

As I approach Your throne of grace today, I am grateful that You care about the things that concern me and that You want me to offer them up to You.

Who makes me different from anyone else? And what do I have that I did not receive? And if I did receive it, why I should I boast as though I had not received it? (1 Corinthians 4:7)

May Your merciful kindness be my comfort,
According to Your promise to Your servant. (Psalm 119:76)

Take a moment to share your personal needs with God, including your physical, emotional, relational, and spiritual concerns.

THANK YOU, LORD, FOR WHAT YOU HAVE DONE

I will sing of Your lovingkindness and justice; to You, O Lord, I will sing praises. (Psalm 101:1)

357
❧

As the gospel spread to the Gentiles, many rejoiced and glorified the word of the Lord, and all who were appointed for eternal life believed. (Acts 13:48)

LORD, I LISTEN TO YOUR WORDS OF TRUTH

By this is Your Father glorified, that I bear much fruit, showing myself to be Your disciple. (John 15:8)

LORD, I RESPOND TO YOUR INSTRUCTION

God is not mocked, for whatever a man sows, this he will also reap. The one who sows to please his flesh will reap corruption; the one who sows to please the Spirit will of the Spirit reap eternal life. (Galatians 6:7-8)

Whatever is not from faith is sin. (Romans 14:23)

❧

Lord, I thank You for Your lovingkindness and justice and for the good news of eternal life through Your Son. I pray that I would glorify You by bearing much fruit. Help me to please Your Spirit and thereby reap eternal life.

DAY 348

HONORING GOD IN MY WORDS AND DEEDS

❧

LORD, I DRAW NEAR TO YOU

Lord, You have invited me to pray for the needs of others, and since You desire what is best for them, I take this opportunity to bring these requests to You.

May I speak words of encouragement to other believers. (Acts 20:2)

Remember us, O my God, and do not blot out what we have done in Your name. Remember us, O my God, for good. (Nehemiah 13:14,31)

Take a moment to lift up the needs of your family and friends, and to offer up any additional burdens for others that the Lord brings to mind.

THANK YOU, LORD, FOR WHAT YOU HAVE DONE

The Lord executes righteousness and justice for all who are oppressed. The Lord is compassionate and gracious, slow to anger, and abounding in lovingkindness. (Psalm 103:6, 8)

Both Jews and Greeks must turn to God in repentance and have faith in our Lord Jesus Christ. (Acts 20:21)

LORD, I LISTEN TO YOUR WORDS OF TRUTH

If a man dies, will he live again? All the days of my hard service, I will wait for my renewal to come. (Job 14:14)

LORD, I RESPOND TO YOUR INSTRUCTION

Whatever I do, whether in word or in deed, I will do all in the name of the Lord Jesus, giving thanks to God the Father through Him. (Colossians 3:17)

I will not neglect my spiritual gifts. (1 Timothy 4:14)

❧

Lord, I thank You for Your compassion and grace and for the gift of repentance and faith in the Lord Jesus Christ. I thank You for the hope of the resurrection. I will do all things in the name of Jesus and serve others by cultivating my spiritual gifts.

DAY 349

INTERNALIZING GOD'S COMMANDMENTS

❧

LORD, I DRAW NEAR TO YOU

Lord, I want Your Word to be deeply implanted in me so that I will know the truth and be able to express it in the way I live.

Now listen to me, O sons,
For blessed are those who keep my ways.
Hear instruction and be wise;
Do not refuse it. (Proverbs 8:32-33)

Take a moment to affirm the truth of these words from Scripture and ask God to make them a growing reality in your life.

THANK YOU, LORD, FOR WHAT YOU HAVE DONE

The Lord's lovingkindness is great toward us, and the truth of the Lord endures forever. Praise the Lord! (Psalm 117:2)

Those who show contempt for the riches of God's kindness, forbearance, and patience do not realize that the kindness of God leads toward repentance. (Romans 2:4)

359
❧

LORD, I LISTEN TO YOUR WORDS OF TRUTH

I will sing praises to the Lord and give thanks at the remembrance of His holy name. For His anger lasts only a moment, but His favor is for a lifetime; weeping may endure for a night, but joy comes in the morning. (Psalm 30:4-5)

LORD, I RESPOND TO YOUR INSTRUCTION

Your commandments will be upon my heart, and I will teach them diligently to my children and talk about them when I sit in my house and when I walk along the way and when I lie down and when I rise up. (Deuteronomy 6:6-7)

❧

Lord, I thank You for Your great lovingkindness and truth and for the riches of Your forbearance and patience. I pray for the joy of Your favor. Help me to internalize Your commandments and teach them to others.

DAY 350
PURSUING VIRTUE

LORD, I DRAW NEAR TO YOU

O Lord, I am deeply grateful for Your wonderful acts, for Your abundant promises, and for the gift of my relationship with You through the merits of Christ.

I will give thanks to the Lord, for He is good;
His love endures forever. (1 Chronicles 16:34)

Take a moment to express your gratitude for the many blessings that you have received from the Lord.

THANK YOU, LORD, FOR WHAT YOU HAVE DONE

The sum of Your words is truth, and all of Your righteous judgments are eternal. (Psalm 119:160)

You will punish the world for its evil, the wicked for their iniquity. You will put an end to the arrogance of the haughty and will humble the pride of the ruthless. (Isaiah 13:11)

LORD, I LISTEN TO YOUR WORDS OF TRUTH

You are my hiding place and my shield; I have put my hope in Your Word. (Psalm 119:114)

LORD, I RESPOND TO YOUR INSTRUCTION

I will be diligent to add to my faith, virtue; and to virtue, knowledge; and to knowledge, self-control; and to self-control, perseverance; and to perseverance, godliness; and to godliness, brotherly kindness; and to brotherly kindness, love. For if these qualities are mine in increasing measure, they will keep me from being barren and unfruitful in the full knowledge of our Lord Jesus Christ. (2 Peter 1:5-8)

Lord, I thank You that Your righteous judgments are eternal and that You will put an end to iniquity. I thank You for being my hiding place and shield. I will add to my faith, virtue, knowledge, self-control, perseverance, godliness, kindness, and love.

DAY 351

FIXING MY CONFIDENCE ON GOD

LORD, I DRAW NEAR TO YOU

Lord, I give thanks for Your greatness, Your goodness, and Your love, and I now draw near to enjoy Your presence.

The Lord gives the sun for light by day,
And decrees the moon and stars for light by night;
He stirs up the sea so that its waves roar;
The Lord of hosts is His name. (Jeremiah 31:35)

Take a moment to consider God's awesome majesty and thank Him that He loves you and wants an intimate relationship with you.

THANK YOU, LORD, FOR WHAT YOU HAVE DONE

O Lord of hosts, You judge righteously and test the heart and mind; to You I have committed my cause. (Jeremiah 11:20)

The Lord of hosts has planned it, to bring low the pride of all glory and to humble all who are renowned on the earth. (Isaiah 23:9)

361

LORD, I LISTEN TO YOUR WORDS OF TRUTH

I will watch in hope for the Lord; I will wait for the God of my salvation; my God will hear me. (Micah 7:7)

LORD, I RESPOND TO YOUR INSTRUCTION

I will not boast about tomorrow, for I do not know what a day may bring forth. (Proverbs 27:1)

Thus says the Lord: "Let not the wise man boast of his wisdom, and let not the strong man boast of his strength, and let not the rich man boast of his riches; but let him who boasts boast about this: that he understands and knows Me, that I am the Lord, Who exercises lovingkindness, justice, and righteousness on earth; for in these I delight," declares the Lord. (Jeremiah 9:23-24)

Lord, I thank You that I can commit my cause to You and that You bring Your justice to the earth. I will fix my hope and confidence in You, and I will not be proud or presumptuous but boast only in the knowledge of You.

DAY 352

DISCOVERING THE RICHNESS OF GOD'S PROMISES

❧

LORD, I DRAW NEAR TO YOU

I am grateful to You, O God, for the blessing of Your forgiveness. I thank You that in Christ, You set me free from the guilt of the past and give me hope for the future.

O Lord, God of heaven, You are the great and awesome God, keeping Your covenant of loyal love with those who love You and obey Your commands. Let Your ear be attentive and Your eyes open so that You may hear the prayer Your servant is praying before You day and night. I confess the sins I have committed against You. (Nehemiah 1:5-6)

Take a moment to ask the Spirit to search your heart and reveal any areas of unconfessed sin. Acknowledge these to the Lord and thank Him for His forgiveness.

THANK YOU, LORD, FOR WHAT YOU HAVE DONE

I call this to mind, and therefore I have hope: The Lord's mercies never cease, for His compassions never fail. They are new every morning; great is Your faithfulness. (Lamentations 3:21-23)

LORD, I LISTEN TO YOUR WORDS OF TRUTH

Everyone who has left houses or brothers or sisters or father or mother or children or fields for Your sake will receive a hundred times as much and will inherit eternal life. (Matthew 19:29)

LORD, I RESPOND TO YOUR INSTRUCTION

He who pursues righteousness and love finds life, righteousness, and honor. (Proverbs 21:21)

I will not imitate what is evil but what is good. The one who does good is of God; the one who does evil has not seen God. (3 John 11)

❧

Lord, I thank You that Your mercies never cease and that Your compassions never fail. I thank You for the richness of Your promises. I will pursue righteousness, goodness, and love.

DAY 353

WALKING IN HUMILITY AND PATIENCE

~&~

LORD, I DRAW NEAR TO YOU

I praise You, Lord, that You are intimately acquainted with my ways and that You always love me and have my best interests at heart.

Those who live according to the flesh set their minds on the things of the flesh; but those who live according to the Spirit set their minds on the things of the Spirit. The mind of the flesh is death, but the mind of the Spirit is life and peace. (Romans 8:5-6)

Take a moment to offer this day to the Lord and ask Him for the grace to grow in your knowledge and love for Him.

THANK YOU, LORD, FOR WHAT YOU HAVE DONE

Your eyes are too pure to look at evil; You cannot look on wickedness. (Habakkuk 1:13)

God is jealous and the Lord avenges; the Lord takes vengeance and is filled with wrath. The Lord takes vengeance on His adversaries, and He reserves wrath for His enemies. The Lord is slow to anger and great in power and will not leave the guilty unpunished. His way is in the whirlwind and the storm, and clouds are the dust of His feet. (Nahum 1:2-3)

363

LORD, I LISTEN TO YOUR WORDS OF TRUTH

I have been called by God my Savior, and Christ Jesus is my hope. (1 Timothy 1:1)

LORD, I RESPOND TO YOUR INSTRUCTION

If anyone thinks he is something when he is nothing, he deceives himself. (Galatians 6:3)

I want to walk in a way that is worthy of the calling with which I was called, with all humility and meekness and patience. (Ephesians 4:1-2)

~&~

Lord, I thank You for the perfection of Your character and for Your promise to bring all things under Your perfect judgment. I thank You for calling me into the hope of Christ Jesus. I will walk in humility and patience.

DAY 354

ABOUNDING IN THE GRACE
OF GIVING

LORD, I DRAW NEAR TO YOU

---

*As I approach Your throne of grace today, I am grateful that You care about the
things that concern me and that You want me to offer them up to You.*

I will call upon You in the day of trouble,
And You will deliver me, and I will honor You. (Psalm 50:15)

*Take a moment to share your personal needs with God, including your physical,
emotional, relational, and spiritual concerns.*

THANK YOU, LORD, FOR WHAT YOU HAVE DONE

Oh, the depth of the riches both of the wisdom and knowledge of God!
How unsearchable are His judgments, and His ways past finding out!
For who has known the mind of the Lord? Or who has been His
counselor? Or who has first given to Him, that He should repay him?
For from Him and through Him and to Him are all things. To Him be
the glory forever! Amen. (Romans 11:33-36)

There is one God and one Mediator between God and men, the Man
Christ Jesus, who gave Himself as a ransom for all, the testimony given
in its proper time. (1 Timothy 2:5-6)

LORD, I LISTEN TO YOUR WORDS OF TRUTH

I will hold fast the confession of my hope, for He Who promised is
faithful. (Hebrews 10:23)

LORD, I RESPOND TO YOUR INSTRUCTION

I want to abound in faith, in speech, in knowledge, in all diligence, in
love, and in the grace of giving. (2 Corinthians 8:7)

I want to abound in love and faith toward the Lord Jesus and to all the
saints. (Philemon 5)

*Lord, I thank You for the depth of Your wisdom and knowledge and for the
ransom that Christ Jesus provided. I thank You for the faithfulness of Your
promises. Help me to abound in love and faith and in the grace of giving.*

DAY 355

RESISTING THE DEVIL

~❧~

Lord, You have invited me to pray for the needs of others, and since You desire what is best for them, I take this opportunity to bring these requests to You.

I was called to freedom, but may I not use my freedom to indulge the flesh, but through love let me serve others. For the whole law is summed up in this word: "You shall love your neighbor as yourself." (Galatians 5:13-14)

Take a moment to lift up the needs of your family and friends, and to offer up any additional burdens for others that the Lord brings to mind.

T H A N K   Y O U ,   L O R D ,   F O R   W H A T   Y O U   H A V E   D O N E

The Lord is not slow concerning His promise, as some count slowness, but is patient with us, not wanting anyone to perish, but for all to come to repentance. (2 Peter 3:9)

The Father has sent the Son to be the Savior of the world. Whoever confesses that Jesus is the Son of God, God abides in him and he in God. (1 John 4:14-15)

365
~❧~

L O R D ,   I   L I S T E N   T O   Y O U R   W O R D S   O F   T R U T H

Like Abraham, I am looking for a city which has foundations, Whose architect and builder is God. (Hebrews 11:10)

L O R D ,   I   R E S P O N D   T O   Y O U R   I N S T R U C T I O N

Before I was afflicted I went astray, but now I keep Your Word. It was good for me to be afflicted, so that I might learn Your statutes. (Psalm 119:67,71)

I will submit myself to God and resist the devil, and he will flee from me. I will humble myself before the Lord, and He will exalt me. (James 4:7,10)

~❧~

Lord, I thank You for Your patience and for Your desire that people would find life by confessing that Jesus is Your Son. I thank You for the city that You are preparing for Your children. I ask that my afflictions would drive me to You, as I submit myself to You and resist the devil.

DAY 356

GOING ON TO MATURITY

LORD, I DRAW NEAR TO YOU

Lord, I want Your Word to be deeply implanted in me so that I will know the truth and be able to express it in the way I live.

These are the things I want to do: speak the truth to others, judge with truth and justice for peace, not plot evil against my neighbor, and not love a false oath; for all these things the Lord hates. (Zechariah 8:16-17)

Take a moment to affirm the truth of these words from Scripture and ask God to make them a growing reality in your life.

THANK YOU, LORD, FOR WHAT YOU HAVE DONE

I will proclaim the name of the Lord and praise the greatness of my God. (Deuteronomy 32:3)

By this the love of God was manifested to us, that God has sent His only begotten Son into the world that we might live through Him. In this is love, not that we loved God, but that He loved us and sent His Son to be the propitiation for our sins. (1 John 4:9-10)

LORD, I LISTEN TO YOUR WORDS OF TRUTH

God is able to keep me from falling and to present me before His glorious presence faultless and with great joy. (Jude 24)

LORD, I RESPOND TO YOUR INSTRUCTION

I will keep the feast of Christ, my Passover, not with old leaven, or with the leaven of malice and wickedness, but with the unleavened bread of sincerity and truth. (1 Corinthians 5:7-8)

Anyone who partakes only of milk is not accustomed to the Word of righteousness, for he is an infant. But solid food is for the mature, who because of use have their senses trained to distinguish good from evil. Therefore, I will leave the elementary teachings about Christ and go on to maturity. (Hebrews 5:13-6:1)

Lord, I thank You for the greatness of Your name and for the love You manifested through the gift of Your only begotten Son. Help me to live in sincerity and truth and grow into maturity in Christ.

DAY 357

WALKING IN THE LIGHT
OF GOD'S PRESENCE

꒜

LORD, I DRAW NEAR TO YOU

O Lord, I am deeply grateful for Your wonderful acts, for Your abundant promises, and for the gift of my relationship with You through the merits of Christ.

We are looking for the blessed hope and the glorious appearing of our great God and Savior, Christ Jesus, who gave Himself for us to redeem us from all iniquity and to purify for Himself a people for His own possession, zealous for good works. (Titus 2:13-14)

Take a moment to express your gratitude for the many blessings that you have received from the Lord.

THANK YOU, LORD, FOR WHAT YOU HAVE DONE

"The Lord lives! Blessed be my Rock! Exalted be God, the Rock of my salvation! (2 Samuel 22:47)

367
꒜

If the blood of goats and bulls and the ashes of a heifer sprinkled on those who are ceremonially unclean sanctify them so that they are outwardly clean, how much more will the blood of Christ, who through the eternal Spirit offered Himself unblemished to God, cleanse our consciences from acts that lead to death, so that we may serve the living God? (Hebrews 9:13-14)

LORD, I LISTEN TO YOUR WORDS OF TRUTH

Blessed are those who have learned to acclaim You, who walk in the light of Your presence, O Lord. They rejoice in Your name all day long, and they are exalted in Your righteousness. (Psalm 89:15-16)

LORD, I RESPOND TO YOUR INSTRUCTION

The way of a fool is right in his own eyes, but a wise man listens to counsel. (Proverbs 12:15)

꒜

Lord, I thank You that You are the exalted Rock of my salvation and that the blood of Christ cleanses me from all impurity. I thank You for the light of Your presence. Help me to be wise and listen to counsel.

DAY 358

RECEIVING AN UNSHAKEABLE KINGDOM

❧

Lord, I give thanks for Your greatness, Your goodness, and Your love, and I now draw near to enjoy Your presence.

O Lord, my Lord,
How majestic is Your name in all the earth!
You have set Your glory above the heavens! (Psalm 8:1)

Take a moment to consider God's awesome majesty and thank Him that He loves you and wants an intimate relationship with you.

T H A N K   Y O U ,   L O R D ,   F O R   W H A T   Y O U   H A V E   D O N E

God is exalted beyond our understanding; the number of His years is unsearchable. (Job 36:26)

368

When Christ came as high priest of the good things that have come, He went through the greater and more perfect tabernacle that is not made with hands, that is to say, not a part of this creation. Not through the blood of goats and calves but through His own blood, He entered the Most Holy Place once for all, having obtained eternal redemption. (Hebrews 9:11-12)

L O R D ,   I   L I S T E N   T O   Y O U R   W O R D S   O F   T R U T H

Since I am receiving a kingdom that cannot be shaken, I will be thankful and so worship God acceptably with reverence and awe, for my God is a consuming fire. (Hebrews 12:28-29)

L O R D ,   I   R E S P O N D   T O   Y O U R   I N S T R U C T I O N

I do not want even a hint of immorality, or any impurity, or greed in my life, as is proper for a saint. Nor will I give myself to obscenity, foolish talk, or coarse joking, which are not fitting, but rather to giving of thanks. (Ephesians 5:3-4)

❧

Lord, I thank You that You are exalted and that Christ obtained eternal redemption once for all. I thank You that I am receiving a kingdom that cannot be shaken. I will never give myself to those things that are not fitting.

DAY 359
CRUCIFYING THE OLD SELF

LORD, I DRAW NEAR TO YOU

I am grateful to You, O God, for the blessing of Your forgiveness. I thank You that in Christ, You set me free from the guilt of the past and give me hope for the future.

If I say that I have fellowship with Christ and yet walk in the darkness, I lie and do not practice the truth. But if I walk in the light, as He is in the light, we have fellowship with one another, and the blood of Jesus His Son purifies me from all sin. (1 John 1:6-7)

Take a moment to ask the Spirit to search your heart and reveal any areas of unconfessed sin. Acknowledge these to the Lord and thank Him for His forgiveness.

THANK YOU, LORD, FOR WHAT YOU HAVE DONE

You will magnify Yourself and sanctify Yourself, and You will make Yourself known in the sight of many nations, and they will know that You are the Lord. (Ezekiel 38:23)

369

LORD, I LISTEN TO YOUR WORDS OF TRUTH

I know that my old self was crucified with Christ, so that the body of sin might be done away with, that I should no longer be a slave to sin; for the one who has died has been freed from sin. (Romans 6:6-7)

LORD, I RESPOND TO YOUR INSTRUCTION

If we have any encouragement from being united with Christ, if any comfort from His love, if any fellowship of the Spirit, if any affection and compassion, we should also be like-minded, having the same love, being one in spirit and one in purpose. (Philippians 2:1-2)

Just as the body is one, but has many members, and all the members of the body, being many, are one body; so also is Christ. (1 Corinthians 12:12)

Lord, I thank You that You will be exalted in all the earth and all people will know You are the Lord. I thank You that because I was crucified with Christ, I am no longer a slave to sin. I will seek unity of spirit with other believers as a member of the same body.

DAY 360
DWELLING IN GOD'S PRESENCE

LORD, I DRAW NEAR TO YOU

I praise You, Lord, that You are intimately acquainted with my ways and that You always love me and have my best interests at heart.

I have not been made perfect, but I press on to lay hold of that for which Christ Jesus also laid hold of me. I do not consider myself yet to have attained it, but one thing I do: forgetting what is behind and stretching forward to what is ahead, I press on toward the goal to win the prize of the upward call of God in Christ Jesus. (Philippians 3:12-14)

Take a moment to offer this day to the Lord and ask Him for the grace to grow in your knowledge and love for Him.

THANK YOU, LORD, FOR WHAT YOU HAVE DONE

One generation shall praise Your works to another, and shall declare Your mighty acts. I will meditate on the glorious splendor of Your majesty and on Your wonderful works. People shall speak of the might of Your awesome works, and I will proclaim Your great deeds. (Psalm 145:4-6)

LORD, I LISTEN TO YOUR WORDS OF TRUTH

I have become dead to the law through the body of Christ, that I might belong to another, to Him who was raised from the dead, in order that I might bear fruit to God. But now, by dying to what once bound me, I have been released from the law so that I serve in newness of the Spirit and not in oldness of the letter. (Romans 7:4,6)

LORD, I RESPOND TO YOUR INSTRUCTION

I will let my eyes look straight ahead, and fix my gaze straight before me. I will ponder the path of my feet so that all my ways will be established. I will not turn to the right or to the left but keep my foot from evil. (Proverbs 4:25-27)

Lord, I thank You for the glorious splendor of Your majesty and for Your wonderful works. I thank You that I now belong to Christ Who freed me from bondage to that which condemned me, and I ask that I would keep my foot from evil.

DAY 361

PUTTING AWAY CONDEMNATION

❧

LORD, I DRAW NEAR TO YOU

As I approach Your throne of grace today, I am grateful that You care about the things that concern me and that You want me to offer them up to You.

My body is a temple of the Holy Spirit, Who is in me, Whom I have from God, and I am not my own. For I was bought at a price; therefore, may I glorify God in my body. (1 Corinthians 6:19-20)

Take a moment to share your personal needs with God, including your physical, emotional, relational, and spiritual concerns.

THANK YOU, LORD, FOR WHAT YOU HAVE DONE

Great is the Lord, and most worthy of praise in the city of our God, His holy mountain. As is Your name, O God, so is Your praise to the ends of the earth; Your right hand is filled with righteousness. (Psalm 48:1,10)

You will create new heavens and a new earth. The former things will not be remembered, nor will they come to mind. (Isaiah 65:17)

371
❧

LORD, I LISTEN TO YOUR WORDS OF TRUTH

There is now no condemnation for those who are in Christ Jesus, because the law of the Spirit of life in Christ Jesus has set me free from the law of sin and death. (Romans 8:1-2)

LORD, I RESPOND TO YOUR INSTRUCTION

The heart of the prudent acquires knowledge, and the ear of the wise seeks knowledge. (Proverbs 18:15)

He who heeds the Word prospers, and blessed is he who trusts in the Lord. (Proverbs 16:20)

❧

Lord, I thank You that You are most worthy of praise and that You will create new heavens and a new earth. I thank You that there is no condemnation for those who are in Christ Jesus. Help me to acquire knowledge from Your Word and trust in You.

DAY 362

SPEAKING WHAT IS JUST

LORD, I DRAW NEAR TO YOU

Lord, You have invited me to pray for the needs of others, and since You desire what is best for them, I take this opportunity to bring these requests to You.

May we rejoice, become complete, be of good comfort, be of one mind, and live in peace; and the God of love and peace will be with us. (2 Corinthians 13:11)

Take a moment to lift up the needs of your family and friends, and to offer up any additional burdens for others that the Lord brings to mind.

THANK YOU, LORD, FOR WHAT YOU HAVE DONE

I will trust in the Lord forever, for in Yahweh, the Lord, I have an everlasting Rock. (Isaiah 26:4)

To us a Child is born, to us a Son is given, and the government will be on His shoulders. And He will be called Wonderful, Counselor, Mighty God, Everlasting Father, Prince of Peace. Of the increase of His government and peace there will be no end. He will reign on the throne of David and over His kingdom, establishing and upholding it with justice and righteousness from that time on and forever. The zeal of the Lord of hosts will accomplish this. (Isaiah 9:6-7)

LORD, I LISTEN TO YOUR WORDS OF TRUTH

None of us lives to himself alone and none of us dies to himself alone. If we live, we live to the Lord; and if we die, we die to the Lord. So, whether we live or die, we belong to the Lord. (Romans 14:7-8)

LORD, I RESPOND TO YOUR INSTRUCTION

The mouth of the righteous speaks wisdom, and his tongue speaks what is just. The law of his God is in his heart; his steps do not slide. (Psalm 37:30-31)

Lord, I thank You I can always trust in You and for sending Your mighty Son into the world in fulfillment of Your promises. I thank You I belong to You. Teach me to speak what is wise and just.

DAY 363

FULFILLING THE LAW OF CHRIST

LORD, I DRAW NEAR TO YOU

Lord, I want Your Word to be deeply implanted in me so that I will know the truth and be able to express it in the way I live.

As the Father has loved You, You also have loved me. May I abide in Your love. If I keep Your commandments, I will abide in Your love, just as You kept Your Father's commandments and abide in His love. You have told me this so that Your joy may be in me and that my joy may be full. (John 15:9-11)

Take a moment to affirm the truth of these words from Scripture and ask God to make them a growing reality in your life.

THANK YOU, LORD, FOR WHAT YOU HAVE DONE

You are He; You are the first, and You are also the last. (Isaiah 48:12)

LORD, I LISTEN TO YOUR WORDS OF TRUTH

Who will bring a charge against those whom God has chosen? It is God who justifies. Who is he who condemns? It is Christ Jesus Who died, Who was furthermore raised to life, Who is at the right hand of God and is also interceding for me. (Romans 8:33-34)

LORD, I RESPOND TO YOUR INSTRUCTION

I will endure discipline, for God is treating me as a son. For what son is not disciplined by his father? If I am without discipline, of which all have become partakers, then I am an illegitimate child and not a true son. Moreover, we have all had human fathers who disciplined us, and we respected them; how much more should I be subjected to the Father of spirits and live? (Hebrews 12:7-9)

We should bear one another's burdens and so fulfill the law of Christ. (Galatians 6:2)

Lord, I thank You for being the first and the last and that Christ Jesus intercedes on my behalf. I will endure Your discipline with joy. Help me to bear the burdens of others thus fulfilling the law of Christ.

DAY 364

COMMITTING MYSELF TO MY FAITHFUL CREATOR

～❧

LORD, I DRAW NEAR TO YOU

O Lord, I am deeply grateful for Your wonderful acts, for Your abundant promises, and for the gift of my relationship with You through the merits of Christ.

In Your unfailing love You have led the people You have redeemed.
In Your strength You have guided them to Your holy dwelling.
You brought them in and planted them in the mountain of Your inheritance —
The place, O Lord, You made for Your dwelling;
The sanctuary, O Lord, Your hands have established. (Exodus 15:13,17)

Take a moment to express your gratitude for the many blessings that you have received from the Lord.

～❧

THANK YOU, LORD, FOR WHAT YOU HAVE DONE

The kingdom of the world has become the kingdom of our Lord and of His Christ, and He will reign for ever and ever. (Revelation 11:15)

LORD, I LISTEN TO YOUR WORDS OF TRUTH

We all, with unveiled face beholding as in a mirror the glory of the Lord, are being transformed into the same image from glory to glory, which comes from the Lord, Who is the Spirit. (2 Corinthians 3:18)

LORD, I RESPOND TO YOUR INSTRUCTION

Those who suffer according to the will of God should commit themselves to their faithful Creator in doing good. (1 Peter 4:19)
Being built up in the most holy faith and praying in the Holy Spirit, I want to keep myself in the love of God as I wait for the mercy of our Lord Jesus Christ to eternal life. (Jude 20-21)

～❧

Lord, I thank You that all glory and honor belong to You and that the kingdom of Your Christ will continue forever. I thank You for the process of transforming me into the image of Your Son. I commit myself to You and will abide in Your love during times of suffering.

DAY 365

LIVING BY FAITH IN
THE SON OF GOD

ﻋ

LORD, I DRAW NEAR TO YOU

---

*Lord, I give thanks for Your greatness, Your goodness, and Your love, and I now
draw near to enjoy Your presence.*

I will praise You, O Lord, with all my heart;
I will tell of all Your wonders.
I will be glad and rejoice in You;
I will sing praise to Your name, O Most High. (Psalm 9:1-2)

*Take a moment to consider God's awesome majesty and thank Him that He loves
you and wants an intimate relationship with you.*

THANK YOU, LORD, FOR WHAT YOU HAVE DONE

At the name of Jesus every knee should bow, in heaven and on earth
and under the earth, and every tongue should confess that Jesus Christ
is Lord, to the glory of God the Father. (Philippians 2:10-11)

375
ﻋ

LORD, I LISTEN TO YOUR WORDS OF TRUTH

I have been crucified with Christ; and it is no longer I who live, but
Christ lives in me; and the life which I now live in the flesh, I live by
faith in the Son of God, Who loved me and gave Himself for me.
(Galatians 2:20)

LORD, I RESPOND TO YOUR INSTRUCTION

Since I have a great cloud of witnesses surrounding me, I want to lay
aside every impediment and the sin that so easily entangles, and run
with endurance the race that is set before me, fixing my eyes on Jesus,
the author and perfecter of my faith, Who for the joy set before Him
endured the cross, despising the shame, and sat down at the right hand
of the throne of God. I will consider Him Who endured such hostility
from sinners, so that I will not grow weary and lose heart. (Hebrews
12:1-3)

ﻋ

*Lord, I thank You that Christ gave Himself for me and lives in me. I will lay
aside all entanglements and run with endurance the race that is set before me.*

ABOUT THE AUTHORS

Kenneth Boa is engaged in a ministry of relational evangelism, discipleship, teaching, writing, and speaking. He holds a B.S. from Case Institute of Technology, a Th.M. from Dallas Theological Seminary, a Ph.D. from New York University, and a D.Phil. from the University of Oxford in England.

Dr. Boa is the president of Reflections Ministries, an organization that seeks to provide safe places for people to consider the claims of Christ and help them mature and bear fruit in their relationship with Him. He is also president of Trinity House Publishers, a publishing company that is dedicated to the creation of tools that will help people manifest eternal values in a temporal arena by drawing them to intimacy with God and a better understanding of the culture in which they live.

Publications by Dr. Boa include *Cults, World Religions, and the Occult; I'm Glad You Asked; Talk Thru the Bible; Visual Survey of the Bible; Drawing Near; Unraveling the Big Questions About God; Night Light; Handbook to Prayer; Handbook to Renewal.* He is a contributing editor to *The Open Bible* and *The Promise Keeper's Men's Study Bible*, and the sole contributor to *The Two-Year Daily Reading and Prayer Bible*.

Karen Boa has a B.A. from Montclair State University in English and has done graduate work at New York University in comparative literature. She continues to develop her interests in literature, film, music, and art; and she is an avid gardener.

Kenneth Boa writes a free monthly teaching letter called *Reflections*. If you would like to be on the mailing list, call:

(800) DRAW NEAR
(372-9632)

Or, if you would like to write the authors, address your correspondence to:

Kenneth and Karen Boa
4600 Morton Road
Alpharetta, Georgia 30022

Additional copies of this book
are available from your local bookstore.

Honor Books
Tulsa, Oklahoma